Contents

Emancipations, Modern and Postmodern

edited by

Jan Nederveen Pieterse

SAGE Publications
London • Newbury Park • New Delhi

First published 1992

SAGE Publications Ltd
6 Bonhill Street
London EC2A 4PU

SAGE Publications Inc
2455 Teller Road
Newbury Park, California 91320

SAGE Publications India Pvt Ltd
32, M-Block Market
Greater Kailash – I
New Delhi 110 048

British Library Cataloguing in Publication data

A catalogue record for this book is available from the British Library

ISBN 0 8039 8777 3
ISBN 0 8039 8781 1 (pbk)

Library of Congress catalog card number 92-050450

Typeset by Colset Pte Ltd, Singapore
Printed in Great Britain by J. W. Arrowsmith Ltd, Bristol

Foreword

Times change. So do people's collective projects, priorities, paradigms. But the same is true for the broader processes and structures that determine shifting patterns of hegemony and incorporation, and for the search for autonomy and a decent existence they invariably engender. As patterns of domination reshape themselves in the wake of changing priorities and justifications, so do the foci and strategies of emancipatory movements or indeed all social action seeking to define liberation, equality, social justice. Thus, state and civil society today increasingly compete with capital and class for primary attention, as part of an unending succession of subtle but definite shifts in the foci and rationale of modes of maintaining or creating 'order' on the one hand and the focal point for efforts at preserving or enlarging social 'space' on the other. But whereas opposite foci — power versus freedom, oppression versus liberation, incorporation versus autonomy - may change in tandem, opposition *per se* and the relevance of the counterpoint in socio-political processes will remain. Continuous change equals no change in this fundamental respect. The process will never be completed. That would mean the end of history.

At a juncture such as the present one, when major visions of an alternative future society have bleakened while there is also a rapidly shifting ground at the level of ideas and of perceptions of reality, the question of what conceptions of emancipation are remaining or emerging seems particularly pertinent. Is postmodern also to be understood as post-emancipatory; i.e. does postmodernism signify the dwindling and denial of emancipatory projects and ideals? Or does it instead offer uneasy but compelling grounds for radical rethinking of emancipation? What is the paradigmatic significance of the 'new' social movements — feminism, ecology, non-party political movements — in this context? And what content is there for the concept of 'development', if this is still to be a relevant signifier? These and other related questions are of a kind of first order magnitude at the present time, which accounts for their being

Development and Change (SAGE, London, Newbury Park and New Delhi), Vol. 23 (1992) No. 3, 1–4.

raised and debated in a whole range of centres of social and philosophical enquiry at least in the Northern Hemisphere – though their implications for the South, and for orientations to the South and in the South, are yet to become more transparent.

The contributions to the present volume form part of this current movement of enquiry and debate. They address the crucial question of rethinking emancipation and engage in a critical inventory of our concepts of liberation. They were first presented and discussed at an international workshop titled Rethinking Emancipation: Concepts of Liberation which was convened at the Institute of Social Studies, The Hague, in collaboration with the Institute of Philosophy at the University of Groningen, at the initiative of the Editors of *Development and Change* in 1991.

As Editors, our motivations in convening this workshop and preparing this volume based on it were basically twofold. One, functioning as monitors of multiple concurrent streams of reflection on macro and micro processes of social transformation, we were intent on promoting an increased understanding of the implications of the present paradigmatic shifts in social theorizing for current emancipatory thought and praxis generally. Are these shifts to last? If so, what lessons should one draw from them and in what ways, if at all, should we revise our perspectives on social processes, politics and alternative development strategies in the light of them? Second, given our specific brief in the area of development studies, we were especially interested in coming to a critical juxtaposition and reappraisal of notions of emancipation and of development. Are they still valid? Can they still be related? If so, in what ways? To what extent, for example, have the implications been thought through of a shift away from a primary focus on poverty alleviation in current discussions on development strategies to one on the (re)creation of 'civil society' and the formation of middle cadres? Are these both, and similarly, 'emancipatory' intervention strategies?

But images of New Societies are no monopoly of the Left, as witnessed by a whole array of blueprints for green lands of promise issued by political leaders not primarily known for their emancipatory ethos: Marcos's New Society, Suharto's New Order, Ghadaffi's Green Book principles, Pinochet's project, etc. Revolutionary violence adds to the problematic. Pol Pot promised a New Society of sorts, though demanding a staggering toll for it in terms of human sacrifice. In Peru today, the most horrendous crimes are perpetrated in the name of the poor and of 'emancipation' by

Sendero Luminoso, though with such narrow and gruesome fixation on the capture of power *per se* that non-violent self-organizations and development programmes by and for the poor are seen as its greatest obstacles and chief targets for elimination. What extent of violence, and to whom, do emancipatory social movements and theory actually accept, if any at all? There is a continuous threat of corruption and erosion of emancipatory thinking and premises and one would like to be reassured that no such contaminations will be condoned within the pluriformity of perspectives that seem to be inaugurated by contemporary paradigmatic shifts.

In the light of current queries as to the future trajectories of emancipatory and critical development thinking, a select group of social theorists and actors was invited to make explicit what generally remains implicit in their work, that is, to bring out the underlying notion or concept of emancipation which so often is kept hidden behind the 'if only' element in social analysis. 'if only' this or that basic structural constraint could be overcome, vistas of emancipation would more readily unfold themselves. Or would it no longer be the case that there is an image of a better world implied in contemporary social theory — if only?

Such an inventory, it was anticipated, might give an indication as to whether emancipatory thinking is still intrinsic to social theory, and in what directions it appears to be evolving. The aim of the exercise, however, was in no way an attempt to promote the construction of any new consensus. Instead, if a bouquet of differently coloured and structured conceptualizations of and reflections on emancipation were to emerge as its result, we would consider our objective realized. Predictably, perhaps, this is what has happened. Thanks to the perceptive and pertinent discussions by all contributors an exceptionally rich and illuminating overview of current trends in the rethinking of concepts of emancipation and liberation has resulted. Moreover, through this project we had wanted to re-establish an intellectual link to the pioneering work on emancipatory processes as the pulsating substance and core of longitudinal societal change by the Dutch sociologist Wim Wertheim during an earlier generation of critical scholarship, and also in this respect the collection that has emerged has met our expectations.

The points of divergence in the contributions that follow are as instructive as their common ground, and one lesson they collectively drive home is that we shall indeed have to get used to thinking in terms of emancipations rather than emancipation. The other, admittedly tentative conclusion, is that the scope for non-contaminated emancipatory thinking as a basic ingredient of social theory is upheld, confirmed and, who knows, might even be widening in a changing context. We are confident that the spirited responses to our invitation to reflect and debate on the theme of the contemporary relevance of emancipatory thinking and social movements of which this collection gives evidence, will be found stimulating by readers way beyond those within the regular circuit of *Development and Change*.

Martin Doornbos

Emancipations, Modern and Postmodern

Jan Nederveen Pieterse

There is no shortage of reasons for rethinking emancipation. Theory lags behind practice. New social movements have generated new practices and theorizing, much of which has not filtered through to social theory. Some of the developments which can be summed up as the poststructuralist turn are significant to emancipatory thought and practice, yet most of this goes on as if these developments were taking place on another planet. A tendency towards de-ideologization and scepticism has become widely prevalent, if not routine. All the same some developments continue to be referred to as 'progressive' while others are termed conservative. Apparently some standard and sense of direction still exist. Obviously it does for social movements. Obviously it does in development efforts. It may be, however, a sense of direction far more subtle, multiple and modest than the 'modern' views. It's a matter of progress against the backdrop of pragmatism and emancipation in the no-nonsense era.

While the 1960s are on record for being 'liberation' oriented, the actual conceptions of liberation developed at the time were often vague and unreflected. Prominent in the Western world were the themes of the Freudian left, the encounter of Freud and Marx, questions of class mingling with individual liberation (e.g. Cooper, 1967). In the Third World the keynotes were national liberation and variations on the theme of anti-imperialism. While the 1970s and 1980s saw new politics and new theorizing, the key concepts of 'progressive' thought, except for the problematic of class, were rarely reflected on with any degree of thoroughness. Flagwords in political analysis and policy, such as participation, emancipation, empowerment, have rarely been clearly defined, or for that matter referred to in indexes, another indication of their unreflected use. The cornerstones of analysis have often been the most casual elements.

Development and Change (SAGE, London, Newbury Park and New Delhi), Vol. 23 (1992) No. 3, 5–41.

This is a volume of reflections on reorientations in emancipatory thought and on the meanings of emancipation. The term 'emancipation' has been used increasingly widely in recent years, possibly as a reflection on the limitations of class analysis in the face of collective actions which are not reducible to class, and on the limitations of postmodern discourse whose generalized indirection impairs differentiation among types of collective action. The appeal of emancipation is that as a concept broader than class struggle it can potentially embrace the projects of old and new social movements. Even so, as a concept, emancipation has been closely linked to the Enlightenment tradition and it remains to be seen whether it can survive the poststructuralist turn.

The various terms used to describe collective action carry many different inflections. They include attitudinal terms such as dissent, opposition, resistance, protest, defiance; terms emphasizing methods of action such as riot, violence, *jacquerie*, rebellion, mutiny, revolution, petition, demonstration, consciousness raising; general terms with normative or political overtones such as class struggle, liberation, emancipation, participation, empowerment; and social science terminology such as collective behaviour, collective action, social movement.

Also among the latter there are distinct differences: collective behaviour is neutral and suggests distance, while collective action emphasizes the importance of agency, subjectivity. Collective behaviour, a term used by structural fuctionalists (Smelser, 1962), can accommodate negative and conservative interpretations of 'mass behaviour'. A substantial tradition in social science views collective behaviour, particularly violence and revolution, as manifestations of the breakdown of systems of social integration. Durkheim and his notion of anomie (normlessness) is one of the main lineages of this tradition. Along with the Durkheimian perspective, as part of its cultural assumptions, come negative, anxiety-ridden views of the 'masses', the crowd or mob – the threatening imagery of social pathology and collective criminality as laid down in the works of Le Bon, Sighele and Tarde (van Ginneken, 1992). The Durkheimian perspective interprets collective mobilization as the consequence of the breakdown of social control, or social disequilibrium; this results in individual disorientation, which in turn leads to violent protest. Psychologizing protest, in terms such as frustration, anger, panic, alienation, tends to discredit the motives of protesters. The imagery of the masses uprooted by rapid social change, of crises, of alienation, suggests an ambience close to that of disease and crime.

In his studies of social movements in European history, Charles Tilly uses the concept of collective action, charting a course diametrically opposed to the Durkheimian view, also on the part of American representatives of the Durkheimian tradition such as Ted Gurr and Chalmers Johnson. Instead of social disintegration, uprootedness, alienation and assorted emotional states, Tilly's extensive empirically documented studies emphasize the role of solidarity and organization in collective action (Tilly, 1978; Hunt, 1984).

In structural functionalism collective behaviour is viewed primarily in terms of the 'problem of order', or the Hobbesian problem. A breakdown of social order, it must be remedied by the reimposition of order. Collective mobilization in this view easily exceeds the bounds of law and order. Thus the social movements of the 1960s were regarded as an 'excess of democracy', resulting in the 'ungovernability' of Western societies (Huntington, 1975). In like manner, the 'revolution of rising expectations' and consequent large-scale mobilization in developing countries were viewed negatively – as an obstacle to the process of modernization (Eisenstadt, 1966). As a general perspective, emancipation belongs to the collective action end of this theoretical spectrum as against the social pathology or breakdown view.

EMANCIPATION

As a political term emancipation dates from the Enlightenment. By the turn of the nineteenth century emancipation was associated with a view of progress as a movement towards freedom and equality. In this way Condorcet formulated the general character of progress in the cause of reason – inequality among nations will disappear, equality will increase within each nation (Condorcet, 1794; Gay, 1969: 119–20). Progress defined as a process of increasing equality, in other words, a process of emancipation, was a common denominator of nineteenth-century liberal and radical perspectives (Greiffenhagen, 1973). A series of collective mobilizations was recognized in these terms: the emancipation of the bourgeoisie, workers, slaves, women, Catholics, Jews and serfs. All of these concern a two-fold process of the extension of political rights to subaltern groups and subaltern groups acting as agents of history.

At the time the understanding of emancipation as a general process of which these movements were specific manifestations seemed unproblematical. Emancipation was a grand unifying theme; in the words of Heinrich Heine: 'Not simply the emancipation of the Irish, the Greeks, Frankfurt Jews, West Indian blacks, and all such oppressed peoples, but the emancipation of the whole world, and especially of Europe, which has now come of age, and is tearing itself loose from the apron-strings of the privileged classes' (quoted in Feuerlicht, 1983: 41). While there were vast ideological differences as to the prime mover, manner and direction of the process among liberals, Owenites, Saint-Simonians, Blanquists, Marxists, national movements and anarchists, there was little doubt as to its overall momentum. Mankind was on the way to freedom, inexorably so. These various views did not so much dispute this central tenet as the modalities in which it would work out. The tenet was questioned by those who disbelieved in the momentum of modernization – by conservatives, Romantics, aristocrats, élite theorists and all those to whom decadence was a matter of greater concern than progress. For the rise of the bourgeois order coincided with the decline of the aristocratic order, bemoaned by those taking a racial view such as Gobineau, or nihilist in outlook such as Nietzsche. The interrogation of the Enlightenment and modernity did not have to wait for critical theory or postmodernism: it was part and parcel of the Enlightenment and modernization itself, which were heterogeneous all along – from the 'Romantic Enlightenment' to 'conservative modernization' (e.g. Seidman, 1983; Kondylis, 1986).

Emancipation does not have a fixed meaning. Over time it has been undergoing several changes. Since becoming a political flagword at the time of the French revolution, from a relationship between individuals (father and son, master and slave) it came to refer to relations between groups; from a formal process controlled from above, or a gift (manumission), it came to refer to the self-liberation of the non-privileged (Lempert, 1973).

EMANCIPATION OR EMPOWERMENT

Emancipation is used more often as an explanatory term (e.g. 'emancipatory project') than it is explained, more often as a qualification than it is qualified. As such it refers to a general implicit understanding rather than to an explicit, defined body of theory. What definitions are given tend to be particularistic (e.g. women's emancipation is the improvement of conditions and life opportunities for women) rather than general. Emancipation tends to be used in two related ways: the process of the disadvantaged entering the mainstream, including women's liberation, and in a general sense of 'becoming free', the character of which varies according to the understanding of constraint.

In 'Capitalism and Human Emancipation', Ellen Meiksins Wood (1988) argues that race and gender discrimination, unlike class, are not intrinsic to capitalism but contingent, and that therefore class struggle remains the central issue. Unger (1987: 52ff) uses emancipation in a general sense, as 'emancipation from false necessity', from various forms of closure. Bob Marley's 'emancipate yourself from mental slavery' makes the connection between a specific and a general process.

Wertheim (1983: 11, 2) refers to emancipation as 'liberation of creative human potentialities from suffocating social structures' or 'liberation, from both natural and man-made shackles'. An explicit definition is that 'emancipation refers to a collective struggle on the part of a thus far underprivileged group or category' (see article by Wertheim, p. 258).

This provides little basis for distinguishing between different kinds of collective action. There is no distinction between an excluded group entering into dominance and a change of the rules of the game; between a minority's struggle for integration and a revolution, or between a political and a social revolution.[1] Another group, previously disadvantaged and underprivileged, joins the game. White sahib becomes brown sahib – as the classic description of the outcome of the anti-colonial struggle for independence goes. In other words, power itself has not changed; power is not problematized. If emancipation is to be a critical concept it must enable us to make such distinctions.

In his classic work on liberation theology, Gutiérrez distinguishes three interpenetrating levels of meaning of *liberation*: as the aspirations of oppressed peoples and social classes; as an understanding of history in which 'man is seen as assuming conscious responsibility for his own destiny'; and in a spiritual sense where it matches salvation from sin (Gutiérrez, 1973: 36–7, 176–8). The first meaning refers to national liberation and class struggle in one breath, the second is equivalent to progress, while the third refers to spiritual redemption. The scripts of Enlightenment, Marxism, national liberation and Christianity are fused in a single theology of interdependent liberations.

Participation is a term widely used in liberal democratic theory (participatory democracy), community organizing, in development projects (popular participation) and forms of research (participatory action research). A more egalitarian-sounding term than mobilization (with its vanguardist connotations), it has been criticized for its neo-populist character (Dahl, 1970; Kothari, 1984). It refers to integration rather than transformation – taking part in something which itself is not necessarily changing – unless the notion is full participation, a notion which has been criticized for invoking the illusion of primary democracy. The weakness of participation is what it leaves out: 'the issue is not simply whether or not certain groups participate, but whether the mass of the population has the means to define the terms and nature of their participation' (Kaufman, 1991:n. 11).[2]

A fashionable term that gained currency over recent years is *empowerment*, used in development projects, women's movements, education, welfare and family support programmes. Its defining feature is a participatory approach which aims to 'enable people to emancipate themselves' (Kronenburg, 1986: 229–33). Definitions of empowerment tend to be soft, for instance: 'empowerment is a process aimed at consolidating, maintaining or changing the nature and distribution of power in a particular cultural context' (Bookman and Morgen, 1988: 4). This is not particularly helpful since the direction of the change in the distribution of power is not indicated. According to another account, empowerment 'is taken to mean a group process where people who lack an equal share of valued resources gain greater access to, and control over, those resources' ('Empowerment', 1990: 2). This is so broad that it might refer, for instance, to any method for getting rich. The term has also been used in a populist sense, as in the empowerment of the Philippine people through 'People Power'. More critical is the view of Sen and Grown (1988: 80, 81) for whom empowerment begins with 'self-definition' and is concerned with the 'transformation of the structures of subordination'.

Part of the appeal of empowerment is the aura of power. But it does not necessarily problematize power. It does not differentiate between 'power to' (ability) and 'power over' (control), between empowerment as acquiring skills or as seeking control. It can denote anything from individual self-assertion to upward mobility through adaptation and conformism to established rules (e.g. sanskritization might be considered a process of empowerment). Accordingly empowerment may carry conservative implications, or more precisely, it is politically neutral. It does not necessarily imply a critical consciousness. Empowerment may relate to emancipation as a necessary but not a sufficient condition: emancipation implies empowerment, but not every form of empowerment is emancipatory.

The various definitions of emancipation, liberation, participation and empowerment show a tendency towards circularity, one being defined in terms of the other. Emancipation is a form of liberation, liberation a form of emancipation, etc. Some terms do not imply transformation. Clegg (1989) does refer to 're-fixing power' but does not specify the terms of re-fixing. We may try to gain further clarity by juxtaposing emancipation to resistance.

RESISTANCE OR EMANCIPATION

It is striking how fundamental the imagery of resistance is to radical discourse. Stuart Hall's (1988: 237) observation that 'Socialism has been so long on the defensive in Britain that it has by now acquired a permanent negative posture', might as well apply to the left in general, although one might argue whether it applies since 1848, 1870, 1930 or the post-war era. Resistance is the default discourse of the left, casually embedded in terms such as cultures of resistance. In France a grouping of left-wing forces may be referred to as a *cartel de non*. All of this suggests a general attitude in which being progressive is identified with saying no, keeping things from happening, and in fact with a profound tendency towards cultural conservatism.

Closer consideration shows that resistance implies a complex register of notions. First, resistance is not simply negative but also affirmative – as in the basic understanding of *critique* as opening, and in critical theory's 'negation of the negation', monumentalized in Marcuse's Great Refusal. Next, resistance may reflect a commitment to and defence of an existing 'moral economy' or notion of social justice and collective rights. In this way Thompson (1971) interpreted the actions of crowds in eighteenth-century England. Scott (1976) used the term to explain peasant attitudes in twentieth-century South-East Asia. Resistance in this sense is also affirmative, but in a conservative sense. In terms of action it may motivate rebellion, quietism or anti-emancipatory actions. For instance, the familialism of the anti-feminist movement in the United States has been interpreted in this way: 'as an attempt to reinstate an older patriarchal bargain, with feminists providing a convenient scapegoat on whom to blame current disaffection and alienation among men' (Kandiyoti, 1988: 284). In other words, emancipation efforts may be resisted in the name of a moral economy, which itself may be the crystallization of a previous wave of emancipation.

The currency of the term 'resistance' also derives from the legacy of anti-colonial struggles. Here resistance is conservative in the sense that the intention is to preserve community life as it existed before the colonizers intervened; its future is in the past. In the terminology of primary, secondary and tertiary resistance (as in Davidson, 1978), the latter refers to nationalism.

The 'everyday forms of peasant resistance' (1985) and the 'arts of resistance' (1991) are themes of James Scott's work. 'Everyday resistance' avoids overt confrontation and defiance of élites and authorities, and instead applies the 'weapons of the weak' such as foot-dragging, arson, sabotage, pilfering and gossip. The way some women use spirit possession has also been regarded a weapon of the weak (Moore, 1988: 181). Is resistance, then, a weapon of the weak and emancipation a project of the not-so-weak? This is an impression one might gain from Scott's work or from some studies of poor people's movements in the Western world (e.g. Piven and Cloward, 1977). The problem with this kind of analysis is that it renders invisible what transformative element there is to poor people's actions — even in the process of withdrawal and evasion, new solidarities may be created and new cultural understandings and counterpoints take shape.

In his work on European social movements Tilly distinguishes between *competitive* actions, which claim resources also claimed by rival groups and take the typical form of village fights and brawls; *reactive* ones in which people act in the name of threatened rights, taking forms such as food riots and tax rebellions; and *proactive* forms which assert group claims not previously exercised, taking forms such as the demonstration and the strike. In the period from 1600 to 1850, in the context of large-scale structural change, proactive forms of collective action gradually replaced reactive ones (Tilly, 1978: 143–71). Touraine (1985) distinguishes between defensive and offensive conflicts.

The common ground of resistance and emancipation is the concern with autonomy or self-definition (self-determination in an international context). The difference between resistance and emancipation seems to parallel in a general way the distinction between protest and transformation. Resistance is negative *tout court*; its politics are opaque, they must be decoded from context. Emancipation is negative in that it is a process of a group freeing itself from restriction. Emancipation is concerned with 'freedom from' rather than 'freedom to'. It is proactive, but in an unfinished sense, as a negative commitment of transgression rather than a positive blueprint.

Emancipation is a matter of critique *and* construction, of which resistance represents the first step and transformation, in the sense of structural change, the second.[3] Resistance and emancipation are interdependent, with the proviso that not every form of resistance opens the way to emancipation and some block it. What sets emancipation as a concept apart from resistance is the proactive, transformative element. Foucault's understandings of power break with traditional political theory in showing that 'power's function is not merely prohibitive and repressive but productive, positive, educative' (Cocks, 1989: 51). Similarly, emancipation is not simply about saying no, reacting, refusing, resisting, but also and primarily about social creativity, introducing new values and aims, new forms of co-operation and action.

Most representations of emancipatory processes, however, also on the part of the left, stress the negative and not the creative moment. While in many cases the vocabulary of resistance reflects the cultural conservatism of the left, in others it is tied up with a particular argument. Often resistance implicitly passes for emancipation, or at least the two are not clearly distinguished; in other cases they are consciously set apart, as in views which present resistance as an alternative to emancipation.

Habermas interprets the new social movements as forms of resistance to increasing commodification, bureaucratization and other processes of colonization of the life-world by capitalist and state interventions. The emphasis is on the defensive character of the new social movements. Are the new movements then solely motivated by the defence of existing claims? Habermas does acknowledge the proactive claims made by the new politics: 'The new problems have to do with quality of life, equal rights, individual self-realization, participation, and human rights' (Habermas,

1987: 392). If these proactive features are recognized and yet the overriding discourse remains that of the defensiveness of social movements, perhaps this may be accounted for by Habermas's view that the movements are concerned with developing the unfinished project of the Enlightenment. An evolutionary teleology is inscribed in the social movements: a telos of collective agreement underlies Habermas's perspective (Dews, 1986: 22; Lyotard, 1984: 66). In other words, according to Habermas resistance *is* emancipation.

Foucault opts for the vocabulary of resistance for entirely different reasons. Foucault differentiates between three forms of power and three forms of struggle: against *domination*, predominant in feudalism, taking the form of ethnic, religious struggles; against *exploitation*, dominant in capitalism, taking the form of class struggle; and against *subjugation*, which is dominant now, taking the form of struggles in the name of identity. For the latter Foucault's chosen vocabulary is that of resistance, rather than emancipation. Instead of proposing a theory of total liberation, Foucault (1980, 1981) speaks of a series of local resistances, local struggles. For Foucault there is no transcendence, there is only an alteration of discourse: another truth, another power. Struggle produces a new domination. Hence resistance is the appropriate vocabulary, not liberation or emancipation for there is no emancipation from the nexus between truth and power itself: in this sense there is no future which is different in a radical way.

Habermas opts for the vocabulary of resistance because the future is prefigured in the communicative rationality which is part of the Enlightenment project – the future is past; Foucault opts for resistance because there is no future. The latter is the essential poststructuralist criticism of emancipation discourse; a criticism which is rearticulated upon another arc of meaning by the postmodern critics. Lyotard (1988) also opts for the term resistance. Henceforth emancipatory thinking is thinking *after* the poststructuralist turn. One of the keynotes of rethinking emancipation is whether emancipation can survive this turn, and if so, what kind of emancipation.

EMANCIPATIONS AND MODERNITY

A basic error that has been made in emancipatory thought time and again is to generalize from particular contexts towards a general model, theory, strategy and agenda of emancipation. Therefore it is not merely illustrative but essential to historicize emancipation and show the plural character of emancipations. These emancipations, at the same time, may not be simply isolated processes but may be correlated in several ways.

Table 1 gives a loose list of emancipation projects from *c.* 1800. (It would not be difficult to add others but the list only seeks to cover the main projects and those which play a part in the literature. The table is not chronological in the sense that later projects annul former ones. Neither is the implication that later is better. Blank spaces under the subheadings indicate the absence of specific information on that point.)

Initially, the momentum of the age of the democratic revolution (Palmer, 1964) inspired emancipatory movements of different kinds. For a long time egalitarianism in the name of reason, the liberal ideas of the Rights of Man and bourgeois emancipation were the matrix for other projects, although it is important to note that they were never the sole source of emancipatory momentum. Thus, the emancipation movements of black slaves of North America were inspired by dissident Christian movements such as the Quakers, before riding piggy-back on the discourse of the democratic revolution. The abolitionist movements stemmed from similar multiple, heterogeneous sources. The nineteenth-century women's movements were motivated by the discourse of equal rights and, in the American Republic and England, by the example of black emancipation and abolitionism. In many respects the emancipation of workers followed in the footsteps of the emancipation of the bourgeoisie. The emancipations of Catholics and Jews depended on the climate of secularization. The theme of popular sovereignty, perhaps the central motif of the democratic revolution, inspired the momentum of 1848 and the 'springtime of peoples', or the national question, as it was termed at the time.[4]

By the mid-nineteenth century two terrains of emancipation that were explicitly recognized were those concerned with the 'national question' and the 'social question'. For the generation between 1830 and 1848 it was not clear where the line between them was drawn or which was the most important. There was considerable cross-over between them; for instance, before the First International turned to Karl Marx it asked Giuseppe Mazzini, the leader of the Young Italy movement for the unification of Italy, to be its president (Billington, 1980: 148).

Table 1. *Emancipation projects over time (c. 1800 to present)*

Emancipations	**Subjects**	**Methods**	**Projects**
Liberalism	Bourgeoisie	Democratic struggles	Liberal democracy
Marxisms	Proletariat	Class struggle Union, Party Proletarian revolution	Socialism
Anarchisms	Working class and anti-authoritarians	Syndicalism co-operatives insurgency terrorism	Co-operative society Libertarian socialism
Social democracy	Multiclass	Democratic struggles	Social democracy
Leninism	Working class and revolutionaries Anti-colonial movements	Vanguard party Agitprop, etc. Internationalism (Comintern)	Dictatorship of proletariat, Socialism World revolution
Maoism	Peasants and workers	Party, Mass line	Socialism
National liberation	Multiclass United/national front	armed struggle civil disobedience	Self-determination
Indigenous peoples	Indigenous	Multiple	Self-determination
Guevarism (Focismo)	Peasants, workers and revolutionaries	Foco Armed struggle	Socialism and self-determination

Gramsci	Workers, intellectuals and peasants	War of manoeuvre War of position Hegemonic struggle	Socialist hegemony
Frankfurt School		Critique Psychoanalysis	Authenticity
Habermas		Communicative action	Democratic socialism
Feminisms	Feminists and women	Liberal: rights Socialist: class Radical: autonomy Poststructuralist: symbolic struggles	Equality and socialism Autonomy Difference
Community organizing (US)	Community and labour	Power structure analysis, organization, lobbying	Empowerment
Liberation theology	Poor, people and clergy	Popular education Conscientization	Peace and justice
Anti-racism	Minorities and people	Consciousness raising Collective action	Autonomy or integration
Ecological movements	Plural	Democratic struggle	Survival, quality of life
Holistic humanism	Plural	Democratic struggle	Democratic socialism
Post-Marxism	Plural		Radical democracy
Poststructuralisms	Plural Plural	Local resistance Deconstruction	Identity Difference without domination
Postmodernisms	Plural	Little narratives Struggle against totality	Piecemeal change Resistance

By the second half of the century the 'social question' and class-based movements were widely considered to be the most important in the eyes of participants as well as the powers that be, from Bismarck to the Pope. Yet, particularly during the last quarter of the century, nationalism was a growth industry and there were many attempts to outflank the class struggle and the importance of working-class parties and trade unions with the trappings of nationalism, political anti-Semitism, popular imperialism and racism. Discussions on class and nation loomed large through much of the twentieth century: on the question of national self-determination, taken up by Lenin and Stalin; the relationship between socialism and nationalism, taken up by Kautsky, Luxemburg and the Austrian Marxists; and the anti-colonial movements (e.g. Amin, 1980). What the movements based on the themes of class and nation shared is that they set up formal organizations, were organized on a national basis, focused on the state and on acquiring state power and converged on revolution, in either social or national guise (Wallerstein, 1990).

After the growing disillusionment with socialism in the Eastern bloc, class and national liberation lived on as twin themes in 'Third Worldism'. After liberation, the new nations were to transform nationalist consciousness into a new social consciousness (e.g. Fanon, 1967: Ch. 3). This meant that class served as the centre of gravity in emancipation writ large. It was the centre of gravity theoretically, as the chief instrument of analysis of national and international situations, and in terms of praxis, as the main avenue of mobilization. This generated a large literature of the 'and class' variety which sought to establish the relationship to class of various questions and subject positions: nation and class, state and class, power and class, capital and class, gender and class, race and class, caste and class, village and class, ideology and class, culture and class, religion and class, and so forth. Besides being theoretically meaningful in articulating a field of forces centred around class it was politically meaningful in formulating a rank order of emancipations in terms of a 'line of march' led by class projects. International relations were annexed into the class paradigm by equating imperialism with capitalism.

All along, the representation of the 'old' social movements centred on and dominated by the tension between class and nation was itself a highly ideologized definition of the terrain of forces that was by no means undisputed. The emancipations grounded in ethnicity, gender or religion were marginalized or excluded in the class-or-nation schema. The peasantry and the countryside were either left out or squeezed in. And where did democratic reform movements such as the Chartists in England belong? The class paradigm was disputed by anarchists, by third world nationalists such as Gandhi, and generally by those who were left out by the hegemony over emancipatory projects sought by organizations claiming to represent the working class.

By logic emancipation is a terrain highly susceptible to the politics of theory. Annexationist theories abound.[5] Each paradigm of emancipation turns emancipations plural into emancipation singular: it enlists the range and variety of emancipatory projects in the notion of a central momentum of progress. Ultimately, the question of emancipation hinges on the question of progress. It is a matter of the hierarchy among the projects challenging hierarchy. What is the spearpoint of emancipation considered as an overall project? The question of the 'privileged revolutionary subject' has long been dominated by the class paradigm. Politically this concerns the ranking of emancipations, which organization is to exercise leadership, what are the terms of co-operation in alliances, coalitions, fronts?

In the 1960s, in the wake of the embourgeoisement or 'privatization' of the Western working class, Third Worldism fulfilled the desire for a new historical subject. Marcuse, on the cusp of two eras, pinned his hopes on a combination of the disaffected in the West and the disinherited in the Third World (Marcuse, 1964). The disillusionment with post-revolutionary societies, not only in the socialist bloc but also in the Third World, again created a demand for a new historical emancipatory subject. For a while it seemed that the new social movements which came into focus from the 1970s fulfilled this role.

EMANCIPATION AND THE NEW SOCIAL MOVEMENTS

The new social movements (NSM) have been considered under several analytical models. They have been viewed in terms of social pathology – for instance, as expressions of an 'excess of democracy'. They have been annexed to the old movements and analysed in terms of the class paradigm – as in structural Marxism and variations on the 'and class' type of literature. Among the new theoretical approaches formulated in relation to the NSM, we can distinguish perspectives which ignore or reject a notion of emancipation (resource mobilization theory and several forms of poststructuralism and postmodernism), those which uphold it with reservations (European social movement theories) and those which reconstruct emancipation (forms of poststructuralism, post-Marxism). While these approaches differ on the point of emancipation they converge on other points relevant to rethinking emancipation.

Resource mobilization theory departs from the social pathology or breakdown of the integration approach in regarding conflictual behaviour not as an abnormal condition in society but as normal and in viewing the actors in collective mobilization not as an irrational 'crowd' but as rational agents (e.g. Oberschall, 1973; Zald and McCarthy, 1979). Keynotes of this approach are rationality, organization and 'objective' variables such as interests, resources, opportunities and strategies. The framework of analysis is neo-utilitarian logic with actors engaging in cost–benefit analyses and following a 'Clausewitzian' understanding of politics. Social movements are the outcome of the strategic mobilization of resources in a political marketplace where actors perform rationally in pursuit of their interests.

It has been argued that this market model of social mobilization overemphasizes the role of rational calculation, leadership and formal organization in movements (Foss and Larkin, 1986). While the critique of the breakdown thesis is valid, excluding the analysis of values, ideologies, projects, culture and identity in other than instrumental terms is not (Cohen, 1985: 688). Resource mobilization theory may be relevant with respect to the bargaining strategies of organized groups capable of negotiating demands, but it does not account for the processes of identity formation, which involve non-negotiable demands or demands which are in the process of taking shape (Cohen, 1985: 692). Problems which this paradigm does not address are identity (how does a group identity come about?), consciousness (how do actors become aware of common interests?) and solidarity (how do collective interests command loyalty?).

By contrast, in the perspectives developed in Europe, the interests pursued by social movements are viewed not as givens but as constructions which take shape in the process of social action. The essentialism of the subject is replaced with the construction of identity. As historically new dimensions of NSM, Touraine (1981) identifies the concern with democratization and the expansion of civil society, with cultural issues, reflexivity concerning identity and self-limitation. According to Melucci (1989: 205–6), while the contemporary social movements as such are not new, novel structural elements are information-orientation, process-oriented action, integration of the private and the public spheres and planetary consciousness. In these approaches the emphasis is not on structure or on agency, but on action itself.

Some exponents of European action sociology are quite sanguine about the emancipatory impetus of NSM, in particular those of the 1980s. According to Zsuzsa Hegedus (1989: 19), the 1980s have witnessed

> . . . the massive emergence throughout the world of collective actions which are non-violent and pragmatic in their methods, non-integrated and multiple in their structures, anti-hierarchical and networking in their organizations, heterogeneous (cross-class, cross-ideology, cross-age) in their constituencies, non-coercive in people participation and non-exclusive in their adherence . . .

This profile of organizational methods and structures can be supplemented with other tendencies. In most perspectives there is no longer a privileged subject for radical collective action. Class struggle as a general framework is left behind. Whether or not in specific conditions class-based movements are the most significant actors, depends not solely on objective conditions but on logics of identity formation and mobilization, part of which are cultural in character. In addition, the state is no longer the obvious target of transformative action. Social action tends to become 'movementist' rather than statist in orientation. The terrain is civil society as much as the state, and cultural as much as political. Transformation is no longer conceived as total. 'Self-limiting radicalism' (Touraine, 1981; Cohen, 1985) is the predominant note. In the imagery of social transformation revolution as total rupture is abandoned in favour of changing hegemony, and expanding civil society as against state and market along with structural reform.

A common query is what the relationship is, or should be, between the old and new movements. For instance: 'new social movements can coalesce with other political groupings much more easily when a new ideological common denominator is found. By that I mean a social project, a notion of a new ordering of the polity and the community that calls into play ideas of order and equity, of historical opportunity and cultural consensus. The discrete addition of separate demands will not serve' (Birnbaum, 1988: 103). According to Michael Harrington (1987: 193), 'What is needed in the late twentieth century is not just another program. What is needed is a restatement of the basic moral vision of the Western Left.'

In these views fragmentation is posed as a problem and a return to an overarching narrative as a solution. There are structural reasons why class is unlikely to return as the central paradigm and provide such a unified solution, the most significant being the onset of post-Fordism or flexible accumulation (Harvey, 1989). Sivanandan (1990) refers to this as the 'emancipation of capital from labour'. The retreat of class and the dispersion of subject positions is a tendency widely observed. Clark and Lipset (1991) document the 'fragmentation of stratification' in the Western world: the weakening of class stratification, the decline of economic determinism and the increased importance of social and cultural factors, and the fact that politics is less organized by class and more by other loyalties. This does not mean that class loses relevance but that it is no longer necessarily the single overriding dimension. Terms change in meaning according to context; whether class is one feature among others or the most salient, overdetermined, all-encompassing dimension implies a world of difference: it is only the latter that constitutes a 'class society' (Laclau, 1990: 163–6).

Chantal Mouffe (1988: 98) cautions that 'it is both dangerous and mistaken to see a "privileged revolutionary subject" constituted in the new social movements, a subject who would take the place formerly occupied by the now fallen worker class'.

> Like those of the workers, these struggles are not necessarily socialist or even progressive. Their articulation depends on discourses existing at a given moment and on the type of subject the resistances construct. They can, therefore, be as easily assimilated by the discourses of the anti-status quo Right as by those of the Left, or be simply absorbed into the dominant system, which thereby neutralizes them or even utilizes them for its own modernization.

In this view the features of the NSM do not *per se* add up to a new profile of emancipation, although there are common tendencies. According to Melucci (see his article, pp. 67–8), concepts like liberation or emancipation 'are too strictly connected to the conceptual and linguistic horizon of industrial society to be used without metacommunicating about them'. Social movements have 'enlightened the new potential for democracy in the contemporary world, together with new powers and new risks'.

EMANCIPATION AND THE POSTMODERN TURN

The themes and sensibilities of the NSM overlap with those of poststructuralism and postmodernism. In postmodernism the plurality which is a matter of practice of the new movements has become a point of theory. If the grand theme of modernity is human beings taking responsibility for their own destiny, that is the conscious programming and production of society, poststructuralism and postmodernism may be considered as reflections upon that project. They are reflections on what really happened and what went wrong, and as such they are essentially pleas for self-reflexiveness, particularly as regards the role of reason, knowledge and power, the exclusions of modernity, the dark side of the Enlightenment.

Since emancipation looms large in the project of modernity, poststructuralism and postmodernism are also reflections on emancipation – rejecting, deconstructing and redefining it. If modernity is about the logic of order produced as against order received, or custom replaced by reason, postmodernism is about the logics of producing order. If modernity is about the promise of power, postmodernism is about the problem of power. As such it represents heightened sensibilities. Unlike Marxism, it is not an 'in-house' critique of the Enlightenment project but it brackets the premises of modernity and the Enlightenment itself. It interrupts the familiar duets of liberals and radicals. Since it is concerned with paradigmatic transgression it generates irritability among paradigm partisans. Since its concerns are central to the question of the making and the makeability of society, they are also central to the questions of development, which is after all nothing but the Enlightenment applied or modernization operationalized.

This is not the occasion for a methodical engagement with poststructuralism and postmodernism, but only a very brief reflection on some of its findings in relation to emancipation, put in relief by comparison to past paradigms. The work inspired by linguistics, literary theory, psychoanalyis and culture studies which is grouped under the headings of semiotics, poststructuralism and deconstruction is itself too heterogeneous, self-reflexive and self-critical to invite comfortable generalizations.

Part of the poststructuralist turn is the concern with culture as a terrain of politics. Evident already in the work of Gramsci and Walter Benjamin, this concern has been elaborated by Foucault, Raymond Williams and Edward Said and has resulted in different understandings of power as hegemony (Gramsci), as discourse (Foucault) and as representation (Said). In this light the idea of a ruling class comes across as superficial and old-fashioned: 'the dominant social class is not the given order's master but its creature at least as much as the subordinate class is' (Cocks, 1989: 47). It follows that the relationship between power and emancipation can no longer be conceived as a simple adversarial relationship:

> There is not, on the one side, a discourse of power, and opposite it, another discourse that runs counter to it. Discourses are tactical elements or blocks operating in the field of force relations; there can run different and even contradictory discourses within the same strategy; they can, on the contrary, circulate without changing their form from one strategy to another, opposing strategy. (Foucault, 1981: 101–2)

Understanding power and emancipation as discursive contestations in a field of forces opens up terrains beyond conventional social theory. The boundary between power and emancipation itself becomes fluid. Poststructuralism is about the fluidity of boundaries, the unfixity of fixations, the partiality of totalities.

No doubt there is an emancipatory project underlying poststructuralism. But it is a kind of project that implies emancipation *from* the Enlightenment tradition and received notions of emancipation. With Foucault this is tied up with the question of transgression[6] and hinted at, for instance, in his statement that 'modern thought is advancing toward that region where man's Other must become the same as himself' (Foucault, 1970: 328). This concern ranges from the project of anti-psychiatry (or breaking down the barrier between madness and sanity, in other words, madness as a construction) to that of critical anthropology (or breaking down the barrier between savagery and civilization, in other words, savagery as a construction).

That poststructuralism is not just concerned with deconstructing emancipation but also with reconstructing it, is apparent, for instance, in poststructuralist feminism (e.g. Weedon, 1987; Nicholson, 1990; Diamond and Quinby, 1988). We can emphasize either the discontinuities or the continuities between Marxism and poststructuralism. One of the themes of poststructuralism is the 'question of the Other'. In Marxist terms the 'other' is the working class and in this reading Marxism is a project of disidentification with bourgeois political economy and élite culture, and identification with working-class aspirations. Thus, according to Amilcar

Cabral (1969: 110), petty bourgeois intellectuals who want to join the struggle of the subaltern classes have to commit suicide as a class 'in order to be reborn as revolutionary workers'. The others of poststructuralism and deconstruction are women, blacks, orientals, natives, gays, prisoners or mad people. The poststructuralist sensibility is one of disidentification with the dominant culture, whether in its imperial or 'white malestream' forms, and identification with the other. In this vein Sandra Harding (1991; see also her article on pp. 175–93) proposes that we 'reinvent ourselves as other'.

In this regard the overall movement in Marxism and poststructuralism is similar: it concerns the self-awareness and mobilization of subaltern identities by transgressing boundaries of exclusion and inverting hierarchies. The continuity comes across in Nancy Hartsock's (1987) proposal to reconstruct Marxism as a 'minority' project. In this light the poststructuralist turn implies the planetarization of emancipation (the conscientization of Western imperialism) and the inversion of the Enlightenment (the conscientization of its shadow side). The former matches the sensibilities of the post-imperial era and the latter the epistemology of constructivism.

The objection that deconstruction 'offers no alternative' cuts two ways. Deconstruction parallels the Marxist contradiction for it is likewise concerned with underlying tensions and conflicts, but differs from contradiction in that it is not part of a dialectical process which resolves the conflict in a synthesis. Therefore Marxism could give rise to 'real existing socialism'. Deconstruction provides no such unified solution. But if we reconsider Marxism, the difference, at least in theory, is slim: for the synthesis is the start of another dialectical round, the process does not cease. Therefore Marxism also gives rise to notions such as 'permanent revolution' and 'continuous revolution' (cf. Ryan, 1982).

The discontinuities lie in the epistemology – which is no longer that of determinist materialism but of multidimensionality and constructivism; in the terrain – no longer that of political economy but of the political writ large comprising civil society and culture; in the project – no longer that of the future dictatorship of the subaltern but of inclusive democratization; in the conception of the future – which begins with the 'end of the future'.

Emancipation has long been associated with transcendence and utopianism (as in Mannheim, Bloch, Buber, Marcuse, Ricoeur). The critique of utopianism is by no means new (Dahrendorf, 1967);

what is new is that the abdication from claiming the future recurs as a left-wing theme. For Foucault the era of the universalist prophetic intellectual is past. For Laclau, anti-utopia becomes the starting point: 'Utopia is essentially asceptic, since it is a "model" of society conceived independently of the struggles needed to impose it' (Laclau, 1990: 232). In the perspective of post-Marxism the present juncture is

> . . . a moment in which new generations, without the prejudices of the past, without theories presenting themselves as 'absolute truths' of history, are constructing new emancipatory discourses, more human, diversified and democratic. The eschatological and epistemological ambitions are more modest, but the liberating aspirations are wider and deeper. (Laclau and Mouffe, in Laclau, 1990: 98)

It is not without irony that we find that this attitude of modesty and anti-utopia brings us back to Popper's (1966) critiques of the radical schemes and blueprints of utopianism and Marxism. In what way does this anti-utopia differ from Popper's plea for 'piecemeal social engineering'? In Lyotard we find a similar attitude: what remains after the end of metanarratives in science and imagination are 'little narratives'.

Postmodern sensibilities are plural, protean, not reducible to a single view – not even to that most often cited assertion, that postmodernism equals the 'incredulity towards metanarratives' (Lyotard, 1984). Lyotard, in one reading, has produced 'the dark night of the metanarrative to end all metanarratives' (Montag, 1988: 93). Postmodernism cannot simply be presented as the refutation of modernity's 'grand récits', without in turn exposing itself as a total theory of postmodernity. It is difficult to avoid giving a modern definition of the postmodern; in fact, virtually any definition of postmodernism will turn out to be modernist.

The postmodern involves a heightened sensibility to instability, indeterminacy and transience. Rather than being the solvent of modernity's woes, the postmodern is another terrain of contestation: indeed postmodernism is available in neo-conservative, liberal or radical versions (Hudson, 1989). There are several attempts to link the postmodern to radical politics, a relationship that has been referred to as 'the most pressing problem of contemporary social science' (Turner, 1990: 10). Postmodernism is, virtually per definition, a matter of looking in the rearview mirror: as postmodernism, or a reflection on modernity. What matters is what it means to turn one's back on modernity – whether the dominant note is one of relief or nostalgia.

Central preoccupations of the moderns have been causality and determination as the logics of producing order. The emerging paradigm is a reflection not on the determined (order received) but on the constructed (order produced) character of social realities and on the contingencies involved in the process. The epistemology of constructivism is as central to poststructuralism and postmodernism as the epistemology of causality, determinism and mechanical models of social change have been to modernity – the project of Bacon, Hobbes, Descartes, Condorcet and Comte makes place for the world of Wiener (cybernetics), Luhmann (systems theory), Bateson (ecology) and Bohr, Bohm and Prigogine (quantum physics).

Poststructuralism and postmodernism are not without their silences and exclusions. Criticisms advanced against poststructuralism are the tendency to 'theorrea' (Merquior, 1986), the predilection for high theory, ethnocentrism (see article by Slater, pp. 283–319), ignoring the Third World (Nederveen Pieterse, 1989/1990: Ch. 3) and actual relations of power, and the weakness of economic analysis, or 'throwing out the tool of economic analysis along with the ideological baggage of economism' (Sivanandan, 1990: 5).

Is poststructuralism an expression of the embourgeoisement of social theory? Is it not obvious that culturalism is to the disadvantage of subaltern groups who are better served by a materialist outlook? There seems to be little space indeed between the Scylla of economism and the Charybdis of culturalism. What is rightly being questioned, however, is the very dichotomy of base and superstructure, the material and the cultural, as, among other things, a variation on the dualism of body and mind (Mitchell, 1990). Materialism itself is a particular cultural politics, and one that provides for a very narrow understanding of the logics of political mobilization.

There are, in fact, numerous accounts of the political economy of the postmodern. A general observation is that postmodernity correlates with the condition variously termed post-Fordism, disorganized capitalism, just-in-time capitalism or flexible accumulation (Harvey, 1989). Others, like Jameson, interpret postmodernism as the culture of late capitalism and in terms of the commodification of culture (Lash, 1990; Featherstone, 1990).

Along with the relations of production the technologies too have changed, from strong power controls to weak power controls, which use much less energy relative to the processes they control (e.g.

compare mechanical machines to touch button power). Mulgan (1988) argues that

> . . . the replacement of strong power by weak power controls in the physical machinery of post-Fordism is being matched by a parallel transformation of social organization and control, a transformation that is also one from strong to weak types of control. . . The weak power structures of the 'new times' . . . tend to be decentralised without a single point of leadership; communication is horizontal; structures are cellular rather than pyramid like, a shifting mosaic rather than the kind of structure that can be drawn as a diagram.

Strong power relationships of hierarchical command were the model both for control and for emancipation in the industrial and Fordist era. In this reading, according to Mulgan, the present crisis of socialism is not a crisis of values but of structures.

Diverse and heterogeneous as these reorientations are, is there a pattern which separates the 'modern' views on emancipation from the 'postmodern'? Do the reorientations add up to the contours of a new emancipatory perspective on the horizon? The question itself may imply a 'modern' urge for a clear-cut inventory, a sense of direction, an order of change – a nostalgia for overdetermination.

The total theory and universal vision of emancipation may not be succeeded by another total theory, but by an awareness of plurality. There is no need to rush in the search for a new paradigm. A recent volume on Third World politics argues for 'a more detached, eclectic attitude towards paradigms' (Manor, 1991: 7). As Laclau (1990: 225) puts it, 'we would today speak of "emancipations" rather than "Emancipation"'.[7] As an objection to Laclau it has been pointed out that his perspective gives no indication which articulations among movements are more possible than others (Mouzelis, 1988). One question is whether open-endedness is to be taken as a problem or as an opportunity, but still more basic a question is whether there is an alternative at all.

Among the new perspectives there is no lack of dissonants. To mention just one example, in most interpretations the postmodern sense is one of fragmentation and the breakup of totalities, while another sensibility, which is also in evidence among NSM, is holism. Holism as a perspective is found in Green movements, in social ecology (Bookchin, 1982) and as a theme uniting feminism and ecology (Capra and Spretnak, 1984). Complementary holism, a view inspired by developments in quantum physics, has also given rise to a political theory (Albert et al., 1986).

To what extent are these reorientations 'universalizable' across the globe? A point often made with respect to the 'old' liberation theories is that they have been Eurocentric (Joshi, 1988). Furthermore, it is often made to appear that the NSM are specific to Western, post-industrial societies, or that if the NSM are planetary, they play only a marginal role in third world settings.

In India, for instance, the role played by NSM concerned with issues of ecology, health and gender is regarded as 'complementary to the more powerful class-based movements': 'Compared to class-based struggles – the trade union movement, peasant movements of the Sharad Joshi/Mahendra Tikait variety, and Naxalite-led movements of the landless agricultural labourers and tribals – the popular support enjoyed by the new social movements is negligible' (Guha, 1989: 15). The new movements are advised to retain their identity while being assigned 'a valuable role to play in *enlarging* the scope of lower class movements'. Kothari (1984), on the other hand, sees for the 'nonparty political formations' a role both more profound and more limited than the political parties.

A typology of social settings, along with the question of which are the leading types of collective action, would yield a simple ranking of emancipations. In agricultural settings, social agents tend to be defined by cultural criteria such as religion and ethnicity and by ascribed status such as kinship or caste, and collective action tends to be structured along these lines. In industrial settings social agents defined by class are the most salient and class-based movements take the lead, while in post-industrial settings new social movements would take the lead. A consequence of this approach is *stageism* with respect to agents of social change, in other words, an emancipation evolutionism, which means that we still toe the line of unilear progress. Obviously, the typologies themselves stem from prioritizing the relations of production and are predicated upon the class paradigm. We are reminded of Hegel's 'peoples without history' and Fukuyama's (1989) distinction between those 'mired in history' and those in the 'post-historical' stage.

While seeming commonsensical this approach is deceptive in several ways. An empirical objection is that post-Fordism and flexible accumulation affect all societies whether directly or indirectly. Besides, all societies, North and South, are programmed societies, in which planning and social engineering play an important part.[8] Furthermore, each setting, third world societies included, is a *mélange* of agricultural, industrial and post-industrial sectors. The multisectoral quality of combined and uneven development affects the nature and dispersion of subject positions and the multiplication of sites of conflict. Quantitative assessments of the strengths of social forces bypass the unevenness in social networks. Judgements as to which movements are most numerous or powerful in a society may homogenize and simplify the social terrain and ignore its uneven and composite network character.

In fact, it should come as no surprise that some forms of action of NSM match those of peoples outside the Western framework, and that postmodern sensibilities have been voiced earlier or independently in non-Western points of view, as part of the critique of modernity-for-export. Thus, Ashis Nandy exposes the rendezvous with power and control that is implicit in liberation as a project; the old liberation theories figure as a mode of control – 'the victim must first learn the oppressors language and worldview before qualifying as a proper dissenter' (Nandy, 1988: 167, 1987).

In comparing Gandhi's views to those of Habermas, Pantham notes the extra-rational elements in Gandhi's approach of truth-centred direct action. According to Gandhi, the 'attribution of omnipotence to reason is as bad a piece of idolatry as is worship of stick and stone believing it to be God' (quoted in Pantham, 1986a: 203). Gandhi's approach requires participation in action and involves the abdication of persuasion even by argumentation: 'everyone should follow his or her own inner voice'. These views overlap with other emancipatory perspectives. They match a widely shared understanding that liberation must first of all be the liberation of oneself (a theme in existentialism, Erich Fromm and the Freudian left). With his contemporary Gramsci, Gandhi shares the concern with popular religion and with merging the national and the popular (Pantham, 1986b). The latter concern we also find with other contemporaries, such as the Peruvian Mariátegui (see article by Slater, pp. 283–319). The shift from persuasion to dialogue is a matter of principle in Paulo Freire's (1972) popular education approach.

The sensibility of the postmodern is one of emancipation from emancipation, or emancipation from modernity. Part of what this entails is expressed by Ashis Nandy (1988: 171): 'Human nature being what it is, while everyone likes to be a social engineer, few like to be the objects of social engineering.'

EMANCIPATIONS OR EMANCIPATION

Several episodes of emancipation have passed review: social movements in the wake of the democratic revolution, class struggles and national liberation (from the Young movements to the colonial question), and new social movements, in the context of poststructuralism and the postmodern. What comes across most strongly is the impression of *movement* and ever shifting horizons: whichever the social context, emancipation challenges the prevailing codes. A theory of emancipation must be, above all, a theory of the relativity of the social.

If we try to distil a minimum profile of emancipation as it emerges from contemporary reorientations, it includes, as regards aims, the concern with autonomy, in terms of organization, a tendency towards network forms, and, in terms of mentality, a tendency towards self-limitation. The main differences between the modern and the postmodern emancipations appears to be that the former situate themselves within the Enlightenment tradition and secondly that they take an instrumental attitude to power, whereas the latter problematize power to a much greater degree. How the politics of autonomy work out depends on the way it relates to other political dimensions. Autonomy takes on different forms ranging from self-definition, self-determination, identity or difference.

At any rate it involves self-organization, and this relates to the issue of democracy, which is another recurrent theme in the contemporary reorientations of emancipatory thought. Democracy has become a central terrain of rethinking in critical liberal democratic theory (McPherson, 1977), in merging democracy and socialism (Cunningham, 1987), notions of radical democracy (Laclau and Mouffe, 1985) and in development thinking (Kothari, 1988). Some prefer to speak of 'new democratic movements' rather than NSM.[9] The democratic theme can be interpreted as part of a wider trend towards a reconvergence of liberalism and Marxism, of Tocqueville and Marx — nineteenth-century enemy ideologies, both Enlightenment offspring, separated by the Cold War, reborn as twins in the late twentieth century. We further recognize this in the comeback of classical liberal themes such as autonomy, citizenship and human rights as part of the new politics.

While contemporary emancipations are framed against the horizon of democracy, there are also tensions between democracy and emancipation (see article by Apter, pp. 139–73). According to Laclau (1990: 169):

> The central obstacle preventing the democratization of emancipatory discourses is the fact that . . . while ambiguity and indeterminacy are central features of democracy, emancipatory discourses tend to manifest themselves as total ideologies which seek to define and master the foundations of the social.

This responds, according to Laclau, 'to a deep psychological need': it follows from the very process of constructing a collective will and a hegemony. 'Democratic universalism' as the 'universalism of indeterminacy' is cast as a way out of the dilemma because it means that no form of social organization 'can take on the paradigmatic value of a model' (Laclau, 1990: 170). This being the case, then, what is the content of radical democracy itself?

In some respects the minimum profile of emancipation also matches that of particularism, chauvinism and fundamentalism, which are likewise preoccupied with autonomy. There remains a fundamental tension between emancipations in a particularistic sense and emancipation in a general sense, or between emancipations and emancipation. If there is no guideline but 'universal indeterminacy', then what is the difference between a particular process of emancipation, in the sense of a new group entering into dominance, and the 'circulation of élites'? Emancipation in the sense of a new group entering into dominance without the 'rules of practice' being altered, may in the last instance not be distinguishable from the reshuffling of élites. Thus, a neo-fascist organization organizing local youth and the unemployed, gaining votes and entering legislative bodies might be considered a process of emancipation from the point of view of the group in question.

It follows that emancipations plural must in some fashion refer to emancipation in a general sense: not every process of empowerment is emancipatory. A working definition I propose is that emancipation refers to collective actions which seek to level and disperse power, or seek to install more inclusive values than the prevailing ones. This means that emancipation, postmodern turn or not, involves a moral horizon.

The articles in this publication span the terrains of social and political theory, social movements and development. Starting out from the central theme of rethinking emancipation, the overall tendency is towards reflection and social theory. Together the contributions represent a variety of views on emancipation straddling modern and poststructuralist views. The distinction between old and new movements, old and new paradigms, modern and postmodern plays a part in most contributions.

Self-limiting understandings of rationality and emancipation are a thread running through several reflections. Reviewing developments in the study of social movements in terms of their wider implications, Alberto Melucci brings out the theme of self-limitation. The loss of certainties is the starting point and the potential foundation of a new awareness: 'if we can accept that in social relations everything is not subject to the calculus of an absolute rationality, diversity and uncertainty can become the basis for a new solidarity. From this condition of conscious fragility could come the changes in ethical values that form the basis for coexistence' (p. 53). This is the point of departure in rethinking emancipation: 'We need a self-limiting concept of emancipation, mindful of the dark side of the modern myths, like progress, liberation and revolution' (p. 73).

Sudipta Kaviraj turns to the 'dark' tradition of the Enlightenment to find a self-limiting or minimalist rationality. In this light he reviews Marxism as discourse and as a field of contestation. Rereading the Marxist theory of history leads to rereading of the history of Marxist theory and practice, one that shows the consequences of maximalist rationalism for instance as regards party and state structures, and views on the peasantry.

Reflecting on Marxism and the problem of violence, Bhikhu Parekh argues for a radical self-critique of Marxism if it is to remain a theory of emancipation. His reflections raise the question to what extent Marxist theory can be used to legitimize state terrorism, in the name of what has been termed the 'calculus of progress' and what might be regarded as the 'utilitarianism of the left'.

Likewise Ernesto Laclau's reflections concern the awareness of self-limitation and its ramifications: examining the logical claims made according to 'the classic concept of emancipation' they are found logically incompatible. 'The relation between particularity and universality is an essentially unstable and undecidable one' (p. 134). For Laclau the awareness of 'our own finitude' is 'the beginning of freedom'.

Collective actions, according to Melucci, act as 'revealers'; 'Collective mobilization forces power into the open and exposes the interests behind the apparent neutrality of its rationality' (p. 68).

This notion is also taken up by David Apter, who examines the interplay of institutional democracy and emancipation movements. Apter's centre ground and touchstone is democracy, which itself represents an emancipation process as it emerges out of the evolution from an order model to a choice model. Apter emphasizes the totalizing face of emancipation and its 'politics of the moral moment'. Seeking to '"liberate" the mainstream from itself' and favouring 'total uprooting', contemporary movements such as the Situationists engage in the 'postmodern politics' of 'inversionary discourse'. Hence the interplay between emancipation and democracy is precarious.

For Sandra Harding, the logic of difference developed by the new social movements poses a different kind of problem. What kind of knowledge, what kind of epistemology is needed to bring together today's multiple subject positions in a 'rainbow politics'? Harding argues that 'we must "reinvent ourselves as other" in order to develop those kinds of doubly multiple subjectivites that are capable of understanding objectively their own social location, not just imagining that they understand the social locations of others' (p. 190). This contradictory position is the landscape of Virginia Vargas's reflections on the development of feminism in Latin America, where, in addition, modernization has only been an incomplete, truncated process. Vargas analyses the recent development of the feminist movement in Latin America by looking, from the inside, at the series of Feminist Encounters which have been held every two or three years since 1981. The observations made by others, in particular Melucci and Harding, in generic terms are concretized and driven home in Vargas's article, which is thus a vivid illustration and discussion of the precarious transition and interaction between old and new, modern and postmodern emancipations in Latin America.

Several discussions of emancipation and development conclude this volume, some of which elaborate modern and one engages postmodern views. Taking a Marxist-feminist perspective on the questions of women in development, Valentine Moghadam argues that in the 'belt of classic patriarchy', which stretches from North Africa across the Middle East and the northern plains of the Indian subcontinent to rural China, development has been beneficial to women — genuine development, that is, as against distorted development. Development erodes classic patriarchy and in providing women with education, paid employment and a wider range of life-options, contributes to women's emancipation. In other words, in this particular context modernization furthers women's emancipation.

Expanding on his previous work on emancipation, Wim Wertheim turns to the role of the state in development and to the question of the dialectic of the state and emancipation: under what circumstances do states act as allies of emancipation and when do they become a brake upon emancipation? In criticizing the tenets of neoliberalism he reviews the historical role states have played in the development of Western countries and the neo-mercantilist policies of communist states and highlights the underlying need for developing countries to protect themselves from foreign economic and political domination. This, along with the pressing problems of development, creates the demand for a strong state; the state however is likely to become an end in itself and thus a brake upon further emancipation.

No doubt the ramifications of poststructuralist and postmodern thought for the questions of development will become an area of major debate. If development follows the logic of modernity, operates within the framework of modernity, postmodernity is likely to affect the practice and theory of development quite profoundly. With David Slater this project itself is undergoing redefinition. Slater's concern is to 'open up Marxist development theory so that new territory can be explored' and he does so by exploring the relevance of the poststructuralist and postmodern turn for critical development theory. The postmodern sense is emancipatory inrelation to the certitudes of modern universalism and modernization theory and 'enabling in its destructuring of Marxist totality', but when the realities of oppression and subordination in global politics are occluded or anaesthetized, postmodern politics becomes a barrier to emancipation (p. 290). While criticizing postmodern authors for residual universalism and ethnocentrism, Slater argues for taking the postmodern in its enabling sense – for the sake of its iconoclasm, openness and reproblematization of fixities.

NOTES

The articles in this publication are the selected and revised proceedings of a seminar which took place at the Institute of Social Studies in The Hague in 1991. Only Bhikhu Parekh's article has been added later. I am indebted to the editors of the journal *Development and Change* for their consistent support of this project. In particular, to Martin Doornbos with whom the idea to organize the seminar on emancipation orginates, who co-organized it and helped edit this volume; likewise to Henk van

Roosmalen, in particular for his editorial support; and to Paula Bownas for her patient assistance.

1. These distinctions play an important role in Wertheim's work (e.g. Wertheim, 1974), but his concept of emancipation is open ended on these points.

2. More critical is the definition of popular participation used by the Popular Participation Programme of the UN Research Institute for Social Development: 'the organized efforts to increase control over resources and regulative institutions in given social situations, on the part of groups and movements hitherto excluded from such control' (Pearse and Stiefel, 1979, quoted in Turton, 1987: 3).

3. For instance, Laclau and Mouffe (1985: 152–3) note: 'Only in certain cases do these forms of resistance take on a political character and become struggles directed toward putting an end to relations of subordination as such.'

4. Several of these movements and their interdependence are discussed in Nederveen Pieterse 1989/1990. On links between black and women's emancipation concerns and movements see, for example, Lerner (1979) and Nederveen Pieterse (1992: Ch. 14).

5. Thus, in presenting social movements as 'antisystemic movements', world-system theorists prioritize their world-system definition of the global situation (Arrighi et al., 1989). Here capitalism has been renamed the 'world-system' and class struggle 'antisystemic struggle'.

6. Foucault's transgression is not the same as transcendence but more akin to Nietzsche's 'beyond' as in *Jenseits von Gut und Böse* (see Boyne, 1990: 84).

7. 'While the socialist project was presented as the global emancipation of humanity and the result of a single revolutionary act of institution, such a "fundamentalist" perspective has today gone into crisis. Any struggle is, by definition, a *partial* struggle – even the violent overthrow of an authoritarian regime – and none can claim to embody the "global liberation of man"' (Laclau, 1990: 225).

8. For this point I am indebted to Michael Chai (see Touraine, 1977).

9. 'Democratic discourse questions all forms of inequality and subordination. That is why I propose to call those new social movements "new democratic struggles" because they are extensions of the democratic revolution to new forms of subordination. Democracy is our most subversive idea because it interrupts all existing discourses and practices of subordination' (Mouffe, 1988: 96; cf. Laclau and Mouffe, 1985: 159–60).

BIBLIOGRAPHY

Albert, Michael et al. (1986) *Liberating Theory*. Boston, MA: South End Press.

Amin, S. (1980) *Class and Nation*. New York: Monthly Review Press.

Arrighi, G., Hopkins, T.K. and Wallerstein, I. (1989) *Antisystemic Movements*. London: Verso.

Bauman, Z. (1976) *Towards a Critical Sociology: An Essay on Commonsense and Emancipation*. London: Routledge.

Bay, C. (1981) *Strategies of Political Emancipation*. Notre Dame, IN: University of Notre Dame Press.

Billington, J.H. (1980) *Fire in the Minds of Men: The Origins of the Revolutionary Faith*. New York: Basic Books.

Birnbaum, N. (1988) *The Radical Renewal*. New York: Pantheon.

Bookchin, M. (1982) *The Ecology of Freedom*. Palo Alto, CA: Cheshire Books.

Bookman, A. and Morgen, S. (1988) *Women and the Politics of Empowerment*. Philadelphia, PA: Temple University Press.

Boyne, R. (1990) *Foucault and Derrida: The Other Side of Reason*. London: Unwin Hyman.

Cabral, A. (1969) *Revolution in Guinea*. New York: Monthly Review Press.

Capra, F. and Spretnak, C. (1984) *Green Politics*. New York: Dutton.

Clark, T.N. and Lipset, S.M. (1991) 'Are Social Classes Dying?', *International Sociology* VI(4): 397–411.

Clegg, S. (1989) *Frameworks of Power*. London: Sage.

Cocks, J. (1989) *The Oppositional Imagination*. London: Routledge.

Cohen, J.L. (1985) 'Strategy or Identity: New Theoretical Paradigms and Contemporary Social Movements', *Social Research* 52(4): 663–716.

Condorcet, A.N. de (1794) *Esquisse d'un tableau historique des progrès de l'esprit humain*. Paris.

Cooper, D. (ed.) (1967) *The Dialectics of Liberation*. Harmondsworth: Penguin.

Cunningham, F. (1987) *Democratic Theory and Socialism*. Cambridge: Cambridge University Press.

Dahl, R.A. (1970) *After the Revolution? Authority in a Good Society*. New Haven, CT: Yale University Press.

Dahrendorf, R. (1967) *Pfade aus Utopia*. Munich: Piper.

Davidson, B. (1978) *Africa in Modern History*. Harmondsworth: Penguin.

Dews, P. (ed.) (1986) 'Introduction', in Jürgen Habermas, *Autonomy and Solidarity*, pp. 1–34. London: Verso.

Diamond, I. and Quinby, L. (eds) (1988) *Feminism and Foucault: Reflections on Resistance*. Boston, MA: Northeastern University Press.

Eisenstadt S.N. (1966) *Modernization: Protest and Change*. Englewood Cliffs, NJ: Prentice Hall.

'Empowerment: A Process of Change' (1990) *Bernard van Leer Foundation Newsletter* 57 (January): 1–9.

Fanon, F. (1967) *The Wretched of the Earth*. Harmondsworth: Penguin.

Featherstone, M. (1990) *Consumer Culture and Postmodernism*. London: Sage.

Feuerlicht, R.S. (1983) *The Fate of the Jews*. London: Quartet.

Foss, D.A. and Larkin, R. (1986) *Beyond Revolution: A New Theory of Social Movements*. South Hadley, MA: Bergin and Garvey.

Foucault, M. (1970) *The Order of Things*. London: Tavistock.

Foucault, M. (1980) in C. Gordon (ed.) *Power/Knowledge*. New York: Pantheon.

Foucault, M. (1981) *The History of Sexuality*, Vol 1. Harmondsworth: Penguin.

Freire, P. (1972) *Pedagogy of the Oppressed*. Harmondsworth: Penguin.

Fukuyama, F. (1989) 'The End of History?', *The National Interest* (Summer): 3–18.

Gay, P. (1969) *The Enlightenment*. New York: Norton.

van Ginneken, J. (1992) *Crowds, Psychology and Politics, 1871–1899*. New York: Cambridge University Press.

Greiffenhagen, M. (ed.) (1973) *Emanzipation*. Hamburg: Hoffman and Campe.

Guha, R. (1989) 'The Problem', *Seminar* on New Social Movements, No. 355 (March): 12–15.

Gutiérrez, G. (1973) *A Theology of Liberation*. Maryknoll, NY: Orbis.

Habermas, J. (1987) *The Theory of Communicative Action*, 2 Vols. Cambridge: Polity Press.

Hall, S. (1988) *The Hard Road to Renewal*. London: Verso.

Harding, S. (1991) *Whose Science? Whose Knowledge*? Ithaca, NY: Cornell University Press.

Harrington, M. (1987) *The Next Left: The History of a Future*. London: Tauris.

Hartsock, N.C.M. (1987) 'Reconstituting Marxism for the Eighties', *New Politics* II(2): 83–96.

Harvey, D. (1989) *The Condition of Postmodernity*. Oxford: Blackwell.

Hegedus, Z. (1989) 'Social Movements and Social Change in Self-creative Society: New Civil Initiatives in the International Arena', *International Sociology* IV(1): 19–36.

Hudson, W. (1989) 'Postmodernity and Contemporary Social Thought', in P. Lassman (ed.) *Politics and Social Theory*, pp. 138–60. London: Routledge.

Hunt, L. (1984) 'Charles Tilly's Collective Action', in T. Skocpol (ed.) *Vision and Method in Historical Sociology*, pp. 244–75. Cambridge: Cambridge University Press.

Huntington, S.P. (1975) in Michel Crozier, S.P. Huntington, and J. Watanuki (eds) *The Crisis of Democracy: Report on the Governability of Democracies to the Trilateral Commission*. New York: New York University Press.

Joshi, P.C. (1988) 'Notes on Gandhi's Contribution to Liberation Thought and Practice', in Lelio Basso International Foundation (ed.) *Theory and Practice of Liberation at the End of the 20th Century*, pp. 151–64. Brussels: Bruylant.

Kandyoti, D. (1988) 'Bargaining with Patriarchy', *Gender and Society* II(3): 174–90.

Kaufman, M. (1991) 'Differential Participation: Men, Women and Popular Power', CEDLA/CERLAC Workshop Paper (unpublished).

Kondylis, P. (1986) *Die Aufklärung in Rahmen des neuzeitlichen Rationalismus*. Munich: DTV; Stuttgart: Klett-Cotta.

Kothari, R. (1984) 'Party and State in Our Times: The Rise of Non-party Political Formations', *Alternatives* IX(54): 542–64.

Kothari, R. (1988) *State against Democracy*. Delhi: Ajanta.

Kronenburg, J. (1986) *Empowerment of the Poor: A Comparative Analysis of Two Development Endeavours in Kenya*. Amsterdam: Koninklijk Instituut voor de Tropen.

Laclau, E. (1990) *New Reflections on the Revolution of Our Time*. London: Verso.

Laclau, E. and Mouffe, C. (1985) *Hegemony and Socialist Strategy: Towards a Radical Democratic Politics*. London: Verso.

Lash, S. (1990) *Sociology of Postmodernism*. London: Routledge.

Lempert, W. (1973) 'Zum Begriff der Emanzipation', in M. Greiffenhagen (ed.) *Emanzipation*, pp. 216–27. Hamburg: Hoffman and Campe.

Lerner, G. (1979) *The Majority Finds its Past: Placing Women in History*. Oxford: Oxford University Press.

Lyotard, J.-F. (1984) *The Postmodern Condition*. Manchester: Manchester University Press.

Lyotard, J.-F. (1988) Interview, *Theory, Culture and Society* V(2–3): 277–309.

McPherson, C. (1977) *The Life and Times of Liberal Democracy*. Oxford: Oxford University Press.

Manor, J. (ed.) (1991) *Rethinking Third World Politics*. London: Longman.

Marcuse, H. (1964) *One Dimensional Man*. Boston, MA: Beacon Press.

Melucci, A. (1989) in J. Keane and P. Mier (eds) *Nomads of the Present*. London: Hutchinson Radius.

Merquior, J.G. (1986) *From Prague to Paris*. London: Verso.

Mitchell, T. (1990) 'Everyday Metaphors of Power', *Theory and Society* 19(5): 545–77.

Montag, W. (1988) 'What is at Stake in the Debate on Postmodernism?', in E.A. Kaplan (ed.) *Postmodernism and its Discontents*, pp. 88–103. London: Verso.

Moore, H.L. (1988) *Feminism and Anthropology*. Oxford: Blackwell.

Mouffe, C. (1988) 'Hegemony and New Political Subjects: Towards a New Concept of Democracy', in C. Nelson and L. Grossberg (eds) *Marxism and the Interpretation of Culture*, pp. 89–104. Basingstoke: Macmillan.

Mouzelis, N. (1988) 'Marxism or Post-Marxism?', *New Left Review* (167): 107–23.

Mulgan, G. (1988) 'Collapse of the Pyramid of Power', *Marxism Today* (December).

Nandy, A. (1987) *Traditions, Tyranny, and Utopias*. Delhi and Oxford: Oxford University Press.

Nandy, A. (1988) 'Liberation of Those Who Do Not Speak the Language of Liberation', in Lelio Basso International Foundation (ed.) *Theory and Practice of Liberation at the End of the 20th Century*, pp. 165–73. Brussels: Bruylant.

Nederveen Pieterse, J. (1989/1990) *Empire and Emancipation: Power and Liberation on a World Scale*. New York: Praeger; London: Pluto Press.

Nederveen Pieterse, J. (1992) *White on Black: Images of Africa and Blacks in Western Popular Culture*. New Haven, CT and London: Yale University Press.

Nicholson, L. (ed.) (1990) *Feminism/Postmodernism*. London: Routledge.

Oberschall, A. (1973) *Social Conflict and Social Movements*. Englewood Cliffs, NJ: Prentice Hall.

Palmer, R.R. (1964) *The Age of the Democratic Revolution*. Princeton, NJ: Princeton University Press.

Pantham, T. (1986a) 'Habermas's Practical Discourse and Gandhi's Satyagraha', *Praxis International* VI(2): 190–205.

Pantham, T. (1986b) 'Proletarian Pedagogy, Satyagraha and Charisma: Gramsci and Gandhi', in R. Roy (ed.) *Contemporary Crisis and Gandhi*, pp. 165–89. Delhi: Discovery.

Pearse, A. and Stiefel, M. (1979) *Inquiry into Participation*. Geneva: UNRISD.

Piven, F.F. and Cloward, R.A. (1977) *Poor People's Movements*. New York: Pantheon.

Platt, R. (1989) 'Reflexivity, Recursion and Social Life: Elements for a Postmodern Sociology', *The Sociological Review* 37(4): 636–67.

Popper, K.R. (1966) *The Open Society and its Enemies*, Vol 2, 5th rev. edn. London: Routledge and Kegan Paul.

Ryan, M. (1982) *Marxism and Deconstruction*. Baltimore, MA: Johns Hopkins University Press.

Scott, A. (1990) *Ideology and the New Social Movements*. London: Unwin Hyman.

Scott, J.C. (1976) *The Moral Economy of the Peasant: Rebellion and Subsistence in Southeast Asia*. New Haven, CT and London: Yale University Press.

Scott, J.C. (1985) *Weapons of the Weak: Everyday Forms of Peasant Resistance*. New Haven, CT and London: Yale University Press.

Scott, J.C. (1991) *Domination and the Arts of Resistance: Hidden Transcripts*. New Haven, CT and London: Yale University Press.

Seidman, S. (1983) *Liberalism and the Origins of European Social Theory*. Berkeley, CA: University of California Press.

Sen, G. and Grown, C. (1988) *Development, Crises and Alternative Visions*. London: Earthscan.

Sivanandan, A. (1990) 'All that Melts into Air is Solid: The Hokum of New Times', *Race and Class* 31(3): 1–30.

Sivanandan, A. (1991) *Communities of Resistance*. London: Verso.

Slater, D. (ed.) (1985) *New Social Movements and the State in Latin America*. Amsterdam: CEDLA.

Slater, D. (1991) 'New Social Movements and Old Political Questions', *International Journal of Political Economy* 21(1): 32–65.

Smelser, N. (1962) *The Theory of Collective Behaviour*. London: Routledge and Kegan Paul.

Thompson, E.P. (1971) 'The Moral of the English Crowd in the Eighteenth Century', *Past and Present* 50.

Tilly, C. (1978) *From Mobilization to Revolution*. Reading, MA: Addison-Wesley.

Touraine, A. (1977) *The Self-production of Society*. Chicago, IL: University of Chicago Press.

Touraine, A. (1981) *The Voice and the Eye*. Cambridge: Cambridge University Press.

Touraine, A. (1985) 'An Introduction to the Study of Social Movements', *Social Research* 52(4): 749–88.

Turner, B.S. (1990) 'Periodization and Politics in the Postmodern', in B.S. Turner (ed.) *Theories of Modernity and Postmodernity*, pp. 1–14. London: Sage.

Turton, A. (1987) *Production, Power and Participation in Rural Thailand*. Geneva: UNRISD.

Unger, R.M. (1987) *Social Theory: Its Situation and its Task*. Cambridge: Cambridge University Press.

Wallerstein, I. (1990) 'Dilemmas of Antisystemic Movements', in S. Amin, G. Arrighi, A.G. Frank and I. Wallerstein (eds) *Transforming the Revolution: Social Movements and the World-system*, pp. 13–53. New York: Monthly Review Press.

Weedon, C. (1987) *Feminist Practice and Poststructuralist Theory*. Oxford: Blackwell.

Wertheim, W.F. (1974) *Evolution and Revolution: The Rising Waves of Emancipation*. Harmondsworth: Penguin.

Wertheim, W.F. (1983) 'Emancipation as Motive Power of Human Evolution and Survival', in W.F. Wertheim (ed.) *Emancipation in Asia: Positive and Negative Lessons from China*, pp. 1–26. Rotterdam: Comparative Asian Studies Programme.

Wood, E. Meiksins (1988) 'Capitalism and Human Emancipation', *New Left Review* (167): 1–21.

Zald, M.N. and McCarthy, J. (eds) (1979) *The Dynamics of Social Movements*. Cambridge, MA: Winthrop.

Jan Nederveen Pieterse is the author of *Empire and Emancipation* (New York, 1989; London, 1990) and *White on Black: Images of Africa and Blacks in Western Popular Culture* (New Haven, CT and London, 1992), and editor of *Christianity and Hegemony: Religion and Politics on the Frontiers of Social Change* (Oxford and New York, 1991). He has lectured in sociology at the University of Amsterdam, the University of Cape Coast, Ghana, the State University of New York, Binghamton, and is presently Senior Lecturer at the Institute of Social Studies, PO Box 90733, 2509 LS The Hague.

Liberation or Meaning? Social Movements, Culture and Democracy

Alberto Melucci

COLLECTIVE ACTION BETWEEN ACTORS AND SYSTEMS

The study of collective action represents an object of knowledge analytically constructed, whose significance goes well beyond the specific topic and relates to many other areas of sociological theory and research. In contemporary social systems whose capacity for self-generation is incomparably superior to any of the past, the forms of action which are less regulated by social order can be read as signals, warnings of processes which can affect the entire system. Thus the analysis of social movements offers theoretical and methodological keys that can be applied far beyond the empirical field of collective action. Movements help us to understand the creation of social action, and thus also of individual action, in systems where the available resources for self-production far exceed today's reproductive needs.

If social action in complex systems is moving closer to the constructed, and farther away from the inherited, society can no longer be conceived as the transcription of a given order in institutions and roles, but should instead be seen as a field of cognitive, motivational and relational investments, which generates its own orientation and meaning. Social movements are a form of action which distance themselves most from the inherited and signal the sites and ways in which society constructs itself. The analysis of collective action is thus a special territory for the exploration of new possibilities.

It is useful first of all to ask why the last twenty years have occasioned such a development of research on collective action and social movements that the field is now becoming an increasingly

Development and.Change (SAGE, London, Newbury Park and New Delhi), Vol. 23 (1992) No. 3, 43–77.

institutionalized disciplinary sector. What is the origin of the interest which has produced such a quantity of contributions and actual schools (McCarthy and Zald, 1977, 1981; Alberoni, 1977; Cohen, 1985; Gamson, 1990; Jenkins, 1983; Klandermans et al., 1988; Tilly, 1978, 1986; Turner and Killian, 1987)?

The answer must be of a sociological nature because in the scenario of complexity the construction of social phenomena and the construction of knowledge have a circular relationship. The interest is due above all to the obvious fact that over the last three decades, in all developed societies, there have been collective mobilizations (among the young, among women, around environmental, peace or minority issues) which forced a re-examination of the previous analytical frameworks. The inadequacy of the available conceptualizations became progressively obvious, as the emerging movements revealed their non-conjunctural nature, and the impossibility of reducing them to mere variations on known forms of collective action became apparent. Researchers found themselves in the uncomfortable position of a hiker on unfamiliar ground without a map. Some turned back to consult the old maps, trying to get their vague impressions of the new terrain to strike a chord with the familiar outlines of the map worn out by habitual use; others struck out blindly, expending great amounts of energy to walk around in circles; still others sought out the nearest reference point (a hill, a tree, a riverbank) and proceeded to draw maps, rudimentary and limited, but reliable, of the new zone.

A second reason for the interest in social movements must be the fact that this field of sociological research is like a gymnasium for those students who wish to take on the challenge of examining the relationship between systems and actors. In no other area of sociology is the weight of the dualistic tradition inherited from the nineteenth century so incongruous with the object of study. Mobile and 'in action', often the expression of emerging needs and conflicts, social movements stand at the frontier, at the opposite pole from that dense and opaque visibility of institutions which suggests that a society can be identified with its established order. Perhaps this is why collective action has either been seen as the expression of a kind of occult energy, a collective *élan vital*, which causes change to appear in the heart of order; or it has been relegated to the margins, where certain social phenomena are exiled, not so much because they resist the established order as because they escape from it. Or, yet again, social movements have been forced into the impossible role of interpreter and flag carrier for 'contradictions' written in the thick fabric of the social structure.

Structural density or the mobility of the actors, 'objective' determinism or revolutionary voluntarism, have been the recurring extremes of a theoretical oscillation inherited from the nineteenth century, indelibly marking the conceptual models in the area of collective action.

DUALISM AND THE METAPHYSICS OF THE ACTOR

The various empirical phenomena which have entered the study of collective action and social movements (from panic to political violence, from fashion to revolution) are traditionally explained in two parallel ways. On the one hand, they are considered to be the sum of atomized events, which due to one circumstance or another, come together to form a collective reality. In the tradition of the crowd psychology, which prolonged its influence up to the theories of mass society of the 1950s (Kornhauser, 1959; Moscovici, 1981), they are attributed to an imbalance in the social order and their collective character depends on the spatial/temporal coincidence of individual behaviours. One could speak in this case of *an action without an actor*.

On the other hand, the Marxist tradition sees collective action as the expression of a structural class condition from which behaviour springs: it expresses (although not always completely) the structural contradictions to which the actor is subjected. The 'true' interests of the actors depend upon these contradictions, even if they are not conscious of their motivations. Here we meet *an actor without an action*. The structural condition 'objectively' selects the actor, without being able to bridge the gap between the 'objective' potential and the action effectively observed. Concrete action always differs from the 'objective' interests and cannot be deduced from the actor's condition. This is the old Marxist problem of the passage from a class-in-itself to a class-for-itself, from the material roots of class interests in capitalist relationships to revolutionary action (or, more often, to the lack of such an action). This immense chasm was inevitably filled up by a kind of *deus ex machina* (the party, the intellectuals) that serves as the external supplier of that consciousness which the actor is lacking. Leninism as a theoretical construct, before political practice, is an inevitable consequence of this dualism.

These two perspectives, here greatly simplified for the purpose of discussion, have been progressively thrown into crisis by changes in historical conditions, but also by the evolution of theory. First, the type of collective action on the basis of which most models, including those still dominant today, were historically constructed, was that of working-class movements during the process of capitalist industrialization. It was around this historical reference point that both the idea of the actor as a revolutionary embodiment of the destiny of the social structure and that of the manipulated mob, under the influence of the suggestive power of a few agitators, were given form: movements as interpreters of history or as expressions of social pathology.

Today, historical and sociological research helps us to understand that the popular movements of the industrialization period combined two different processes, analytically distinct from one another, although empirically linked. One was the actual industrial conflict, tied to the capitalist mode of production and to the factory system: a social conflict putting the working class, the new producers, in opposition to the capitalists, in a struggle for controlling the ends, means and organization of industrial production. The second process, also marked by conflicts, was the progressive integration into the citizenship of social categories which had been excluded from the construction of the modern nation-state: an eminently political process, which widened the base of legitimacy of the state and extended political democracy (Bendix, 1964, 1978).

In the working-class action of the nineteenth century these two processes, a class struggle and a fight for citizenship and the extension of political rights, combine and complement one another. But they seem to draw further apart as the systems grow in complexity and differentiation. The struggle for democracy and citizenship and the conflict that impacts the central resources of the system no longer follow the same path and no longer involve the same actors. Here begins also the separation of theoretical approaches dealing with one or the other of these processes. Concern about citizenship and the extension of democratic rights has not ceased to be important, nor are the claims to civil spaces in modern democracies exhausted. This is, however, a different point of view from that concerned with the forms of conflict with regard to the crucial resources of contemporary systems.

Together with changes in the historical conditions, there has been considerable evolution in the social sciences, which has changed our outlook and our approach to collective phenomena:

• The development of macro-theories which seek to link contemporary collective action to a system analysis of 'post-industrial' or 'post-material' society (Habermas, 1984; Touraine, 1973, 1978, 1984; Giddens, 1984).

• The enormous growth of organizational theory and research, which has come a long way from Weber and the functionalist model; organization is now conceived as a field of resources and limits with an autonomous capacity of mediating between 'objective' constraints and the actual organizational output (Crozier and Friedberg, 1977).

• This emergence of a constructivist view on organizations has been significantly paralleled by the development of cognitive theories according to which action is closely connected to the capacity of the actors to construct their 'scripts' of reality, to influence each other, to negotiate the meanings of their experience (Abelson, 1981; Eiser, 1980; Neisser, 1976; Bateson, 1972, 1979).

Historical change to the phenomena observed and changes in conceptual models help us to formulate new questions which could not be posed in the dualistic context: through which processes do the actors construct their collective action? When we observe an empirical collective phenomena, how is the unity which we observe formed? To answer these questions one must give up the dualistic assumption right from the start, because the possibility of eventually reuniting the 'subjective' and 'objective' elements has proved to be inaccessible. Dualistic thinking attributed collective action to the structural background or to the values, motivations and ideologies of the actors. Action brought to light some deep essence of systems or actors. Today we are more aware that if the analysis is not able to establish a circular relationship between the actor and the system, the choice of determinism or voluntarism becomes only a question of taste and circumstance. Thus the introduction of a tertium cannot be avoided. Perhaps this third party will no longer be the revolutionary party; perhaps it will be the sociologist him- or herself, who, in a dream of omnipotence, will imagine that s/he must reconcile the constraints of the system with the consciousness of the actors.

One of the most resistant heredities of the nineteenth century is the tendency to attribute a kind of substantial unity to the observed actor. The idea of social movements as unified subjects acting on the stage of history, oriented towards luminous destinies or pledged to an inevitable collapse, this essentialist and teleological idea is the last expression of a philosophy of history and of a metaphysical assumption. That which one observes as unity, as a given reality, is actually the result of multiple processes, of different orientations, of a constructive dynamic which the actors bring about (or fail to bring about): in any case it is thanks to this dynamic that an action is developed or fails to develop, evolves or is arrested, reaches its objectives or falls apart.

A collective actor is a composite, constructed reality, which nevertheless presents itself empirically as a unity. It does so in a dual sense. On the one hand, the actors tend to give themselves a unified definition which reinforces, at least in terms of ideology, their capacity for action and their relationship to their opponents, allies and potential supporters. On the other hand, observers tend to attribute this unity to an empirical collective phenomenon, simplifying it and transforming it into a homogeneous 'subject' according to the logic of common sense. Thus this unity is currently viewed as a given both because of the tendency of the actors to attribute it to themselves and because the observers interact with the actors in a high complicity with the assumptions of common sense.

This unity is merely an empirical starting point. This is no doubt that we can observe a group of individuals who, acting together, define themselves as 'we', and to whom we tend to attribute the same unity. But everyday common sense becomes naïve realism when it assumes the 'metaphysical' existence of the actor. From the analytical point of view, it is precisely this datum which needs to be questioned. The unity is a result of exchanges, negotiations, decisions and conflicts that the actors continually bring about, but which are never in the foreground. Such processes are not immediately visible, as the actors tend to hide their fragmentation. But when unification is realized, this in itself is already a product. The process of construction can have more or less successful results, but when it is manifested in actual collective action it means that it is active and has been sustained over time. The unity that we observe is the fact that must be investigated, rather than the evidence to be used as a point of departure. In asking ourselves the questions formulated above, collective action ceases to be an object. It can instead be thought of as a purposive orientation built by means of social relationships, within a field of possibilities and limits which the actors perceive.

In reconstructing the genesis and the development of an empirical, collective actor current historical analyses of social movements often provide useful information about specific subjects, but they nearly always take place in the context of that naïve realism which I criticize above. That is, they assume that the collective actor exists, for example that the 'women's movement' exists, that like an historical figure it is born in a certain period, develops in another, manifests such and such kinds of behaviour. But *who* acted, *who* spoke for the movement and what happened inside the collective actor in the meantime? If we try to answer these questions we will discover that the sociological reality of the actor is far from the unity attributed to it by the observer.

The analysis should focus on the process through which the actors produce an interactive and shared definition of the goals of their action and the field in which it is to take place. To speak of goals means putting the accent on ends and on meaning, while the notion of a field refers to the possibilities and limits in which the goals are pursued. The definition which the actors produce is not a representation, or the reflection of structural determinism. It is an active relational process. I call it 'collective identity' (Melucci, 1984, 1989), although I am not entirely satisfied with this term which seems extremely static and does not account for the process of social construction which is the dimension I intend to emphasize. Collective identity is a definition constructed and negotiated through an activation of the social relationships connecting the members of a group or movement. This implies the presence of cognitive frames, of dense interactions, of emotional and affective exchanges. What holds the individuals together in the form of a 'we' is never completely translated in the logic of a means–ends calculation, or of a political rationality, but always carries with it margins of non-negotiability in the reasons for and ways of acting together. The question is, therefore, how a 'we' becomes a we.

CULTURE AND ACTION

In the study of social movements *action itself* (not structures or opinions) should be a meaningful subject for research. A possible way out of the difficulties mentioned above is by explicitly surpassing the dualistic premises which form the basis of the modern thought. Instead, it is necessary first to recognize that the actors understand the meaning of their actions, independent of the redeeming or manipulative intentions of the researchers. Secondly, we must recognize the fact that the researcher–actor relationship is itself subject to observation, itself included in the field of action and therefore subject of an explicit negotiation, a contract between the two parts. This implies the assumption of the non-identification of interests and roles in the game. Finally, we must recognize that any research practice which requires an intervention in the field of action of a given actor creates an artificial situation which must be explicitly acknowledged. The researcher cannot pretend that phenomena impacted by his or her practices are natural, but must be capable of moving the level of observation and communication. It is necessary to introduce into the field of research a capacity for metacommunication, regarding the relationship between the observer and the observed.

A conscious practice which is able to respond to these requirements needs to concentrate more upon processes and less upon their contents. It is in this direction that my research experiences in the field of collective action have been directed. This experience has resulted in my conviction that the three directions I have indicated above constitute a proving ground for any method that wishes to find a way out of dualism: the need to recognize that the actors are able to define the meaning of what they are doing; the need to make the research relationship an explicit object of observation, negotiation and contract, in the assumption of a non-identification between analyst and actor; finally, the need to recognize that research constructs an artificial field which can be controlled only through a capacity for metacommunication.

Thus social research on collective action loses the illusion of being a reflection of the 'true' reality and begins to come closer to understanding its very nature. Namely that it is a self-reflecting process socially constructed within the limits of an ecosystem. The particular form of action which we call research introduces new cognitive inputs into the field of social relations, derived from the action itself and from the observation of its processes and effects. In complex societies research could be conceived as a process of deutero-learning, as the development of those formal abilities which an era of accelerated change such as ours requires of knowledge.

This is also the place for new reflection on the social function of social knowledge. The collective actor, in fact, is never completely in control of his/her own actions. S/he is acted upon and lived by the process of the construction of a 'we', even as s/he acts and lives it. There is an opaque, hidden part of collective action which is due to the impossibility of the actor to simultaneously assume the position of actor and the point of view of the relationship which s/he is involved in and contributes to. The relational point of view is not inaccessible for the actor, but s/he cannot simultaneously act and be their own analyst, as each of us knows from our own personal experience. Analysis requires that distance which permits us to assume the point of view of the relationship and to metacommunicate about the constraints and the possibilities by which our action is delimited.

In systems of great differentiation and variability, knowledge becomes a desirable resource for the actors, and this allows the recognition of a difference between actors and researchers, in terms of skills and interests. The researcher is that particular type of actor who can provide cognitive resources, which help to make the relational point of view more transparent. This brings about the possibility of a negotiated relationship between certain actors, on the one hand, who professionally control some cognitive resources, and other actors, on the other hand, who need to clarify their capacity for action, but in turn control expertise and information relative to the action itself. Their meeting point is necessarily contractual. There is nothing missionary about it, and it does not imply expectations about the destiny of the actors on the part of the researchers. This might be true of the researchers as individuals, as citizens, as political activists, but not as scientists. In the latter institutional role they are called upon to carry out the function of producing knowledge. Thus they have the ethical and political responsibility for the production and destination of cognitive resources; they do not have the privilege of being able to guide the destiny of the society as advisors to the rulers or ideologues of protest. The meeting ground between actors and researchers – and in this case I am not thinking merely about social movements – is the recognition of a demand for cognitive resources. Two distinct interests, that of the researcher to gather information and that of the actor to improve his/her capacity to act consciously and meaningfully, can temporarily meet and create the possibility for an exchange.

The relationship with researchers can provide a different view of the action involved, not because there exists any such task or mission on the part of the researchers, but because a contractual agreement permits metacommunication about the relations between the actor and his/her partners and opponents. These relations delimit a field of action and at the same time create opportunities. But possibilities and constraints are never 'objective'; they can only be recognized (or not!) according to the actors' cognitive, motivational and perceptional investments. Knowledge thus assumes a decisive role in rendering accessible a certain potential for action. And it can function as a multiplier of processes for change, because it gives the actors the responsibility for their choices.

In the field of social conflicts we are witnessing the decline of the great collective forms of identification and the emergence of fragmented and multiple collective actors. This apparent 'weakness' of social actors can provoke regret that the heroic era is finished, in which the course of history assigned to each a role and the job of the researcher was to reveal this plot. But if the pluralism, transience and variety of the actors is not merely the sign of a decadent situation, then the observer's viewpoint must undergo a modification of its pretexts and ask itself about the meaning of these changes. The decline of the figure of the actor/personage, conceived as an 'essentialist' subject of history, forces us to transfer our attention to the constructionist processes of social action.

The most recent reflections on the closure of systems encounter this need and bring to the foreground the necessity to define human action as the construction of possibilities within boundaries. The reference to boundaries should be understood in a dual sense. Boundary means a finite condition, a recognition of corporal nature and of death as the space of the human condition. But at the same time, boundary means frontier, separation, therefore also the recognition of the other, that which is diverse, irreducible.

The accent on possibility signals, in the first case, the uncontainable drive of human action to overcome the limits of pain and death. Secondly, it bears witness to the tendency of the species towards 'cerebralization', the growth of cognitive capacities, which elevates the body into the realm of meaning produced by human superior faculties. Finally, it makes visible the dimension of solidarity and communication, as a drive to make diversity less opaque and insurmountable.

Consequently, our knowledge of social action should increasingly incorporate body and nature, emotions and desires; dealing with sex and gender, time and space, communication and otherness; placing the fragility and diversity of social actors in their ecosystemic fields (Gilligan, 1981). The tension between limits and possibilities has a particularly strong impact on our concept of rationality, as it was defined in the context of modern Western thought. While pointing out the precariousness of a rationality based exclusively on a means/ends calculation, it opens the way to new kinds of knowledge. The emotions, intuition and creativity, the 'feminine' perception of the world, can all become legitimate elements of the process through which social reality is constructed. This means acknowledging their role in social action and not attempting to hide their presence.

Even the ethical capacity loses its certainty of absolute ends and finds itself consigned to the responsibility and the risk of coexistence: how to *exist with the other* in a planetary world is the moral challenge of our time. When human relations are increasingly based more upon choice than necessity, the social contract becomes fragile and precarious. The threat of a catastrophic disintegration is a part of our horizon. But if we can accept that in social relations everything is not subject to the calculus of an absolute rationality, diversity and uncertainty can become the basis for a new solidarity. From this condition of conscious fragility could come the changes in ethical values that form the basis for coexistence.

Thus social action should be thought of as a construct, putting an end to the structure–intentions duality. Action is an interactive, constructive process within a field of possibilities and limits recognized by the actors. The accent on the limits to the process of construction, which always take place within the boundaries of an ecosystem, avoids the risk of a radical constructivism which would be difficult to sustain. Nevertheless, without the capability of perceiving and making sense of its boundaries, action would not be possible. In fact, radical constructivism finishes by destroying the relational dimension of social action and presents itself as the ultimate version, perhaps more sophisticated, of a voluntaristic paradigm.

Scientific knowledge itself enters into the constructive process, as a particular form of social action with a high self-reflective capacity. Knowledge is not a mirror revealing in a linear way the causal chains that govern reality. Instead, it is a circular process of modelling (of its subjects) and self-modelling (of its instruments). A process that is anything but 'pure', in which interact in a decisive manner the contaminating factors of emotions, subjective evaluations and the limitations of the observer. But in which also interacts, to an ever greater degree, the contamination of different fields of knowledge, continuously calling into question the conventional disciplinary boundaries and their institutional settings. Thus defined, scientific knowledge takes on the aspect of a *bricolage*, the gathering and combining of cues, whose meanings depend upon variations in point of view, from the particular perspective of the observer.

This means redefining the relationship between the observer and the observed. Acknowledging in ourselves as scientists and in the actors the limited rationality which characterizes social action, the researchers can no longer apply the criteria of truth or morality defined *a priori*, outside the relationship. Researchers must also participate in the uncertainty, testing the limits of their instruments and of their ethical values.

Thus the two models which have always characterized the relationship between researcher and actor in social sciences fall to pieces before our very eyes: that of *identification*, and that of *distance*. The 'understanding' or 'empathetic' researcher shares with the ideologue, from whom s/he nevertheless intends to stand at a distance, the illusion of the power to destroy the gap between reflection and action. The myth of transparence or of total communication seems to feed in a recurrent manner the need to transform the scientific work into maieutics or into pedagogy, exposing the 'cold' body of science to the fire of action.

But the model of distance, of the neutrality of the researcher, high priest of a 'truth' and a 'reality' that are beyond the comprehension of the actors, also seems to be obsolete. After all, what is this reality of which the researcher speaks, if not constructed together in a circular interaction with his or her 'subjects'? We are facing the crisis of sociological models centred around opinion and representation as opposed to the action itself; based on a model of the rationality of the actor that relegates the emotional and intuitive dimensions of behaviour to a marginal status; marked by a pretext of 'objectivity' which fails to include the observer in the field of observation.

In highly differentiated and variable systems, the need to predict and control uncertainty increases. Research inevitably enters into the game of the questions, expectations and interests that link or oppose actors, researchers and those who fund the research. It is difficult to imagine how social research can meet the new challenges that await it without a strong level of self-reflexivity which makes ever more explicit, as part of the research process itself, the social relations and options which are the basis for the practice adopted and that make it possible. A sort of situational epistemology which is needed more than ever in the field of social research, if it wants to escape from the illusion that it is outside, or above, the circular game of the observer and the actor. This is not a vicious circle, if it is capable of acknowledging the limitations of the points of view of the participants and of metacommunicating it.

The relationship between the observer and the observed becomes a terrain of responsibilities, the space for a cognitive and ethical contract between the researcher and the actor. This is a difficult encounter because it entails recognition between diverse elements. It is also difficult because it means holding together two requirements imposed upon us by the era of complexity: that of existing and that of coexisting. Responsibility is above all the capacity to assume one's own existence, finite nature and value. But this assumption of self opens and requires responsibility towards the other, the definition of a space in which to coexist. *Time to be* and *time to care* become inextricably intertwined, the projects and imperatives of a liveable human life.

Giving up the role of the demiurge, the great suggestor or the eye of God, the researcher nevertheless cannot go back to being the sorcerer's apprentice, naïve manipulator of forces beyond his/her control. The reference to the 'weakness' of the actors does not reflect only the necessary redemption from a vision which insisted upon giving them a metaphysical consistence. Within this weakness are also condensed new imbalances, submission to new powers, where the actor is excluded and deprived of his/her voice.

In a world in which 'naming' is becoming the equivalent of 'bringing into existence', the weakness of actors is too often a *deprivation or deformation of the power of naming*. The flow of signs is meaningless, if there is no access to the dominant codes. A contract could not exist without being preceded by a restitution/reappropriation of the power over languages and codes. The work of the researcher can escape from the role of demiurge or pedagogue, without giving up the responsibility to make the power of naming available, which means enabling even the weakest actors to take part in a contract. The researcher does not have a monopoly on cognitive resources, but by his or her work s/he can offer the actors a possibility to develop their capacity to learn how to learn, to produce their own codes. The researcher's responsibility concerns the ways in which s/he constructs the objects of knowledge, but also the omissions, the silences, the empty spaces in his or her practice. The acknowledgment of both sides of this responsibility opens the way to a new ethics and politics of scientific work, in a planetary world where social actors are not the bearers of a final meaning of history and researchers are not devoted to disclosing that meaning. This reasoning thus necessarily brings us to a discussion of ideology and ambivalence in collective action.

THE REPRESENTATION OF COLLECTIVE ACTION

Framing processes, as discussed in the recent literature on social movements (Snow et al., 1986; Snow and Benford, 1988; Gamson and Modigliani, 1989), are part of the symbolic production of a social movement and they make sense within a theory of ideology. Even after Mannheim (1936), sociological thought is still prisoner of its dualistic inheritance, which considered symbolic production either as a transparent expression of beliefs and values or as a pure reflex of material interests. Recent advances in theory (for a synthesis see Habermas, 1984; Thompson, 1984; Wutnow et al., 1984) have contributed to a new awareness of the complexity of cultural and symbolic levels in individual and collective action.

Ideology is thus a key analytical level for the understanding of social movements. The way in which the actors represent their own actions is not a simple reflection of more profound mechanisms (economic constraints or psychological unconscious motivations, for example), but it carries the meaning of the action itself, although removed from the system of social relationships of which it is a part. Ideology can neither be written off as false conscience, simply mystifying real social relationships, nor as the transparent representation of shared social values.

Ideology is a set of symbolic frames which collective actors use to represent their own actions to themselves and to the others, within a system of social relationships. This symbolic production is a constituent part of these relationships, but at the same time the actor tends to separate it from the system of which it is a part, turning it to the defence of his/her own particular interests. Hence the interweaving of truth and falsehood that characterizes ideology because it reproduces real social relationships, but at the same time it hides and negates them. The symbolic elaboration 'rationalizes' social relationships according to the interests of the actor. It provides a representation which tends to legitimate and reinforce those interests while at the same time defining the relational field of collective action. The meaning of this action, which is to be found in the system of relations of which the actor is a part, is instead identified with the actor's particular point of view: the field of social relationships, which is always made up of a network of tensions and oppositions, is restructured according to the position occupied by the actor. When sociological analysis takes these representations back to the system of relationships in which they are produced, and there tries to discover the meaning of collective action, it becomes a critique of ideology.

Let me now examine more directly the role and the form of ideology within a social movement, during its formative phase and its organizational consolidation. At the most general level the ideology of a movement always includes, as Touraine (1973) has pointed out, a (more or less clearly articulated) definition of the actor, the identification of an adversary and an indication of ends, goals and objectives for which to fight. But ideology also stabilizes a set of relationships among these elements which serve, on the one hand, to legitimize the actor, and, on the other, to negate any social identity to the opponent. By declaring that s/he fights for a goal which belongs to him/her, but which goes beyond his/her own immediate interests, a collective actor always tries to affirm the general legitimacy of the action. By at the same time indicating the opponent as the major obstacle to the attainment of this goal or to the realization of this objective, the actor negates the adversary's right to a social statute or to any form of legitimacy.

The connection between the particularism of the actor and some general values (truth, freedom, justice, emancipation, etc.) is a key mechanism of the framing activity of a collective actor. A link of necessity is established between the role of the actor and some kind of totality to be reached through his/her action. The actor is the true interpreter of this totality, which always has positive attributes, in cultural, political or moral terms. On the other hand, the adversary is seen as only having a negative relationship to the totality: s/he is in fact the very obstacle that prevents general needs from being satisfied, or social goals from being attained.

It is then always possible to identify, more or less explicitly, in the ideology of a social movement, a definition of the social actor who is mobilized, of the adversary against whom the movement must struggle and of the collective objectives of the struggle. These three analytical elements are combined in a complex system of representations, that defines the position of the collective actor with respect to the opponent and the collective goals: (1) the definition of the social group in whose name actions are undertaken determines the limits of collective identity and the legitimacy of the movement; (2) the undesirable situation which has given rise to the need for collective action is attributed to an adversary, usually identified in non-social terms, without any legitimacy; (3) objectives, or desirable goals, exist for society as a whole, for which it is necessary to fight; (4) there is a positive relationship between the actor and the general goals of the society, and therefore the actions of the movement go beyond the particular interests of the actor; (5) the adversary is seen as an obstacle to the general goals of the society; (6) thus there is an irreconcilable opposition between actor and adversary.

These constituent elements of the ideology of a social movement take on different cultural contents and vary during the course of collective action. As far as the birth of a collective actor is concerned, Alberoni's (1977) work has pointed out the many ways in which the fundamental experience of the nascent state is framed into different ideological contents. In the formative phase, I consider that two elements permanently characterize the ideology of a movement. The first is the *negation of the gap* between expectations and reality. The birth of a movement is marked by 'moments of madness' (Zolberg, 1972), when all things seem possible, and collective enthusiasm looks forward to action, certain of positive results. Ideology overcomes the inadequacy of practice: the less capacity for action the movement, as yet weak and unorganized, has, the greater will be the production of symbolism. This is the moment of the fusion of the various components of a movement into a new form of solidarity, where the expressive dimensions and emotional identification with collective goals prevail.

The second characteristic is the central role of the theme of *rebirth*. Collective actors often make reference to a 'mother society' or to a golden age, temporarily rewriting the chronicle of the group's infancy. The ideology of rebirth, of a return to an intemporal past, is closely tied to the need for a totalizing legitimacy mentioned above. In the moment of its formation, the movement restructures old social allegiances in a new collective framework, combining the defence of an identity still referring back to the past and the emerging new problems. In this situation the only sure points of reference, the only known language, the only images to be entrusted with the new claims, belong to the past.

A return to a situation of original purity, which can assume a variety of cultural connotations in different cases, allows collective action to combine the precedent components into a new solidarity, and restructures existing identities projecting them towards the prospect of change. A movement joins past and future, the defence of a social group with a demand for transformation. Symbols and cultural models are sought in the traditions of the group and of the social movements that came before the movement presently taking form. Symbolic referents and the language in which new collective demands are expressed come from the past. A new movement always views its own action as a rebirth: a regeneration of the present through a mythic reaffirmation of the past, which in reality is the 'cocoon' in which new needs and new conflicts are formed.

For a long time, the labour movement spoke the language of the French Revolution, and dreamed of a return to the community and the solidarity of corporations. Marx's analysis, which tried to define scientifically the specific characteristics of the movement within the capitalist mode of production, was accepted only at a certain phase of the movement's development, and still had to deal with the other components – utopian, humanitarian, religious, solidaristic – which existed within the movement. The evoking of a Leninist purism or Maoism on the part of many small sects which came out of the youth movement of the 1960s reflects, analogously, this tiring, intolerant search for an identity which looks to the past, on the part of a movement in the formative stage. The profound crisis of so many of the political groups stemming from 1968 does not indicate, as many would have it, the end of the movement or its integration, but rather the end of a utopian, fragmentary phase of collective action. In the late 1970s the movement left the myths and symbols which had helped to bring it about in the first place; in the 1980s the new problems and new conflicts which the movement carried with it emerged and began to manifest their real contents.

I would call this situation of movements in formation *regressive utopia*. The general characteristic of utopia is the immediate identification between the actor and the goals of a global society. The cultural model of transformation of the society coincides, in the utopian view, with the action of a particular actor, who thus becomes the direct agent of general change. A utopia is regressive when the transformation is equated with a return to the past and the myth of rebirth. After the nascent phase, these utopian components do not disappear, but progressively give way to an ideological elaboration which is more directly linked to the specific problems of the movement. New languages and new symbols are created to define the field and the actors of the conflict. The mobilized social group, the adversary and the collective goals are redefined in a more pertinent manner; ideology becomes a complex and detailed symbolic system, which can also include many elements of scientific analysis. At the same time, the movement finds that it is faced with the necessity to ensure internal integration and to improve its position in the environment.

INTEGRATION AND STRATEGY

When the movement grows, two essential aspects of ideology are thus called into play. First of all, ideology fulfils a function of integration for the movement as a whole: this function is accomplished by a repeated proposal of values and norms, the control of deviant behaviours and the stabilizing of certain rituals. Secondly, ideology has a strategic function in relation to the environment. Ideology is one of the resources that can be used to reduce the costs and maximize the benefits of action. This process can take place in two ways. On the one hand, there is an effort to widen the margins in which the movement acts within the political system, increasing the possibility that it will have some influence. On the other, ideology tries to widen the movement's base and to push the groups which were previously outside the conflict to get involved in it. Both of these processes imply a complex game, in which ideological messages are inserted in an effort to turn social interactions to the actor's advantage. In particular, one of the fundamental tasks is that of making the illegitimacy of the adversary, and the negative nature of his/her position, evident in the eyes of both neutral observers and potential supporters.

Let me first have a look at the integrative function of ideology. A movement is subject to strong centrifugal pressures, both due to its own internal fragmentation and to the initiatives of the adversary. The need to maintain organizational unity becomes stronger as the movement consolidates. Ideology is one of the main tools which can be used to guarantee integration. The multiplicity of interests and demands which are always to be found in an organized movement must be mediated and unified. Ideology co-ordinates, articulates and makes coherent these demands, associating them with general principles. By reformulating values and norms of the group, ideology consolidates the collective identity and prevents internal conflicts from destroying unity. At the same time, it determines the criteria for the identification and punishment of those who deviate from these norms.

Nevertheless, the ideological apparatus of a movement is not a static entity: it is also influenced by tensions, and is a field of conflict between groups and factions. The control of ideology and, more generally, of the flow of information, is an important leadership resource, in which there is a continuous adapting of symbolic representations to the present state of the movement. The bottom-line balance between costs and benefits cannot always be directly calculated, particularly when dealing with non-material resources. Thus ideology comes into play, utilized to minimize costs, to increase the perception of rewards, to cover losses or to substitute for resources which are in short supply. The relative rigidity or flexibility of the ideological frames will make the adjustments more or less difficult in turn.

A last aspect of the integrative function of ideology can be found in rituals. Every movement creates rituals which serve to consolidate its components. The adoption of linguistic or gestural codes, of costumes or ways of dressing, become common traits to those who are part of the movement. Actual ceremonies, governed by codified procedures, represent the synthesis of a shared culture. These rituals, through the nearly sacred crystallization of the norms of the group, tend to guarantee the continuity and the efficacy of ideology, in spite of the tensions which are at work within it.

Let me consider now the second fundamental need for a movement which is in the phase of consolidation: that of improving its position in the environment, on the one hand increasing its influence within the political system, while on the other widening the base of consensus it can count on within the society. In this sense ideology has a strategic function, because it is through the articulation of the symbolic meaning of his/her action that the actor can increase his/her advantage over the others. In particular, this means gaining the consensus of components of other organizations and the support of groups who are not directly involved in the conflict, against the initiatives of the adversary.

With respect to other organizations, ideology must call forth loyalty to the general aims of the movement, while at the same time differentiating the image and the contents of the single organization. Competition between organizations can increase the differentiation of symbolic contents without any real corresponding conflict in practice. In a situation in which the market of potential supporters is a limited one, and there are restrictive margins for action, different organizations will tend to accentuate competition on an ideological level.

As far as the adversary is concerned, ideology will tend to assign the blame for the negative situation to the initiatives of the adversary, and attempt to deny him/her any legitimacy. At the same time it will try to improve the position of the actor *vis-à-vis* his/her opponent, in the eyes of a public from whom support or favour is sought. The contrast must be symbolically articulated in such a way as to turn to the actor's advantage the imbalance of the power relationship. Ideology can be used to obtain a positive identification with the movement on the part of potential supporters and neutral observers, deflecting all negative feedback onto the adversary. In these 'dramatic encounters' (Klapp, 1965), different situations may occur with a variety of symbolic meanings, but which follow one or another of a few common scripts. In the 'victory of the hero' script the actor tries to present him/herself as culturally or morally superior to the opponent; this symbolic tool is often complemented by the 'vanquishing of the villain' script in which a temporary or occasional disadvantage of the opponent is presented as a due and deserved punishment. When the actor is in an uncomfortable or disadvantaged position, then the 'unfair tactics' or 'dirty fighting' or even the 'oppression of the weak' scenarios are used as symbolic means to re-establish a fairly balanced confrontation with the opponent. And if by any chance these efforts do not succeed, the 'defeat without dishonour' script is often the last resort to maintain or recapture the attention and support of the potential followers.

All of these symbolic scenarios framing the relationship between a movement and its opponents respond to the strategic function of ideology, which aims at widening the support base of a movement and the space in which it can act within the political system, at the same time denying any legitimacy to the adversary and to his/her action. The role of ideology is that of making sure that the actor comes out of every confrontation with the most positive image possible. In the case of a positive outcome to the conflict, the situation will be symbolically articulated as the victory of the good and the righteous over arbitrary injustice. In the case of a defeat, ideology will speak of the battle of the weak against the powerful, and of unfair tactics. In either case, ideology intervenes on behalf of the actor in an attempt to increase the consensus mobilization (Klandermans et al., 1988; Gamson et al., 1982; Gamson, 1990).

It should not be forgotten that these mechanisms also operate, with even greater efficacy, in the area of social control. The attempt to discredit collective forms of protest, to turn public resentment against a movement, thus legitimizing repression, is one of the essential components of the framing activity of the ruling groups. Control over the flow of information and the media guarantees a structural advantage to the powers that be, because in social conflict, even in competition for public consensus, the game is never fair and the positions are not those of parity.

THE AMBIVALENCE OF COLLECTIVE FRAMES

In collective mobilizations individuals and groups act together by defining in cognitive terms the possibilities and limits of their action and by constructing through interactions the meaning of what they are doing. Such definitions are not linear because they are produced by internal negotiations and conflicts: individuals and groups within a movement 'construct' their action, laboriously adjusting the different orientations that express multiple and contrasting requirements of a collective field (Melucci, 1984, 1989; for a general discussion of a constructionist paradigm, see Von Foerster, 1973; Watzlawick, 1981).

But this deep constructive activity of a collective actor is not visible, particularly because some unity and effectiveness must be maintained over time. Ideological patterns and leadership functions are always at work in an attempt to give a durable and predictable order to this continuously negotiated process. One of the main tasks of the leaders is precisely that of producing ideological frames to reinforce the unity and to improve the effectiveness of the collective actor.

Ideology and framing processes are therefore necessarily ambivalent because on the one hand they express the actual meaning and goals of collective action, but on the other they cover and hide the plurality of orientations and tensions corresponding to the different components of the movement. Leaders claim a unity that they rarely achieve and tend to present the movement as homogeneous and coherent.

There is another sense, even more important, in which frames produced by a collective actor are ambivalent. The very idea of a social conflict implies the opposition of two actors struggling for the same resources, symbolic or material, which they consider valuable. The adversaries share the same field but they interpret it in opposite ways, trying to submit it to their control. They identify themselves to the entire field, while denying any legitimacy and role to the opponent. Conflict is a social relationship, but the actors tend to reify it: each pole wants to cancel the other and labels it in non-social terms. A relational field, constructed by conflicting orientations, is thus reduced to the particularism of a single actor. The ideology of a movement carries with it this ambivalence because it is an interpretation of a social field but also a misinterpretation, guided by the particularism of the actor. It reveals and covers what is at stake in a conflict. Sociological analysis should be able to discover the field behind the actors' ideologies.

Let me take the 'ecological question' as an example. Both environmentalists and their opponents speak the same language, they define a common field from opposite poles. In fact they address the same basic dilemmas of social life in a planetary world: problems which have no solutions, and which define the cultural and social boundaries of complexity; polarities which present impossible choices, inasmuch as their tension is the source of equilibrium of a highly differentiated system; problems that society cannot help trying to solve, but whose solutions only transfer the uncertainty elsewhere. Society tries to deal with them by making decisions, which attempt to reduce uncertainty within the range of possible action. But the decision, which permits action, is also an attempt at escape, a denial and cover-up of the dilemmas implicit in the decision itself. It can mean avoidance of a tension which has become unbearable, a means of neither seeing nor speaking of these dilemmas.

Both environmentalists and technocrats deal with these dilemmas but frame them in opposite ways, while denying any truth to the opponents' frames. Sociological analysis can detect the ambivalence of these ideologies and recognize a conflictual field which is common to the adversaries. Behind the 'ecological question', the first dilemma is that between *autonomy and control*, between the enormous expansion of individual capacities and choices, and the tendency to create capillary systems of behaviour manipulation, which today impact both the brain and the genetic structure itself.

The second dilemma is related to the fact that social systems have extended their power beyond the boundaries of any society of the past. Nuclear energy and genetic engineering bear witness in different ways to the extreme capacity of contemporary societies to produce themselves to the point of self-destruction. This gives birth to a new dilemma, that between *responsibility and omnipotence*, between the tendency to expand the capacity of human systems to intervene in their own development, and the need to respond (response-ability) to the limits of internal and external 'nature'.

This power is immediately tied to another dilemma. The influence of the human species upon itself and upon its environment is based on irreversible scientific knowledge, which can no longer be erased (except in the case of a regressive catastrophe which brings evolutionary progress back to zero). At the same time the way this knowledge is utilized is based upon choices which are revocable, tied to energetic, scientific and military policies and to the administrative rationality of the political apparatuses. The dilemma *irreversible information/reversible choices* opens up the field for debates and struggles on new public ethics in the post-nuclear era.

Finally, the planetarization of the world system means that there is no longer an 'outside world': territories and cultures exist only as internal dimensions of the same system. But this 'internalization' opens up another dilemma, that between *inclusion and exclusion*. Inclusion tends towards a levelling of cultural differences, and transforms peripheral or marginal cultures into insignificant folkloric or ethnic accessories of the few major centres which govern the elaboration of cultural codes and their dissemination to the great media market. Resistances to this pressure towards homogeneity produce self-exclusion or marginalization, which often means being reduced to silence and cultural death.

Environmental and pacifist movements deal with these dilemmas. They challenge the technocratic power on a symbolic ground, they oppose to its instrumental rationality cultural codes which reverse the logic of the dominant scientific, political, military apparatuses: the need for autonomy and meaning, the limits of human action, the search for a new scientific paradigm, the respect due to the 'margins' of human cultures. Revealing the shadowy side of technological power, movements allow society to take responsibility for its own action.

But when they produce their challenging codes, movements also frame the dilemmas mentioned above according to their particular standpoint: they deny the field of which they are part and which includes the shared trust in science, rationalization and effectiveness. The affirmative and negative sides of ideology, the revealing and the covering functions, are simultaneously present: ambivalence marks the consciousness of collective actors and reminds us that social action is never transparent.

METHODOLOGICAL ISSUES

From the framework outlined above I would draw some methodological consequences for sociological research on social movements. I assume that collective actors are able to define the meaning of what they are doing; but at the same time they are never completely in control of their own actions. They are acted upon and lived by the construction of a collective field, even as they act and live it.

The current research practices on social movements still reflect the actor/system dualism that characterized the theoretical inheritance of the nineteenth century. When dealing with ideology and framing processes, empirical research is often based on surveys or on the analysis of documents produced by collective actors (that is, of those parts of the movement ideology which have been articulated in written form). In the first case, since the attention is mainly focused on individual opinions, the analysis ends up reinforcing the naïve assumption that the meaning of a collective action will be the sum of the representations of individual actors. The second case entails working on organized representations (and also organizational ones, given the fact that these documents are usually produced by organizations). In this case, for the most part, one takes the framing activity of the leaders as if it represented the whole movement.

Each of these research practices collects useful information and clarifies some aspects of the framing processes. But in both cases, what disappears from the scene is *the field* of collective action: ideological representations are part of this field and their ambivalence can appear only if they are placed in the system of relationships to which they belong.

The analysis should take the point of view of the field and reveal the hidden ambivalence of ideology. By reconstructing the network of internal tensions covered by unifying frames, the analysis can help to redefine the actor's identity. By making more visible the system of relationships connecting the adversaries in a conflictual field, the researcher can contribute to a better understanding of this field in terms of opportunities and constraints. S/he could provide a different view of the collective action, not because there exists any specific enlightening task or mission (as, for instance, still pursued by Touraine, 1978, 1984), but because the work favours metacommunication (Bateson, 1972, 1979) about the relations between the actor and his/her partners and opponents.

These relations delimit a field of action and at the same time create opportunities. But possibilities and constraints are never 'objective'. The opportunity structures, as defined by the recent literature on social movements (Klandermans et al., 1988; Tarrow, 1989), can only be recognized (or not) according to the actors' cognitive, motivational and perceptional frames (Neisser, 1976; Eiser, 1980). Knowledge thus assumes a decisive role in rendering accessible a certain potential for action. And it can function as a multiplier of processes for change, because it gives the actors the responsibility for their choices.

Action is a process whose meanings are established through interaction. The researcher interested in social movements should not forget that the collective actors are not the object of analysis; rather they produce the object of analysis and supply its meanings. The research techniques should be designed to uncover this active and ambivalent construction (see Gamson and Modigliani, 1989; Melucci, 1989). However homogeneous or contradictory they might appear, ideological frames correspond to an intrinsic rationale, to orientations and strategies that the actors set in motion within the system of relations to which they belong. In order to get at this meaning the researcher has to try and enter the actors' interior world, to reconstruct from the inside the logic of the frames as lived and experienced by the actors themselves (Crozier and Friedberg, 1977). Then the researcher must emerge from the ideological contents and identify the logic and games that structure the field itself. During this process then the researcher alternates between two poles: the critical position of external observer and the 'viewpoint' of the actors within the field. Here the role of researcher is rid of all pedagogic intention and becomes a scientific function from which may arise metacommunication.

MAKING ENDS NEGOTIABLE

What kind of political consequences should one draw from this framework? Are concepts like liberation or emancipation still useful? I shall argue that they are too strictly connected to the conceptual and linguistic horizon of industrial society to be used without metacommunicating about them. The planetarization of the world system has called into question a restricted view of democracy as based simply on a competition for governmental resources and it has revealed the inadequacy of political institutions when facing the dramatic challenges of our time. Social movements have strongly contributed to this awareness and their action has enlightened the new potential for democracy in the contemporary world, together with new powers and new risks.

Complex systems are characterized by uncertainty, exposed as they are to change and differentiation. Decision-making is a crucial part of their government because a plurality of interests can confront each other within an accepted framework of rules. Selection and risk allow choice between alternatives, and the narrowing of uncertainty. Selection is therefore the price to be paid for reducing uncertainty, but it is also the least transparent part of the process, where power relations are concentrated and hidden.

Contemporary forms of collective action act as 'revealers', exposing that which is hidden or excluded by the decision-making process. Collective protest and mobilization bring to light the silent, obscure or arbitrary elements that frequently arise in complex systems' decisions. Decisions may present themselves as mere procedures, based on a consensus and guaranteed by rules. In the decision-making process power tends to be masked behind procedures: the greater and the more continuous the need for decisions, and the more these depend upon a growing mass of technical data, the less visible power becomes. It seems to disappear behind a neutral mask of rational measures to achieve the given goals, of technical evidence provided by available facts. Collective mobilization forces power into the open and exposes the interests behind the apparent neutrality of its rationality.

Decisions also present themselves as a series of means, of operations and techniques, whose effectiveness must be maximized. As the range of options broadens and the value of problem-solving techniques grows, the decision-making process tends to avoid the question of ends altogether, concentrating instead on the choice and optimization of means alone. Collective mobilization and protest opens the discussion of ends, revealing non-negotiable needs and creating an area of debate in which the presumed neutrality of means is thrown into question.

Decisions are essential in governing any large or complex systems, but they mask important dilemmas. The first consists in the necessity of constant change while at the same time maintaining a stable normative and prescriptive nucleus. In complex systems, it is necessary, on the one hand, to take into account changeable interests, a wide distribution of social actors and the variability of their aggregated interests while, on the other hand, guaranteeing systems of rules and prescriptions which ensure a certain predictability in behaviour and procedures.

Secondly, in complex systems there is an increase in the number of groups capable of organizing themselves, representing their interests and extracting advantages from processes of political exchange; there is also a fragmentation of political decision-making structures, giving rise to numerous partial governments that are difficult to co-ordinate. At the same time, there is a consolidation of uncontrolled and invisible decision-making centres within which decisions about ends are made. Hence the second dilemma: while too many decisions are made, it becomes increasingly difficult to openly decide about ends.

The extension of citizenship and participation, together with an increasing need for the planning of society as a whole by means of bureaucratic-administrative organizations gives rise to a third dilemma. The extension of the sphere of individual and collective rights necessitates planning, in order to co-ordinate the plurality of interests and decisions and to protect the corresponding rights of representation and decision-making. But each planning intervention necessitates a technocratic decision-making power, which inevitably curtails participation and effective rights.

These dilemmas are linked to profound transformations of the complex social systems. These systems are forced to mobilize and control individual resources in order to enable their high-density and highly differentiated organizational, informational and decision-making networks to function. At the same time, however, individual action acquires an elective character, because individuals are attributed an increasing possibility of controlling and defining the conditions of their personal and social experience. The process of individualization – the possibility for every individual potentially to act as an individual – is thus two edged: while there is an extension of social control by means of an increase of socializing pressures on individuals' motivational and cognitive structures, there is also a demand for the appropriation of the meaning of social action by these same individuals who are provided with broader possibilities of being individuals. The paradoxes of post-industrial democracy are linked to both the pressures for integration and the needs for identity building. The dilemmas mentioned above, variability and predictability, fragmentation and concentration, participation and planning, represent in the political sphere, two sides of a more general systemic problem.

A DEMOCRACY OF MEANINGS

To believe that the essence of democracy still consists in securing the competition of interests and the rules that make their representation possible is to fail to appreciate the scope of the transformations that are taking place within the complex systems. The conception of democracy as a pure competition for government resources corresponded to a capitalist system founded on the separation of the state from civil society, a system in which the state simply translated the private interests formed in civil society into the terms of public institutions.

Today, this distinction between the state and civil society, upon which the political experience of capitalism was based, is fading. As a unitary agent of intervention and action, the state has dissolved. It has been replaced, from above, by a tightly interdependent system of transnational relationships, as well as subdivided, from below, into a multiplicity of partial governments, which are defined both by their own systems of representation and decision-making, and by an ensemble of interwoven organizations which combine inextricably the public and private. Even civil society, at least as it was defined by the early modern tradition, appears to have lost its substance. The private interests once belonging to it no longer have the permanence and visibility of stable social groups sharing a definite position in the hierarchy of power and influence. The former unity (and homogeneity) of social interests has exploded. From above they assume the form of general cultural and symbolic orientations which cannot be attributed to specific social groups; from below, these interests are subdivided into a multiplicity of primary needs, including those which were once considered to be natural.

The simple distinction between state and civil society is replaced by a more complex situation (Keane, 1988). Processes of differentiation and secularization of mass parties have transformed them increasingly into catch-all parties which are institutionally incorporated into the structures of government; at the same time, the parliamentary system tends to accentuate both its selective processing of demands and its merely formal decision-making functions. On another plane, there is an evident multiplication and increasing autonomy of systems of representation and decision-making; this process results in the pluralization of decision-making centres, but also carries with it the undoubted advantages associated with the diffusion of decision-making instances. Finally, on a further plane, there is an evident formation of collective demand and conflicts which assume the form of social movements aiming at the reappropriation of the motivation and sense of action in everyday life.

Under these conditions, it would be illusory to think that democracy consists merely in the competition for access to governmental resources. Democracy in complex societies requires conditions which enable individuals and social groups to affirm themselves and to be recognized for what they are or wish to be. That is, it requires conditions for enhancing the recognition and autonomy of individual and collective signifying processes in everyday life. The formation, maintenance and alteration through time of a self-reflexive identity requires social spaces free from control or repression.

The necessary conditions of such a democracy include public spaces independent of the institutions of government, the party system and state structures. These spaces assume the form of an articulated system of decision-making, negotiation and representation, in which the signifying practices developed in everyday life can be expressed and heard independently of formal political institutions. Public spaces of this kind should include some guarantees that individual and collective identities are able to exist; soft institutionalized systems favouring the appropriation of knowledge and the production of symbolic resources; and open systems in which information can be circulated and controlled. Public spaces are characterized by a great fluidity, and their size may increase or diminish according to the independence they are accorded: they are by definition a mobile system of instances kept open only by creative confrontation between collective action and institutions. Inasmuch as public spaces are intermediate between the levels of political power and decision-making and networks of everyday life, they are structurally ambivalent: they express the double meaning of the terms representation and participation. Representation means the possibility of presenting interests and demands; but it also means remaining different and never being heard entirely. Participation also has a double meaning. It means both taking part, that is, acting so as to promote the interests and the needs of an actor, as well as belonging to a system, identifying with the general interests of the community.

The main function of public spaces is that of rendering visible and collective the questions raised by the movements. They enable the movements to avoid being institutionalized as such and, conversely, ensure that society as a whole is able to assume responsibility for (i.e. institutionally process) the issues, demands and conflicts concerning the goals and meaning of social action raised by the movements. In this sense, the consolidation of independent public spaces is a vital condition of keeping open — without seeking to falsely resolve — the paradoxical dimension of post-industrial democracy. For when society assumes responsibility for its own issues, demands and conflicts, it subjects them openly to negotiation and to decisions, and transforms them into possibilities of change. It thereby makes possible a democracy of everyday life, without either annulling the specificity and the independence of the movements or concealing the use of power behind allegedly neutral decision-making procedures.

Political relationships have never been so important as in complex systems. Never before has it been so necessary to regulate complexity by means of decisions, choices and policies, the frequency and diffusion of which must be ensured if the uncertainty of systems subject to exceptionally rapid change is to be reduced. Complexity and change produce the need for decisions, and create a plurality of variable interests which cannot be compared to situations of the past; the multiplicity and changeability of interests results in a multiplicity and changeability of problems to be solved. Hence the need for decisions, and for decisions which are continually subject to verification and are exposed to the limitations and risks of consensus in conditions of rapid change.

In complex societies we are in fact witnessing a process of multiplication and diffusion of political instances. In different areas of social life, and within institutions and organizations of many kinds, a process of transformation of authoritarian regulations into political relationships is taking place. The process of politicization is linked to the complexity of the information systems, the need to cope with a changeable environment and the multiplication of requirements of balance within the system itself. The problem of decision-making processes, which function by means of representation, was underestimated or ignored by the Marxist tradition, which reduced representation to its bourgeois forms and in so doing annulled the problem of how to mediate and represent a plurality of interests. The problem of representation is tied to complexity and it therefore cannot be annulled, whatever model of political organization is envisaged. Representation involves an inevitable difference between representatives and those whom they represent, between the interests of each and between their concurrent or divergent logic of action. Any process of democratic transformation must necessarily take into account this difference between the structures of representation and the demands or interests of the represented.

Change in complex societies becomes discontinuous, articulated, differentiated. These systems never change at the same time and in the same way at their various levels. The political system, by means of decisions, can reduce the uncertainty and increase the transformation potential produced by conflicts. But this involves a separation of the agents of change from those who manage the transformation. The actors who produce the change and those who manage, that is, institutionalize the transformation are not the same. Social movements can prevent the system from closing in upon itself by obliging the ruling groups to innovate, to permit changes among élites, to admit what was previously excluded from the decision-making arena and to expose the shadowy zones of invisible power and silence which a system and its dominant interests inevitably tend to create. By their action they are already contributing to making visible the planetary challenges and to establishing a new transnational political arena in which people and governments can take responsibility for the dramatic choices human beings are facing for the first time.

MOVEMENTS AND EMANCIPATION

The concept of emancipation still belongs to a culture that thinks of a future society. We need a self-limiting concept of emancipation, mindful of the dark side of the modern myths, like progress, liberation and revolution. For developing societies the future is still open to development, but they are at the same time entirely involved in the planetary system based on information. So it is at the *political level* that a project of 'emancipation' can be discussed. Free of any metaphysical assumption, we can openly discuss our future, our hopes and our limitations. In this *civil debate* social movements play a central role.

In a planetary system of high information density, individuals and groups must possess a certain degree of autonomy and formal capacities for learning and acting which enable them to function as reliable, self-regulating units. Simultaneously, highly differentiated systems exert strong pressure for integration. They shift social control from the content of action to its languages, from the external regulation of behaviour to interference in the cognitive and motivational preconditions for it. Conflicts tend to arise in those areas of the system most directly involved in the production of information and communicative resources but at the same time subjected to intense pressures for integration. The crucial dimensions of daily life (time and space, interpersonal relations, birth and death), the satisfying of individual needs within welfare systems, the shaping of personal and social identity in educational systems – these today are constructed through the production and processing of information. Individuals and groups are allocated increasing amounts of information resources with which to define themselves and to construct their life spaces. At the same time, however, these same processes are regulated by a diffuse social control which passes beyond the public sphere to invade the very domain where the sense of individual action takes shape. Dimensions that were traditionally regarded as 'private' (the body, sexuality, affective relations), or 'subjective' (cognitive and emotional processes, motives, desires), or even 'biological' (the structure of the brain, the genetic code, reproductive capacity) now undergo social control and manipulation. Over these domains the technico-scientific apparatus, the agencies of information and communication, the decision-making centres which determine 'policies', wield their power. But these are precisely the areas where individuals and groups lay claim to their autonomy, where they conduct their search for identity by transforming them into a space where they reappropriate, self-realize and themselves construct the meaning of what they are and what they do.

Conflicts are therefore carried forward by temporary actors who bring to light the crucial dilemmas of a society. The conflicts I describe here (which do not exhaust the range of social conflicts) concern the production and the appropriation of resources which are crucial for a global society based on information. These same processes generate both new forms of power and new forms of opposition: conflict only emerges in so far as actors fight for control and the allocation of socially produced potential for action. This potential is no longer exclusively based on material resources or on forms of social organization, but to an increasing extent on the ability to produce information.

Conflicts do not chiefly express themselves through action designed to achieve outcomes in the political system. Rather, they raise a challenge which recasts the language and cultural codes which organize information. The ceaseless flow of messages only acquires meaning through the codes that order the flux and allow its meanings to be read. The forms of power now emerging in contemporary societies are grounded in an ability to 'inform' (give form). The action of movements occupies the same terrain and is in itself a message broadcast to society conveying symbolic forms and relational patterns which cast light on 'the dark side of the moon' – a system of meanings which runs counter to the sense that the apparatuses seek to impose on individual and collective events. This type of action affects institutions because it selects new élites, it modernizes organizational forms, it creates new goals and new languages. At the same time, however, it challenges the apparatuses that govern the production of information, and prevents the channels of representation and decision-making in pluralist societies from adopting instrumental rationality as the only logic with which to govern complexity. Such rationality applies solely to procedures, and imposes the criterion of efficiency and effectiveness as the only measure of sense. The action of movements reveals that the neutral rationality of means masks interests and forms of power; that it is impossible to confront the massive challenge of living together on a planet by now become a global society without openly discussing the 'ends' and 'values' that make such cohabitation possible. They highlight the insuperable dilemmas facing complex societies, and by doing so, force them openly to assume responsibility for their choices, their conflicts and their limitations.

By drawing on forms of action that relate to daily life and individual identity, contemporary movements detach themselves from the traditional model of political organization, and they increasingly distance themselves from political systems. They move in to occupy an intermediate space of social life where individual needs and the pressures of political innovation mesh together. Because of the particular features of movements, social conflicts can only become effective through the mediation of political actors, even though they will never restrict themselves to only this. The innovative thrust of movements, therefore, does not exhaust itself in changes to the political system brought about by institutional actors. Nevertheless, the ability of collective demands to expand and to find expression depends on the way in which political actors are able to translate them into democratic guarantees.

NOTE

I am grateful to Jan Nederveen Pieterse for his perceptive comments on a previous version of this paper.

REFERENCES

Abelson, R.A. (1981) 'Psychological Status of the Script Concept', *American Psychologist* 36.

Alberoni, F. (1977) *Movimento e istituzione*. Bologna: IL Mulino.

Bateson, G. (1972) *Steps to an Ecology of Mind*. New York: Ballantine.

Bateson, G. (1979) *Mind and Nature*. New York: Dutton.

Bendix, R. (1964) *Nation-Building and Citizenship*. New York: Wiley.

Bendix, R. (1978) *Kings or People*. Berkeley, CA: University of California Press.

Cohen, J.L. (1985) 'Strategy or Identity: New Theoretical Paradigms and Contemporary Social Movements', *Social Research* 52(4).

Crozier, M. and Friedberg, E. (1977) *L'Acteur et le système*. Paris: Seuil.

Eiser, J.R. (1980) *Cognitive Social Psychology*. London: McGraw-Hill.

Gamson, W.A. (1990) *The Strategy of Social Protest*, 2nd edn. Belmont, CA: Wadsworth.

Gamson, W.A. and Modigliani, A. (1989) 'Media Discourse and Public Opinion on Nuclear Power: A Constructionist Approach', *American Journal of Sociology* 95.

Gamson, W.A., Fireman, B. and Rytina, S. (1982) *Encounters with Unjust Authorities*. Homewood, IL: Dorsey Press.

Giddens, A. (1984) *The Constitution of Society*. Berkeley, CA: University of California Press.

Gilligan, C. (1981) *In a Different Voice*. Cambridge, MA: Harvard University Press.

Habermas, J. (1984) *Theory of Communicative Action*. Boston, MA: Beacon Press.

Jenkins, J.C. (1983) 'Resource Mobilization Theory and the Study of Social Movements', *Annual Review of Sociology* 9.

Keane, J. (ed.) (1988) *Civil Society and the State*. London: Verso.

Klandermans, B., Kriesi, H. and Tarrow, S. (eds) (1988) *From Structure to Action*. New York: JAI Press.

Klapp, O. (1965) *Symbolic Leaders*. Chicago, IL: Aldine.

Kornhauser, W. (1959) *The Politics of Mass Society*. Glencoe, IL: Free Press.

McCarthy, J.D. and Zald, M.N. (1977) 'Resource Mobilization and Social Movements: A Partial Theory', *American Journal of Sociology* 86(6).

McCarthy, J.D. and Zald, M.N. (1981) *Social Movements in Organizational Society*. New Brunswick, NJ: Transaction Books.

Mannheim, K. (1936) *Ideology and Utopia*. London: Routledge and Kegan Paul.

Melucci, A. (1984) *Altri Codici*. Bologna: Il Mulino.

Melucci, A. (1989) *Nomads of the Present*. London: Hutchinson; Philadelphia: Temple University Press.

Moscovici, S. (1981) *L'Age des foules*. Paris: Fayard.

Neisser, U. (1976) *Cognition and Reality*. San Francisco, CA: Freeman.

Snow, D.A. and Benford, R.D. (1988) 'Ideology, Frame Resonance, and Participant Mobilization', in B. Klandermans et al. (eds) *From Structure to Action*. New York: JAI Press.

Snow, D.A., Rochford, E.B., Worden, S.K. and Benford, R.D. (1986) 'Frame Alignment Processes, Micromobilization, and Movement Participation', *American Sociological Review* 51.

Tarrow, S. (1989) *Democracy and Disorder*. Oxford: Clarendon Press.

Thompson, J.B. (1984) *Studies in the Theory of Ideology*. Berkeley and Los Angeles, CA: University of California Press.

Tilly, C. (1978) *From Mobilization to Revolution*. Chicago, IL: Addison-Wesley.

Tilly, C. (1986) *The Contentious French*. Cambridge, MA: Harvard University Press.

Touraine, A. (1973) *La Production de la société*. Paris: Seuil.

Touraine, A. (1978) *La Voix et le regard*. Paris: Seuil.

Touraine, A. (1984) *Le Retour de l'acteur*. Paris: Fayard.

Turner, R.H. and Killian, L.M. (1987) *Collective Behavior*, 3rd edn. Englewood Cliffs, NJ: Prentice Hall.

Von Foerster, H. (1973) 'On Constructing Reality', in W.F.E. Preiser (ed.) *Environmental Design Research*. Stroudsbourg: Dowden, Hutchinson and Ross.

Watzlawick, P. (ed.) (1981) *Die Erlundene Wirlichkeit*. Munich: Piper Verlag.

Wutnow, R., Davison Hunter, J., Bergensen, A. and Kurweil, E. (1984) *Cultural Analysis*. London: Routledge and Kegan Paul.

Zolberg, A.R. (1972) 'Moments of Madness', *Politics and Society* 2(2).

Alberto Melucci is Professor of Sociology and Clinical Pyschology at the University of Milan, Department of Sociology, Via Conservatorio 7, 20122 Milano. For the last twenty years he has been working on social movements, cultural change and the relation between collective and individual identity. He is the author of more than ten books, including *Nomads of the Present* (1989) and *Il gioco dell'io* (1991), and many articles in international journals and readers.

Marxism and the Darkness of History

Sudipta Kaviraj

Philosophers have shed too much light on the process called history. The point now is to shed some kindly darkness on it to make it habitable. Then we might be able to recognize it again as something familiar yet intractable, something we always live within but never quite control. It would not appear as something ideal, rational, perfectly designed though imperfectly executed, but as the tragic, ironic, part transparent, part obscure process we encounter every day and at all times. This article seeks to show how the Marxist theory of history, traditionally seen as an obstinately optimistic construct, would look with a coat of dark philosophic paint.

At the end of his great elucidatory exercise on modernity, de Tocqueville ended on this surprising puzzled note:

> . . . in the presence of so great a subject, my sight is troubled, my reason fails. . . . Although the revolution which is taking place in social conditions, the laws, the opinions and the feelings of men is still far from being terminated, yet its results already admit of no comparison with anything the world has ever before witnessed. I go back from age to age, to the remotest antiquity but I find no parallel to what is occurring before my eyes; as the past has ceased to throw light on the future, the mind of man wanders around in obscurity. (de Tocqueville, 1951: 331)

I would like to call this sense of cognitive intractability the darkness of history. It recognizes the limits of the rational explanatory enterprise in the face of history's intrinsic complexity, yet does not fall into cognitive despair.

This illustrates two aspects of the intellectual configuration of the nineteenth century from which Marxism emerged. It represents graphically the sense of bewilderment in the face of the unfolding logic of modernity — an age created by supposedly rational acts, driven by rational impulses, yet appearing to be unmasterable by ordinary processes of reasoning. It is this darkness of history which

Development and Change (SAGE, London, Newbury Park and New Delhi), Vol. 23 (1992) No. 3, 79–102.

ideologies of the nineteenth century try to understand and dispel. Of the great variety of responses to this problem, from exultant optimism about an imminent clarification of history to unrelieved pessimism and despair, de Tocqueville's response seems to be the most pragmatically sound and morally attractive. For it suggests against both extremes an attitude of cognitive modesty without abandoning the general possibility of historical understanding. I see this approach to the possibility and limits of human constructions as coming down from a 'dark' tradition of rationality in European social thought, which exists in creative tension with the mainstream trends of rationalist enlightenment.

Finally, I still think Marxist theory, seen as a discourse, provides a fertile point of departure for understanding the historical destiny of the modern world. To understand the world and its own history within it, however, Marxism must be read as a discourse; and its central historical theorems of rationality must be mediated through this dark tradition instead of the seductive optimism of the Enlightenment.

Before entering into a consideration of the history of Marxism we must set some provisional rules about how to define its boundary. Before we enter into a consideration of history it is essential to state clearly which history we are seeking to understand. This is a textual problem; but without denying its significance in the proper context, I shall not take a textual line here. There is a temptation for those who still declare their indebtedness to Marxism to take a simple recourse, and try to limit the history of Marxism to the history (though it is not easy to see what this could mean) of Marx's own direct statements, to draw a clear boundary around Marxism by referring to lines of intentionality of the author. But we should accept the general argument of Foucault that this denies a realistic view of the text's mode of being in history. Or to put it in his terms, it is essential to see Marx as the originator of a discourse, not just the creator of a social theory (Foucault, 1977: 113–38). Such a view of what thinking does to the world must then include not only the purity of intentions of the original author or his texts, but also the far murkier realm of the strange, often tragic consequences — ways in which these statements influence other intentions and practices, some of which would surely have surprised or dismayed him. Yet there is no denying that these constitute parts of Marxism's history. To deal with this adequately we shall require a subtle theory of the relation between responsibility and consequence. To take a historical view, the theory must be seen as being responsible even for those things which were done illegitimately in its name. It then becomes impossible to use the easy solution of denying by textual analyses the historical significance of major setbacks for Marxian socialism, either by claiming that Marx's intentions were realized in those institutions, or that they were not and that their collapse should not, therefore, overly concern real Marxists. It becomes necessary to understand Marxism itself historically, as a theory or discourse that is capable of contending readings and configurations, reflecting occasionally contending trends; to ask why one type of configuration came to dominate its subsequent history, what other possible configurations could be and whether these are still recoverable from the historical crisis that the collapse of Soviet communism has brought about.

Every crisis opens up history in a double way, only one side of which we usually consider. A crisis not only opens up the future dramatically by forcing us to abandon the lines of extrapolations from the present which we specially favour and to understand the range of possibilities, but in a significant sense it also opens up the past as well. It forces us to look into complexities of the past and reconsider lines of possible development which existed but might not have materialized, or towards which we may have been indifferent. Lines of argument, suggestions or initiatives on institutionalization which did not attract attention at the time might now appear as historically interesting.

Social theories also have hidden autobiographies; they subtly offer historical suggestions in the course of their self-presentation. Their favourite likings, hatreds, questions, anxieties and metaphors often indicate how they construct their own historical genealogy. Marx constantly warns against taking people and theories at their word, against accepting too trustingly their self-presentation or their self-understanding; and though communists are exceptionally skilful at self-exempting arguments (by distinguishing, for instance, between ideology and science) we must apply to Marxism this simple general rule. This is not a judgement about truth and falsehood: to say that a theory's self-presentation should not be taken too literally does not necessarily imply that it lies about itself, only that the structure of the self also structures knowledge about the self, and puts some limit to its cognitive powers. Autobiographies respond to situations, and what may be quite true among the complex influences of a theory at a certain historical juncture might not be apposite in another.

Conventionally, the standard histories of Marxist thought emphasize the sequential or longitudinal continuity between Marx and earlier radical, socialist thinking; without denying this, it could be said that Marx must be set in terms of a different, more lateral context of puzzles shared with others. Some thinkers who did not share his political commitments but did share his historical curiosity, sought to unravel, in Koselleck's terms, the peculiar temporality of modernity (Koselleck, 1985: 3–20). All those who undertook this project shared in some form the complex inheritance of European rationalism (in a general sense here, not in the narrower technical sense of philosophical disputes), as rationality was involved at two distinct levels in this project. First, the spectacle of events to be explained was driven by rationalist aspirations.[1] The major difference between earlier revolutions and those after the French Revolution, it was widely held, was that while earlier political disorders seemed condemned to accepting political changes within something like the Polybian cycle of constitutions, the modern revolutions happened in a linear consciousness of time, and attempted not a temporary relief from the sufferings of bad government but the apocalyptic beginning of unprecedented social constitutions, conceived and perfected by reason (Arendt, 1963: Ch. 1). Secondly, this historical record was to be explained rationally; and the more subtle optimists among the early modern social thinkers transferred to history a form of argument common among rational theologians of the previous century. Rational enquiry by human thought, perfected by science, discovered the rationality of the infinite design of the universe. Similarly, Hegel asserted 'to him who looks upon the world rationally, the world in its turn presents a rational aspect. The relation is mutual' (Hegel, 1956: 13). Since this social theory is pervaded by the arguments and rhetoric of rationality, it becomes necessary to analyse what this rationalist inheritance was, whether it was entirely homogeneous, as the mainstream Enlightenment tradition asserted, or whether the history of the idea of rationality itself was internally diverse, with dissonant traditions and tendencies which had tried to either limit theorems of rationality or extend them in different directions with different theoretical results.

What is invariant in all forms of rationalist thought is an optimism about the cognitive amenability of the worlds of nature and history:

despite complexity and difficulties, knowledge about these infinite entities is held to be eventually possible. Later trends in rationalist thought were to attach a pragmatic or technical dimension to this knowledge; not only can nature and history be known, but this knowledge can be used to human advantage in both cases.

Clearly, this picture of the shared core beliefs of rationalism is highly abstract, and capable of very different inflections. The history of rationalism in fact shows a great deal of experimentalism with these essential ideas and their implications, rather than a gradual defeat of alternative tendencies and constructions by a dominant Enlightenment rationality due to its incontrovertible scientific superiority. The optimism was related to the Cartesian model of successful knowledge – of clarity, precision, economy, uniformity. The initial doubt was a necessary point of departure to be overcome, circumvented, laid to rest. Extreme dogmatism, as Hobbes maintained, could rest only on extreme scepticism. Doubting everything was merely a necessary step towards ascertaining the form of a nature in which everything was known beyond a shadow of doubt, a world of causalities which are established and explained with certainty. Given the nature of human reason, there was always some remaining area of doubt, but this was only provisional, to be slowly conquered by the advance of rationality.

Enlightenment accepts and declares its complete affiliation to this model of rationality and knowledge in the metaphorical name given to it. What exists is the 'book of nature', and it was not, as with Hegel, written in the 'hieroglyph of reason'. In high Enlightenment, this idea of a knowledge that slowly spreads across the world and lights up all areas from nature to history reaches its final triumph. Enlightenment is acquired through the method of criticism, subjecting the beliefs of traditional, especially religious, thought systems to the merciless process of critical testing, rejection of what Enlightenment called 'prejudice' (Gadamer, 1989: 265–300). Enlightenment and the whole rationalist project for the transformation of nature and society was irresistible, in this view, because it was based on the critical principle of unconditional doubt of all premises. It has been convincingly shown now that there were significant limitations to this self-image of rationalism; its own initial premises were often not subjected to equally severe or merciless critical examination, and one of the major faults of the mainstream tradition of Enlightenment was its tendency to invent excuses and self-exempting rules by which the emancipating, liberating, corrosive light of reason that it threw on the rest of the world did not fall on the foundations of its own cognitive and pragmatic enterprises. It is on this point that the difference between the two ways of constructing rationality is seen most vividly. The idea of critique or of critical knowledge was articulated differently by what I would like to call a 'dark tradition'. In the standard historical view – especially that conventionally favoured by Marxists – this tradition is wholly and unjustly overshadowed by the other. As a first step in rethinking Marxism, it becomes necessary to see this history from the other side, to open up and reconsider its suppressions, problematize its victories and read its history, in Benjamin's phrase, 'against the grain' (Benjamin, 1973: 258–9).

Exaggerated claims of intellectual traditions often invite their own parodies. Similarly, the mainstream tradition of rationalism, whose perfect metaphor was the Enlightenment, can be aptly opposed by the answering metaphor of darkness with its general metaphorical association with liminality, tragedy and irony which both the Enlightenment tradition and the Marxist trend which followed it lacked entirely (to their own impoverishment). The way this 'dark' tradition looked upon itself and its place in the world is illustrated by a celebrated passage from Pascal's *Pensées*: 'Reason's last step is the recognition that there are an infinite number of things which are beyond it. It is merely feeble if it does not go as far as to realise that' (Pascal, 1981: 85). He concludes: 'such is our true state. That is what makes us incapable of certain knowledge or absolute ignorance' (p. 92). Surely it would be inappropriate to claim that the deeply tragic pessimism of the later Pascal is compatible with Marx's optimistic emancipatory theory of history. I use this passage to make an elementary distinction between two views of rationality. In one view criticism, the major principle of rational knowledge, gradually opens up the world and creates an enlightenment that is cumulative and without residue (those parts of the world's working which are clarified by knowledge do not fall back into obscurity and mystery), and its epistemic theories are based on a strong idea of bivalence. But there is a second tradition which differs from the first in two major respects. It turns the principle of critique on itself, making its claims to rationality self-limiting and fallible; it uses, for purposes of historical reasoning at least (and in cases like Hegel, for all reasoning), a gradational theory of truth-adequacy. What is important in this difference is not just the more likeable mood of modesty, which might only be contingently present in one person's views as distinct from others, but rather the principle of self-doubt and self-limitation as a constituent of rationality.

Since Marx's intellectual enterprise was to apply the rationalist programme to the newly opened field of history, much depends on how we construct the principles of rationalist thinking, which particular model of cognitive rationality we consider preferable. Of the main principles of rationalism, three of its central tenets can be read significantly differently by the two forms: (1) all things are knowable with certainty; (2) everything known must form an interconnected system; and (3) the knowledge of infinite objects like nature or history (as a totality) must transcend mere empirical investigation, and must primarily be theoretical. The alternative tradition held that certain things, created or caused by human agency, may be precisely known but that this knowledge may not be final; the constant presence of unrealized intentions and unintended results prevents a perfect transparency of the historical process. This was not seen as a dishonourable failure of epistemology of social science, but as the first principle of an adequate ontology of the historical world. Some things were such that they could not be perfectly known, and to register this agnostic non-finality was not the failure of a theory of knowledge, but actually the mark of its maturity. For the fact that these things could not be known perfectly, exhaustively or in advance,[2] or be subjected to reliable control, did not mean that human beings could not relate to them rationally. To attempt to know, predict and predictively control them was false on two counts: firstly, it was a regrettable rationalist conceit; and secondly, by equating rationality with control, it implicitly presented too narrow a picture of what it was to be rational. This condemned all non-instrumental attitudes *ipso facto* as irrational.

Consequently, the two trends of rationalism developed rather different cognitive stances towards history. Enlightenment rationalism held that the basic laws of history could eventually be discovered and, by their intelligent manipulation, humanity would be able to achieve a control and mastery over its own patterns of collective action comparable to its control over processes of nature. Interestingly, it is possible to find in Marx, especially his relatively early works, several assertions which incline towards this cognitive optimism. After his discussion of communism in the *Economic and Philosophic Manuscripts*, he exults: 'communism is the riddle of history solved', and 'it knows itself to be this solution' (Marx, 1972: 148). I wish to claim that Marx's later writings, though inclined more towards discovery of structural forms and tendencies, seem to be marked by a historical theory which is not more pessimistic, but certainly more complex. Laws of history are still sought but they are, as is well known, not laws of finality but of tendency. The relation between structure in history and human agency or between laws and actions which constitute them is now seen as an internal relation. In his later works, he seems more ready to admit that 'men make their history but they do not do as they please' (Marx, 1977: 96).

This restores into the heart of the historical process a darkness or obscurity remarkably similar to the one that de Tocqueville had seen around him in the paradoxical history of modernity. Indeed, any reader of Marx would notice that we meet in his historical narratives two types of people, or rather people in two very different historical stances. Men as representatives of their species, whom we meet in the *Economic and Philosophical Manuscripts* or *Capital* seem to be endowed with more insight, energy, rationality and control than the puny individuals, much like the small men in Piranesi's drawings (Clark, 1973: Ch. 1), whom we meet in the chronicles of French or German politics. Their initiatives constantly miscarry, their deliberate designs are seldom straightforwardly fulfilled but return to haunt their lives in grotesque forms. The history of modernity was peculiarly difficult to understand because of this disjunction between greater collective competence of the human species and individual inability of sectors to control their destiny. It was this great problem of translation or intransitivity from one level of rationality to another, and between one aspect and another, which formed the main cognitive problem of modern history. It can be contended that the history of modernity cannot be easily clarified, or rationally explained without residue, due to a peculiar character of social action that the modern period has introduced. We can illustrate this better by using an argument derived from Weber's distinction between traditional and rational action.

De Tocqueville's work, and especially the passage quoted (see p. 79), shows these difficulties through its internal structure of interconnected metaphors. First, earlier periods are easier to understand because they are over; the historical theorist of modernity faces a problem in trying to obtain an historical view of a process which is unconcluded: he must do without the advantages of the owl of Minerva. He cannot wait for the dusk of history to fall because, due to the aspiration of rationality, his attempted knowledge is related to the historical process in a radically different way. Neither de Tocqueville nor Marx was drawn towards the Hegelian solution of positing a 'closure' to make rational understanding of history possible. How could human beings who are being carried in the flux of history caused by their own uncoordinated and uncontrolled deliberate acts achieve a rational understanding of its structure and tendency? De Tocqueville's passage suggests a second reason for this cognitive intractability. Besides the fact that modernity is an unconcluded process, he notes that 'the past has ceased to throw light on the future', which can be given a more complex, partly Weberian, construction.

The difficulty of earlier history might have lain in inaccessibility of material or evidence; the intractability of knowledge about modernity lies in the structure of historical action. Past societies were marked by repetitive forms of action, and this was logically reflected in the way in which history was seen to be an instructor in life. Machiavelli, writing about Renaissance Italy, could line up illustrations of conspiracies in the long chapter of the *Discourses*, because he assumed conspiracies to be a part of the general business of statecraft, which had an immutable structure and form. Acting in the name of rationality, in modern times, humanity had achieved a peculiar plasticity of its own existence, at once exhilarating, frustrating and frightening, which made traditional forms of historical knowledge obsolete at one stroke. Modern actions were difficult to understand because they were unprecedented in the sense that in earlier periods men did not act like this. They were unprecedented in a second sense as well: modern action was driven by a logic of perfectibility and instrumental improvement, a constant search for more efficient action which meant that the same act performed a second time tended to be different from the first occasion. Thus the scholarship of history must change in a most radical way: instead of reading the 'line of events', those hoping to understand history must try to read the 'logic of process' (Koselleck, 1985: 39–54). Conventional understanding of history must give way to social theory.

If we accept this way of reading the problem of modernity in historical cognition, the optimism of the early Marx has to be seriously qualified. In any case, to the complexities arising out of recursiveness we must also add the problem of unintended consequences, where causation and intention do not coincide in historical action. A certain riddle-like quality may attach to modernity precisely because of its aspiration towards rationality in its actions. Marx's works in the more mature period present us with an increasingly complex picture: while he seems confident that it is possible to unravel laws and trends, 'the logic of processes', it is increasingly evident that the relation between this logic and the 'line of events' is not unproblematic or simply transitive. If read through these constructions, it is possible to make the case for a Marxian theory of history that was more self-limiting because more self-critical. Marxist historical praxis then should not claim self-exemption because it has the status of science, but accept that it is subject to the same general logic of recursive criticism and alteration that all other trends and aspects of modernity required. History was something to which men must relate rationally, but that did not imply either having ultimate knowledge or technical-rational control. I do not deny the possibility, indeed, the plausibility of the other, Enlightenment-oriented construction; but I wish to restore the picture of the Marxist theory of history as a complex, internally contested discursive field which, for historical reasons, came gradually to be completely dominated by one political tendency of an immodest rationalism. It is important to see Marxism like any other discourse as a field of contestation. This is true not because contradictory elements were wrongly brought into what should have been an ideally pure, symmetrical theory, but rather because its moment of origin was itself rich in complexity and suggestiveness. Thus going back to its origins would not restore purity, but a sense of ambiguity and diverse possibilities – which may be reassuring for other reasons and to other tastes.

In the institutional history of Marxism, for reasons that are well known and documented, one tradition came to acquire an exclusive predominance; but the other trend was not wholly extinguished. Like the historical relation between rationalism and romanticism, an asymmetric contest and exchange continues between the central and the marginal tendencies, in which the marginal tradition never acquires sufficient strength to dislodge the mainstream tendency, but works away as a constantly bothersome, ineradicable critique.[3] At times of crisis of the mainstream paradigm, it forces upon it certain criticisms, worries, corrections, some central redefinitions of its concepts, and a deflection of the axis of theoretical construction. It is a constant, if suppressed subterranean presence, and since Marxism has rarely faced a crisis of such proportions as that which it faces today, it is necessary to reconsider some of the primary theses of Marxist political theory in the light of this second tradition.[4] How would a Marxism informed by this tradition look? What would be its central theses about rationality in history?

The problem of 'reason in history' concerned first of all the relation between the causal field and the horizon of intentional rationality associated with a particular individual or collective action. The late clarificatory letters of Engels suggest that he still accepted the structure of the elucidation of this problem in terms of Hegel's classic exposition on the cunning of reason in the introduction of the *Philosophy of History*.[5] Rational designs of actors and their intentions must be reconstructed correctly, not because they are carried through, but because they show us the basic intentional identifications of social acts, without which this social analysis simply cannot begin to work.[6] Historical events have to be explained by their summation; this is not a simple linear realization of designs but a complex process of mutual restrictions and production of emergent properties which cannot be attributed to the original basic intentions. The historical process is a sum of these events, but if this level of the historical record shows any 'logic' or design which can be seen *ex post facto* as 'rational', this could not be attributed to the rationality of the original actors. To arrive at a non-Hegelian solution to this inherited problem Marxism had to settle its account, not surprisingly, with 'the Hegelian dialectic and philosophy as a whole'.

A solution to the riddle of history meant in that case keeping the consequences of political actions consonant with the rational intentions in which they originated. Since this, to be realistic, was to be seen as a horizon, a range of possibilities, rather than the occurrence or non-occurrence of a single line of events, the exact meaning of 'keeping control over events' had to be modified. Indeed, the concept of revolution came to be associated with this model of action after it had undergone the strange transformation in its conceptual meaning, from being an upheaval in a cyclical order which restricted possibilities, to a deliberately caused disturbance in a linear, typically modern temporality (Koselleck, 1985: Ch. 7). There could be two forms of solution to the riddle of history, the first of which can be called maximal, the second minimal. The first model of revolutionary action involved some firm fundamental beliefs: (1) that revolutionary parties knew with certainty the preferred direction of change and the preferable state of affairs, and this did not require any fundamental correction; (2) that the course of history could be altered in this preferred direction through a massive act of submergence of individual into collective intentionality represented by a political party which 'acted as one man'; and (3) that once this preferred state was achieved through a revolutionary act, society must be held down to that condition and that social form, by a pattern of rational control – preferably ideological, but if necessary, also forcible. Clearly, this model of political action implied strong rationality claims on several counts; it ruled out as a fatal weakness any possibility, not to mention requirement, of self-doubting criticism, the possibility of error, of unconsidered or unintended consequence as an ineradicable dimension of historical action.

The second approach to history, using a more modest conception of historical rationality and an inherent principle of philosophical self-criticism, would clearly build up the model quite differently, seeing recursive self-correction as central to the whole enterprise. It would perhaps claim that revolutionary politics could establish with certainty what the preferred state of affairs would be. It might also concede that a massive deliberate collective act could move historical processes in that general direction, though it would hardly be confident about taking it along the exact trajectory. It would be willing to admit that 'successful' revolutionaries are often successful in making revolutions different from the ones they had intended and initiated, and would claim that there is nothing peculiarly dishonourable about such loss of control. But it would maintain that once the change had taken place, its very success would create an altered political world which would require a review of the structure of its theory and its constituent programmes. In other words, it is not only historical political failure which necessitates a change in theory but, paradoxically, also its success.

Two implications of this argument of self-limiting rationality appear to me to be of some interest. The first is the notion of recursiveness as a constituent of a rational relation to history – keeping in touch with history by 'changing with the times' instead of trying to hold it down to an impassable state of affairs. This is opposed to a notion of final truth. Secondly, if radicals do not claim the possession of such infallible truth, the preservation of a structure of intellectual freedom becomes an essential mechanism for keeping up with history. Since the principles of organization of the radical party in Marxism are basically connected to this notion of truth, this has implications which are not merely cognitive and intellectual, but also relevant for party and state construction. In this view, construction of a totalitarian party and state becomes a guaranteed way of ensuring that the intellectual resources of the society to cope with both unwanted and premeditated change would decline. As events in the former Soviet Union show dramatically, the party and the state can carry on with a massive pretence of rationality through the enormous structure of state planning; but this becomes pitifully out of touch with a reality it has itself successfully changed. Maximalist doctrine tends to argue that because a particular policy has been successful in the past, it would be irrational to alter it. Minimalist thinking would suggest the opposite, and argue that in case of either failure or success recursive correction and change are needed. In the case of failure, the reasons for theoretical correction are obvious. If successful, this success would itself, over time, alter the structure of the world in such a way that the earlier 'correct' policies would start yielding diminishing returns, until the very success of the policy causes the conditions for its eventual abandonment.

It is hardly possible in a short article to provide an outline of what such a minimalist rationalism would do to the shape of the Marxist theory of history. In the rest of this article, I shall try very briefly to sketch its implications for some central concerns of radical social theory. It will not be difficult to anticipate my conclusion. I shall advocate that in the present crisis, taking advantage of the at least temporary disarray of the dominant maximalist model, Marxists interested in emancipation should try to excavate and liberate the second tradition of Marxian radicalism.

The first consequence of this would of course be that our way of looking at history and making broad judgements about it must change. Most human endeavours of any significance neither simply succeed nor simply fail; and if we become too committed to that form of bivalence, we make it appear that what happened in history most of the time goes beyond the descriptive power of human language. A Marxism that has not totally forgotten its Hegelian heritage will not find itself out of depth in encountering such puzzles. It would use the entire repertory of metaphors from poetics – of tragedy, irony, farce, travesty, misunderstanding, catachresis – to characterize this persistent disjunction between incontrovertible causal connection and rational inappropriateness. This can perhaps be called miscausation, or simply 'irony'. History does not use irony occasionally to relieve dramatic tedium as in literary stories; it is history's major mode, it is the main, predominant form of what can be called the poetics of history. Thus there is nothing dishonourable in radical men, acting more or less rationally, losing control of what they set in motion, even if it turns in unintended ways and assumes grotesque forms which seem not only to escape from, but also to mock the intentions that lay at their origins.

In modernity, rationality enters into the realm of history with an unprecedented force, in two interconnected forms. The first is the ability to conceive of and argue for preferable states; the second is the rationality of bringing causation sufficiently in consonance with rational intentions so that by concerted collective action such states can be brought about. Shrewd observers noticed quite early in the period of modernity that the claim to control did not impart actual control, but affected the relation between acts, intentions and consequences in peculiar, unfamiliar ways. The gradual ascendancy of the scientific-technical conception of rationality in historical thinking led to a situation in which control over history meant simply control of end-states, the ability to control outcomes, as in scientific experimental procedures. The truth of Marx's statements about the future lay not in accurate predictions about future states of industrial societies, but in the identification of incontrovertibly real processes. The picture of Soviet society was declared to fit Marx's future scenarios, assisted in this dubious enterprise by the sketchiness of those scenarios themselves. Marx wrote so insubstantially about what socialism meant to him institutionally that any society in which woefully inadequate capitalist orders had been successfully overthrown could be interpreted as a preliminary realization of his dreams – although it was granted that these were still short of the stage in which socialist man could conduct scientific experiments in the morning and write poetry in the afternoon.

In fact, a social theory like Marx's immediately sets in motion both self-fulfilling and self-falsifying practical effects. When a future state is predicted, this can become a self-fulfilling prophecy. By implication, the fact that a state of affairs has been realized does not necessarily indicate that the initial historical statements were empirically or tendentially correct (Merton, 1968: Ch. 8). Thus the coming of revolutions which looked like those Marx predicted was a matter of belief rather than of truth. However, the other side of this picture has been less well presented. Marxist theory also set in motion a logic of practical self-falsification. Once a prediction is made about the probable causes of a catastrophic crisis in the capitalist economy, the entire pragmatic ingenuity of those whose interests this might injure become focused on exactly those processes. Since every society is a complex field of strategic action in which there are several players with contending interests, it is unlikely that a system would ever break down on the exact points predicted. If the system does collapse, it may do so for quite different reasons, and through stress at quite other points. This illustrates a contradictory relation between the truth of historical statements and the probability of occurrence. Precisely because the statement is true, or is feared or believed to be so, the probability of the occurrence of that state of affairs decreases.

The history of Marxism shows the operation of both these types of predictive logic, though orthodox communists are apt to forget the second part of this historical narrative. In fact, chronologically, it is the self-falsifying trend which came about first. The emergence of Marxism set off two processes: the organization of socialist parties and movements committed to bringing the prediction about; and, simultaneously, the introduction of major countercyclical reforms and welfare measures by the organized forces of capital, which took the prediction seriously enough to attempt to alter the structure of developed capitalist economies. One of the historic victories of Marxism, viewed from this angle, was precisely that restructuring of capitalism in a more humane direction, because the attribution of such changes to purely endogenous forces of rational decisions within capitalist production is not an entirely credible story. In standard Marxist histories, however, this process has been seen derisively as the growth of reformism, a theory which unwittingly gives credit to capitalist regimes for something that was not their achievement.

When Marxism travels to the political culture of Czarist Russia, the tendencies of an alternative construction are seen as weaknesses, uneradicated residues from ideologies which scientific socialists were to weed out and destroy. Sociologically, the fascination of radical intellectuals in less developed capitalist societies for rationalist certainties is not difficult to explain; but after the success of the revolution, and in the absence of similar transformations elsewhere, its local mistrusts came to crystallize into the orthodoxies of the entire international communist movement. There appears to be a strong inverse relation between the development of a society and its need for utopias of maximalist rationality.

Yet Leninism shows some interesting features which are neglected because we are apt to take too trustingly its self-understanding and intellectual genealogy. In purely doctrinal terms, Lenin's major thesis bore a deeply paradoxical relation to Marxism. Leninism could be seen as a valid extension of Marxism only if recursive self-correction is seen as an ineradicable constituent of modernity. Since the historical structure of capitalist political economy had changed fundamentally, an obdurate adherence to Marx's theoretical statements was woefully inadequate: both the revisionism of the reformists and the revisionism of the left, the responses of Lenin and Bernstein, recognized this. The very possibility of such a successful recoordination depended on the existence of pluralism, the unobstructed working out of these alternative hypotheses. Lenin was not suppressed because the structure of radicalism was not Leninist. The theoretical space created by the contest between Marxist reformism and radicalism was a precondition for this successful reinterpretation of Marx's theory. It would follow that Marxism, to stay alive as a theory of history, required a political constellation which allowed radically different hypotheses to be entertained and articulated. It is no small irony that Lenin's legacy so utterly misconstrued the relation between historical rationality, recursive correction and plurality and went against the grain of its own history. The institutional apparatus of the Comintern systematically hunted down and eradicated all hints of unorthodoxy, making it impossible for Leninism to have a sequel theory which bore to it the same relationship that Leninism bore to Marxism.

This has clear implications again for the theory of organization of radical politics. While a revolutionary breakdown of power might need a disciplined party that acts 'like one man', the logic of long-term historical rationality goes against this. Precisely in order to preserve its intellectual resources, to retain its position in a politically changing world, the radical movement requires constant generation of possible scenarios, because there is one single certainty in the historical world of modernity — that human beings will reconstruct their world. Indeed, the structure of political organizations must be like the structure of successful science which arranges its fallible cognitive programme by having a central core of normative, puzzle-solving activity surrounded by small enterprises of more radical anticipation of paradigmatic change. To think like one man is indeed a certain recipe for historical disaster. The crisis of Soviet society is frightening, not only in its political and economic aspects. A society which in the nineteenth century prided itself on its intellectual diversity has, in seventy years of rational planning, completely divested itself of all dissenting intellectual resources. Now that the dominant paradigm has collapsed, it becomes clear that Russian society had not allowed any form of alternative thinking to develop new scenarios in the dark corners and margins of the system. The system policed itself so successfully and so completely, in fact, that there were no dark corners left in which its own resources of intellectual renewal could be secretly nurtured. The collapse of the Soviet order should force radicals to rethink some of the basic issues of Marxist theory, only some of which are indicated below.

It is impossible to give a detailed account of the central theoretical questions on which Marxists should try to recover their own second or alternative traditions of thought. However, some can be briefly mentioned, all of which are concerned with different domains of rationality. On all of these questions, the communist tradition of Marxist theory probably exercised its collective choice in the wrong direction. By implication, if the socialist position on all these questions is reconsidered, it may be possible to construct the outline of a fundamentally different type of theory of modernity.

Although Marx's treatment of the theme of technology under capitalism was mixed, occasionally ambiguous, his theory of history welcomed the development of technology in the form of productive forces – which does not necessarily imply an unrestricted welcome to technological instrumental rationality. The later Marxist tradition, however, embraced technology indiscriminately. Under Stalin, the fascination of the Soviet system with gigantic structures reflected a primitive equation of high technology not with subtlety and more minute control but with sheer scale. Slowly, communists all over the world imitated this and transformed Marx's mixed position on technology, which had made rethinking and different inflections possible, into a wholly uncritical acceptance of technology itself as evidence of man's conquest of nature. The practical consequence of this theory in terms of environmental degradation has been enormous; Marxist thinking outside socialist countries became deeply biased against environmental issues.

The way Marxists have regarded capitalist expansion across the world is not unrelated to this theoretical view. There were two problematic aspects here: Marxists too often tended to welcome uncritically the entry of a superficial, predatory travesty of capitalism into the colonial world as unproblematically 'progressive'. But they made a more empirical mistake as well, grossly overestimating the ability of capitalist production to invade and restructure traditional rural societies. People who lived in other parts of the world and were the objects of bourgeois rationalist apparatuses of economic and political control were not resourceless to the extent implied by traditional

Marxism. Peasant societies and social groups living in cultures of illiteracy, in communities produced by shared productive labour on a common physical world, had resources and subtle techniques of 'hiding' their social structures from the invading forces and their agents. They could not defeat the forces of capitalist rationalism, but they could try to cheat them out of their victory. They often used the intangible frontiers of culture with great effect and saved their social world by inducing a belief in the colonial power and its local allies that they had submitted to the demands of its superior rationality. Until recently, Marxists underestimated this successful 'resistance' of peasant societies, with their distinctive ontologies, attitudes towards nature, towards technology, towards the modern state. Emancipation theorists like Wertheim were more prescient on this question, while Marxists continued to treat peasants as a class of inferior subalterns who had failed to become rational workers. They did not recognize the possibility of alternative rationalities of peasant societies, nor did they realize that peasant opposition to capitalism had often been as successful as the workers'. Indeed, Lenin's own filiation to the earlier Russian radical tradition is itself quite paradoxical; it might be necessary, in a rereading of Marxist theory, to turn it upside down. The earlier tradition of Chernyshevsky, Herzen and Dobrolyubov was more deeply sympathetic to the peasant traditions of an unworried, convivial community. There is a clear connection between this tradition and Bakhtin's celebration of a peasant humour and the laughter of a thousand years (Bakhtin, 1984). He saw in peasant traditions a carnivalesque, anti-puritan, scatological disruptiveness of the solemnity and rationalist puritanism of Soviet communism itself. It appears that in the final analysis, the Weberian discipline of the modern system failed to get the better of the deceiving indiscipline of the traditional Russian *muzhik* who seems to have defeated the process of collectivization by a strategic lack of productivity. Bakhtin's work is thus of incalculable significance if we begin such an excavation in search of Marxism's complex history.

The question of rationality is inextricably connected in Marxism with another question – what were the reliable instruments of rationality in social life as instruments of producing rational collective decisions? This would involve discussions about the political institutions of modernity, the question of states, markets and civil societies.

A curious aspect here is the strange and unintended ways in which internal arrangements of a theory can change over time. Marx was concerned in his reflections about capitalist modernity with the two major instruments of rational allocation of resources which this civilization had slowly brought into being: the market and the state. He spent more time analysing market structures and emphasized that though trade and exchange had existed in practically all human social forms, the capitalist market was in fact a new type of structure of rational action. While he neglected to make a similar statement about the modern state, it is clearly appropriate to extend Marx's idea to this arena. Although in a very general sense states had existed in history for a long time, the specific organization of force represented by the modern state was inextricably connected to the needs of bourgeois modernity. Nothing is clearer than Marx's simultaneous opposition to the claims of both these institutions of modern rationality. In certain realms of ideological dispute, the claims of the market and the state might be represented as conflicting; but if we try to discern the structure of a whole discourse, the joint or complementary claim is astonishingly large. It is claimed that either the market or the state or some combination of the two will produce rational solutions to all problems of modernity. It would obviously be historically inappropriate to suggest that Marx saw their relation in this way, or that he would be troubled by the distinctly post-Foucauldian worry about the two configurations of the state and the market swallowing up the entire space of possibilities of social arrangements, so that conceiving of other possibilities becomes extremely difficult. Yet I would argue that one can see such an opposition in Marx's unremitting hostility to both.

Historically, of course, in the context of the political theory all around him, Marx saw the state and the market as two complementary instruments of capitalist domination, which supported and covered for each other; he did not foresee the later innovation of using them as foils to each other's excesses. His hostility and critical rejection of both the market and the state is never in doubt. Utilitarian and other individualist theories expected the market to produce a rational ordering of society, because it contained an internal mechanism that corrected overallocation and imbalances. Accordingly, these traditions emphasized the self-regulating aspects of the civil society. The Hegelian tradition equated the civil society with an unhindered pursuit of self-interest and private desires, but was sceptical of its ability to produce unaided any rational civil order. Civil society, thus, could be seen as an implement which produced rational action only in a restricted sense, if at all. It therefore relied increasingly heavily on the state as the mechanism which would produce a rational social order, as distinct from the rational behaviour of maximizing individuals and groups.

Marx's thinking on the state was seriously underdetermined on crucial points. Consequently, it is difficult to organize it into a systematic, internally consistent argument. Despite textual difficulties of this kind, the drift of his thought and its considerable originality is quite unmistakable. His critique of the market as the rationalizing institution of modern society is well known. But his attitude towards the state was no less sceptical. The state is marked by the stigma of a permanent alienation, making collective activities tractable only through abstract processes, which always bear the sociological danger of congealing into an oppressive social group with pre-emptive powers of control, and producing cognitive estrangement by making the process of planning collective life impenetrable to ordinary men. That is why its utility to the emancipation of the proletariat is merely transient and instrumental. Since the enormously powerful structure of bourgeois states cannot be destroyed by a movement dissolving into instant anarchism, there is an historic necessity for a proletarian state. But Marx's insistence on the eventual waning of state power, in the *Critique of the Gothat Programme*, indicated that he did not expect the state, suitably restructured, to function as a crucial, irreplaceable instrument for the allocation of goods, capacities and rewards. In a developed socialist society, according to Marx's sketchy outlines of the future, a rational productive and distributive system would have to be worked out in which the state did not have a central, and certainly not an ever expanding role. In view of this, the state could not have appeared to Marx as the predominant instrument of social rationality. So what does the Marxist tradition of thinking about the state offer us? The devoted statism of Marxist movements is clear; at the same time, this position appears not only practically fatal but also theoretically illegitimate because Marx's thinking was clearly as much opposed to the state as to the market.

This might indicate indirectly a major focus of challenge for Marxist social theory. The solution to the problem of the state and the market can be sought in two different ways. An historically sensitive account of the state/market problem may well incline towards a cyclical and contextual theory which could claim that neither the state nor the market has any pre-emptive or universal claim to be the rational mechanism of social ordering. Each has an ability to correct imbalances created by exclusive reliance on the other: it is the state which creates the conditions for the success of the market and vice versa. The history of European industrial development shows how the entry of the state into positions of control enhanced productivity, and subsequently attended to equity needs. The state, in other words, tackled and eased a crisis created by the market. Exclusive reliance on state control in all economic activities, irrespective of their specific character, created the opposite type of crisis in the former Soviet Union, which the market is now expected to ease, if not solve altogether. The gradual control of the market by the state did not occur without political upheavals and structural problems of adjustment; wrenching an economy out of the exclusive control of a bureaucratic state is proving to be extremely difficult. It can be argued, with considerable economic plausibility, that mixed economies have therefore avoided such swings; but even within their more placid histories, one can surely discern cycles of emphasis on the logic of the market or the logic of the state.

Yet there is a subtle impoverishment of social theory in this modestly plausible reading of European reflection on modernity whose richness, complexity and tensions Marx inherited in full measure. In the social theory of the eighteenth and nineteenth centuries, there is a clear distinction between private and public interests reflected in the vigorous discussions on the nature of 'common good' or 'public happiness' and the continual attempts to redefine, in response to new practical needs, what it is that is common, or shared, or public. This is a debate which is still far from over. Undoubtedly, modern technological disasters and ecological degradation have provided stunningly obvious examples of the existence of some forms of common, indivisible interests. Recent history also shows how easily modern liberal states can neglect those commonalities which lie beyond the boundaries of the nation-state within which they are trained to think. Entrusting all common and public interests to the state, even though liberal and democratic, is no solution to such problems. Modern political theory is thus forced back into a more penetrating and more extended consideration of the question of 'common' and 'public'.

Seen this way, Marx's simultaneous opposition to the state and the market might appear institutionally puzzling, but easier to understand. In fact, Marx is simply continuing a line of earlier thinking in political theory. In early modern theory, the dichotomy between the private and the public/common is not immediately translated into the symmetrical dichotomy of the market and the state. Rather, it appears that while the private realm is equated with the play of forces in the market, the picture of the public realm is more complex than the modern one. The public realm consists of two types of principles: only those functions which are so obviously universal as to be mandatory and faintly coercive are entrusted to the state; other activities which are public without being mandatory are given over to a less clearly defined notion of the 'civic'. A major error of later Marxist theory was to abandon this insight, to neglect entirely this continuity between Marx and earlier theoretical traditions of the civic institution, which would share the public quality of the state, but would have a dialogical instead of a monological structure. I argued earlier that crises open up not only the future but also the past; this is true not only of practical initiatives in politics but also in theory. The present crisis should force those who still think through the discourse created by Marxism to open up and explore theoretical suggestions that were neglected – imprudently, it now seems.

Finally, perhaps the concept of emancipation must also undergo a certain change of meaning. It has commonly been seen and theorized as a state of affairs in which a principal cause of suffering and affliction is overcome; or, in more extreme cases, all such causes. But the historical experience of emancipatory theory itself shows that there is something wrong with this conception; either the overcoming does not occur, or where it does happen, other afflictions are always discovered which require equally urgent remedies. This does not indicate that emancipatory theory has pursued a chimerical object; rather, it shows that it has discovered something of utmost significance and reality, although it may have generally misdescribed its own object of discovery. Emancipation theories might have different objects to pursue, often in mutual conflict, but they have this feature of rational dissatisfaction in common.

Marxists must learn to shun a rationalist conceit which was based on an outdated and discredited notion of science, and an insufficient and woefully simplified appreciation of the historical problem of modernity. They must recognize that history can be moved by collective human praxis in the general direction of emancipation, but cannot be forced into a trajectory of our choice. Emancipation comes quite often in forms which might surprise those who had worked for it. The rational response is not to condemn it because it has come in an unexpected form, but to rejoice in its ever complex emergence.

NOTES

1. Political rationality means, minimally, a conceptual ability to posit schemes of a preferred social order, and the pragmatic ability to match actions in such a way that these schemes become realized.

2. It is plausible to argue, after Hegel, for a distinction between what may be called pre- and post-rationality: there are some things about which it is possible to know or act rationally beforehand, and others about which this can only be done after the event.

3. The presence of Gramsci's Marxism alongside Stalin's is best seen this way, instead of the conventional 'solution' of exalting one of these tendencies as the 'true' one and the other as deviant.

4. This dichotomous picture of only two traditions — a single dominant and a single dissenting one — is of course a convenient fable. In the nature of things, the alternatives had to be diverse, less clearly and systematically worked out, and dispersed in Marxism's astonishingly diverse history. I do not at all mean to deny the existence of alternative traditions. I have only taken up for elucidation the one that seems to me to be the most promising in the context of the problem we are discussing.

5. Especially Engels's famous letters to J. Bloch, 21 September 1890, and to Conrad Schmidt, 27 October 1890. See Marx and Engels (1975: 394–6, 396–402).

6. As Hirschman (1977: 128–31) points out, the idea of unintended consequences requires further elaboration. Agent *A* undertook action *a* because he wished to achieve intended result *x*; in actual fact, action *a* leads to the unintended result *y*. In understanding history, it is insufficient merely to say that *a* led to *y*; we must also say that *A* had intended it to lead to *x*, since *A* would probably not have acted at all if he sensed that his action could lead to a non-*x* result.

REFERENCES

Arendt, H. (1963) *On Revolution*. Harmondsworth: Penguin.

Bakhtin, M. (1984) *Rabelais and his World* (trans. H. Iswolsky). Bloomington, IN: Indiana University Press.

Benjamin, W. (1973) *Illuminations* (trans. H. Zohn and H. Arendt). Glasgow: Fontana/Collins.

Clark, K. (1973) *The Romantic Rebellion*. London: J. Murray.

Foucault, M. (1977) *Language, Countermemory, Practice* (trans. D.F. Bouchard and S. Simon). Oxford: Blackwell.

Gadamer, H.G. (1989) *Truth and Method*. New York: Crossroad Publishing.

Hegel, G.W.F. (1956) *The Philosophy of History* (trans. J. Sibree). New York: Dover Publications.

Hirschman, A.O. (1977) *The Passions and the Interests*. Princeton, NJ: Princeton University Press.

Koselleck, R. (1985) *Futures Past* (trans. K. Tribe). Cambridge, MA: MIT Press.
Marx, K. (1972) 'Economic and Philosophical Manuscripts', in David McLellan (ed.) *Karl Marx, Early Texts*, pp. 130–80. Oxford: Blackwell.
Marx, K. (1977) 'The Eighteenth Brumaire of Louis Napoleon', in Karl Marx and Friedrich Engels *Selected Works in One Volume*, pp. 96–179. London: Lawrence and Wishart.
Marx, K. and Engels, F. (1975) *Selected Correspondence*. Moscow: Progress Publishers.
Merton, R. K. (1968) *Social Theory and Social Structure*. New York: Free Press.
Pascal, B. (1981) *Pensées* (trans. A.J. Krailsheimer). Harmondsworth: Penguin.
de Tocqueville, A. (1951) *Democracy in America* (trans. Henry Reeve), 2 Vols. New York: Alfred A. Knopf.

Sudipta Kaviraj was educated at Calcutta and New Delhi. He taught at the University of Burdwan and at Jawaharlal Nehru University, New Delhi, before being appointed Agatha Harrison Fellow at St Antony's College, Oxford (1980–82). He is now at the Department of Political Studies, SOAS, Thornaugh Street, Russell Square, London WC1H 0XG, where his main fields of interest include political theory and the Indian state.

Marxism and the Problem of Violence

Bhikhu Parekh

Marxism represents the greatest emancipatory project in the history of Western and even non-Western thought. No other body of ideas has so closely identified itself with the poor and the oppressed, so passionately championed their cause, devoted so much attention to a systematic study of the causes of their predicament, and dared to construct a vision of the world free from most man-made suffering. The integrity and future of Marxism are therefore a matter of deep philosophical and political concern to all interested in human well-being and progress. Many of the communist societies that he inspired have spectacularly collapsed within a short span of three years. Communism in Eastern Europe was externally imposed, and its collapse may therefore not be so important. But the Russian Revolution of 1917 was quite different. It was indigenous, led by men many of whom were scholars of Marx, and it lasted for over seven decades. Its collapse therefore cannot be easily explained away and raises deeply disturbing questions about the validity of Marx's central insights.

The question as to how the collapse of Soviet communism bears on Marxist thought has received two opposite answers. Some writers, mainly conservative and liberal, have argued that since the Russian Revolution of 1917 was Marxist, its collapse discredits Marxism and reveals it to be a deeply flawed, morally irresponsible and inhuman doctrine. Others, mostly Marxists, contend that since the revolution did not occur in an advanced capitalist society or satisfy any of the basic preconditions laid down by Marx, it was not Marxist in character and that its collapse has no implications for the validity of Marxism. In their view, Russian communism was always a source of ideological and political embarrassment for the Marxists. Now that it has disintegrated and Marxism has been liberated from the clutches of a wholly mistaken interpretation, Marxists can

Development and Change (SAGE, London, Newbury Park and New Delhi), Vol. 23 (1992) No. 3, 103–120.

set about reviving and propagating true or real Marxism.

Neither answer is satisfactory. The first is open to two serious objections. First, as the Marxists have rightly pointed out, albeit with some exaggeration, the Russian Revolution did not fully conform to the Marxist model of a genuinely communist revolution. Its limitations cannot therefore be automatically attributed to Marxism. Secondly, the relation between theory and practice is far more complex than is assumed by the advocates of this view. Marxism is a body of thought, whereas Soviet communism was a set of institutions and practices existing in the real world. The world of practice has its own distinct logic and is subject to its characteristic constraints, pressures and compromises. No body of thought can enter the world of practice without undergoing inevitable changes and distortions. Its fortunes in the practical world cannot therefore be used to discredit its theoretical validity. Even as Christianity was invoked in defence of all manner of practices including colonialism, capitalism and slavery and cannot be said to have been refuted by them, Marxism cannot be discredited simply because it was used to legitimize ugly and ultimately self-defeating practices and policies.

The second answer, which completely uncouples Marxism and Russian communism, is unsatisfactory for opposite reasons. First, while the advocates of the first view identify theory and practice, those of the second disjoin them and fail to perceive their complex relationship. A theory represents a specific way of conceptualizing and understanding the relevant area of experience. It orders, arranges and maps out the area, explains its inner structure and dynamics, and indicates the range of possible responses to it. Marxism performed this role for the Russian communists. It orientated their thoughts and feelings in a certain manner, fostered certain sensibilities and attitudes, framed their expectations, and in general gave them an intellectual and moral compass. It cannot therefore disclaim all responsibility for their actions.

Secondly, although the Russian Revolution did not conform to the Marxist paradigm of a communist revolution, neither did it fall completely outside it. In his agonized responses to the questions raised by Vera Zasulich and other Russian leaders, Marx observed that he was not laying down a 'rigid' and 'unalterable' pattern of historical development valid for all times and places, and that it was possible to proceed from pre- or quasi-capitalism straight to communism without passing through the capitalist stage. The Russian leaders were therefore not wrong to invoke Marx's authority in their support, and the Marxists cannot completely disown them. Even the contemporary Marxists, who considered the Russian Revolution premature and would have liked its leaders to fight for democracy rather than communism, conceded that it had some support in Marx's writings and that it was possible to combine the struggles for democracy and communism.

Thirdly, leaders of the Russian Revolution drew their inspiration from Marx, legitimized their actions and policies on the basis of his writings, and by and large many saw themselves as sincere Marxists. They recognized that from time to time they had to deviate from his ideas in response to unexpected problems and crises, but believed, rightly or wrongly, that they were functioning within the framework of the central principles of his thought. After all Marx himself had repeatedly revised his ideas and urged others to do the same in the light of new situations. The Russian leaders claimed that they were doing just that. There is no 'real' or 'pure' Marxism luminously self-evident and unsullied by interpretations. The Russian leaders read the master in a particular manner. And as long as their reading was plausible and supported by the texts, they were entitled to call themselves Marxists just as much as their critics. If their reading led to morally outrageous deeds, Marx cannot be wholly exonerated. His admirers and followers owe it to him, and to the mankind they claim to serve, to read him afresh and criticize and revise his thought accordingly. To uncouple Marx's thought from the communist praxis is to dehistoricize him, to render him irrelevant to the constantly changing world, and to arrest the growth of a rich tradition. Like the world of practice, a body of thought remains alive and effective only when constantly criticized, revised and rejuvenated in the light of its gaps, silences, ambiguities and potentialities for evil as revealed by the actions of those claiming to act in its name.

The collapse of communism in the erstwhile Soviet Union then neither discredits Marxism nor leaves it untouched, and it raises important questions about its central doctrines. It is in this spirit that I propose to explore one important aspect of his thought, namely his discussion of violence. From its very beginning until its collapse, the Soviet Union practised egregious state violence, direct and indirect, episodic and structural, and evident in all areas of social life including the economic. The violence killed millions, paralysed the society, created a pervasive spirit of numbness, and in one form or another contributed greatly to the discrediting and the eventual disintegration of the Soviet state. Although we do not yet know the exact casualties, we know that they were between 3 and 10 million. Stalin's purges, mass executions, terror and labour camps are too notorious to need reiteration. But Lenin's seven years in power were not blameless either. Although part of his violence was necessitated by the capitalist encirclement and the internal sabotage by the discontented groups, the rest of it was not. He followed policies which he knew would provoke great resistance and lead in turn to state violence, but he did not think it necessary to go slowly or to choose second-best options. This was particularly true of his policies in relation to the peasantry, from which the New Economic Policy represented a belated and 'tactical' retreat. Dzherinsky, his protégé and head of Cheka, used the 'sword and scalpel' of the revolution, with Lenin's approval, to unleash massive violence. It was during Lenin's time that the first batch of inmates were sent to labour camps. He declared a war on such large groups as the landlords, church leaders, the Whites, the Mensheviks, the Socialist Revolutionaries and the bourgeoisie, and saw little wrong in 'liquidating' them. Stalin's successors were not shy of violence either. Khruschev was more concerned about the fact that Stalin had killed his friends and colleagues than about his elimination of millions. Even during the Gorbachev era, the old attitude kept reappearing, and violence was often the first weapon used to put down discontent. Although many a Marxist abroad criticized much of this violence, especially during Stalin's period, the sense of outrage and anger was muted, and there was no real pressure on the Soviet Union to abandon terrorist violence or risk losing external support.

In this article I intend to explore how the Russian leaders were able to justify their massive violence in Marx's name and whether the roots of it lay in his thought. I shall argue that the discussion of violence in the Marxist tradition leaves much to be desired and that part of the responsibility lies at the door of its founder.

Although a peaceful or non-violent revolution is not inherently impossible, as a matter of historical fact every revolution has involved varying degrees of violence. Dominant groups rarely abdicate voluntarily, and violence is needed to overthrow them. Since dominant groups never entirely disappear during the revolutionary struggle and continue to resist the new government, further violence is needed to counter them after the revolution. Even the groups otherwise indifferent or sympathetic to the revolution may turn hostile once the new government's policies begin to affect their interests and that too calls for a limited measure of violence.

If no revolution can dispense with violence altogether, neither can it rely on violence alone either during or, especially, after its successful completion. In most cases the means of violence available to revolutionary groups are insignificant compared to those at the disposal of the established social order, and can rarely succeed in isolation from other methods of struggle with which it must therefore be integrated. When a revolutionary government comes to power, the role of violence in creating a new social order is also necessarily limited. The government needs to mobilize the energies of its citizens in the massive task of social reconstruction. Violence can at best terrorize them into submission, but it can never energize them or evoke their support. The revolution derives its legitimacy from its promise of a more humane social order, and risks forfeiting it if it relies on violence alone.

A revolution requires violence: at the same time it is constantly tempted to misuse it, and runs the risk of losing its legitimacy and sense of direction. Every theory of revolution therefore needs a well-considered theory of violence. This must show why and when violence is justified during the course of the revolutionary struggle and afterwards. While justifying violence, the theory must ensure that its justification is not so vague, permissive and open ended as to condone its indiscriminate use. Since the temptation to use violence both during and after the revolution is great, the theory must insist that although necessary, violence is always regrettable and to be avoided as far as possible. It must show too that violence has its limits, that it can remove obstacles but not transform men, and that it must be subordinated to the central values in whose name the revolution is launched. In the interest of the survival of the revolution itself, not to mention the basic respect for human beings, a revolutionary theory of violence must have built-in theoretical, moral and institutional safeguards against the misuse of violence. No doubt, every theory can be misused, but it can at least minimize and provide criteria for identifying and attacking the misuse. A theory of revolution without a carefully worked out theory of violence is dangerously incoherent. It gives no guidance to its adherents and leaves them free to fill its large gaps as they please.

Surprising as it may seem, Marx, the greatest theorist of revolution in the modern age, has no theory of violence. Nowhere does he systematically discuss the subject and he makes only passing references to it in his discussions of specific historical situations. He did not write much about the French Revolution, on which his own theory of revolution was largely based, and he offered no systematic analysis of the reign of terror in its aftermath – its nature, origins and the way it might have been avoided or minimized. This is particularly surprising since Hegel, whose theory of history greatly influenced Marx, had given the subject considerable attention and a distinctly idealistic interpretation.

There are at least three reasons why Marx failed to provide a well-considered theory of violence. First, a theory of violence is concerned with such questions as whether or why human life is 'sacred' or deserves respect, why and when it may be taken, why a qualitative comparison of lives taken and saved is deeply problematical and how the use of violence is to be balanced against the realization of other goals. Marx dismissed these and such other questions as ideological. Moral questions become important and are even regarded as a distinct class of questions when morality is believed to be autonomous and capable of shaping human conduct. For Marx morality was neither autonomous, being largely an idealization of class interests, nor capable of motivating people. People acted on the basis of their perceptions of their interests and morality neither entered into their definitions of these interests nor acted as an independent factor.[1] To think otherwise was to abstract consciousness from the material relations in which men and women were involved, and to be guilty of 'idealism'. For Marx the bourgeoisie was bound to use all its power to protect its interests, and no amount of argument or moral persuasion made any difference. It might work on isolated individuals, but they were prisoners of and unable to withstand the imperative demands of their class interests. Like the bourgeoisie, the proletariat too fought, and was bound to fight, for its interests, and moral appeal had no meaning. Morality was essentially ideological and epiphenomenal, and the questions it posed were inconsequential. Given these views, Marx's thought had no room for a moral theory, although as we shall see, he could and did develop a normative theory of history. In the absence of a moral theory, there could be no theory of violence either.

Even if Marx had admitted the importance of moral questions, he would not have considered violence as one of them. For him in the capitalist society, as indeed in all class-divided societies, violence was built into its very structure. Human life was held in low regard and society was based on the principle of mutual exploitation rather than mutual completion. Human beings were treated as commodities and bought and sold under the system of what Marx suggestively called wage slavery. In civil society workers appeared as nothing more than their labour power, whose price was determined by the forces of the market. They were made to work under inhuman conditions and died painful and premature deaths. When they protested the state used violence to beat them into submission. In such a society, which was suffused with the spirit of violence and in which human life had no value, the talk of sacredness of life was a cruel joke. Worse, it was a cynical ploy to deny the oppressed the only effective weapon of struggle available to them. The bourgeoisie had a vital interest in turning violence into a moral issue. The bourgeois morality and law defined violence as deliberate killing of human beings. Since bourgeois violence was structural and embedded in practices in which workers 'voluntarily' participated, the bourgeoisie were by definition never guilty of it. By contrast the workers, who could not overthrow capitalism without using violence as defined by the bourgeoisie, were never innocent of it. The bourgeois discourse on violence was thus ideologically biased and had to be avoided. The workers had to fight the bourgeois violence as best they could, and they had to decide for themselves when and how much defensive violence to use. To debate the morality of violence was to remain trapped within the bourgeois discourse and to legitimize and participate in its exploitative practices.

The third reason why Marx did not take the question of violence seriously had to do with his theory of revolution, which implied that the amount of violence involved both in overthrowing capitalism and consolidating the revolution would be extremely small. For him no mode of production disappeared so long as it had room in it for the development of the productive forces, that is, so long as the relations of production were in harmony with the productive forces. A revolution occurred when the dominant class obstructed the development of the productive forces and only the dominated class was able to carry them forward. For Marx communism was 'not a state of affairs which is to be established, an ideal to which reality [will] have to adjust itself', but a 'real movement' developing and gathering momentum within the capitalist society itself (Marx, 1965: 48). Quietly but unmistakably, capitalism created the conditions of its eventual suppression, and both undermined itself and generated the class capable of creating a new society on its ruins. The working classes 'have no ideals to realise but to set free the elements of the new society with which the old collapsing bourgeois society itself is pregnant'. For Marx the communist revolution occurred when capitalism was in a crisis, had lost its legitimacy in the eyes of 'its slaves whom it was no longer to feed', and when the organized and ideologically self-conscious proletariat constituting the majority of the population was ready to give it the final push. In such a situation the proletariat needed to use no more force than was needed by the midwife to deliver the child. As for the new society, pockets of capitalist resistance were bound to be few and weak and could be easily put down. The proletariat would represent the common interests of all classes including the peasantry, and there was no major source of conflict between the two. The culturally developed proletariat, already disciplined into the habits of hard work and co-operation by the 'dull compulsions' of capitalism, did not need to be coerced either. And thanks to its desire for self-expression and trade union experiences, it was bound to demand and evolve new forms of participatory democracy.

For Marx then violence was a fact of life. The dominant classes used it to perpetuate their rule, and the dominated classes responded with counterviolence. So far as the latter were concerned, and Marx was primarily interested in them, they needed to realize that violence was neither a mode of self-expression nor endowed with mysterious regenerative powers as Bakunin and others had argued, but merely a means to be judged in solely instrumental terms. Furthermore, by itself it achieved little, and had to be integrated with other methods of struggle. For Marx a sustained and organized struggle had a great political and educational value. It organized the proletariat, fostered its sense of class solidarity, and trained it for collective action. It also produced revolutionary consciousness 'on a mass scale', rid the proletariat of 'all the muck of the ages', gave it a coherent consciousness of its historic mission and 'fitted [it] to found society anew'. Marx ascribed these qualities not to violence *per se* but to the revolutionary struggle of which it was a part, and he judged acts of violence in terms of whether or not they served the cause of revolutionary struggle and prepared the proletariat for its 'self-emancipation'. While such episodic violence was inevitable and often justified, the premature overthrow of capitalism was to be avoided. Unless the proletariat was politically, ideologically and culturally ready, it risked being defeated; and if it won, it was bound to end up being ideologically dominated by and doing the dirty work of another more self-conscious class. Marx was particularly worried about the influence of the petty bourgeoisie, and thought that the Communist

Party had a vital role to play in refining, sharpening and articulating the true proletarian consciousness.

For Marx each class used violence for its own distinct purposes, and both types of violence were necessary and justified from their specific points of view. Marx did not and could not leave the matter at that, and argued that the violence of the negative class was better or 'progressive' from the 'higher' human point of view, viewing societies and historical epochs from the standpoint of the human species.[2] Man was the highest being for man, and the species point of view was the only valid Archimedean standpoint for assessing societies and historical epochs. The species point of view was purely formal, and Marx needed to specify what human interests or their fullest development consisted of. He thought that the interests could not be defined abstractly in the manner of utopian writers, but only in the light of the possibilities opened up by history as judged by critical reflections on human nature. By various steps, some ingenious and others dubious, Marx concluded that the fullest human development consisted in the conquest of nature, an unmediated unity of the species, the development of intellectual, social, emotional, artistic and other human capacities, and minimum legal, moral and social coercion.

This vision of the fullest development of man formed the basis of Marx's theory of historical judgement. He used it to evaluate different epochs, societies and historical movements. He considered the capitalist mode of production higher than its predecessors because, although it was in some respects more alienated and inhuman, it brought mankind closer to its ultimate goal and was therefore on balance most progressive. Acknowledging that the capitalist society had undermined parental authority and corrupted the relations between the sexes, Marx observed:

> However terrible and disgusting the dissolution, under the capitalist system, of the old family ties may appear, nevertheless, modern industry, by assigning as it does an important part in the process of production, outside the domestic sphere, to women, to young persons, and to children of both sexes, creates a new economic foundation for a higher form of the family and of the relations between the sexes. It is, of course just as absurd to hold the Teutonic christian form of the family to be absolute and final as it would be to apply that character to the ancient Roman, the ancient Greek, or the Eastern forms, which, moreover, taken together form a series in historical development . . . the fact of the collective working group being composed of individuals of both sexes and all ages, must necessarily, under suitable conditions, become a source of humane development; although in its spontaneously developed, brutal, capitalistic form, where the

labourer exists for the process of production, and not the process of production for the labourer, the fact is a pestiferous source of corruption and slavery. (Marx, 1967: Vol. 1, 489–90)

Marx admitted that historical progress had often been achieved at the cost of considerable human suffering, but insisted that the price was necessary and worth paying. To show undue solicitude for the individual:

> . . . is to assert that the development of the species must be arrested in order to safeguard the welfare of the individual, so that, for instance, no war may be waged in which at all events some individuals perish . . . . Apart from the barrenness of such edifying reflections, they reveal a failure to understand the fact that, although at first the development of the capacities of the human species takes place at the cost of the majority of human individuals, and even classes, in the end it breaks through this contradiction and coincides with the development of the individual; the higher development of individuality is thus only achieved by a historical process during which individuals are sacrificed for the interests of the species. (Marx, 1969: Vol. 2, 303–4)

This is also how Marx justified British colonialism in India:

> Now, sickening as it must be to human feeling to witness those myriads of industrious patriarchal and inoffensive social organizations disorganized and dissolved into their units . . . we must not forget that the idyllic village communities, inoffensive though they may appear, had always been the solid foundation of Oriental despotism, that they restrained the human mind within the smallest possible compass, making it the unresisting tool of superstition, enslaving it beneath traditional rules, depriving it of all grandeur and historical energies . . . . We must not forget that the little communities were contaminated by distinctions of caste and by slavery, that they subjugated man to external circumstances instead of elevating man, the sovereign of circumstances, that they transformed a self-developing social state into never changing natural destiny, and thus brought about a brutalizing worship of nature, exhibiting its degradation in the fact that man, the sovereign of nature, fell down on his knees in adoration of Kanuman, the monkey, and Sabbala, the cow.
>
> England, it is true, in causing a social revolution in Hindustan, was actuated only by the vilest interests, and was stupid in her manner of enforcing them. But that is not the question. The question is, can mankind fulfil its destiny without a fundamental revolution in the social state of Asia? If not, whatever may have been the crimes of England she was the unconscious tool of history in bringing about that revolution. (Marx and Engels, 1979b: 132)

It is also the justification Engels used for slavery:

> It is very easy to inveigh against slavery and similar things in antiquity, and to give vent to high moral indignation at such infamies, namely that these institutions

> of antiquity are no longer in accord with our present day conditions and our sentiments, which these conditions determine . . . we are compelled to say – however contradictory and heretical it may sound – that the introduction of slavery at that time was a great step forward. (Engels, 1939: 200)

In all these passages there is a remarkable consistency. The events in question, be they capitalism or colonialism, cause enormous havoc, are terrible and disgusting, are 'sickening . . . to human feeling', and leave us with a sense of 'sadness'. The agents involved behave badly, are 'stupid' and even 'evil', and are driven by 'greed' and the 'crudest forms' of self-interest. Yet the net outcome of these events is 'progressive' and to the long-term advantage of their victims. Hence they are to be welcomed, and such price as has to be paid is worth paying. It would have been nice if the human cost had not been so high, but that is not how history functions in a class-divided society in which men are not in conscious control of their collective actions. As long as the classes lasted, human progress would continue 'to resemble that hideous, pagan idol who would not drink the nectar but from the skulls of the slain'. If we want the nectar, we must accept the violence and the suffering involved.

Marx, then, judges violence from two different points of view. He judges it from the moral or conventional point of view, and regrets it. He also judges it from the historical or species point of view, and fully approves of it. Of the two he considers the latter 'higher' and indeed the only true way of judging political and historical events. Nowhere does he state how his moral judgements are grounded. He clearly disapproves of such things as loss of life, cruelty, destruction of established communities, human suffering, loss of parental authority and disintegration of the family, but he does not explain why. He neither teases out and defends the underlying moral principles, nor relates them to those informing his theory of historical judgement. As a result his disapproval of cruelty, human suffering, and so forth remain little more than expressions of his personal feelings and play no objective role in his thought. Furthermore, although Marx regrets them, he gives them little if any weight. He does not say, for example, that capitalist development or colonialism should take *some* account of the suffering they cause and slow down or, whenever possible, choose less disagreeable options. In other words Marx assigns the underlying moral principles no regulative or moderating role. He is primarily concerned that mankind should reach its ultimate goal as speedily as possible and is in essence an uncompromising historical consequentialist. For him a historical epoch or society is superior if it takes mankind closer to the ultimate goal. And within each epoch or society, that action is better which promotes the development of the productive forces and, at an appropriate stage, furthers the revolutionary struggle.

Since Marx seethed with anger and outrage at the evils of capitalism, he failed to see the human beings behind the capitalist class. He greatly admired the technological achievements of the bourgeoisie, but neither had much praise for their moral, cultural, political and other achievements nor showed much sympathy for them as individuals. Once they had served their historical role, they were to be removed. And if they resisted, they had to be put down. Marx tended to place them outside the pale of moral intercourse, and his humanism lacked universality and depth. Since he saw the bourgeoisie in the context of structures of social relations, he did not hold them personally responsible for the proletarian suffering or share the anarchist's intense hatred of them. But this way of seeing them also meant that they never emerged as individuals entitled to basic humanity and respect. Although Marx personally disapproved of such a conclusion, his thought encouraged the belief that by virtue of their class, the bourgeoisie's humanity need not be taken seriously. His system of thought made it difficult to draw a clear and vitally necessary distinction between 'liquidating' them as a class and 'liquidating' them as individuals.

Marx's discussion of violence left many gaps and ambiguities at crucial places. He made contradictory assumptions about the cultural level of the proletariat on the eve of revolution. He assumed that it would be a genuinely universal class aware of its historic mission, 'noble', technically versatile, looking on labour as a mode of self-expression, truly social and suffused with the spirit of 'the brotherhood of man'. But he also said that it was brutalized, 'mentally and physically dehumanized', 'deformed', 'barbarized' and 'confused', full of 'crude and abstract' needs, and with no family life worth speaking about. The two assumptions have different implications for the post-revolutionary society. In the first case, there is very little role for the Communist Party, very little need to 'educate' the proletariat, and a considerable scope for participatory democracy. In the second case, the Communist Party would have to play a hegemonic role and use the state to enforce a massive programme of educating the proletariat with all the coercion that it involves.

Marx's analysis of the experiences of the Paris Commune led him to conclude that part of its weakness lay in its vacillations and self-restraint. The Commune had been too scrupulous and too afraid to use force lest it should alienate world opinion. It did, of course, use some violence, which Marx considered fully justified. The violence was 'unavoidable and comparatively trifling concomitant to the titanic struggle between a new society arising and an old one breaking down', and was perfectly legitimate 'in the war of the enslaved against their enslavers, the only justifiable war in history' (Marx and Engels, 1980, 303–4). However even this violence was not enough to protect the Commune. Marx concluded that the communist society should not repeat the Commune's mistake. It should 'intimidate' and 'hold down' its opponents, be 'energetic in its use of force', and take 'all necessary' steps to subdue them and consolidate the revolution.[3] This would seem to involve a considerable use of force and could corrupt the revolution. Marx did not think so because his Hegelian theory of revolution led him to assume that in the communist society the proletariat would not encounter serious resistance. He assumed a harmony of interests between the proletariat and the peasantry, and did not appreciate the resistance likely to be put up by the latter. He did not anticipate the difficulties likely to be created by the bureaucracy, the army and the other institutions of the state, which have a vested interest in preserving the autonomy of the state and were bound to resist the attempts to smash it. Marx showed little sensitivity to the fears and interests of minorities and nationalities and assumed that they would neatly divide along class lines. In short, he took a grossly optimistic, almost naïve view of the kinds of problems likely to face the communist state. His followers were not alerted to the enormity of their task or prepared for its challenges, fondly imagining that consolidating revolution involved no more than putting down isolated pockets of demoralized resistance. When reality turned out to be quite different, they were completely at sea.

Marx's view of violence has its obvious strengths and limitations. He rightly stressed that violence must be seen as an integral part of a wider political struggle, and that it was no more than a necessary means to be judged by its results rather than a mystical power endowed with the kinds of ontological, epistemological and moral properties attributed to it by the anarchists and others. He was also right to stress that violence was only effective when used not by isolated individuals but by organized and disciplined groups following a coherent strategy of social transformation. While Marx's understanding of the nature and role of violence was broadly correct, his positivist and consequentialist manner of justifying it was not.

Although morality has its limits, he was wrong to insist that it did not shape or at least influence human behaviour and enter into men's self-definitions and determination of their interests. While he was right to stress the importance of consequences in any evaluation of violence, his consequentialism was too narrow and abstract to be valuable. The fullest human development as he defined it was too general to help us decide when a society or an epoch can be said to be moving closer to it. Since we can never clearly identify the very long-term consequences of human actions and practices, his kind of consequentialism can also be twisted in any direction one chooses. Furthermore Marx's consequentialism admits of no moral checks and permits no trade-offs, and would seem to justify large amounts of human suffering as his discussion of capitalism and British colonialism in India shows. Indeed there is a deep and unresolved tension between his positivism and consequentialism. The oppressed, he says, are *bound* to protest against and try to end their oppression. But his consequentialism implies that they *should* not do so as long as their oppression is historically 'progressive'. The conflict between what people would do anyway and what he thinks they should do is not even appreciated by Marx, let alone resolved. Even worse conclusions follow. As long as a system of oppression, such as capitalism or imperialism, is historically progressive, the inevitable violence of the oppressed is reactionary or regressive, and the oppressors have an historical right and are therefore fully justified in trying to suppress it!

Marx's view of violence formed the basis and determined the conceptual parameters of the subsequent Marxist discourse on violence.[4] Such early Marxists as Kautsky, Lenin, Trotsky, Stalin, Bukharin and Lukács as well as such later and chastened Marxists as Sartre, Marcuse, Althusser and Barrington Moore all continued to share Marx's analysis of the nature and mode of justification of violence. None of them glorified violence, lost sight of its political context, approved of its premature and indiscriminate use, sanctioned its use by isolated individuals acting independently of the revolutionary struggle by organized classes, or tolerated terrorist deeds. All of them, further, evaluated it in positivist and consequentialist terms.

For almost all of them the bourgeois state is nothing but a 'pure power structure', an instrument of 'concentrated legal violence', and the fetishism of legality is to be avoided. The capitalists are bound to use violence to protect their interests, and the proletariat is equally bound to match it. Whether and when it should use violence is a 'mere question of tactics' to be decided 'solely on the basis of utility' as Lukács (1971: 256) put it. Unlike bourgeois violence, proletarian violence leads to a higher stage of human development and is therefore progressive and fully justified. Almost all the Marxists, both classical and contemporary, invoke what Marcuse called a 'calculus of progress', involving a comparative assessment of the number of people likely to be killed during and after the revolution and if the existing order were to be allowed to continue. Barrington Moore's use of such a comparative assessment to compare China favourably with India and Ted Honderich's democratic violence are more recent examples of such a consequentialist calculation. As the Marxist Helmut Fleischer puts it, 'To Marxists the question [is] . . . whether the sacrifices of the revolutionary struggle and subsequent reconstruction are not less than those involved in the continuation of the status quo' (Fleischer, 1973: 105).

The horrors of the Russian Revolution caused the Marxists considerable unease, and some such as Rosa Luxemburg and Karl Kautsky sought to introduce moral checks on the use of violence. They, especially Kautsky, thought that the Marxists must respect and protect human life and other basic rights, and that a theoretical space could be found or created for this in Marxist thought. But they had difficulty doing so within the Marxist framework, and ended up introducing large chunks of ill-digested liberalism. Even this limited attempt was unacceptable to Lenin, Trotsky and others. In his vicious attack on Kautsky, which only differed in tone from Lenin's and later Lukács's criticism of Rosa Luxemburg, Trotsky rejected the 'Kantian-priestly and vegetarian-quaker prattle about the "sacredness of human life" ' (Trotsky, 1961: 63).[5] Such a principle was too abstract and unhistorical; it was 'hypocritical and stupid' in a society in which the worker was daily mutilated; and it was 'a shameful lie uttered with the objective of keeping the oppressed slaves in their chains'. Although Trotsky took an extreme view, his last two arguments echoed some of Marx's. No Marxist so far has been able to ground general principles of the kind Kautsky had in mind within the Marxist framework and to use them to check its historical consequentialist thrust.

In the light of the silences, ambiguities and limitations of Marx's discussion of violence, it is easy to appreciate the dilemmas and modes of thought of the Russian revolutionary leaders. Although their revolution could claim Marxist legitimacy, Marx's entire theory of revolution was predicated on wholly different assumptions and offered them limited guidance. Nor had it theoretically prepared them for the horrendous problems they faced. Not surprisingly they improvized as they went along. Thanks to the basic features of Marx's theory of violence mentioned earlier, they found some support in it for some of their most inhuman deeds. Marx's historical consequentialism meant that the Russian leaders could do 'all that was necessary' to take their society to the next higher stage, and that such violence as they had to use was justified and subject to no moral checks. Thanks to Marx's positivist approach to violence, they insisted that it was pointless to argue with, persuade, accommodate, appeal to the good sense of, and in general seek to win over at least some of the discontented groups. They appealed to Marx's humanism to *deny* the basic humanity of the erstwhile dominant groups, and blurred the vital distinction between the elimination of classes and the murder of their members. Marx had alerted them to the dangers of the Paris Commune's self-restraint, and they knew they had to act 'energetically'. Since the proletariat had a historical mission to fulfil and represented the 'healthy interests of society', it was entitled to beat down the peasantry. And since the proletariat was culturally backward and ideologically muddled, the point repeatedly made by Lenin and Trotsky and later by Stalin, the Communist Party had to exercise hegemony over it.

Karl Marx would most certainly have been horrified by the scale and depth of Soviet violence. He saw the need for revolutionary violence, but not of this magnitude. He allowed for the Communist Party's hegemonic role, but not its contempt for and inhuman treatment of the proletariat. He recognized that history moved in a zigzag manner, but did not think that it could so completely lose its sense of direction. I have argued in this article that although Marx's humanism and commitment to the free, full and non-coercive development of all human beings are genuine, his thought has several features that give some theoretical support to state terrorism. If Marxism is to remain a theory of emancipation, it must undertake a radical self-critique and reformulate some of its central principles in the light of the use which the Soviet leaders made of it. Even after making full allowance for the tortuous logic of the world of practice and the misjudgments, malevolence and sheer vindictiveness of some Soviet leaders, Marxism cannot escape some responsibility for the millions sacrificed in its name.

NOTES

I am most grateful to Jan Nederveen Pieterse and Terry McNeill for discussing with me many of the ideas in this paper.

1. This view is not confined to *The German Ideology* as is generally thought, and is to be found in many of Marx's later writings, including *Capital*.
2. For a detailed discussion of this, see Parekh (1982: Ch. 7).
3. 'We have no compassion and we ask no compassion from you. When our turn comes, we shall make no excuses for the terror' (Marx and Engels, 1979a: 453).
4. There is so far no systematic discussion of the Marxist discourse on violence. For a useful short essay, see Harding (1975).
5. Also see Marx and Engels (1976: 56): 'in a party one must support everything which helps towards progress and have no truck with any tedious moral scruples (*langweiligen moralischen skrupel*)'.

REFERENCES

Engels, F. (1939) *Anti-Duhring*. New York: International Publishers.
Fleischer, H. (1973) *Marxism and History* (trans. Eric Masbacher). London: Allen Lane.
Harding, N. (1975) 'Socialism and Violence', in Bhikhu Parekh (ed.) *The Concept of Socialism*, pp. 192–220. London: Croom Helm.
Lukács, G. (1971) *History and Class Consciousness* (trans. Rodney Livingstone). London: Merlin Press.
Marx, K. (1965) *The German Ideology*. Moscow: Progress Publishers.
Marx, K. (1967) *Capital*. New York: International Publishers.
Marx, K. (1969) *Theories of Surplus Value*. Moscow: Progress Publishers.
Marx, K. and Engels, F. (1976) *Marx–Engels Collected Works*, Volume 6. London: Lawrence and Wishart.
Marx, K. and Engels, F. (1979a) *Marx–Engels Collected Works*, Volume 9. London: Lawrence and Wishart.
Marx, K. and Engels, F. (1979b) *Marx–Engels Collected Works*, Volume 12. London: Lawrence and Wishart.
Marx, K. and Engels, F. (1980) *Marx–Engels Selected Works in One Volume*. London: Lawrence and Wishart.
Parekh, B. (1982) *Marx's Theory of Ideology*. Baltimore, MD: Johns Hopkins University Press.
Trotsky, L. (1961) *Terrorism and Communism*. Ann Arbor, MI: University of Michigan Press.

Bhikhu Parekh is Professor of political theory at the University of Hull, Hull HU6 7RX. He was Deputy Chairman of the Commission for Racial Equality, UK, between 1985 and 1990. His major publications include *Marx's Theory of Ideology* (Johns Hopkins University Press, 1982), *Contemporary Political Thinkers* (Johns Hopkins University Press, 1982), *Gandhi's Political Philosophy* (Macmillan, 1989) and *Colonialism, Tradition and Reform* (Sage, 1989).

Beyond Emancipation

Ernesto Laclau

I see 'emancipation' — a notion which has been part of our political imagery for centuries and whose disintegration we are witnessing today — as being organized around six distinctive dimensions. The first is what we could call the *dichotomic dimension*: between the emancipatory moment and the social order which has preceded it there is an absolute chasm, a radical discontinuity. The second can be considered a *holistic dimension*: emancipation affects all areas of social life and there is a relation of essential imbrication between its various contents in these different areas. The third dimension can be referred to as the *transparency dimension*: if alienation in its various aspects — religious, political, economic, etc. has been radically eradicated, there is only the absolute coincidence of human essence with itself and there is no room for any relation of either power or representation. Emancipation presupposes the elimination of power, the abolition of the subject/object distinction, and the management — without any opaqueness or mediation — of communitarian affairs by social agents identified with the viewpoint of social totality. It is in this sense that in Marxism, for instance, communism and the withering away of the state logically entail each other. A fourth dimension is the *pre-existence* of what has to be emancipated *vis-à-vis* the act of emancipation. There is no emancipation without oppression, and there is no oppression without the presence of something which is impeded in its free development by the oppressive forces. Emancipation is not, in this sense, an act of *creation* but instead of liberation of something which precedes the liberating act. In the fifth place we can speak of a *dimension of ground* which is inherent in the project of any radical emancipation. If the act of emancipation is truly radical, if it is really going to leave behind everything preceding it, it has to take place at the level of the 'ground' of the social. If there was no ground, if the revolutionary

Development and Change (SAGE, London, Newbury Park and New Delhi), Vol. 23 (1992) No. 3, 121–137.

act left a residue which is beyond the transforming abilities of the emancipatory praxis, the very idea of a *radical* emancipation would become contradictory. Finally we can speak of a *rationalistic dimension*. This is the point where the emancipatory discourses of secularized eschatologies part company with the religious ones. For religious eschatologies the absorption of the real within a total system of representation does not require the rationality of the latter: it is enough that the inscrutable designs of God are transmitted to us through revelation. But in a secular eschatology this is not possible. As the idea of an absolute representability of the real cannot appeal to anything external to the real itself, it can only coincide with the principle of an absolute rationality. Thus, full emancipation is simply the moment in which the real ceases to be an opaque positivity confronting us, and in which the latter's distance from the rational is finally cancelled.

To what extent do these six dimensions confirm a logically unified whole? Do they constitute a coherent theoretical structure? I shall try to show that they do not do so, and that the assertion of the classical notion of emancipation in its many variants has involved the advancement of incompatible logical claims. This should not lead us, however, to the simple abandonment of the logic of emancipation. It is, on the contrary, by playing within the system of logical incompatibilities of the latter that we can open the way to new liberating discourses which are no longer hindered by the antinomies and blind alleys to which the classical notion of emancipation has led.

Let us start with the dichotomic dimension. The dichotomy that we are facing here is of a very particular kind. It is not a simple *difference* between two elements or stages which contemporarily or successively coexist with each other and which in that way contribute to the constitution of each other's differential identity. If we are speaking about *real* emancipation, the 'other' opposing the emancipated identity cannot be a purely positive or neutral other but, instead, an 'other' which prevents the full constitution of the identity of the first element. In that sense, the dichotomy involved in the emancipatory act is in a relation of logical solidarity with our fourth dimension – the pre-existence of the identity to be emancipated *vis-à-vis* the act of emancipation. It is easy to see why: without this pre-existence there would be no identity to repress or prevent from fully developing, and the very notion of emancipation would become meaningless. Now, an unavoidable conclusion follows from this: *true* emancipation requires a *real* 'other' – that is, an 'other' who cannot be reduced to any of the figures of the 'same'. But, in that case, between the identity to be emancipated and the 'other' opposing it, there can be no positive objectivity underlying and constituting the identity of both poles of the dichotomy.

A very simple consideration can help to clarify this point. Let us suppose for a moment that there is a deeper objective process giving its meaning to both sides of the dichotomy. If so, the chasm constituting the dichotomy loses its radical character. If the dichotomy is not constitutive but it is rather the *expression* of a positive process, the 'other' cannot be a *real* other: given that the dichotomy is grounded in an objective necessity, the oppositional dimension is also necessary and, in that sense, it is part of the identity of the two forces confronting each other. The perception of the other as a radical other can only be a matter of appearance. If a stone is broken when it clashes with another stone, it would be absurd to say that the second stone negates the identity of the first – on the contrary, being broken in certain circumstances expresses the identity of the stone as much as remaining unaltered if the circumstances are different. The characteristic of an objective process is that it reduces to its own logic the totality of its constitutive moments. The 'other' can only be the result of an internal differentiation of the 'same' and, as a result, it is entirely subordinated to the latter. But this is not the otherness that the chasm of the emancipatory act requires. There would be no break, no true emancipation if the act constitutive of the latter was only the result of the internal differentiation of the oppressing system.

This can be expressed in an only slightly different way by saying that if the emancipation is a true one it will be incompatible with any kind of 'objective' explanation. I can certainly explain a set of circumstances that *made possible* the emergence of an oppressive system. I can also explain *how* forces antagonistic to that system were constituted and evolved. But the strict moment of the confrontation between both of them, *if the chasm is a radical one*, will be refractory to any kind of objective explanation. Between two incompatible discourses, each of them constituting the pole of an antagonism between them both, there is no common measure, and the strict moment of the clash between them cannot be explained in objective terms. Unless, of course, the antagonistic moment is purely a matter of appearance and the conflict between social forces is assimilated to a natural process, as in the clash between the two stones. But, as we said, this is incompatible with the otherness required by the founding act of emancipation.

Now if the dichotomic dimension requires the radical otherness of a past which has to be thrown away, in that case this dimension is incompatible with most of the others which we have presented as constitutive of the classical notion of emancipation. In the first place, dichotomic radicalism and radical ground are incompatible. As we have seen, the condition of the radical chasm that the emancipatory logic requires, is the irreducible otherness of the oppressive system which is rejected. But in that case there can be no single ground explaining *both* the order which is rejected and the order that emancipation inaugurates. The alternative is clear: *either* emancipation is radical, and in that case it has to be its own ground and to confine what it excludes to a radical otherness constituted by evil or irrationality; *or* there is a deeper ground which establishes the rational connections between the pre-emancipatory order, the new 'emancipated' one and the transition between both – in which case emancipation cannot be considered as a true *radical* foundation. The philosophers of the Enlightenment were perfectly consequent when they asserted that if a rational society was a fully fledged order resulting from a radical break with the past, any organization previous to that break could only be conceived as the product of ignorance and of the folly of men, that is as deprived of any rationality. The difficulty, however, is that if the founding act of a truly rational society is conceived as the victory over the irrational forces of the past – forces which have no common measure with the victorious new social order – the founding act itself cannot be rational but is itself utterly contingent and depends on a relation of power. In that case the emancipated social order becomes also purely contingent and cannot be considered as the liberation of any true human essence. We are in the same dilemma as before: if we want to assert the rationality and permanence of the new social order that we are establishing we have to extend that rationality to the founding act itself and, as a result, to the social order which is to be overthrown – but in that case the radicalism of the dichotomic dimension vanishes. If, on the contrary, we assert this latter radicalism, both the founding act and the social order resulting from it become entirely contingent; that is, the conditions for a permanent structural outside have been created and what now vanishes is the dimension of ground of the classical notion of emancipation.

This incompatibility within the discourse of emancipation between the dichotomic dimension and the dimension of ground creates two fundamental matrices around which all the other dimensions are organized. As we have said, the pre-existence of the oppressed *vis-à-vis* the oppressing force is a corollary of the radicalism of the chasm required by the dichotomic dimension; if the oppressed did not pre-exist to the oppressing order it would be an effect of the latter, and in that case the chasm would not be constitutive. (A different matter is whether the chasm is not represented by the oppressed through forms of identification which *presuppose* the presence of the oppressor. We shall return later to this point.) But all the other dimensions logically require the presence of a positive ground and are, consequently, incompatible with the constitutivity of the chasm required by the dichotomic dimension. Holism would be impossible unless a positive ground of the social unifies in a self-contained totality the variety of its partial processes, antagonisms and dichotomies included. But in that case the chasm has to be internal to the social order and not a dividing line separating social order from something outside it. Transparency requires full representability, and there is no possibility of achieving it if the opaqueness inherent in radical otherness is constitutive of social relations. Finally, as we have seen, in secularized eschatologies full representability is equivalent to full knowledge – understood as full reduction of the real to the rational – and this is only achievable if the other is reduced to the same.

So, we can see that the discourses of emancipation have been historically constituted through the putting together of two incompatible lines of thought: one that presupposes the objectivity and full representability of the social, the other whose whole case depends on showing that there is a chasm which makes any social objectivity ultimately impossible. Now the important point is that these two opposite lines of thought are not simple analytical mistakes so that we could choose between one or the other and formulate an emancipatory discourse which would be free of logical inconsistencies. The matter is more complicated than that, because these two lines of thought are equally necessary for the production of an emancipatory discourse. It is by asserting both of them that the notion of emancipation becomes meaningful. Emancipation means *at the same time* radical foundation and radical exclusion; that is, at the same time it postulates a ground of the social and its impossiblity. It is necessary that an emancipated society is fully transparent to itself and at the same time that this transparency is constituted through its demarcation from essential opaqueness, with the result that the demarcating line cannot be thought from the side of transparency and that transparency itself becomes opaqueness. It is necessary that a rational society is a self-enclosed totality which subordinates to itself all its partial processes; but the limits of this holistic configuration – without which there would be no holistic configuration at all – can only be established by differentiating the latter from an exterior which is irrational and formless. We have to conclude that the two lines of thought are logically incompatible and yet require each other: without them the whole notion of emancipation would crumble.

What follows, however, from this logical incompatibility? In what way does the notion of emancipation crumble as its result? It is clear that it only crumbles in a *logical* terrain, but it does not follow at all that this is enough to make it non-operative *socially* – unless, of course, we espouse the absurd hypothesis that the social terrain is structured as a logical one and that contradictory propositions cannot have social effectivity. We must carefully distinguish at this point two very different assertions. The first is that the principle of contradiction does not apply to society and that, as a result, somebody can be and not be in the same place at the same time, or that the same piece of legislation has been both promulgated and not promulgated, etc. I do not think that anybody would be bold enough to formulate this kind of proposition. But it is a completely different proposition to assert that social practices construct concepts and institutions whose inner logic is based on the operation of incompatible logics. And there is obviously here no denial of the principle of contradiction, because to say the opposite would be to assert that it is logically contradictory to formulate contradictory propositions, which certainly is not the case. Now, if the operation of contradictory logics can perfectly well be at the root of many institutions and social practices, the problem arises as to the extent to which this operation is possible. Could it be the case that incompatible logics operate within society but cannot be extended to society as a whole; that is, that formulating contradictory propositions in certain circumstances is a logical requirement for society as a whole not to be contradictory? Here we are close to Hegel's cunning of reason. But it is clear that in this case we are dealing with an *ontological* hypothesis, not with a *logical* requirement. And this ontological hypothesis is nothing other than a new formulation of the 'dimension of ground' that we have already discussed.

But what about the hypothesis itself? Is it logically impeccable and our only task is to determine if it is right or wrong? Evidently not, because everything that we have said about the logic of the ground and its concomitant dimensions – transparency, holism, etc. – fully applies here. Transparency, as we have seen, constitutes itself as a terrain through the act of excluding opaqueness. But what about the act of exclusion itself, what about the constitutive *difference* between transparency and opaqueness: is it transparent or opaque? It is clear that the alternative is undecidable, and that the two equally possible logical moves – to make the opaque transparent or to make the transparent opaque – blur the neatness of the alternative.

This whole digression on the status of logical contradictions in society is important to make us aware of two aspects which have to be taken into account in dealing with the language games that it is possible to play within the logic of emancipation. The first is that if the term 'emancipation' is to remain meaningful, it is impossible to renounce either of its two incompatible sides. We rather have to play one against the other in ways which have to be specified. The second aspect is that this double and contradictory requirement is not simply something that we have to assert *if* emancipation is to be maintained as a relevant political term. If that was the whole problem, we could avoid it just by denying that emancipation is a valid concept and by asserting the validity of either of the two logics taken separately. But this is precisely what is not possible: our analysis has led us to the conclusion that it is the contradictory sides themselves that require the presence and at the same time the exclusion of each other: each is both the condition of possibility and the condition of impossibility of the other. Thus, we are not simply dealing with a logical incompatibility but rather with a real *undecidability* between the two sides. This already indicates to us the way in which the logic of emancipation has to be approached: by looking at the effects which follow from the subversion of each of its two incompatible sides by the other. The very possibility of this analysis results from what we said earlier: that the social operation of two incompatible logics does not consist in a pure and simple annulment of their respective effects but in a specific set of mutual deformations. This is precisely what we understand by subversion. It is as if each of the two incompatible logics presupposes a full operation that the other is denying, and that this denial leads to an unorderly set of subversive effects of the internal structure of both of them. It is clear that in analysing these subversive effects we are not witnessing the rise of something totally new that leaves both logics behind, but rather an orderly drifting away from what would otherwise have been their full operation.

Before we move on to describe the general pattern of this drifting away, we have to consider, however, the way in which classical emancipatory discourses dealt with our basically incompatible dimensions, which certainly did not go entirely unnoticed. A discourse of radical emancipation emerged for the first time with Christianity, and its specific form was *salvation*. With elements partly inherited from Jewish apocalypse, Christianity was going to present the image of a future humanity – or post-humanity – from which all evil would have been eradicted. Both the dichotomic and the ground dimensions are present here: world history is a permanent struggle between the saints and the forces of evil, and there is no common ground between them; the future society will be a perfect one, without any internal splits, any opaqueness or any alienation; the various alternatives in the struggle against the forces of evil and the final triumph of God are known to us by revelation. Now, within this world-embracing picture we see the emergence of a theological difficulty which is nothing but the theological recognition of our two incompatible dimensions. God is almighty and absolute goodness, the creator *ex nihilo* of everything existing and the absolute source and ground of all created beings. In that case, how do we explain the presence of evil in the world? The alternative is clear: either God is almighty and the source of everything existing – and in that case he cannot be absolute goodness because he is responsible for the presence of evil in the world; or he is not responsible for the latter, and therefore is not almighty. We see here emerging the same problem that we posed in non-theological terms: either the dichotomy separating good and evil is a radical one, without common ground between the two poles; or there is such a ground, and in that case the radicalism of the opposition between good and evil is blurred. Christian thought, confronted with this alternative, oscillated between asserting that the designs of God are inscrutable and that the dilemma was the result of the limitation of human reason – so that the problem was set aside without solution – and looking for a solution which, if it was going to be consistent at all, could only maintain an image of God as absolute source by asserting in one way or another the necessary character of evil. Eriugena, asserting in the Carolingian renaissance that God reaches its perfection through necessary phases of transition involving finitude, contingency and evil, started a tradition which, passing through Northern mysticism, Nicholas Cusanus and Spinoza, would reach its highest point in Hegel and Marx.

The Christian vision of history was also confronted with another problem – this time without contradiction – and that is the incommensurability existing between the universality of the tasks to be performed and the limitation of the finite agents in charge of them. The category of incarnation was designed in order to mediate between these two incommensurable realities. The paradigm of all incarnation is, of course, the advent of Christ himself, but each of the universal moments in world history is marked by divine interventions through which finite bodies have to take up universal tasks which were not predetermined in the least by their concrete finitude. The dialectic of incarnation presupposes the infinite distance between the incarnating body and the incarnated task. It is only God's mediation that establishes a bridge between the two, for motives which escape human reason. Returning to our various dimensions of emancipation, we can say that in Christian discourse transparency is ensured at the level of *representation* but not at the level of *knowledge*. Revelation gives us a representation of the totality of history, but the rationality which expresses itself in that story will always escape us. That is why the rationalistic dimension had to be absent from theological accounts of salvation.

It is this chasm between representation and rationality that modern eschatologies will attempt to bridge. Since God is no longer in the foreground as guarantor of total representability, the ground has to show its all-embracing abilities without any appeal to an infinite distance from what it actually embraces. So total representation becomes possible only as total rationality. The first consequence of this modern turn is that the turn insinuated in pantheistic and semi-pantheistic versions of Christianity, is brought now to its logical conclusions. If there is a ground out of which human history shows itself as purely rational – and, as a result, fully transparent to itself – evil, opaqueness, otherness can only be the result of partial and distorted representations. The more the dimension of ground imposes itself, the more the irretrievable alterity of the chasm inherent in the dichotomic dimension has to be dismissed as false consciousness. We have mentioned before the Hegelian 'cunning of reason'. But the Marxian versions of the same principle are not far away. It is enough to remember the description of the emergence and development of antagonistic societies: primitive communism had to disintegrate in order to develop the productive forces of humanity; the latter's development required, as its historical and logical condition, the passage through the hell of the successive exploitative regimes; and it is only at the end of the process, when history reaches the peak of a new communism representing a further development of the productive forces, that the meaning and rationality of all the previous suffering is finally shown. As Hegel said, universal history is not the terrain of happiness. Seen from the vantage point of universal history, everthing – slavery, obscurantism, terrorism, exploitation, Auschwitz – reveals its rational substance. Radical rejection, antagonism, ethical incompatibilities, in sum anything linked to the dichotomic dimension, belong to the realm of the superstructures, to the way in which social actors live (distortedly) their relations to their real conditions. As it was asserted in a famous text:

> The changes in the economic foundation lead sooner or later to the transformation of the whole immense superstructure. In studying such transformations it is always necessary to distinguish between the material transformation of the economic conditions of production, which can be distinguished with the precision of natural science, and the legal, political, religious, artistic or philosophic – in short, ideological forms in which men become conscious of this conflict and fight it out. Just as one does not judge an individual by what he thinks about himself, so one cannot judge such a period of transformation by its consciousness, but, on the contrary, this consciousness must be explained from the contradictions of material life, from the conflict existing between the social forces of production and the relations of production. (Marx, 1971: 21)

So, in this reading the dichotomic dimension becomes a 'superstructure' of the dimension of ground, and emancipation becomes a mere rhetorical ornament of a substantive process which has to be understood in entirely different terms. As a result of that, the second logical requirement of this essentialist turn is that we have to do away altogether with the dialectic of incarnation. As we have seen, incarnation requires connection between two elements through the mediation of a third external to them, in such a way that, left to themselves, there is an unbridgeable distance between the first two elements: without the third element there would be no connection at all between them. So incarnation was possible as long as God was part of the *explanans*, but if he retreats to the background, the connection between incarnated universality and incarnating body becomes impossible. That is, a fully rationalistic and secular eschatology has to show the possibility of a universal actor who is beyond the contradiction between particularity and universality, or rather, one whose particularity expresses in a direct way, without any system of mediations, pure and universal human essence. This actor is for Marx the proletariat, whose particularity expresses universality in such a direct fashion, that his advent is conceived as the end of the need for any process of representation. No incarnation can take place here. But if we look at the matter closely, we shall see that this actor, who is presented as the only one who can carry out a true process of emancipation, is precisely the one for whom 'emancipation' has become a meaningless term. How do we construct the identity of this actor? As we have seen, the agent of emancipation has to be one whose identity is prevented in its constitution/development by an existing oppressive regime. But if the process of disintegration of that regime and the process of formation of the 'emancipatory' actor are the same, then we can hardly say that s/he is oppressed by the same regime that constitutes him or her. We can, of course, perfectly well argue that the proletariat is the product of capitalist development, for only the latter creates the separation between the direct producer and the ownership of the means of production, but this only explains the emergence of the proletariat as a particular subject position within capitalist society, not the emergence of the proletariat as an emancipatory subject. In order to have the latter, we need to show that the capitalist negates in the worker something which is not the mere product of capitalism. In our terminology: we need to show that there is an antagonistic dichotomy which is not reducible to a single ground. That is, that the condition of true emancipation is, as we have mentioned before, a constitutive opaqueness that no grounding can eradicate. This means that the two operations of closure which founded the political discourse of modernity have to be unmade. If, on the one hand, modernity started by strictly tying representability to knowledge, the constitutive opaqueness resulting from the dialectic of emancipation involves not only that society is no longer transparent to knowledge, but also – since God is no longer there to substitute knowledge by revelation – that all representation will be necessarily partial and will take place against the background of an essential unrepresentability. On the other hand, this constitutive opaqueness withdraws the ground which had made it possible to go beyond the dialectic of incarnation, given that there is no longer a transparent society in which the universal can show itself in a direct unmediated way. But again, as God is no longer there, ensuring through his word the knowledge of a universal destiny which escapes human reason, opaqueness cannot lead to a restoration of the dialectic of incarnation either. The death of the ground seems to lead to the death of the universal and to the dissolution of social struggles into mere particularism. This is the other dimension of the emancipatory logic that we stressed before: if the absence of a ground is the condition of radical emancipation, the radicalism of the founding emancipatory act cannot be conceived otherwise but as an act of grounding.

So it looks as if whatever direction we take, emancipation becomes impossible. However, we hesitate before extending a death certificate. For, although we have explored the logical consequences which follow from each of the two alternatives taken separately, we have still said nothing about the effects that could derive from the social interaction of these two symmetrical impossibilities. Let us consider the matter carefully. Emancipation is strictly linked to the destiny of the universal. If the dimension of ground is going to prevail, or if emancipation is going to be a true act of radical foundation, its performance cannot be the work of any particularistic social agency. We have seen that these two dimensions – ground and radical chasm – are actually incompatible, but both alternatives equally require the presence of the universal. Without the emergence of the universal within the historical terrain, emancipation becomes impossible. In theological thought, as we have seen, this presence of the universal was guaranteed by the logic of incarnation, which mediated between particularistic finitude and universal task. In secularized eschatologies the universal had to emerge without any kind of mediation: the 'universal class' in Marx can perform its emancipatory job because it has become, precisely, pure human essence which has abandoned any particularistic belonging. Now, the ultimate logical impossibility of either a chasm which is truly radical, or of the dissolution of emancipation in some version of the 'cunning of reason', seems to destroy the very possibility of any totalizing effects. With this the only terrain in which the universal could emerge – that is, social totality – has apparently disappeared. Does this mean that this death of the universal, with the impossibility of emancipation as its necessary corollary, leaves us in a purely particularistic world in which social actors pursue only limited objectives? One moment of reflection is enough to show us that this is not an adequate conclusion. 'Particularism' is an essentially relational concept: something is particular in relation to other particularities and the ensemble of them presupposes a social totality within which they are constituted. So, if it is the very notion of a social totality that is in question, the notion of 'particular' identities is equally threatened. The category of totality continues haunting us through the effects that derive from its very absence.

This last remark opens the way to a form of conceiving the relationship between universalism and particularism which differs from both an incarnation of one in the other and the cancellation of their difference and which, in fact, creates the possibility of new discourses of liberation. These go, certainly, beyond emancipation, but are constructed by movements taking place within the system of alternatives generated by the latter. Let us start our analysis with the consideration of any social antagonism – for instance, a national minority which is oppressed by an authoritarian state. There is a chasm here between the two, and we already know that there is in all chasms a basic undecidability as to which of its two sides the line separating them belongs. Let us suppose that at some point other antagonistic forces – a foreign invasion, the action of hostile economic forces, etc. – intervene. The national minority will see all the antagonistic forces as *equivalent* threats to its own identity. Now, if there is equivalence, this means that through all the very different antagonistic forces something equally present in all of them is expressed. This common element, however, cannot be something positive, because from the point of view of their concrete positive features each of these forces differs from the other. So it has to be something purely negative: the threat that each of them poses to the national identity. The conclusion is that in a relation of equivalence, each of the equivalent elements functions as a symbol of negativity as such, of a certain universal impossibility which penetrates the identity in question. To put the matter in other terms: in an antagonistic relation that which operates as the negative pole of a certain identity is constitutively split. All its contents express a general negativity transcending them. But for that reason, the 'positive' pole cannot be reduced to its concrete contents either: if that opposing them is the universal form of negativity as such, these contents have to express through their equivalencial relation the universal form of fullness or identity. We are not dealing here with 'determinate negation' in the Hegelian sense: while the latter comes out of the apparent positivity of the concrete and 'circulates' through contents that are always determinate, our notion of negativity depends on the failure in the constitution of all determination.

This constitutive split shows the emergence of the universal within the particular. But it shows as well that the relation between particularity and universality is an essentially unstable and undecidable one. What particular content was going to incarnate universality, was God's decision in Christian eschatologies and was, as a result, entirely fixed and predetermined. As self-transparent universality was a moment in the rational self-development of particularity, what particular actor was going to abolish his or her distance from the universal, was something equally fixed by essential determinations in the Hegelian/Marxist vision of history. But if the universal results from a constitutive split in which the negation of a particular identity transforms this identity in the symbol of identity and fullness as such, in that case we have to conclude that: (1) the universal has no content of its own, but it is an absent fullness or, rather, the signifier of fullness as such, of the very idea of fullness; (2) the universal can only emerge out of the particular, because it is only the negation of a *particular* content that transforms that content in the symbol of a universality transcending it; (3) since, however, the universal – taken by itself – is an empty signifier, *what* particular content is going to symbolize the latter is something which cannot be determined either by an analysis of the particular in itself or of the universal in itself. The relation between the two depends on the context of the antagonism and it is, in the strict sense of the term, a hegemonic operation. It is as if the undecidable line separating the two poles of the dichotomy had expanded its undecidable effects to the interior of the poles themselves, to the very relation between universality and particularity.

Let us now consider, in the light of these conclusions, what happens to the six dimensions of the notion of emancipation with which we started. The dimension of ground, we have shown, is incompatible with emancipation and it also involves us in insurmountable logical aporias. Does this, however, mean that we can have no further dealings with the notion of 'ground', that it has to be merely abandoned? Obviously not, if for no other reason than because disaggregation and particularism, which constitute the only possible alternative, presuppose, at the same time that they deny, the notion of ground. It is possible, however, to make of the interplay of these incompatible logics the very locus of a certain political productivity. Particularity both denies and requires totality, that is, the ground. These contradictory movements express themselves in what we have called the constitutive split of all concrete identity. Totality is impossible and at the same time is required by the particular: in that sense it is present in the particular as that which is absent, as a constitutive lack which constantly forces the particular to be more than itself, to assume a universal role which can only be precarious and unsutured. It is because of that that we can have democratic politics: a succession of finite and particular identities which attempt to assume universal tasks surpassing them; but that, as a result, are never able to entirely conceal the distance between task and identity, and can always be substituted by alternative groups. Incompletion and provisionality belong to the essence of democracy.

It goes without saying that the holistic dimension moves along the same path as the dimension of ground: the two of them are, in fact, the same dimension seen from two different angles. As far as the rationalistic dimension is concerned, we should take into account that the secularist turn of modernity involved both the assertion that the meaning of history is not to be found outside history itself, that there is no supernatural power operating as the ultimate source of everything that exists, and the very different assertion that this purely worldly succession of events is an entirely rational process that human beings can intellectually master. Thus reason reoccupies the terrain that Christianity had attributed to God. But the eclipse of the ground deprives reason of its all-embracing abilities, and only the first assertion (or rather commitment), the intraworldly character of all explanation, remains. Reason is necessary, but it is also impossible. The presence of its absence is shown in the various attempts to 'rationalize' the world that finite social agents carry out. Precariousness and ultimate failure (if we persist in measuring success by an old rationalistic standard) are certainly the destiny of these attempts, but through this failure we gain something perhaps more precious than the certainty that we are losing: a freedom *vis-à-vis* the different forms of identification, which are impotent to imprison us within the network of an unappealable logic. The same applies to the dimension of transparency: total representability is no longer there as a possibility, but this does not mean that its necessity has been eradicated. This unbridgeable gap between possibility and necessity leads straight into what Nietzsche called a 'war of interpretations'. If limited and finite beings try to know, to make the world transparent to themselves, it is impossible that this limitation and finitude is not transmitted to the products of their intellectual activity. In this sense the abandonment of the aspiration to 'absolute' knowledge has exhilarating effects: on the one hand human beings can recognize themselves as the true creators and no longer as the passive recipients of a predetermined structure; on the other hand, as all social agents have to recognize their concrete finitude, nobody can aspire to be the true consciousness of the world. This opens the way to an endless interaction between various perspectives and makes ever more distant the possibility of any totalitarian dream.

What about those aspects that are incompatible with the dimension of ground and the ones depending on it? As we have seen, the dichotomic dimension presupposes the structural location of a ground and, at the same time, makes the latter unthinkable. Only if it takes place at the level of a ground of the social the chasm constituting the dichotomy is radical from the point of view of its *location*, but the operation that the dichotomy performs — the *separation* of emancipation from a totally alien past — is logically incompatible with the notion of such a structural location. Now, as in the case of the other dimensions, some positive consequences follow from this double movement of self-positing and withdrawal of the ground. The most important one is that, if on the one hand no dichotomy is absolute, there can be no act of fully revolutionary foundation; but if, on the other hand, this dichotomization is not the result of an elimination of radical otherness but, on the contrary, of the very impossibility of its total eradication, partial and precarious dichotomies have to be constitutive of the social fabric. This precariousness and incompletion of the frontiers constituting social division are at the root of the contemporary possibility of a general autonomization of social struggles — the so-called new social movements — instead of subordinating them to a unique frontier which would be the only source of a social division. Finally the *pre-existence* of the identity to be emancipated *vis-à-vis* the oppressive forces is also subverted and submitted to the same contradictory movement that the other dimension experiences. In classical discourses, the emancipated identities had to pre-exist the act of emancipation as a result of their radical otherness *vis-à-vis* the forces opposing them. It is true that this is unavoidable in any antagonistic struggle; but if, at the same time, dichotomization is not truly radical — and as we have just seen it cannot be so — then the identity of the oppressive forces has to be in some way inscribed in the identity searching for emancipation. This contradictory situation is expressed in the undecidability between internality and externality of the oppressor in relation to the oppressed: to be oppressed is part of my identity as a subject struggling for emancipation; with the presence of the oppressor my identity would be different. The constitution of the latter requires and at the same time rejects the presence of the other.

Contemporary social struggles are bringing to the fore this contradictory movement that the emancipatory discourse of both religious and modern secularized eschatologies had concealed and repressed. We are today coming to terms with our own finitude and with the political possibilities that it opens. This is the point from which the potentially liberatory discourses of our postmodern age have to start. We can perhaps say that today we are at the end of emancipation and at the beginning of freedom.

REFERENCE

Marx, K. (1971) *A Contribution to the Critique of Political Economy*. London.

Ernesto Laclau is Reader in Politics at the University of Essex, Wivenhoe Park, Colchester CO4 3SQ, where he is also Director of the Centre for Theoretical Studies in the Humanities and the Social Sciences. He is author of *Politics and Ideology in Marxist Theory* (Verso, 1990) and co-author with Chantal Mouffe of *Hegemony and Socialist Strategy, Towards a Radical Democratic Politics* (Verso, 1985).

Democracy and Emancipatory Movements: Notes for a Theory of Inversionary Discourse

David E. Apter

IDEOLOGY, DISCOURSE AND EMANCIPATORY MOVEMENTS

One of the most important and yet elusive concepts in the social science lexicon is ideology. Ideology is all around us. We treat it as a more or less independent form of power, whether as ideas, principles or beliefs. Ideologies of nationalism can build the state: witness the emergence of independent states out of colonial territories. Or they can dismember it, breaking it up into autonomous units, as in Yugoslavia or the Soviet Union. Ideologies can take the form of Plato's 'noble lies', in which attributes of an 'original identity' are accorded to religious, ethnic, racial, linguistic and similar affiliations. They may be considered as false consciousness. They can take the form of 'scientific' thought, as with Althusserian Marxism or theories of free market capitalism. Or they may appear as symbolic templates or pure rationalizations, neither true nor false (Apter, 1964; Geertz, 1964). All these different usages and their chief protagonists have been carefully examined by Raymond Boudon (1989) and there is no need to go over the ground here. However, if we want to find out how, in what form, ideological beliefs come to have power, concretely as well as analytically, it will be necessary to explode the concept itself, and combine a structural analysis with a phenomenological one. Accordingly I shall try to show that ideology becomes important because of the way people interpret certain negative conditions confronting them. Formed in the process of thinking one's way past contradictions and predicaments, ideology in this context means interpreting, and in turn interpreting requires the creation and use of discourses.

The formation of discourses which become consensually

Development and Change (SAGE, London, Newbury Park and New Delhi), Vol. 23 (1992) No. 3, 139–173.

validated, bind people together 'exegetically' in discourse communities. How discourse works in this way is for present purposes more significant than discussions about ideology. I shall therefore examine discourse as a combination of narratives and texts, in the context of transcending or overcoming projects. They take on an independent life of their own whether from above, in the form of the discourse of the state or from below in an anti-discourse directed against the state. The present emphasis is on 'emancipatory movements' from below and the impact of anti-discourses which confront the state. My basic argument is that confrontational acts beyond ordinary institutional rules and mechanisms of politics which challenge the accepted conventional ideologies will alter the scope and meanings of equity and make changes in patterns of allocation. Inclusions and exclusions are revised. In these terms, political discourse is created out of events. This poses the interesting question of the way such events are coded, something which has less to do with ideology *per se* than how people interpret experiences, especially in the context of violence. Which brings us to the matter of social movements themselves.

There are many varieties of social movements, of course. Of special concern are those which, despairing of regularized channels such as electoral or interest politics, organize alternative modes of action. The most common variety is extrainstitutional protest movements using public demonstrations, sit-ins, strikes, etc. to arouse attention and support. Historically linked to the evolution of democracy itself in the form of civil rights, trade unions, women's emancipation and other issues, extrainstitutional protest movements are confrontational without challenging the political system as such. Mainly they are interested in effecting changes in the scope and prevailing definitions of equity.

The second and opposite form is revolutionary insurrection, in which the state is regarded as not only lacking equity but standing as a system for the wrong combination of equity, order and growth. The aim is to generate sufficient mass power to first disrupt the state and then overthrow it root and branch. Such movements can be libertarian and/or democratic, the prototype being the Jacobin phase of the French Revolution.

A third kind of emancipatory movement, where faith in the first kind is lacking and the ability to create the mass following needed for the second has not occurred, is 'terrorism'. This has received considerable attention and publicity but very little analysis which might fall under the rubric of political theory. The phenomenon itself is diverse but so widespread is the use of the term that we shall continue to use it despite its pejorative connotations. Fundamentally it involves small groups committing violent acts against persons and property as symbolic or surrogate for society and state.

All three kinds of movement can be left or right, sacred or secular, particularistic or universalistic, etc. All share one thing in common. As movements *for* they are also movements *against*. In this sense they are provocations, subversive in their own eyes as well as those of the authorities. Theirs is the politics of the moral moment, disjunctive, redemptive or transformational. Claiming legitimacy against current principles as well as excesses of power, the defects of society are interpreted as failures of the state. Movements like these arouse controversy by their very existence and stimulate debates over political fundamentals. Their chief weapon is a discourse capable of threatening prevailing norms and principles of power particularly when combined with confrontational episodes.

Such a discourse is negating and transcending. It is easy to countenance in autocratic and authoritarian societies where emancipation has a self-evident logic, equity being a desire for freedom, independence and equality. But it takes on more troubling characteristics in democratic societies where what is to be negated and transcended is precisely the kind of political system which strives to perfect these three qualities by regularized institutional means. Clearly emancipatory movements of all three types have been intrinsic to the evolution of democracy itself. Equally clearly, it is necessary in each democracy that none of these movements ever fully succeeds on its own terms. It is at this point that the question of emancipatory movements and how to consider them becomes interesting.

To deal with such questions will require a diversion – the examination of democracy as both a model and a discourse – before showing the consequences of emancipatory movements which aim to up-end them. This is necessary for two reasons. In the examination of democracy the role played by emancipatory movements has been given short shrift and treated as a minor factor. By the same token, those favouring such movements have little patience or understanding of democracy. Hence what is important is the interplay between democracy and emancipatory movements; since each has its own dynamics this interplay cannot be understood without knowledge of both as systems.

From the present perspective what makes emancipatory movements interesting is the way in which they try to undermine assumptions on which democracy rests including self-improving assumptions in place since the Enlightenment, such as popular participation, rationality and education (Baudart and Pena-Ruiz, 1991). Just as venues for confrontation have changed over time, for example, from the workplace to the academy, so the emancipatory project has shifted from rectification of inequalities and exclusions, to the undermining of codes and discourses, with real consequences. Education, for example, once a route to social improvement and mobility, is from such a perspective hegemonic, its institutions and instrumentalities prefiguring hierarchy, with the school the locus for discrepancies between the ideally free citizen and the 'real' world of lost opportunities.[1]

Discourse, then, is the focus because discourse is both a method of intellectual expression and a means of intellectual oppression. Any institution using knowledge according to meritocratic principles is thus intrinsically hierarchical. In this sense schooling makes its victims complicit in their condition. The same system which rewards merit with power at one extreme produces marginality at the other.

So considered, the point of departure of today's emancipatory movements is not equality but victimization. This is what distinguishes them from 'old' social movements which fought for equality or greater participation. Today it is the 'negativized other' which takes the moral measure of the whole, especially in democracies. Not surprisingly, movements of this kind are politically irritating even when they are of minor importance. To the extent that they downgrade conventional knowledge while claiming superior moral insight, they challenge order. Critical theory is their privileging weapon. Such movements claim as exclusive their right to purposeful enquiry into what is wrong, bringing the norms and principles embodying the idea of free enquiry into disrepute. Such movements want it both ways, attacking the 'canon' while claiming its protection.

These remarks apply particularly to the more extreme forms of emancipatory movement. Why pay attention to the extreme? It is the extreme which best reveals the more general interplay of conflictual discourse. Inversionary discourse claims 'emancipation' as a moral project rather than a form of alternative organization or structure. By studying its components we can explore a little understood side of democracy, asking how and why it is that such movements seek above all to rupture the discourse of the state by means of an anti-discourse which undermines ordered jurisdictions and stable networks.

INTELLECTUAL PEDIGREES

The intellectual pedigree, if not inspiration, for these movements is diverse and includes such figures as Marx, Foucault, Bataille and Lacan. They provide us with the analytical materials necessary to examine discourse in terms of the processes which make it significant. I shall use notions such as retrieval and projection, story telling and logical construction, metaphor and metonymy, narrative and text. For such movements political action is an engagement with the past of suppressed events and episodes, submerged political upheavals, abortive uprisings which, unregistered in orthodox history, remain in the memory, in the retina of the political eye. How to transform the unhistory of the negativized, to make the anonyms impinge on history is one way to put the matter. To enable those penalized by democracy to gain power through loss is another. Among the aims of such retrievals and the projected outcomes which follow from them are the capture of the moral initiative and net gains in imagination, both necessary to invert the condition of the 'negativized other'.

The common starting point is the 'marginalized'. Even the most economically successful democracies will have some quota of the penalized, the victimized, the marginals. Hence, there will always be opportunities for emancipatory movements of some kind.[2] The question is, what consequences they have for usable social policy. How do democratic societies respond to movements which both violate the law, and refuse to use ordinary institutional rules – especially when, because of the magnitude and audacity of their claims, they polarize the community and force the state to act punitively? Moreover, since they have the disturbing quality of making visible those groups that tend to be politically invisible, they shock the mainstream of society. They 'reveal' negative conditions as more than accidents of individual fortune or collective circumstance and rather as fundamental defects of the system as a whole, and offer a logic to show why democracies depend on such defects in order to survive. They seek to spread the conviction that flaws and gaps in equity are irremedial and decisive in the last instance. The emphasis is not on mere deprivation but on loss, dispossession. The solution is not compensation or remediation but nothing less than the repossession of self, society and the state. So defined the object of emancipatory movements is to provide those forms of discourse that play off Marx and Rousseau, Nietzsche and Sartre, Althusser with Baudrillard (Rey, 1971). The object is to naturalize as self-evident the course of action which leads to the possession of self as a repossession of patrimonies. Inversionary protest movements are thus confrontational and violence prone, and relatively uninterested in rectifying this or that economic, social or political ill, or in providing greater political access to those deprived by reason of religion, gender, ethnicity, race, language, class, role or other affiliations. Such affiliations are interesting only as provocations requiring the violation of standing jurisdictions.

CONCEPTUALIZING POWER: ORDER VERSUS CHOICE

This raises the question of the discourse of democracy itself. Typically characterized as a creature of its institutions and constitutions, examined in terms of decision-making and efficacy, as a system we shall call it a choice model. In these terms the democratic state is an ensemble of individuals and groups representing a prevailing symposium of interests rendered into priorities and preferences of choice by means of the legislative process, with market as the basis for community because it converts individual wants into collective goods (Arrow, 1963). In this, the market is itself a discourse about forces using the language of equilibrium based on a balancing in civil society and the state of recognized needs, wants and desires, a condition of order balancing equity, allocation and growth.

In practice, of course, democracy lurches from crisis to crisis, each of which tests its weakest links. It is precisely in the fluctuations and crises so produced that emancipatory movements have their openings, either to produce crises or in response to them. In short, the predominant 'ideology' of democracy is a discourse embodied in what is called today a rational choice model. Institutionally, the discourse is embodied in mechanisms and instruments which enable choices to be made at different and intersecting levels of state and society. The common consequence of all these mechanisms and instruments is the generation of information. Information refigured in the form of preferential values becomes policies. Markets then are ramified information systems which enable a distribution of choice priorities.[3] To function markets require rules and adherence to those governing choice. It is the discourse which validates these rules.

Democracy in this sense implies freedom to choose within an open-ended political system. Such a system will be relativistic to the degree that it is pluralistic. Precluded is some Platonic concept of justice. Such qualities, built into institutional democracy, represent what might be called, using Foucault's term, the modern political episteme. This *institutional democratic* model is not one among several plausible alternatives. It is not only *the* alternative to all other and previous forms but it appears to have history on its side: built into the discourse is a moral-evolutionary history in which the 'choice model' has emerged out of an 'order model' as morally and institutionally superior to all other forms of polity.

The transition in terms of discourse can be found in Foucault. He compared the modern choice 'episteme' to the order episteme of the 'classical age'.[4] Among the properties of the classical age were a 'general grammar' of the sign; representation meant the names of things; and knowledge, like algebraic transformations, made transitive otherwise fixed but relationally flexible qualities. The theory of wealth depended on use values rather than exchange values. The discourse was composed of permanent relationships fixed in their qualities, ordered nature and social life, regularity in change – teleological in the Aristotelian sense or ideally 'conceptual' in the Platonic sense. Comprised of unity and totality, knowledge consisted of locating and defining the boundaries and ingredients or components of this totality, identifying its elements, classifying them, giving them names, establishing their logical ranks, proportionalities and hierarchies in the social as well as the natural universe. Order was organically rather than mechanically connected. Growth followed form, a telos of the beginning as well as the end.

Such notions as free will and choice were absent. They would have been unthinkable, subversive, revolutionary, explosive. Indeed, as soon as they came to dominate the language of knowledge the old principles of order were destroyed. Wealth was transformed into capital. Use became value. Ranks and hierarchies became functional. Wants and goals became open ended, potentialities open. Teleology disappeared. The natural as well as the human universe became the object of change by conscious design. Order and obligation were removed from the centre of politics. Totality was shattered. The political focus shifted from the collective to the individual.

In contrast, the choice episteme was entirely a discourse based on rationality and exchange, production and reproduction. 'Representation' is political, rather than a business of naming and classifying things. Exchange now includes the realm of value translation, apples measured against pears. Individual preferences are changed into schedules and priorities. Embedded in law and manifested in policies, functional instrumentalities enable exchange and translation to take place under a system of rules where the sole discretionary authority has only limited power. A moving equilibrium replaces centralized power. Balance is represented in the re-equilibration between economic and political marketplaces, the one for goods and services, the other for policies, laws and orders; the one private, dispersing power and other public, concentrating it.

The transition from an order to a choice model was rapid and not without difficulties. For one thing it had to deal with the problem of how to order choice, the solution to which required an entirely new political framework. Hobbes was perhaps the first to recognize it fully.[5] The virtue of his argument was to show clearly just how really fundamental was the conceptual change from an ordered system of mutual obligations and asymmetrical ranks to a universe of rational choice. He made it abundantly clear that order meant protection. But his solution, the conveyance of individual powers to a sole discretionary authority, was too self-limiting. What was needed was a political solution which could provide for authority under maximal choice conditions, i.e. freedom. But freedom, the only totally open-ended value, poses the problem of how to provide for its maximization, and in so doing prevent the strong from prevailing over the weak. To transform a universe of will into a universe of choice requires a new polity. The political becomes a form of order preserving and protecting choice. In this sense the choice model defines the problem of order and the institutional democratic model is a system of order protecting choice.

What is represented is the self-interested individual pursuing interests and by so doing both producing and consuming information. Institutional mechanisms transform information into outputs. Yet because politics is in this sense a transformational grammar in which each institutional form of democracy (presidential or parliamentary, unitary or federal) depends on coalitional games and electoral mechanisms capable of transforming market information into mediating policy outcomes and so enabling the political system to sustain itself as a moving equilibrium, the individuals are all part of the same discourse community.

Despite crises and lurches, then, the two key features of this model are equilibrium as a form of naturalized equity and a community of sharing in the common discourse. Justice is a function of the extent to which the political and economic markets are mutually self-regulating. To prevent the situation from being zero sum, economic growth is essential. As suggested, the choice model represents a shift from a rationality of wealth to a rationality of growth. (Choice for Hobbes was zero sum.) Hence human beings are at one and the same time atomic particles in a field of political force and mutually interactive in a field of discourse. Add growth and the idea of a self-perfecting never-perfected institutional democracy follows.

The evolution of an order model into a choice model is marked not only by a transition from one to the other, but the transition itself is constituted by events which punctuate history and consciousness. Not only different discourses are involved by the ascendancy of the one over the other. Hence democratic discourse takes on the force of truth and history. It is not only an evolution of political theory but, embodied in concrete struggles, revolutions, civil wars, it has a contextual force, the force of human experiences, sufferings and sacrifices. In this sense the discourse of democracy is not only theoretical and abstract, but embedded in the immediacy of people fighting for their beliefs. Embodied in constitutional laws and institutional practices, narratives and text as the distillation of human experiences appear as a triumph of mind over obstacles.

The democratic state is not only a primary or sovereign jurisdiction or the instrument which safeguards all other conventional and legal boundaries of society. It is also a linguistic achievement. That is, it opens up ways of thinking and doing which did not previously exist. It is also the representative of all other lesser group boundaries – interest, class, ethnic, religious, etc. It is both their guardian and their means of entering the market and making their priorities felt. In such a state, governments constitute subsystems which represent the state as an ensemble of functional instrumentalities. Together these make possible an information-generating process whose components include executive accountability, citizen representation, specific and preferred electoral mechanisms, both centralized and decentralized administrative structures, thus providing publicly elected and responsible officials with knowledge of public preferences and priorities. In this sense political decision-making is a function of information, not coercion, with political parties and interest groups performing crucial functions in the agenda-setting process. This, at least in terms of institutional political theory, is the way democracies work, with citizen sovereignty and state sovereignty considered as two sides of the same coin.[6]

THE DEMOCRATIC STATE

Terms like state and civil society, institutions and their linkages, functions and processes, constitute the general political 'grammar' of choice. Because rules restrict choice every concrete institutional democracy represents a particular balance between choice and order according to *rules* rather than *ends*. The choice principle requires that ends remain open. Freedom is the central value. Institutional democracy is a political system in tension between the freedom of choice and rules governing freedom.

The maximal unit of the choice model is the state. The state is the predominant jurisdictional boundary around choice. Civil society (composed of individuals and groups) is constituted primarily of functional need and demands. Principles are converted into negotiable interests (geographical, cultural, business, labour, etc.) whose significance is measured in the dual marketplace in such terms as wealth, saliency and numbers. Serving as a principal basis of political party affiliation the pursuit of interests generates policies and programmes operating through designated bodies representing citizens in their diverse capacities.

With a limited range of alternative constitutional modes (parliamentary, presidential, etc.) institutional-democratic forms of the choice model function in terms of the free exchange of information, the minimization of coercion and the accountability of the executive to representational bodies. All concrete constitutional polities aim to realize the mutual reinforcement of choice and order, tendencies which both repel and attract each other. Each exerts a magnetic pull on the other, generating a field of force within which one finds, sharply posed, the crucial question of how to maximize choice within the limits of order (Barry, 1965; Rawls, 1971). Information in the political sphere is parallel to the same processes in the economic sphere. The same assumptions and the same dynamics which work in the economic marketplace work in the political marketplace. Political parties replace firms. Votes replace money (Downs, 1957; Olson, 1965). Particularly relevant is the private sphere. Civil and property rights are crucially interdependent. Private property is balanced by public need. Public power is diluted by economic power. Political power prevents economic inequality from producing political inequality because numbers (votes) represent the counterweight to wealth (money). An equilibrium of these vectors will be modified by developmental needs with their attendant inequalities, and diluted by shortrun political needs, i.e. compensatory policies favouring access and participation for the relatively disadvantaged.

A key problem arises when provision of information to decision-makers fails because of 'noise' or 'interference' (a failure of institutional linkages). That is where extrainstitutional politics begins. Where compensatory policies fail and equilibrium is skewed, political action, including confrontational social movements, will arise outside of regularized institutional channels. Reform is a process of 'incorporation' of the excluded by means of improvements in linkage instruments (Lawson and Merkl, 1987). The practical or institutional evolution of the model in terms of adaptive change has always included extrainstitutional processes because of information gaps and failures. The power of the powerless is to threaten the choice boundaries of the rationalistic field. By prejudicing choice on the one hand and order on the other, amendment of both the principles and practices of democracy is required. In this sense emancipatory movements are part of self-improvement.[7]

It is also the case that more is required than the purely self-interested rationality of the economic market. As suggested, exchange is also a discourse using a language of equity, allocation, growth and order. The terms of these represent at least a residue of principled discourse defining the nature of political rights and obligations sufficient to produce – to use Shils's term – civility. That is, discourse over the terms of what might be called the equity statement itself generates principles of civic obligation which both incorporate the self-interest principle and embody to some degree the public interest. This was a problem of major concern to Simmel, Durkheim and Pareto more than modern rational choice theorists. For them the question was how to convert functional aggregations into a mutualism of responsibility requiring self-denial in the exercise of self-interested rationality rules.[8]

Above all such mutualism depends on the relationship of rationality and civility to education and knowledge. The two together represent potentiality, i.e. the moral evolution of the community and the individual. Such are the conditions necessary to the exercise of free choice over time. On them depends that necessary confidence without which there would be little sharing of rights, privileges, duties and responsibilities and without which people would be unable to realize preferred ends. In turn, without such confidence the rules which themselves both govern and make choice possible would no longer be independently valued. The normative aspects of the discourse would be undermined. The rules would be less self-monitored than a function of state compliance. In this sense in the model of institutional democracy the normative represents discourse embedded in the rationality rules of the market as well as its political instruments. Such a model of the institutional democratic state is both representational and tutelary.

This does not mean that people must believe in democratic principles. All that is necessary is that people speak, read and act democratically. This suggests that the discourse of democracy is not only a general grammar of the political system, but also a set of 'meta-rules' which include a grammar and a language of politics. Within this framework markets constitute certain boundaries while intersecting others. The aim of the inversionary discourse model is to challenge the meta-rules of democracy, explode the ensemble of choices and disrupt the market. The dialectic with violence constitutes the perpetual negative to this positive notion of the democratic state.

Would the choice model be able to survive without fundamental challenges? Probably not. Too much self-monitoring, too effective equilibration of the market and both the meta-rules and the discourse of choice would lose their validity and meaning. No system of rules is entirely free standing. It is the danger of their violation that gives them vitality. The general tendency in the model would otherwise be to ritualize them and make them perfunctory.

In this sense democracy requires risk from inside as well as outside. But the question is how much risk before democracy is overwhelmed or destroyed? In general I would argue that democracies in which growth is sustained and the discourse derived from it, are much stronger than might appear on the surface. This is first because meta-rules and discourses are embedded in role networks within and between boundaries, and second because membership in discourse communities is both overlapping and socially defined, i.e. interlocking.

This suggests that far from being overwhelmed by them, as long as growth is non-zero sum, democracy as a mediating instrument for open-ended choice depends on emancipatory movements to define its moral trajectory further than the effective participants operating within an equilibrating political and economic market. This suggests that the relationship between choice and order is dialectical. The dialectic operates inside an improving frame within which rational action expresses itself as both self and the collectivity, a function of access to bargaining and negotiation. Decision-making mediates choice and reinforces rules while altering the options and modifying the method. In this process the state is 'privileged'. Without the state, choice would be rendered nugatory.

BOUNDARIES AND STICKY CHANGE

If the practice is bumpy the principle embodied in the democratic meta-rules describes instead a smooth generational transmission of shared values and incorporation into the ensemble of role and role networks centring around the rationality of the double marketplace. In the democratic model choice is open ended but not preordained. The state intersects with society as the sole jurisdiction which sustains all other boundaries. But in democracies the state is also subject to those other boundaries which it is required to protect, since the conventions governing social boundaries change slowly and are rarely challenged. Challenges, when they do arise, cause the state to respond cautiously. Change then tends to be incremental, in Lindblom's sense of the term, and boundary reinforcing. The more things change the more they are the same. The more they are the same, the more they change.[9]

Because of sticky coalitions and entrenched and organized voting blocs, the amendment process is slow. Moreover, within the process, issues must be converted from principle to interests, institutional democratic politics reducing even important concerns to the flat grey of interest and bargaining. Change when it does take place, is more or less imperceptible. Important issues are diluted with the mundane, robbing them of their symbolic or moral significance. An example is afforded by the election of a woman to the presidency of the Irish Republic. Such a choice seems unthinkable: compared to, say, France or the United States, the Irish Republic discriminates against women both in public and private life. It maintains gender boundaries in law as well as custom, reinforced by the doctrines of the Roman Catholic Church. And not only boundaries between men and women. Homosexuality, for example, is – in theory at least – punishable by life imprisonment; abortion and divorce remain illegal; there are no laws against sexual harassment. The Irish are deeply conservative on such matters. Nevertheless, Mary Robinson, member of a small leftist party, was elected president of the Republic. Introducing a certain porousness in the hitherto fixed relationships between men and women in terms of society and state, it is a case of incremental reform by means of institutional modes facilitating boundary changes within the political system by legitimating previously rigoristically regulated 'spaces' between them.[10]

Change by these means is incredibly slow. It presumes a certain satisfaction with things as they are, even a public preference for political lethargy. It is precisely here that emancipatory movements take on significance. Move from the Irish Republic across the border into Northern Ireland and the world turns upside down. Violence, terrorism and national struggle towards an emancipatory end are not only directed against British rule, but against the role of the church, the prevailing relations between men and women, etc. The tragedy is that the conditions for a solution do not exist.

Boundaries exist and boundary changes occur in other than interest, ethnic, ideological or other well-defined groups. Equally significant may be those which form around issues which, while they fluctuate in importance, may burn with a particular intensity and thus intersect with all other groups in powerful ways, becoming focal points of attention and refracting issues to the point where a new discourse is formed. In the United States the matter of abortion can have that effect. Or, to take something much less well defined like changing public tastes, the issue may involve challenges to 'good taste'. Certain 'speech acts' obviously 'transgress' conventional limits. Violation of such boundaries easily leads to demonstrations and protest. The flaunting of sexual mores, or obscenity and pornography in relation to art, for example, tend to be directly disordering. But the long-run effect may be to create a discourse which so reinterprets the meaning of 'speech acts' themselves that these reinforce rather than violate boundaries.

Defining the 'boundary' between life, birth and the definition of the living person is another one of those 'intersecting' issues which redefine equity and by so doing shift the focus of allocation from wealth to power. The state can only mediate such conflicts with difficulty. For those excluded from the process the meaning of incremental change is very different. It is evidence of systemic disparities between the purity of equity claims and the compromises of concrete practices of politics. For them if violence occurs it is both self-righteous and diagnostic. It reveals how glaring these discrepancies may be. The more radical the emancipatory movement, the more it challenges not only the way in which democracy works but the working assumptions that over time and by means of an incremental process, the worst gaps will be bridged.

BOUNDARY SMASHING AND DISCOURSE BREAKS

Emancipatory movements break into the process by challenging both the meta-rules of democracy and its discourse as a political system. We have already described the main characteristic types, of which the most common is extrainstitutional protest, with revolutionary insurrection and terrorism as alternatives. But a great deal of such activity occurs between all three, without in fact being any one of them. They flirt with all, thus exercising the discourse of violence, without necessarily engaging in it. A good example is that of the Situationists who attacking conventional taste, parody social civility at all its most sensitive points and mock the meta-rules on which the choice paradigm itself depends, by calling into question the false consciousness of the choices themselves. They would argue that the basis of rational choice is itself irrational and the moving equilibrium of the institutional democratic model destructive of intelligence and humanity. Hence their actions are designed to alter both the rules governing choice and the nature of choice itself. This requires them to make language performative. Directed against the grammar and language of democratic politics, form smashing and verbal killing are aimed at the principle of rationality itself, an implosion of it by caricature.[11]

Movements other than the Situationists also aim to alter the discourse of institutional democratic politics, its grammar and language, and its surrogate, the state as the boundary of the boundaries. Action is designed to generate new social texts, semiotic, 'sign full'. Occasions, situations and happenings produce signifiers directed at destroying the rationalistic signifieds, i.e. the concepts embedded in the institutional democratic model itself. So startling are the implications of this that no matter how small such a movement might be, it immediately becomes magnified by those in power, blown out of proportion, a manifestation of visible dangers which not only prejudice the transmittal of the discourse of rationality from one generation to the next but introduce chaos and confusion instead. The movements of the 1960s, and indeed early 1970s, in Europe and the United States continue to have ripple effects within universities because they challenged the rationalistic choice episteme. They sought to undermine the *evolutionary* legitimacy of democracy and substitute for it a *revolutionary* legitimacy. To the extent that they see this as an ongoing product they differ from the 'old' social movements which accepted the principles of the democratic political system while seeking to widen their scope. The 'new', employing a critical theory which is continuously inversionary, denies political solutions. So that what might be called the discourse of the post-modern variety has as its aim not only continuous challenging of boundaries but treatment of the democratic discourse as hegemonic. The only possible condition for open-ended choice is in a continuous battle against not only the hegemony of power but the power of the discourse on which it is based.

So considered, the starting point is the perspective of the 'victim' – the thief, the homosexual, the madman, the pariah. Any role which denotes marginality serves as the point of departure for a critical and indeed inversionary discourse different from that of democracy. Pariahs are the heroes of transformational change.

The usual venue is the marginal, or the excluded. More recently, especially in Europe, it is the victim as 'outsider', especially immigrants. From the perspective of the state the problem is how and to what extent immigrants ought to be required to be assimilated in order to enjoy the rights and obligations of citizenship. Or, conversely, to what extent should pluralization prevail so that immigrants will be able to pursue their traditional ways of life in a different terrain. Each alternative involves different limits on choice.

Most states try to integrate outsiders into the political and social life of the country. They define permissible boundaries. Culture and social life fundamentally different from the rest of society becomes 'deviant', hence from the institutional-democratic standpoint, the problem is the 'absorption' of 'difference' – and the difference that difference makes. The flashpoint is reached when there is visible occupation of the same space by 'insiders' and 'outsiders', a condition which magnifies all forms of difference within the same community and raises questions of how much social and cultural boundary 'violation' can be mediated before 'cultural tipping' occurs. In France, for example, such problems have entered the political arena in earnest, in terms of Le Pen and the National Front and other national political parties, with all the implications of fascist revivalism as an 'emancipatory' project.

One sees the predicament virtually every day. A good example of the issue is represented in the recent case of 'veiling' in France. Among the visible signifiers of differences which define the outsider, and which reveal whole social codes, symbolic expressions are clothes, food, language, the movement of the body in public places, the wearing of the veil. The latter is important among many Arabs in much the same way as the skullcap is for Jews. It is provocative as a signifier of difference between Arab and French culture and a demarcation in the status of men and women in terms of modesty, sexuality, eroticism, etc. Veiling is designed to reinforce difference, especially where young girls are incorporated into the secular institutions of the French state.[12]

If the state tries to prevent veiling it imposes on the choice, on the 'rights' of people to live their lives according to their own cherished principles. Yet to the extent that Arab immigration raises the spectre of cultural tipping, it poses the perennial problem of how far the 'tyranny of the majority' should go (Olson, 1965). How far are boundaries to be altered? How can assimilation be balanced by difference? The answers to such questions depend largely on how people define each other. Define 'outsiders' negatively and 'balancing' includes rectifying wrongs. But wrongs tend to be retrieved from the past and imposed on the present. In the French case negative differences redolent of the past as well as those of the present include the residual status of the colonial as pariah. Multiple marginalities – class, religious, ethnic, linguistic – coincide in the case of Muslim Arab immigrants more than in any other group of immigrants in France.

That being the case, a semiotics of 'presence' as a 'presence' of difference radiates throughout the country. The wearing of Arab dress is a signifier for 'violation'. The charm of exotic custom is transformed into provocation. The use of Muslim beads, the very sound of Arabic, the insistence on internally maintained exclusionary boundaries in matters of sexuality, marriage and the restricted nature of exchange between 'communities', all serve to reinforce difference socially and culturally while the official position is how to eliminate difference politically. Public reaction varies, of course. Not a few say in effect, that if foreigners want to live in France permanently they must become French, and if not they should go back where they came from. Others see the matter as people wanting it both ways, to be, say Algerian Arabs enjoying the rights of French citizens, and as French citizens, to be free to impose Arab demands, cultural, educational, etc., on the ways and habits of the French themselves. From the point of view of the French, nothing could be more important to the process of assimilation than the educational system.[13] From this standpoint, French Algerians now face much the same situation as French Jews during the Dreyfus period. Anti-Semitism and anti-Arabism are drawn from much the same source (the followers of Le Pen and the National Front not overly 'discriminating' between the two).

Balancing similarity against difference defines groups rather than individuals as the units of political life, and communities rather than citizens. In these terms, boundary shifting becomes symbolically loaded. Rectifying equity gaps, giving voice to those who for whatever reason are discriminated against or economically disadvantaged, have always been what a good deal of politics is about. But when changing boundaries is no longer a function of individuals but rather of group representation, the basis of the institutional model is undermined. Instead of overlapping roles, cleavages occur. If in the past the evolution of democracy was a function of conflict and confrontation, civil liberties, religious freedom, enfranchisement, trade unionism and collective bargaining, civil rights, feminism, workplace equality, etc., the end was individualization and incorporation. The sustaining power of the political system as a moving equilibrium depends less on the acceptance of differences than their pluralization and individualization. Indeed, what is assumed is that differences will erode (Apter, 1971).

EMANCIPATORY MOVEMENTS AND COLLECTIVE INDIVIDUALISM

This way of putting things should not be taken to imply that the sole or even the predominant way that reform occurs is through emancipatory movements. For the most part it occurs through horse trading, bargaining over interests which one way or another become inputs in the decision-making process. But it emphasizes that such movements do more than simply elevate to the public gaze issues which are troublesome. It emphasizes the symbolic aspects of emancipatory movements and what has been called the symbolic capital this can generate (Bourdieu, 1977; Apter and Sawa, 1984). It is when people are excluded categorically from the market and play a limited role in the political bargaining process more or less permanently that a good many emancipatory movements become inversionary and collectivized.

What that means is, for example, that individualism in the context of the choice model becomes defined as an abdication of responsibility as people refuse to concern themselves with changing the nature of the game itself. Inversionary movements then want to alter the 'taken-for-granted' common sense quality of the political world of interest group bargaining and party politics. In these terms the 'new' emancipatory movements aim at exploding the *doxa* of conventional democracy (Bourdieu, 1977).

For this reason alone they are different from older social movements. The latter believed that their actions would come to have salutary effects on democracy, resulting in net gains in the range and scope of equity, increasing the participation of the hitherto excluded, making the political system more representative, etc. Even when acting outside the boundaries of the legal and appropriate institutional structures of democracy, they raised the question of the moral limitations of the politically possible within those structures.

The difference between 'old' and 'new' social movements can be overemphasized, however. Illegal actions and the question of moral scope have always been troubling questions. Actions outside the boundaries are taken because they are disruptive of order in its most fundamental sense. There is always a question, too, of how much 'emancipation' people can absorb within a limited time frame, before they begin to react negatively. While there is no clear 'absorption limit', how change is mediated is as important as what changes need to be negotiated. In a democracy, majorities may feel that enough is enough, and consider the social fabric more threatened than enhanced by the emancipation process. If too much change is imposed by a minority on a majority, or those in power become threatened with a sudden loss not of power but of authority, they will strike back, using the state as their instrument. Hence, emancipation projects need to be evaluated not only in terms of the worthiness of their projects, goals and objectives, but also of their political consequences. Yet it is precisely this last question which change-oriented emancipatory movements are least likely to address.

Thus the paradox of emancipatory movements is that on the one hand they are intimately connected to the democratization of the state while, on the other, to be effective they promote responses which prejudice the institutionalization of democracy itself. Two concerns immediately arise from this way of defining the situation. Every emancipatory movement poses risks. To consider negative political consequences or pose the needs of democracy against the claims of a movement would emasculate virtually any such movement from the start. Cleavage politics are a necessary consequence because movements need to mobilize support in the face of political risk and danger. A small amount of protest tends to bring about a relatively high degree of reaction from the state. However, confrontational violence leads to more than specific demands and actions. Challenges to power and authority become loaded with emotive and symbolic significance, triggering normative responses on all sides. This being the case, neither the virtues nor the faults of emancipatory movements are to be evaluated with Olympian detachment. But because such movements are better at identifying what needs to be remedied than at providing acceptable remedies themselves, they raise the question of how to regard them. Such evaluation is never easy. Meanings change with events. Events change with meaning. The outrageous emancipatory movement of one generation is the glorious history of another. And this tends to be the case whether one is dealing with 'hard' demands, involving, for example, a specific reallocation of resources – land to the peasants, food to the poor, housing for the homeless – or the larger theoretical and moral factors attending them; how to change 'the system' in order to eliminate marginality, discrimination, the inadequacies of representation; how to alter institutional mechanisms to provide better access, greater accountability; how to open new routes to political access and power, enlarge the rights of minorities, reduce the tyranny of majorities, and so on.

Despite the diversity of the issues and the ambiguities they entail, if we define a political spectrum one end of which represents the erosion of democracy and the other its improvement, then we can think of emancipatory movements not only in terms of the absolute principles they favour or the intrinsic virtue they may claim to represent but their relative effects on democracy as an ongoing process. The same movement in one context may lead to a progressive evolution of democracy, while in another it may seem misplaced, dangerous and inappropriate.

This would suggest that there are no universal standards of judgement that can be meaningfully applied in some purely abstract way without considering other factors. Ethical fine tuning which results from social protest against, say, gender discrimination, race, religion, damage to the environment or against nuclear power plants, may be entirely appropriate in Great Britain or France and involve improvements in the terms of their democracy, while they may impose such burdens in say India or Brazil that they would prejudice democracy itself.

THE NEW EMANCIPATORY MOVEMENTS

While there is nothing new about inversionary discourse, Marxism being a good example, unlike Marxism inversionary discourse theory challenges the assumptions of the rationalistic discourse of both politics and economics. Economics represents commodification and false consciousness. Politics represents the hegemonic power of the state disguised in the discourse of equity and representation. Inversionary discourse seeks to connect the two not as a double marketplace leading to a moving equilibrium but as a double conspiracy against boundary and jurisdiction changing.

Hence such 'inversionary discourse' challenges both the institutional democratic model and modernism as democracy. In doing so its aim is to constitute a new episteme with which to displace the old, and dismantle the privileged role of state, especially its position as the Archimedean lever between choice and rule.

Inversionary discourse is not concerned with formal or representational notions of equality, participation or access precisely because these sustain the boundaries they seek to modify. Nor is it concerned with compensatory responses by the state which merely serve to perpetuate the moving equilibrium which is the basis of the institutional democratic state.

In this sense one might consider inversionary discourse theory as anarchic in character, but without the improving formulae of doctrinal forms of anarchism.[14] These involve the difference between criticism of the democratic state and critical theories of the state.

The whole point to inversionary discourse theory is to exploit what might be called the postmodern paradox. The more finely tuned the concepts of post-Rawlsian equity, the more enlarged the definition and scope of justice, the more hegemonic and dominant the state appears to be. Indeed, the less discriminatory democracy is at the institutional level, unless it explodes the boundaries themselves as distinct from 'merely' giving access to those within them, the more hegemonic the state, because its interest and societal interests are the same.

Since this is presumptuous to the extreme it is important for those engaged in creating an inversionary discourse to use examples where the democratic state denies its own principles – marginalized groups, the poor, the black, the Arab, the Chicano – in terms which involve loss, lack of patrimony, pariahdom, alterity and difference. Since equity gaps can always be found even in the most advanced and successful versions of institutionalized democracy, the social welfare or the social democratic state, inversionary discourse theory both augments the fine tuning of political sensibilities, and casts doubt on both the sincerity and efficacy of remedialism. By the sheer enlarging of participation or the expansion of social services, in so far as it acts to sustain the moving equilibrium, the institutional democratic model also maintains intact the common sense universe of exclusionary boundaries. The point to emancipatory movements is that, in order for them to be effective, they must test the democratic state by threatening to divide it at the point where it normally mediates. They take for granted that even if the outer limits of a democratic polity were reached it is highly doubtful that they would be breached. Democratic solutions are regarded as reductionist and dehumanizing. The more concrete the conditions to be rectified the more one becomes complicit in the bargaining enterprise. Each fresh solution becomes a target. The condition is one in which democracies becoming breeding grounds for discontent. Conventional civilities are boring, restrictive, and self-monitoring the worst consequences.

It has already been suggested that emancipatory movements as such rarely pose great dangers for democratic states and that they should be expected as a form of periodic disturbance. There is no happy condition out there which will eliminate their causes and, indeed, it is among the most privileged that one is likely to find the least satisfied, rather than among the marginals themselves, who on the whole remain relatively inarticulate about their condition. The worst consequence of the new emancipatory movements is the eroding effects of ever more finely tuned standards of equity when applied to the give and take of democratic politics — not to speak of the impact on more fragile and tentative democratic regimes like Czechoslovakia or Argentina today.[15]

It has also been suggested that institutional democracy, because it is democratic, tends to be self-rectifying. It co-opts those who make equity claims. It mollifies and reconciles (without giving too much away in the process), although more often later than sooner. This tension between the co-opting tendencies of political democracy and the resistance to them, one of the most interesting and least explored aspects of democratic political life, involves a process of absorption. The state needs to be able to convert the self-proclaimed principles of the movement into interests and then engage in negotiation and bargaining. But this can only be done when those infuriated by the process can no longer wield principle as their only claim to equity.

THE DIALECTIC OF THE MODELS

This discussion locates emancipatory inversionary discourse at the intersection between state and society and between tendencies towards monolithic beliefs and fragmenting alternatives. The most extreme invent discourses which up-end normal standards of rationality. How threatening they will be to institutional democracies has not been discussed. But it has been suggested that such movements are not likely to succeed on their own terms because of the way the double market works as an information and accountability system. The market, politically and economically, cuts across the most exclusivist boundaries. It stimulates not only a multiplicity of roles but the cross-cutting of their networks. Nothing remains impermeable, neither class nor ethnicity, nor even religion. The political system works because both groups and individuals come to require and indeed rely on funds of practical information that continuously flow throughout the system, from bottom to top and top to bottom. Rhetoric works for a while, and indeed may generate new truths, but it has a way of disappearing in the face of the concrete and the practical. And at that point everything is reversed. The new truths appear as pretentious and false. The old and discredited common sense returns. Once the marketplace begins to work as a choice system it is continuously self-reinforcing. Choice creates wants rather than wants creating choice. Decisions are designed to appeal, please or placate voters, break down cleavages. Continuously reforming coalitions within or between parties, interests and other groups ensures that while no problem is decisively resolved if the solution offends some, few problems are totally ignored if they become politically relevant as information.[16]

This, it might be argued, is too complacent a view which pays insufficient attention to those for whom choice is illusory and access to the market minimal. But it is also the case that the progressive rectification of such conditions for and by particular groups is a good deal of what the democratic process is about. Which poses the question whether today's emancipatory movements are really as different from earlier ones as they might appear.

There certainly are some fundamental differences. As suggested earlier, virtually all the old radical movements accepted the same principles of rationality and equity embodied in institutional democracy. Their demands were for more equal political access leading to compensatory social policies. In today's inversionary discourse movements, emancipation is fundamentally different in the sense that it is aimed not at reducing the negativity of otherness, as embodied in the colonial, the subaltern, the prisoner, *vis-à-vis* the main stream, but to 'liberate' the mainstream from itself. Of course this is also the oldest and most fundamental principle of emancipatory movements, from Christianity to Marxism, i.e. that those suppressed by the normal boundaries of the society will redeem the whole.

Whatever one can say about them, inversionary discourse movements are not content with claiming simply equity or equality. They want to liberate society from its own institutional and ideological structures. They are concerned with fundamental relationships, with Hegel's masters and slaves rather than with the right to vote. They favour the kind of total uprooting that would put the rest of society at risk. They consider the differences between theory and practice in democracies to be so great that only a radical project, continuous and threatening the legitimacy not of this government or that but of the institutional democratic model itself, will suffice. If in theory, for example, institutional democracies see a freed slave as no longer a *slave* but a citizen and an individual, for a good many emancipatory movements he or she remains a freed slave, i.e. neither free, nor slave, nor citizen until the language itself changes and new discourse emerges. Whereas from a state point of view no further 'emancipation' is necessary or desirable, from a movement point of view this represents the myth rather than the substance of democracy. For modern emancipatory movements this is not, and cannot be, good enough.

We have placed in juxtaposition, then, two 'models', inversionary discourse and institutional democracy. We now see them in a permanent struggle. The first challenges the second, attacking it as a system of signs, of signifiers which lead to a reductive consciousness which only genuine inversionary movements can reveal. Such movements draw their inspiration from the broad tradition of critical theory beginning with Marx. To seek out and identify those forms of repression which institutional democracy hides or disguises is to expose the institutional democratic model in theory, revealing its exclusionary and repressive characteristics. Emancipatory movements are seen to rewrite both the history and pedigree of the state itself and impose on it their own specific agenda. Inversionary discourse turns against both the democratic political telos of open ends and self-improvement, and its operating principles: access, participation, accountability and equality.

The point is, of course, that inversionary discourse models pay little attention to the growing range of diversities in the needs and wants of individuals and groups, public and private, and in their dual roles of consumers and citizens. They condense by focusing on those marginalized in the process. This enables them to articulate tensions at the boundaries of social life and the political system. There is revulsion at administered coalition. But in the name of revealed truths one finds also a politics of illusions. Even the most radical social movements of the past understood that no matter how necessary it might be to shove needed changes down the throats of classes or élites anxious to maintain privileges, or get rid of old regimes, there were limits to how far one could go before commonly understood rationality rules were violated.

EMANCIPATION AS POSTMODERN POLITICS

There is a sense in which the new emancipatory movements, as creators of myth and theory, and of symbolic rather than economic capital, represent a kind of postmodern politics. This is true to the extent that they concentrate on action as social text and interpretation as political reality. They are inversionary not only in terms of classes and groups who have less economic and political power or access and are seeking more, but also in regarding the discourse of normal politics as itself disingenuous at best and the information based on the market as false, mystified, commodified and hegemonic. Here the emphasis is not only on shattering the conventional boundaries of political language and discourse but the validity of the boundaries imposed by nations and states. This then is the permanently subversive project, which has less to do with the question of institutional democracy no matter how well it performs, than with the irritations imposed by social life and the impositions it makes on unconventional forms of freedom. The role of emancipatory movements in terms of struggles between state and society is an old one. But the question is whether this new postmodern form as I have described it is really a claim based on the old form, i.e. a moral claim, which has a new object, the displacement of all forms of social discipline and a return of the ideal of emancipation as the liberated being. If so no state is tolerable because it represents a 'veil of ignorance' behind which power itself lies. Institutional democracy then is nothing more than a politics of disguise, dissimulation, spectacle and manipulation. It is the job of emancipatory movements following an inversionary discourse model to explode democracy as a mode of consciousness, and with it the market principle and information itself, and so weaken the hegemony exercised by the state that its legitimacy will be destroyed. People will become aware of what is going on in the name of democracy. Democracy itself will be radically altered – precisely how hardly matters. The grand design is in the attack, not in the solution. In terms of inversionary discourse, democracy is the highest stage of false consciousness, the mystified shell of institutional democracy hiding its rationalistic core.[17]

These then are some of the objects of critical theory as inversionary discourse. To reveal the audacity of the enterprise it has been necessary to describe how the institutional democratic model works on *its* own terms, explicating the ingredients of its discourse and state which inversionary discourse theory aims to up-end. By showing the dynamics of the inversionary discourse model we can also see how the more sweeping and far-reaching its scope and aims, the more likely it is that power gained will be abused. But what I have also tried to show is that the more fundamental the desired transformation, and the more 'fundamentalist' the movement, the more a conversion will occur for which its leaders are not prepared. That is, if initially they are so able to mobilize public support that they come to represent society against the state, once in power the situation will be reversed. For then it is the public which needs to be transformed. The new state is quickly at odds with the society. Rigoristic and authoritarian methods are used in the name of principle. Hence emancipatory movements, where they succeed, are likely to become the problem rather than its solution, the Soviet Union being a good example. One can hardly think of a more dramatic inversionary, totalizing, emancipatory project than the Chinese Revolution, especially in its moral moment in Yan'an in the years 1936–47, where in caves the survivors of the Long March created the simulacrum of a new society, formed doctrines out of the dialectical interpretation of their experiences, modified Marxism to fit local conditions and indeed, through a process of learning and literacy, poring over texts in the midst of war with the Japanese and revolution against the Kuomintang, formed a discourse community on the basis of a process of exegetical bonding. A revolutionary people of the book, they found in Yan'an their Archimedean point for overturning the world as they found it. By the same token, today those former Yan'anites now represent the oppressive state. Once liberating principles became hegemonic for those who, in Tiananmen Square, tried to create their own miniaturized version of a democratic alternative.

Inversionary discourse then is always potentially explosive and never innocent. Morever, since much of the self-evidential superiority of democracy is attached to moral development through knowledge and education, it is not surprising that a prime venue for confrontations involving inversionary discourse has been educational institutions. In the 1960s it was not only a question of power but also a transformation of the discourse, the smashing of conventional languages and the creation of situations which up-ended all forms of conventionality. It is not an accident that the evolution of action into theory along these lines, the text of language smashing, was best personified by the Situationists, who saw in spectacle, the possibilites opened up by semiotic mobilization. There are plenty of those in authority who consider this radical project in the university in terms of conflicts over the curriculum, the canon and what subjects should or should not be taught, but there was also the question of who shall define the nature of educational experience. Which leads us to what might be called the current state of the debate. If institutional democracy and inversionary discourse constitute adversarial models, they also provide an opening for a third discourse, 'neo-institutionalism'.

Here we can find critics on both sides of the conflict. Concerned with the inadequate scope of the state in the fine tuning of social justice, they are aware that the more the state widens its arenas of responsibility on behalf of citizens and enlarges the scope of its jurisdiction, the more such intervention spills over, infringes and imposes the public upon the private sphere. The result is that the state becomes more an instrument of its own than of societal interests.

This introduces an interesting paradox. The more institutional democracy is a project of perpetual reform, the more reform reduces its responsiveness, that is, it becomes less responsive, less accountable and more bureaucratic. Decision-makers are separated further from those whom they are supposed to serve and the state becomes a vast glacial administration. Not that Evans, Skocpol, Birnbaum, Offe and others would suggest that reform movements, enlarging civil rights, enfranchisement of the working class and women, trade unionism and the wide range of other social movements which characterized the evolution of democratic institutions, make the state less democratic. Rather, in considering the gaps between theory and practice and the history of resistance by the state to reform, they see it as necessarily duplicitous.

Whatever one's specific political preference there is a genuine problem here. Democracy tends to separate the state from society at a decision-making level even as it becomes closer to it in terms of public support. In so far as this renders the content of politics relatively empty of meaning, it becomes precisely what critical theorists consider false consciousness. That is, if democracy which is based on the principle of choice, offers the illusion of choices, then the differences between substance and reality become the focal point of attack. Hence emancipatory movements using inversionary discourse find ways to show how meaning loss occurs, how the language, discourse, signs and signifiers of democracy become a form of 'magic realism'. It is precisely this kind of attack which leads one to consider emancipatory movements using inversionary discourse as a postmodern phenomenon, the more so as a good many modern democracies move further away from social democracy and socialism, and towards greater privatization and the broadening of interest group politics (Leca and Papini, 1985; Apter, 1987: Ch. 1).

CONCLUSION

This leads to a not very satisfactory conclusion to this already overextended discussion. For all the talk and on all sides, there are still very few ideas about how the design of the state might be altered specifically to reflect or respond to its critics. If much critical theory has revealed hidden and hegemonic aspects of conventional rationality as it takes different forms – expertise, knowledge, technique, innovation, etc. – it has been short on prescriptive solutions.[18] Hence its main value is to provide us with terms for evaluating democracy in ways it does not evaluate itself. Such a view suggests that one ought to accept or reject the propriety of demands, the righting of wrongs, the reclaiming of lost patrimonies or pretensions to some higher truth, in terms of impacts on democracy itself, that is the enlargement of choice such that it strengthens the relationship between equity, allocation, growth and order.

By the same token one ought never to take emancipatory movements at face value, that is in terms of their solutions. Experience shows that movements which best define some overarching or transcendental goal and pursue it in the name of some overriding truth end up as hegemonic and restrictive, reducing rather than enlarging choice. Such movements need to act in this way if they have any hopes of being successful. But widely different experiences in Africa or in Latin America, or revolutionary transformations as in the former USSR and China, show that no matter how principled the ends or admirable the purposes, most movements demonstrate a remarkable lack of success in promoting democratic regimes by any definition of the term. The problem with emancipatory movements is that even when they bring up the right issues they wind up with the wrong solutions. Having said that, one hastens to add that this may also denigrate too much and too sweepingly. One needs to know about specific emancipatory movements, examine their internal system tendencies, their discourses and symbolic power and the larger political contexts in which they act before assessing whether the result will generate reform, redefine equity, in a fashion broadening the scope of democracy itself.[19]

But the value of inversionary discourse is that by defining marginality, victimness and otherness are the starting points of inversionary discourse – homosexual, prisoner, black, female, 'orientalism', colonialism, etc. One becomes aware of the many levels and layers of sensitivity there are to forms of domination and hegemony which are obscure or entirely lacking from the perspective of the state, even the most democratic state. For example, inversionary discourse is rarely content with establishing straightforward legal notions of equity or equality, one in which say women have the same rights as men, or blacks as whites, but aim at that network of 'dominations' built into the total range of customary boundaries which society and the state take for granted. Inversionary discourse sees the power of the state in its 'taken-for-grantedness'.

In these terms, the hidden major premise is that the more democratic a society becomes, the more of a facade it really is, a mere expression of popular culture masking hidden power interests. By reflecting institutions as they perpetuate hegemony in the name of democracy, the public is complicit in its own foolishness. Hence, as with Hegel's master and slave, it can only be through the articulation of alternative and subversive discourses that this complicity will be revealed, and democracy made, indeed, more democratic. So behind the notion of inversionary discourse is the idea of a transcending insight. Just as the slave, the victim, transcends the knowledge of the master, and understands how limited the latter's understanding is, so that insight becomes a form of empowerment.

I began this discussion with two kinds of question. One had to do with ideology, the other with the absorption limits of democracy, the question of how far it can change in response to demands. Both the concept of ideology and the grammar or structure of democracy were 'exploded' by means of a theory of discourse. I showed how emancipatory movements were designed to break that discourse with its implication of order as an equity both defined by and naturalized in a market producing a moving equilibrium. I also suggested how such movements punctured the language of rationality, self-interest and bargaining that a choice model implies, as well as how they redefine boundaries and go beyond limits imposed by the democratic state.

All this raises far larger theoretical questions. How far ought one to go in using marginality, victimness or otherness, or any outrageous condition, as the basis for evaluating democracy as a system? To what extent should a whole society be held hostage to inversionary discourse? On the other hand, despite the apparent dangers to the institutional democratic state posed by inversionary discourse, in the long term is its consequence not an improving one, advancing the scope and meaning of the equity statement (equity, allocation, growth and order)?

To answer this we should distinguish between orders of inversionary discourse. First-order inversionary discourse based on direct confrontation seems to be the most directly threatening but, in fact, usually leads to mediation. Second-order inversionary discourse is more threatening because it discounts the conventional discourse and seeks to displace it. By the time it reaches the third order, it becomes a thing in itself, a displacing claim which discredits the entire structure of mediating discourse on which the institutional democratic model depends. One might say then that the least activist and the most intellectual is in fact the most dangerous except for the fact that it is largely the plaything of intellectuals whose pieties are longer than their remedies.

That said, it is not the whole story. So long as there is a certain deadpan quality to the common-sense world, an imperviousness to injustices that go deeper than ameliorative reform can rectify, inversionary discourse theory will be required to shock, to get people to pay attention.[20] One needs inversionary discourse no matter how infuriating and insufferable its protagonists. But to accept this point of view requires one to take the long view. It is especially difficult to accept when its immediacy, and its desire to shock, both the text and violence, raw anger, violation, of place and circumstances, body and soul, the stuff of which inversionary discourse is made, force one's attention to what one might prefer to ignore, not to see, to keep invisible. In this respect inversionary discourse violates everything that appears to be ordinary, stable and taken for granted. Hence the implication of this analysis is that one must take both the choice model and democracy and inversionary discourse in juxtaposition, to see their alterity as in some sense mutually necessary. Inversionary discourse by the very challenges it poses, forces people to react, to respond and sometimes to think even when such responses are more reflexive than reflective. This suggests too that by providing information left out by the double marketplace, inversionary discourse models provide an alternative means to checking and balancing by stimulating continuous change and alteration of boundaries (Mudimbe, 1988; Asad, 1973). Change in this sense is a bumpy process, the product of threats, reactions to threats and eventual accommodations.

The genius of the democratic model, and its principle of moving equilibrium, is that along with the balancing of interests between the economic and political market it also absorbs these bumps which are as necessary to democracy as the smoother process of coalition formation and bargaining. For in this way it eventually includes or incorporates even while it appears to exclude. Because inversionary discourses challenge in particular those negativized boundaries whose real consequence is to delimit too narrowly choice for some, democracy re-engages the limits of choice for all. Movements which seek to change the meaning of the rules by changing the terms of choice in effect affirm the rules themselves.

NOTES

1. The special significance of education is that it enables people to make personal predictions based on relevant information, to deal with the conditions of their immediate circumstances and connect causes to effects.

2. As, for example, the bitter protest movements in Japan despite its extraordinary economic accomplishments; see Apter and Sawa (1984).

3. The economic market is coterminous with the political one, but it follows its own dynamics. A modern version equivalent of Adam Smith's assumption that everyone has a 'natural propensity to truck, barter and exchange', it represents a presumption of universal rationality – a rationality applying to individuals everywhere in their roles as producers and consumers. Without it the political marketplace alone, as applied to citizens, would lead to a Hobbesian choice, a survivalist notion of self-protection, making an institutional democratic polity impossible.

4. See Foucault (1970). The chief quality of the classical age is the representation and organization of signs as resemblances. The discourse was a function of recognizing what those signs signified. See especially pp. 56–69.

5. Ruthlessly following out the implications of the dissolution of the old episteme, his redefinition of order in terms of centralized power was consonant more with protecting rather than maximizing choice. Hobbes sought the institutional ground for a minimal definition of choice.

6. For a fuller treatment of such matters, see Apter (1991).

7. In these terms, the main improved versions are social welfare and the social democratic state. The first evolved out of classic liberal capitalism as the political market assumed greater significance. The result has been an enlargement of the state itself and especially its compensatory and entitlement programmes to those 'marginal' in terms of effective political participation. In the US and elsewhere this has been done on a more or less temporary or *ad hoc* basis, with fiscal and monetary policy a major mechanism of decisional efficacy, i.e. the social welfare state. In the social welfare state equity and justice are realized first in terms of the political market and then in law, the rights of citizens being universalistic.

The other tradition, deriving from class-based socialism, is social democracy. Inspired by the recognition that working-class power could be realized by party politics and electoral superiority rather than revolution it derived from a diverse pedigree – Engels (after 1895), revisionism, Lassalleanism, utopianism – and aimed less at revolution than capturing parliamentary majorities, thus taking executive power. By this means, social democracy could then use the authority of the state to eliminate private property and increase social justice. Today, however, social democracy is no longer class based. It accepts private property. It relies less on nationalization and planning and has moved away from socialism except in terms of an appropriate definition of equality. Social democracy assumes that there will be social casualties which result from the private sector and assumes that accordingly compensatory or entitlement programmes are necessary and permanent obligations of the state.

8. Something which Adam Smith recognized in his *Theory of Moral Sentiments* (Smith, 1966). Even in his day the rationality of the economic marketplace alone was too primitive a notion, too unadorned a view of human nature. Economic rationality defines a world of insupportable principles: hence his notion of 'sympathy'.

9. If by the very nature of the choice-vector process it can only utilize processes which are slow, cumbersome and complex, and 'boundaries' can only be readjusted haltingly, this is because choice involves changing boundaries while order means sustaining them.

10. Variations in form but not in principle include parliamentary and presidential systems, consociationalism, pluralism, Dahl's polyarchy and Shil's civic culture. On a right–left spectrum one can include liberal utilitarianism and socialist transformationalism, the centre-left social democracy and the centre-right social welfare state, as well as Birnbaum's distinctions between strong and weak states. The institutional outputs so generated are designed to make the political system self-perpetuating in the form of a moving equilibrium. This political system contains and reinforces all social boundaries within its jurisdiction, and provides rules while leaving choices or ends open.

11. A good example is found in Goodman (1970).

12. The veiling issue was significant because it called into question a number of these assumptions. Moreover, it extended 'difference' into the next generation, among those born in France. It infringes on a principle of French education which since Durkheim's day has been virtually sacrosanct, that secular educational institutions are designed to socialize and integrate students into the civic culture of France. Hence veiling, the demarcation of difference for a next generation in the school system, is a provocation.

13. Moreover, this was also the case in colonial territories. One could be assimilated in a colony by becoming 'evolved'. One became an *évolué* mainly in terms of education, and in French language, culture and social role, as well as dress, etc. Assimilation was a legal status. In Algeria those who became assimilated enjoyed the rights and privileges of being French, but in France there were no such rights for Algerians as Algerians, or Muslims as Muslims, nor was it anticipated that there would be.

14. Among the characteristics of inversionary discourse are the uses of spectacle and the spectacular, including visual alterations that violate conventional boundaries, whether in dress, smearing of bodies and faces, hair, gestures, occupation of space, the use of graffiti, etc. See for example Marcus (1989).

15. Fragility in this sense means that democratic principles of the state are weakly institutionalized in society and while forms and even practices may be observed, these are only instrumental, that is, they work as long as they work.

16. The private sphere includes individual rights as well as property. The public sphere is secured by law and authority. The private sector is separate from but not autonomous of the state. The state sector is more or less accountable to the private. The individual is both a citizen and a consumer. As a consumer he or she is a voter

registering political preferences for leaders, policies and parties. The two roles intersect in the double marketplace of goods and services and leadership preference.

17. The theory behind this interpretation goes back of course to Marx. More contemporary renditions can be found in the work of Foucault, Baudrillard, Lyotard, Jameson and Offe. See, in particular, Offe (1984).

18. For example, Foucault's work on institutions of the insane, prisons, not to speak of his analysis of sexuality, identifies the oppressive boundaries in society which the state represents 'democratically', or how authority and power, validated as 'expertise', perpetuate the hegemony of those who define madness, criminality and sustain conventional boundaries. Those whose job it is to relieve the condition of the poor derive power from the principle of responsibility rather than the responsible exercise of it. Hence the tyranny of insane asylums, prisons and the boundaries that define the very nature of male and female, and their appropriate relations.

19. It is interesting in this regard that Joseph A. Schumpeter made a somewhat similar argument years ago, i.e. that capitalism would give way to socialism not because it is an economically inferior system to the latter, but because its inability to resolve the unemployment problem would generate alienation and antagonism especially from intellectuals and others whose support is necessary for it to survive. See Schumpeter (1947).

20. This was particularly the discovery of such figures as Bataille, Sartre and others who in the 1930s in France belonged to the 'Secret Society', the 'College of Sociology'. See Hollier (1979).

REFERENCES

Apter, D.E. (1964) 'Introduction', in D.E. Apter (ed.) *Ideology and Discontent*, pp. 15–46. New York: Macmillan/Free Press.

Apter, D.E. (1971) *Choice and the Politics of Allocation*. New Haven, CT: Yale University Press.

Apter, D.E. (1987) *Rethinking Development*. Newbury Park, CA: Sage.

Apter, D.E. (1991) 'Institutionalism Reconsidered', *International Social Science Journal* 129: 493–513.

Apter, D.E. and Sawa, N. (1984) *Against the State*. Cambridge, MA: Harvard University Press.

Arrow, K.J. (1963) *Social Choice and Individual Values*. New Haven, CT: Yale University Press.

Asad, T. (ed.) (1973) *Anthropology and the Colonial Encounter*. New York: Humanities Press.

Barry, B. (1965) *Political Argument*. London: Routledge and Kegan Paul.

Baudart, A. and Pena-Ruiz, H. (eds) (1991) *Les Preaux de la Republique*. Paris: Minerve.

Boudon, R. (1989) *The Analysis of Ideology*. Chicago, IL: University of Chicago Press.

Bourdieu, P. (1977) *Outline of a Theory of Practice*. Cambridge: Cambridge University Press.

Downs, A. (1957) *An Economic Theory of Democracy*. New York: Harpers.

Foucault, M. (1970) *The Order of Things*. New York: Pantheon.

Geertz, C. (1964) 'Ideology as a Cultural System', in D.E. Apter (ed.) *Ideology and Discontent*, pp. 47–76. New York: Macmillan/Free Press.
Goodman, M. (1970) *The Movement Towards a New America*. New York: Alfred A. Knopf.
Hollier, D. (ed.) (1979) *The College of Sociology 1937–1939*. Minneapolis, MN: The University of Minnesota Press.
Lawson, K. and Merkl, P. (eds) (1987) *When Parties Fail*. Princeton, NJ: Princeton University Press.
Leca, J. and Papini, R. (1985) *Les Democraties sont elles gouvernables?* Paris: Economica.
Marcus, G. (1989) *Lipstick Traces. A Secret History of the Twentieth Century*. Cambridge, MA: Harvard University Press.
Mudimbe, V.Y. (1988) *The Invention of Africa: Gnosis, Philosophy and the Order of Knowledge*. Bloomington, IL and Indianapolis, IN: Indiana University Press.
Offe, C. (1984) *Contradictions of the Welfare State*. Cambridge, MA: MIT Press.
Olson, M., Jr (1965) *The Logic of Collective Action*. Cambridge, MA: Harvard University Press.
Rawls, J. (1971) *A Theory of Justice*. Cambridge, MA: Harvard University Press.
Rey, J.-M. (1971) *L'Enjeu des signes*. Paris: Editions du Seuil.
Schumpeter, J.A. (1947) *Capitalism, Socialism and Democracy*. New York: Harpers.
Smith, A. (1966) *A Theory of Moral Sentiments*. New York: Kelley (first edn 1759).

David E. Apter is the Henry J. Heinz II Professor of Comparative Political and Social Development at Yale University (Department of Political Science, PO Box 3532, Yale Station, New Haven, CT 06520–3532). He has published monographic studies and articles on nationalist movements and state formation in Africa, emancipatory movements in Japan, and revolutionary transformation in China. He has been particularly interested in the connection between developmental change and radical political discourse. His most recent books are *Against the State* (with Nagayo Sawa, Harvard, 1984) and *Rethinking Development* (Sage, 1987). He is currently working on two books, *Mao's Republic* and *Violence and Democracy*.

Subjectivity, Experience and Knowledge: An Epistemology from/for Rainbow Coalition Politics

Sandra Harding

INTRODUCTION

'Difference' has come to play a complex role in feminist theory and politics, as is increasingly the case in other liberatory social movements in the US. Feminists criticized the idea of 'universal man' and his transhistorical rationality; what has been claimed to be true for 'man' and 'reason' is in fact characteristic (at best) only of men in the dominant groups in the West and the forms of reason that they favour.[1] Neo-Marxists and post-Marxists have continued the older critique of 'rational economic man' and his bourgeois reason;[2] critics identified the distinctively Eurocentric character of Western assumptions about man and reason (Mudimbe, 1988; Amin, 1989; Said, 1978); and criticisms of the 'straight mind' have added compulsory heterosexuality to the coercive social structures that generated partial and distorted accounts of nature and social life (Wittig, 1980; Frye, 1983).

However, these groups are increasingly forced to recognize that the logic of each of these critiques also undermines the legitimacy of generalizations from the speaker's situation to *all* women, or workers, or people of colour, or lesbians/gays, as the case may be. If there is no universal or even typical man and his transcendental reason, then there also can be no universal or typical woman, worker, person of colour, lesbian or gay person and her or his unified and uniquely legitimate reason either. Many different feminisms are generated from different conditions of women's lives. Feminism and the other new social movements must have multiple subjects of their history and knowledge projects. In so far as women,

Development and Change (SAGE, London, Newbury Park and New Delhi), Vol. 23 (1992) No. 3, 175–193.

for example, live in oppositional race, class and sexuality relations to each other, the subject of feminist knowledge will be not just multiple, but also contradictory or 'incoherent'. I shall refer to this second difference concern as one about the multiple subjects of liberatory knowledge and politics.

Since Western thought has assumed only unitary and coherent subjects, it can feel as if one has dropped through Alice's rabbit hole when one tries to pursue the consequences of multiple subjectivity for conventional philosophic issues and conventional understandings of progressive politics: assumptions that appeared virtually unquestionable suddenly appear quite problematic. Here I want to explore some consequences of the logic of multiple subjects for thinking about who can make liberatory knowledge and history, the relationship between experience and knowledge, between subjectivity and experience, and between subjectivity and objectivity. These are huge topics, but I hope to make at least some small progress towards clarifying and complexifying them even in so brief a discussion. I begin by reviewing what is meant by the claim that the subject of feminist (or any other kind of liberatory) knowledge is multiple.

MULTIPLE SUBJECTS OF KNOWLEDGE AND HISTORY

The logic of difference developed by the new social movements in opposition to the dominant culture returns to undermine tendencies within those movements to generalize from the patterns of life and thought of an imagined 'revolutionary subject' to all of the marginalized peoples for whom the movement purportedly speaks. Not only is there no typical 'woman' about whom feminism can make claims regarding her situation in family life or wage labour, her sexuality or her political priorities; there is also no such typical or ideal woman who is the author/subject/agent/speaker of feminist thought. Gender is supposed to be both the distinctive subject matter and analytic tool of feminism. But the logic of multiple subjects has led some feminists to think that feminism must choose between this logic and feminism's focus on gender. This perception leads some feminists in the dominant groups to feel threatened by the insistence of women of colour, poor women, lesbians and 'ethnic' women that difference must be centred within feminist analyses, and not just between them and the dominant culture, so to speak. Of course the same kind of point can be made about the archetypal worker who is the political and epistemological subject of Marxism, and about 'the African-American', 'the lesbian', etc. Indeed, many analysts and political workers in the other new social movements (but certainly not all of them) consistently resist dealing with the sexism, racism, Eurocentrism, classism and/or heterosexism that infest their analyses and politics. Moreover, the bad consequences of relegating difference only to the object of study within these movements has been widely criticized. Of course, an 'imbalance of historic ignorance'[3] leaves white women ignorant about the material conditions, feelings and thoughts of women of colour, and this uneven development of knowledge must be straightened out. However, my concern here is with difference in the *subject* of knowledge, not as its object.

Two unfortunate tendencies have prevailed in mainstream feminist attempts to deal with the differences between women as subjects of knowledge only by including (adding to) the mainstream analyses the perspectives of marginalized women. The first tendency notes the necessity of acknowledging difference, but then offers a number of reasons for actually refraining from providing any analysis of difference and its consequences.

1. The speaker does not have enough information to carry out such a project. Now it is indeed true that processes of marginalization succeed in part by silencing the marginalized (denying them literacy, public voice, 'history', etc.);[4] but it is rare for the marginalized to be quite as silent as this excuse claims, as mainstream feminist scholarship itself has testified when faced with analogous claims by sexists.

2. There is not enough time or space available to provide such an analysis just now or here.

3. It is not the speaker's main concern here, which is to provide a 'feminist analysis' *rather* than one that considers perspectives from the lives of marginalized women on the topic of concern or why it is that marginalized women are *not* concerned with this topic. However, even the briefest reflection on the history of feminist responses to similar claims by sexists should lead immediately to the recognition that temptations to these responses show that there is something wrong with conceptualizing the issue as an additive one.

4. The speaker is not qualified to engage in such a project since the speaker has not had the experience of, say, African-Americans; and so only African-Americans can speak to (or from)

the conditions of African–American lives, etc. Articulating experience is a crucial means of creating knowledge for everyone, and in special ways (to be discussed below) for marginalized peoples. But this reasoning about the relationship between experience and knowledge asks us to accept the counterintuitive claim that we should speak *only* of what we have directly experienced. While eyewitness accounts are valuable indeed, following such a principle would have serious consequences. For example, it would shut down science, since no scientist could possibly directly certify the reliability of every claim or assumption s/he made about her or his instruments, the irrelevance of background phenomena, the empirical support for the theories s/he used, etc. Whatever vulgar readings of scientific method may lead one to think about the relation between experience and knowledge, this claim would seem to limit everyone to a kind of solipsism or, at least, relativism. It would have the depressing and counterhistorical consequences that whites cannot create anti-racist knowledge, men cannot create anti-sexist knowledge, etc. – in short, that no one can ever learn anything from *anyone else's* experience.

A second unfortunate tendency actually carries out the additive project only called for by the first. However, while these accounts often provide plenty of descriptive details that marginalized women have reported about their lives, little attempt is made to explain the origins of such patterns of difference beyond references to the sexism of the men in these other cultures or the relation between the lives of marginalized women and women at the centre. Consequently, they do not reflect on the challenges to the speaker's agenda and conceptual scheme created when marginalized women can structure the research or political agenda rather than only 'appear' in feminist agendas constructed by dominant group women. These accounts frequently take the form of only 'studying down'. The speaker refrains from analysing how racism, imperialism, class exploitation and compulsory heterosexuality also structure the lives and thoughts of women in the favoured groups, such as the speaker's.

Popular opinion, supported by the dominant tendencies in US social science, conceptualizes gender, race, ethnicity and sexual orientation in ways that make it difficult to move past these additive approaches to difference. In order to do so, it is helpful to keep in mind three points. First, each must be reconceptualized as a relationship rather than as a 'thing' or inherent property of people. Race, gender, ethnicity and sexuality do not designate any fixed set of qualities or properties of individuals, social or biological, such that if one possesses these and only these properties then one is African-American, a man, an 'ethnic' or heterosexual.[5] Instead, masculinity is continuously defined and redefined as 'not femininity', 'coloured' as 'not white', etc. Second, these relations are deeply embedded in the structures of societies. Thus, sexism, racism, the politics of ethnicity (starting with who gets counted as ethnic) and compulsory heterosexuality are fundamentally matters of social structure, not of prejudice – that is of individual bad attitudes and false beliefs. The tendency to define racism as 'race prejudice' settles for an account that lodges responsibility for racism only on the already economically disadvantaged poor whites – the Archie Bunkers – who have not learned to avoid making overtly racist statements or have been rewarded for doing so as have middle-class people, and who are forced to bear a disproportionately large share of the burdens of affirmative action and equal opportunity programmes. Racism is enacted in many different ways, and overt individual prejudice is just one of them. It is fundamentally a political relationship, a strategy that 'systematically provides economic, political, psychological, and social advantages for whites at the expense of Blacks and other people of colour' (Wellman, 1977: 37), and it is a dynamic relationship that is flexible enough to adapt to changing historical conditions. Individuals *should* be held responsible for their beliefs and behaviours; it is wrong to express or enact these kinds of prejudices. But to rest satisfied with this analysis and its recommended remedies is to fail to come to grips with the institutional race (or gender, ethnicity or sexuality) supremacy that non-prejudiced individual beliefs and behaviours support and maintain.

Racism, sexism, class exploitation, ethnic subordination and heterosexism have their own distinctive histories, institutional forms and dynamics; they are not identical in their histories or structures, as my account here might suggest. Nevertheless, they are widely recognized to be similar enough that they can be understood in these common ways. Indeed, analogical reasoning from the theories and analytical strategies developed within one new social movement to the situation of those apparently intended to be included as 'revolutionary subjects' but, in fact, marginalized within that movement, provides an important resource for grasping the logic of multiple subjects. Thus, analogous accounts can be provided of sexism, class exploitation, the oppression of ethnic groups, racism and heterosexism.

These two points lead to a third. Systems of political hierarchy based on differences of gender, race, class, ethnicity and sexual orientation are not parallel to each other, as the preceding analysis suggests, but interlocked and mutually creating and maintaining.[6] A setback or advance in one reverberates through the whole network of hierarchy creating consequences far away from where such change began. This point clarifies why, for example, feminism can and must try to centre analyses from the perspective of marginalized women's lives. There are determinate causal relations between the lives of Third World and Western women, economically privileged and poor women, heterosexual women and lesbians, ethnic and 'non-ethnic' women, as well as between the men and women who have been the focus of feminist concern. From the perspective of this kind of understanding, it appears odd that some feminists have thought that the consequence of starting from a conceptual framework that centres differences between women must be to abandon gender as an analytic category and, thus, the attempt to produce distinctively feminist analyses. It is only 'transcendental gender' that would have been abandoned, and that is no more real than the 'transcendental man' feminists have criticized. If women and men can only be found in historically determinate races, classes, ethnicities and sexualities, then a gender analysis — one that is from the perspective of women's lives — must scrutinize gender *as it exists* and from the perspective of *all* women's lives. There is no other defensible choice. Refraining from centring multiple subjects in feminist analyses distorts not only the lives of marginalized women, but also of those at the centre. I cannot understand my own life or the causal social influences on my thought if I cannot understand how my actions and beliefs are shaped by institutional relations of race, class and heterosexist supremacy as well as by male supremacy. Indeed, to understand the latter just *is* to understand the former.

This brings us to the next challenge: if I must understand my life from the perspective of, say Third World women's lives, it cannot be that I am to speak *as* or *for* Third World women. Men must learn to see themselves as they appear from the perspective of women's lives, but it cannot be that men are to speak *as* women or *for* women. How does the logic of multiple subjects work itself out in terms of such anxiety-producing concerns?

BECOMING A MULTIPLE SUBJECT

Western thought has 'started out' from the lives of men in the dominant groups. It is their agendas and issues that have energized and structured this thought. Western thought is not the pinnacle of human thought, but only of the thought of that particular social group whose concerns it centres. All human thought is partial in the senses both of interested and of socially situated. But some interests and social situations are worse than others with respect to the degree of narrowness and distortion that tends to be generated in the thought they produce.

One main tendency in feminist epistemology has insisted that starting thought from women's lives decreases the partiality and distortion in our images of nature and social relations. It creates knowledge – not just opinion – that is, nevertheless, socially situated. It is still partial in both senses of the word, but less distorting than thought originating in the agendas and perspectives of the lives of dominant group men. This is the feminist standpoint theory developed by Dorothy Smith (1987), Nancy Hartsock (1983), Hilary Rose (1983), Alison Jaggar (1983: Ch. 1), Harding (1983, 1986: Ch. 6) and others. But, of course, as we have already discussed, women lead different lives from each other; there is no typical 'woman's life' from which feminists should start thought. Moreover, in many cases women's lives are not just different from each other's, but structurally opposed. For example, in the US, African-American and European-American women's lives are defined against each other by racist policy. African-American and European-American women often 'collude' in this oppositional strategy by defining themselves as 'not her'. (I do not mean to give equal weight on moral or intellectual scales to such creations of self: the European-American woman generates racism in such opposition; the African-American woman generates potentially revolutionary understandings of womanhood.) Nevertheless, all of these women's lives are in different respects valuable starting points for generating feminist knowledge. Thought that starts off from each of these different kinds of lives can generate less partial and distorted accounts of nature and social life. Thus, as explored above, there is not just one unitary and coherent 'speech' that is feminist thought or knowledge, but instead, these multiple and frequently contradictory knowings. Other liberatory movements have developed similar standpoint epistemology projects, whether or not they articulate them as such.

However, the subject/agent of feminist knowledge is multiple and frequently contradictory in a second way that mirrors the situation for women as a class. It is the thinker whose consciousness is bifurcated,[7] the outsider within,[8] the marginal person now also located at the centre,[9] the person who is committed to two agendas that are themselves at least partially in conflict – the liberal feminist, socialist feminist, Nicaraguan feminist, Jewish feminist or woman scientist – who has generated feminist sciences and new knowledge. It is thinking from a contradictory social position that generates feminist knowledge. So the logic of the directive to 'start thought from women's lives' requires that one start one's thought from multiple lives that are in many ways in conflict with each other, and each of which itself has multiple and contradictory commitments. In contrast, the subject of knowledge for both the conventional liberal/empiricist philosophy and for Marxism was supposed to be unitary and coherent. The condition of one kind of idealized knower – the rational man and the male proletarian, respectively – were to be created and generalized for all who would know.

This logic leads to the recognition that the subject of liberatory feminist knowledge must also be, in an important if controversial sense, the subject of every other liberatory knowledge project. This is true in the collective sense of 'subject of knowledge', for since lesbian, poor and racially marginalized women are all women, all feminists will have to grasp how gender, race, class and sexuality are used to construct each other. It will have to do so if feminism is to be liberatory for marginalized women, but also if it is to avoid deluding dominant group women about their/our own situations. If this were not so, there would be no way to distinguish between feminism and the narrow self-interest of dominant group women – just as conventional androcentric thought permits no criterion for distinguishing between 'best beliefs' and those that serve the self-interest of men as men. (Bourgeois thought permits no criterion for identifying specifically bourgeois self-interest; racist thought for identifying racist self-interest, etc.)

But the subject of every other liberatory movement must also learn how gender, race, class and sexuality are used to construct each other *in order to accomplish their goals*. That is, analysts of class relations must look at their agendas from the perspective of women's lives, too. In the first place, women, too, hold class positions.

Moreover, as many critics have pointed out, left agendas need to deal with the fact that bosses regularly and all too successfully attempt to divide the working class against itself by manipulating gender hostilities. If women are forced to tolerate lower wages and double-days of work, employers can fire men and hire women to make more profit, as they have frequently done. Anti-racist movements must look at their issues from the perspective of the lives of women of colour, too. And so forth. Everything that feminist thought must know must also inform the thought of every other liberatory movement – and vice versa. It is not just the *women* in those other movements who must know the world from the perspective of women's lives. Everyone must do so if the movements are to succeed at their own goals. Most importantly, this requires that women be active directors of the agendas of these movements. But it also requires that men in those movements be able to generate original feminist knowledge from the perspective of women's lives as, for example, John Stuart Mill, Marx and Engels, Frederick Douglass and later male feminists have done.

However, if every other liberatory movement must generate feminist knowledge, it cannot be that women are the unique generators of feminist knowledge. Women cannot claim this ability to be uniquely theirs, and men must not be permitted to claim that because they are not women, they are not obligated to produce fully feminist analyses. Men, too, must contribute distinctive forms of specifically feminist knowledge from their particular social situation. Men's thought, too, will begin first from women's lives in all the ways that feminist theory, with its rich and contradictory tendencies, has shown us all – women as well as men – how to do. It will start there in order to gain the maximally objective theoretical frameworks within which men can begin to describe and explain their own and women's lives in less partial and distorted ways. This is necessary if men are to produce more than that male supremacist 'folk belief' about themselves and the world they live in, to which female feminists object. Women have had to learn how to substitute the generation of feminist thought for the 'gender nativism' androcentric cultures encourage in them; female feminists are made, not born. Men, too, must learn to take historic responsibility for the social position from which they speak.

But if having women's experiences – being a woman – is not a necessary condition for generating feminist knowledge, what is the relation between experience and knowledge for the liberatory social movements? Is there no significant *epistemological* difference between a female feminist and a male feminist? Can whites produce 'African–American knowledge'? (Whether they should *claim* to do so is quite another matter!) From the perspective of conventional thought about the relations between subjectivity, experience and knowledge, an epistemological hornet's nest appears when one follows through the logic of multiple subjects and directs *everyone*, not just women, to start their thought from women's lives.

ACHIEVING SUBJECTIVITY AND GROUNDING KNOWLEDGE

Some feminists, and also some of their critics, have assumed that feminist-guided research and scholarship must be grounded in women's *experiences*. This assumption has been made for several reasons. First, feminism has argued that only the experiences of men in the dominant groups have grounded Western knowledge, so the generation of knowledge agendas and problematics, concepts, and interpretations of data originating in women's experiences would appear to provide a needed corrective for the distortions of androcentric thought. Second, consciousness raising – whether or not it is called that – has been an important *method* of gaining feminist understanding.[10] Central to consciousness raising is the act of articulating perceptions of one's experiences that are usually censured by the culture. Thus women articulated their 'illicit' ambivalence about their husbands, male co-workers, teachers, marriage, sexuality, families, children, mothers, etc. The shared knowledge created through such practices appears to be grounded in women's experience. Third, the terms 'standpoint', 'perspective', 'view' and 'experience' are often used interchangeably in everyday talk. If women are to speak, if their voices are to be heard in this culture, will they not be speaking from *their* standpoint, perspective, view and experience? Thus critics of feminist standpoint theory, too, have appeared to assume that those theorists are arguing that women's experiences must provide some sort of absolute grounds for feminist research and scholarship.[11]

Certainly one can learn from experience – and from others' reports of their experiences too. So experience must play some role in the creation of knowledge. However, I think that there is a second and crucial role that speaking of one's experience plays in the generation of knowledge for marginalized people. But in neither case does experience *ground* knowledge in any conventional sense. The reason why this relationship between experience and knowledge for the knowledge projects of the new social movements is so troublesome is, I suggest, because the prevailing theories of that relationship are those that have been produced from the perspective only of dominant group lives.

First, note the relationship between experience and knowledge required by the logic of standpoint epistemology. All women have women's experiences, but only at certain historical moments do any of us ever produce feminist knowledge. Our experience lies to us, and the dominant gender, class, race and sexuality experiences produce more airtight, comprehensive, widely believed and tenacious lies. Dominant group experience generates the 'common sense' of the age that is such fascinating subject matter to anthropologists and historians. Subjugated groups, especially, are forced to internalize and act out what dominant groups believe of them.[12] All of us must live in social relations that naturalize, or make appear necessary, social arrangements that are, in fact, optional at the cultural level; they have been created and made to appear natural by the power of the dominant groups.

Women's reports of their experiences illuminate aspects of human social relations that would not be visible if women did not speak of their experiences. We learn from our own and reports of others' experiences. But it cannot be that women's experiences or 'what women say' in themselves provide reliable grounds for knowledge claims about nature and social relations. Women say all kinds of things – misogynist statements, illogical arguments, misleading statements about an only partially understood situation, racist, class-biased and heterosexist claims. Feminists have been discovered to be making all these kinds of politically and scientifically inadequate claims. Women, and feminists, certainly are no worse in these respects than anyone else, but we, too, are often blind to the social constraints on our belief systems. Furthermore, there are many feminisms, and these can be understood to be starting off their analyses from the lives of different historical groups of women. Liberal feminism initially started off its analyses from the lives of women in the eighteenth- and nineteenth-century European and US educated classes; Marxist feminism from the lives of wage-working women in the nineteenth- and early twentieth-century industrializing or 'modernizing' societies; Third World feminism from the lives of late twentieth-century women of Third World descent, and so forth. Moreover, we all change our minds about all kinds of issues. As Uma Narayan (1988) has put it, women's 'epistemic privilege' does not include a privileged knowledge of the *causes* of their situation; nor does it mean that their understandings are incorrigible, that is, in principle immune from revision by them or anyone else; or that their dominators can *never* come to understand what women understand; nor is the claim to epistemic privilege the same as the claim that the oppressed should speak for themselves.[13] So women's experiences and what women say make important contributions to the creation of knowledge without providing conventional epistemic grounds for deciding just which among competing claims to knowledge should be regarded as preferable.

However, for women to name and describe their experiences in their own terms is a crucial scientific and epistemological act in another respect upon which the above discussion has not yet touched. Members of marginalized groups must *struggle* to name their own experiences *for* themselves in order to claim the subjectivity, the possibility of historical agency, that is given to members of dominant groups at birth (or at least, as psychoanalytic theorists report, in infancy). Dominant group males are inserted into language, history and culture as legitimate speakers and historical agents through no acts of their own, so to speak. They do not have to exert effort in order to 'see themselves in history', or to imagine themselves as authoritative speakers and actors. Their 'Dick and Jane' books, television programmes, observable family and community social relations and, perhaps most importantly, the structure of language itself already tell them that they are the 'right stuff' to make community, history and the subjects of sentences. They simply *are* the subjectivities who *have* experience that provides the raw material for creating dominant group conceptions of knowledge and history. For women and other marginalized groups, subjectivity and its possibility of 'experience' must be achieved; they are made, not born.[14]

This denial of subjectivity has material conditions. It has been illegal for slaves to read and write. Through formal and informal exclusionary policies, it has been difficult even for women in the dominant groups to gain access to read the languages used to create and report knowledge, social theory and public policy. It has been illegal for women to speak in public, difficult for them to publish their thoughts or to travel without male chaperones. It is hard to teach philosophy without books, note several of the contributors to a special issue of *Philosophical Forum* (1987) on apartheid.

But even this way of putting the point is not quite right. It is too tame. It too quickly integrates the difficult and often painful struggle of marginalized people to name their experience and so to gain a self-defined self into the epistemological, scientific and political projects of élites. For marginalized people, naming one's experience publicly is a cry for survival. As the African-American literary critic Barbara Christian (1987: 61) writes, 'what I write and how I write is done in order to save my own life. And I mean that literally. For me literature is a way of knowing that I am not hallucinating, that whatever I feel/know *is*.'[15] Henry Louis Gates argues that Frederick Douglass, like other narrators of slave autobiographies, faced the difficult task of writing into subjectivity and into history both himself and all of the other slaves whose lives would be represented by his story.

> . . . the black slave's narrative came to be a communal utterance, a collective tale, rather than merely an individual's autobiography. Each slave author, in writing about his or her personal life's experiences, simultaneously wrote on behalf of the millions of silent slaves still held captive throughout the South. Each author, then, knew that *all* black slaves would be judged – on their character, integrity, intelligence, manners and morals, and their claims to warrant emancipation – on this published evidence provided by one of their number. (Gates, 1987: x)

For Douglass, his own survival and that of millions of others depended on his ability and that of other ex-slaves to fashion their self-understandings into narratives that voiced/'created' the humanity of the silent slaves. Abdul JanMohammed (1987) notes that for Richard Wright, the choices were literally death or the recovery/creation of his own subjectivity. So for marginalized peoples to speak of their experiences is a crucial ontological and political act, the act that creates them as the kind of people who can make knowledge and history. Knowledge from the perspective of women's lives could not occur without this public act of women naming their experience in their terms. It is subjectivities that legitimate knowledge claims, but it takes difficult, painful and frequently violent struggles to create these subjectivities. Marginal subjectivity is exactly what the dominant groups cannot permit.[16]

Nor is the naming and articulating of marginalized experience a task completed at any particular moment in history. It is a continuous process, as long as oppression, exclusion and silencing exist.

Unless, for example, African-Americans have the resources continuously to name their experience in their terms – the literacy, the university positions, the government consultancies, the policy directorates, etc. – all of us, African-American or not, will be able to generate only partial and distorted accounts of nature and social relations.

TRANSFORMING SUBJECTIVITIES

But if the subjectivities required to create knowledge can be *made* through social processes, then they can also be transformed through such processes. Members of the dominant groups, too, can learn how to see the world from the perspective of experiences and lives that are not theirs. After all, no woman was born with a feminist subjectivity. Women have had to learn to think from perspectives about women's lives that were not initially visible to them from 'their' perspective on 'their' life. 'Their' lives and perspectives were structured by the patriarchal ideology of femininity, not by feminism. In order to transform feminine into feminist lives, they have had to listen to themselves and to other women telling about their lives, to reflect on the gender (and class, race and sexuality) aspects of their lives, to take on acts of resistance to male supremacy, to reflect on the consequences of those acts, to learn various feminist theories about gender relations that provided contexts into which they could insert their own experiences and perspectives, and so forth. They have had to *become* feminists. And if they are, say, European-Americans, they have had to start listening to women of colour – and then themselves in contrast – tell about their lives, reflect on the race aspects of their experiences, take on acts of resistance to race supremacy, reflect on the consequences of those acts, learn various theories produced by people of colour about race relations and imperialism that provided contexts into which they could insert their own experiences and perspectives, and so forth. That is, they have had to learn how to become feminists who can function effectively as anti-racists (who *are* anti-racist), rather than ones who, intentionally or not, perpetuate race supremacy. They have had to learn to take historical responsibility for their race, for the white skins from which they speak and act.

But there is nowhere in this process where it would be appropriate to say that such a white person spoke *as* or *for* women of colour.

Only a woman of colour can speak *as* such; and women of colour must be heard speaking *for* themselves. The reasons for this are many. Even though the claims of women of colour are not incorrigible, nor can they any more than anyone else be expected to grasp the causes of their experiences, they do have a certain epistemic privilege about their own experiences. They can more easily detect the subtle forms in which they are discriminated against and marginalized. They often feel differently than do whites or the men in their own groups about what is and is not oppression. Moreover, they will be more alert to issues of their marginalization and will tend to raise such issues more quickly than will white women. Furthermore, they must be heard as 'equal voices' in order to be equal voices in discussions (Narayan, 1988). The logic of multiple subjects requires that all of our subjectivities be transformed in the manner described, but it does not permit subjectivities to be interchangeable, or, most importantly, permit members of dominant groups to speak *as* or *for* the dominated. Thus I am not arguing that *being other* and *reinventing ourselves as other* are epistemically equal social locations. They can never be so. But members of dominant groups – all of us who are white, ethnically privileged, or men, or economically privileged, or heterosexual (have I excluded any reader of this article from this list?!) – can learn to take historic responsibility for the social locations from which our speech and actions issue. This is a scientific and epistemological issue as well as a moral and political one.

CONCLUSION

The recognition and exploration of the existence of multiple subjects of knowledge in all of the new social movements reveal that the relations between subjectivity, experience and knowledge entrenched in conventional epistemology and political philosophy appear reasonable only from the perspective of dominant group lives. There subjectivity appears on the one hand, in so far as it bears the markers of its social location and, especially, of the social location of 'others', as something to be excluded or at least rigorously controlled in the production of knowledge. Socially situated subjectivity threatens to overwhelm or pollute 'pure knowledge'. Marginalized peoples are thought to be the most irretrievably mired in their social situation; women, 'natives', the poor and other 'others' are the models for the irrationality, the social passions, the immersion in the bodily, and the subjective against which dispassionate reason, social justice, historical progress and the objective pursuit of knowledge have been defined. On the other hand, 'rational man's' subjectivity is to be activated, nourished and encouraged to range freely in the pursuit of truth, justice and social progress. But if we critically examine these imagined relations between experience, subjectivity and knowledge from the perspective of those marginalized lives, these relations, too, begin to move back into the particular historical social locations that make them appear reasonable to the dominant social groups.

'Understanding reality' is supposed to require not just knowing what we think of ourselves and the world, but also what others think of us and our beliefs (Mura, 1988: 152). We must 'reinvent ourselves as other' in order to develop those kinds of doubly multiple subjectivities that are capable of understanding objectively their own social location, not just imagining that they understand the social locations of others.[17] This project will require sciences with stronger and more competent criteria of objectivity, rationality and reflexivity than the only semi-sciences with their weak objectivity, rationality and reflexivity that the West has centred. But this is a topic for another time (Harding, 1991).

NOTES

Since this paper was written, my 1991 book, *Whose Science? Whose Knowledge?* has appeared. Parts of this article draw on that material, especially Chapter 11 (pp. 268–95).

1. See, for example, Lloyd (1984) and Hartsock (1983), especially her discussion of 'abstract masculinity' (p. 296ff).

2. For such a 'neo-Marxist' critique see, for example, Aronowitz (1988). For a 'post-Marxist' one (with 'equal weight on both words', they say) see Laclau and Mouffe (1985).

3. This phrase is Uma Narayan's (n.d.).

4. For discussions of the silencing of marginal peoples – denial to them of literacy, of access to dissemination of writing, of institutional resources, and even of the right to consciousness, 'experience', subjectivity and history – see Spivak (1988), Gates (1987) and Wolf (1982).

5. It is not that long ago that class, too, was claimed to be biologically determined.

6. The literature on this topic is by now large and diverse. For a couple of representative examples, see Mies (1986) and Enloe (1990) on how gender is maintained by and maintains imperialism; D'Emilio and Freedman (1988) on how sexuality reproduced and was reproduced by class, race and ethnicity in the US.

7. This phrase comes from Dorothy Smith (1987).

8. This is Patricia Hill Collins's (1986) phrase.

9. bell hook's (1983) concept.

10. Catherine MacKinnon (1982) argues that consciousness raising simply *is* feminist method. For alternative understandings of feminist method, see Harding (1987).

11. See, for example, Mary Hawkesworth (1989).

12. See the interesting discussion of how African-American novelist, Richard Wright, came to this understanding, in JanMohammed (1987).

13. See Narayan (1988). Narayan's illuminating arguments for the importance in the creation of knowledge of expressions of the emotions of the oppressed as they report their experiences may be read as providing additional arguments to those above for the important role that experiences play in the creation of knowledge from the standpoint of oppressed lives, and without claiming that experience *grounds* that knowledge.

14. See Spivak (1988) and Belenky et al. (1986). Belenky et al. point out that 'It's my opinion' means 'I have a right to my opinion' for men, but it means 'it's just my opinion' for women. They also discuss the 'women of silence' who do not yet 'have' self, voice or mind, whom some of their interviewees report having been.

15. See the discussion of this issue in Ellsworth (1989: especially 301ff, where she also cites the Christian passage quoted) and Lugones and Spelman (1983).

16. Hence I 'read' the early feminist standpoint writings that give considerable attention to articulating the different 'human' experiences that women have through their socially assigned activity in mothering, housework, emotional labour and caring of others' bodies (e.g. Hartsock, 1983; Smith, 1987; Rose, 1983) as making this point: there is a different subjectivity from 'the human' (i.e. the ruling group men's). It is created through certain different 'material' activities. That is, 'women's experience' function in these accounts both as something to be explained, and as a clue to the different 'social location' from which much feminist research has emerged, and from which everyone – not just the women who have some particular experiences or other – should start off thought. 'Women's experience' does not function as the *grounds* for feminist claims on these standpoint accounts any more than 'proletarian experience' provides the grounds for Marx's *Capital*. In contrast, it does function as the grounds for knowledge in some feminist phenomenological sociology and radical feminist writings.

17. V.Y. Mudimbe (1988) argues that African philosophers must reinvent the West as a bizarre and alien tradition from which they can learn important techniques but also ambiguously define their alterity. I am arguing that Westerners – and, more generally, members of dominant social groups – can also engage in this reclamation of self and historical agency.

REFERENCES

Amin, S. (1989) *Eurocentrism*. New York: Monthly Review Press.

Aronowitz, S. (1988) *Science as Power: Discourse and Ideology in Modern Society*. Minneapolis, MN: University of Minnesota Press.

Belenky, M.G., Clinchy, B.M., Goldberger, N.R. and Tarule, J.M. (1986) *Women's*

Ways of Knowing: The Development of Self, Voice and Mind. New York: Basic Books.

Christian, B. (1987) 'The Race for Theory', *Cultural Critique* 6: 51–63.

D'Emilio, J. and Freedman, E. (1988) *Intimate Matters: A History of Sexuality in America*. New York: Harper and Row.

Ellsworth, E. (1989) 'Why Doesn't this Feel Empowering? Working through the Repressive Myths of Critical Pedagogy', *Harvard Educational Review* 59(3): 297–324.

Enloe, C. (1990) *Bananas, Beaches and Bases: Making Feminist Sense of International Politics*. Berkeley, CA: University of California Press.

Frye, M. (1983) *The Politics of Reality*. Trumansburg, NY: The Crossing Press.

Gates, H.L., Jr (1987) 'Introduction', in H.L. Gates Jr (ed.) *The Classic Slave Narratives*, pp ix–xvii. New York: New American Library.

Harding, S. (1983) 'Why Has the Sex/Gender System Become Visible only Now', in S. Harding and M. Hintikka (eds) *Discovering Reality: Feminist Perspectives on Epistemology, Metaphysics, Methodology and Philosophy of Science*, pp. 311–24. Dordrecht: Reidel.

Harding, S. (1986) *The Science Question in Feminism*. Ithaca, NY: Cornell University Press.

Harding, S. (ed.) (1987) *Feminism and Methodology: Social Science Issues*. Bloomington, IN: Indiana University Press.

Harding, S. (1991) *Whose Science? Whose Knowledge? Thinking from Women's Lives*. Ithaca, NY: Cornell University Press.

Hartsock, N. (1983) 'The Feminist Standpoint: Developing the Ground for a Specifically Feminism Historical Materialism', in S. Harding and M. Hintikka (eds) *Discovering Reality: Feminist Perspectives on Epistemology, Metaphysics, Methodology and Philosophy of Science*, pp. 283–310. Dordrecht: Reidel Publishing.

Hawkesworth, M. (1989) 'Knowers, Knowing, Known: Feminist Theory and Claims of Truth', *Signs: Journal of Women in Culture and Society* 14(3): 533–57.

Hill Collins, P. (1986) 'Learning from the Outsider Within: The Sociological Significance of Black Feminist Thought', *Social Problems* 33: S. 14–32.

hook, b. (1983) *Feminist Theory: From Margin to Center*. Boston, MA: South End Press.

Jaggar, A. (1983) *Feminist Politics and Human Nature*. Totowa, NJ: Rowman and Allenheld.

JanMohammed, A.R. (1987) 'Negating the Negation as a Form of Affirmation in Minority Discourse: the Construction of Richard Wright as Subject', *Cultural Critique* (7): 245–66.

Laclau, E. and Mouffe, C. (1985) *Hegemony and Socialist Strategy: Towards a Radical Democratic Politics*. London: Verso.

Lloyd, G. (1984) *The Man of Reason: 'Male' and 'Female' in Western Philosophy*. Minneapolis, MN: University of Minnesota Press.

Lugones, M. and Spelman, E.V. (1983) 'Have We Got a Theory for You! Feminist Theory, Cultural Imperialism and the Demand for "Woman's Voice" ', *Hypatia* (1), published as a special issue of *Women's Studies International Forum* 6(6): 573–81.

MacKinnon, C. (1982) 'Feminism, Marxism, Method and the State', Parts 1 and 2, *Signs: Journal of Women in Culture and Society* 7(3): 515–44; 8(4): 635–58.

Mies, M. (1986) *Patriarchy and Accumulation on a World Scale: Women in the International Division of Labor.* Atlantic Highlands, NJ: Zed Books.
Mudimbe, V.Y. (1988) *The Invention of Africa.* Bloomington, IN: Indiana University Press.
Mura, D. (1988) 'Strangers in the Village', in R. Simonson and S. Walker (eds) *The Graywolf Annual Five: Multi-Cultural Literacy.* St Paul, MN: Graywolf Press.
Narayan, U. (1988) 'Working Together across Difference: Some Considerations on Emotions and Political Practice', *Hypatia: A Journal of Feminist Philosophy* 3(2): 31–48.
Narayan, U. (n.d.) 'The Need for Non-Western Contributions to Global Feminism', unpublished paper.
Philosophical Forum (1987) special issue on 'Apartheid, Racism in South Africa', XVIII (2–3): 71–271.
Rose, H. (1983) 'Hand, Brain and Heart: A Feminist Epistemology for the Natural Sciences', *Signs: Journal of Women in Culture and Society* 9(1): 73–90.
Said, E. (1978) *Orientalism.* New York: Pantheon.
Smith, D. (1987) *The Everyday World as Problematic: A Feminist Sociology.* Boston, MA: Northeastern University Press.
Spivak, G. (1988) 'Can the Subaltern Speak?', in C. Nelson and L. Grossberg (eds) *Marxism and the Interpretation of Culture.* Chicago, IL: University of Illinois Press.
Wellman, D. (1977) *Portraits of White Racism.* New York: Cambridge University Press.
Wittig, M. (1980) 'The Straight Mind', *Feminist Issues* 1(1).
Wolf, E. (1982) *Europe and the People without a History.* Berkeley, CA: California University Press.

Sandra Harding is Professor of Philosophy at the University of Delaware (Newark, DE 19716) and the author or editor of many books on feminist theory, science and epistemology, including *Whose Science? Whose Knowledge? Thinking from Women's Lives* (Cornell University Press, 1991), *The Science Question in Feminism* (Cornell, 1986) and *Feminism and Methodology* (Indiana University Press, 1987).

The Feminist Movement in Latin America: Between Hope and Disenchantment

Virginia Vargas

The feminist movement in Latin America has had a visible, audacious and creative development. Nourished by hundreds of initiatives, by networks of themes and actions that interlink and unite the strength of women all over the continent it has, for the last fifteen years, displayed an immensely challenging social practice. Like all social practices, it is also ambiguous. Since 1981 there have been five Latin American and Caribbean Feminist Encounters – first held every two years and later every three – which have provided rich interchanges permitting us to devise joint strategies and explore national differences in an intellectual and social movement that is, quite possibly, the liveliest in Latin America.

Of the Encounters, Julieta Kirkwood has said:

> Latin American women tear open the national curtains in order to proclaim – in a thousand ways and a thousand languages – the validity of their dissent and their emancipation . . . no matter where it was born – whether from the harsh processes in which political violence is deeply rooted or from others, tangled up in more subtle machinations. (Kirkwood, 1986: 207)

But the Encounters have also left some 'knots': 'dis-encounters' such as impatience, intolerance, paradoxes and confrontations. This is because 'Numerous expectations rise up with our revolution and many of them bear the seal of the absolute. Not seeing the other – in this case, the other women – is also one of our habits' (Kirkwood, 1986: 213–14).

This seal of the absolute is the more uncomfortable because the Latin American feminist movement grew out of the modernist project of emancipation, but in the course of its growth it questioned the basis of this project, questioned the transcendental subject and

Development and Change (SAGE, London, Newbury Park and New Delhi), Vol. 23 (1992) No. 3, 195–214.

found that no transformative project can be conceived on the basis of a monological proposal.

In the light of the experience of the Latin American Feminist Encounters, I analyse the difficulties the movement is facing in trying to escape from this 'seal of the absolute' and recognize the interconnections among hierarchical systems based on gender, class, race, ethnicity, age, etc. The change involves abandoning what Harding (1990) calls the 'transcendental gender', that is, the conception of gender as the primary contradiction.

The development of the Latin American women's movement shows that it is no longer possible to speak of women's identity, anchored and built on their experiences as a subordinate gender. Instead, we need to recognize the plurality of experiences, the possibility of multiple representations and identities. We are living in a time, not only in Latin America, characterized by the simultaneous emergence of new social subjects, multiple rationalities and identities, expressed in the social movements. This opens up more individual and collective possibilities for transforming social values. It also reflects the fact that experiences of oppression and subordination, and the resistance to them, are expressed in so many different ways that there cannot be one global explanation which encompasses all social conflicts. The acknowledgment of these multiple and diverse rationalities refutes the idea of an emancipatory process that articulates aspirations within one dynamic only and through an exclusive and privileged axis (Vega, 1988: 28).

This article attempts to disentangle the knots that have at times been an obstacle to the development of our emancipatory projects. I analyse these knots through a reconstruction of the Feminist Encounters as spaces where the scope and limitations of the movement are crystallized. At the same time, it is necessary to look beyond the Encounters and to analyse the conditions of growth of the feminist movement, its inheritance and theoretical sources and the foundation of its dissent.

MODERNISM AND MIXED TIMES

Since the first decades of this century, Latin America has experienced a complex and contradictory process of modernization. This has been characterized by many authors as the passing from a received order to a produced order. In this sense, modernization refers to the growing disenchantment with the religious organization of the world, a rupture with transcendental foundations, and the acknowledgment of social reality as an order determined and defined by people (Lechner, 1988: 130).

Modernization took different paths in Latin America, including socialist, populist and liberal projects, of which the latter was the least significant. Although each country experienced different histories, all attempted to confront the conservatism of the oligarchies. For a number of reasons, the populist proposal generally won in most Latin American countries (López, 1990). Charismatic leaders rose to the top and established relationships with the masses which, although based on manipulation, did give people a way of expressing themselves politically (Weffort, 1970),[1] thus strengthening the participatory character of Latin American politics.

Marxism and its various socialist expressions represent another fundamental current of modernist thought. Some of these have had a decisive influence on modern consciousness in Latin America. Because of the mixture of Marxism and populism as the leading theories of opposition to oligarchical domination, Latin American societies experienced an idiosyncratic and truncated development as modern societies. Modernization had ambivalent effects. Even as it created and increased the marginalization of large sectors of society, regions and cultures, it also facilitated the process of integration and the widening of the reference horizon and social subjectivity. Although modernization was truncated, aspirations for political self-determination and moral autonomy (Quijano, 1988) influenced large sectors of society. This truncated modernization, in combination with Latin America's multicultural and multi-ethnic nature, its growing poverty and the effects of the drug trade and terrorism in many countries, has created a singular situation in which several processes coexist, 'some completing modernism, others developing the confusing post-modernism and still others holding to pre-modernism' (Calderón, 1988: 227).

The Feminist Movement: One More Expression of the Transition towards Modernity

The feminist movement surges forward as part of the modernization process, receiving its impetus from it but at the same time strained by its logic. The movement has benefited from women's greater access to education, from mass migration, accelerated urbanization, the enlargement of the workforce and from the political antagonisms arising from the contradictory discourses that rely on subordination and those which promote emancipation.

In this context, the feminist movement unfolded strongly throughout Latin America, especially after 1980. Its growth fed on the decline of certainties the continent had lived with for many decades. From the end of the 1970s and throughout the 1980s, confidence in the benefits of progress for all citizens and nations, the capacity of the charismatic leader to face his nation's problems, confidence in the state, in the power structures and in the political parties, began to weaken. The region's dictatorships undermined the myth of progress, the myth of the inevitability of socialism and the myth of populism. Political thought moved increasingly towards considerations of how to recreate civil society (Guzmán, 1990). The rise of diverse social subjects and social movements contributed to challenging some of the certainties that modernism, in its populist and Marxist expressions, had disseminated. What became increasingly manifest was modernity's fundamental contradiction, of stimulating individualization, of opening up individual and multiple values on the one hand, while on the other imprisoning them in monological and summative structures, thus reducing plurality to a single standard (Yeatman, 1990).

This contradiction is also apparent in the feminist movement, in its view of women and in its self-perception and social practices. Because feminism was born as both a part of and an answer to modernity, it criticized the old paradigms of action and knowledge, while at the same time being influenced by them.

UNIVERSALITY WITHOUT DIFFERENTIATION?

In this context, the feminist movement sought to develop new paradigms of criticism, showing that certain 'truths' which claimed to be universal, were in fact partial, contingent and historically situated. But the weight of the dominant cultural moment and the ghost of old paradigms have been so strong that, within the feminist movement, they shared polar and overlapping visions. At one pole were the greatness of vision, the subversive proposals in the face of the authoritarian logic of Latin American societies, the recognition of differences, the emergence of more than one voice, the politicization of daily life – that which we perceive as the fundamental contribution of the feminist movement in Latin America; at the other pole, causal explanations, exclusionary logics, reductionism, myths and partial experiences that attempted to become universal.

This tension is all the more challenging because the feminist movement assumes diversity and democracy as the intrinsic and vital reasons for its own existence and development. This is because the feminist movement is an expression of a much broader women's social movement that is composed of at least three basic streams: the feminist stream; the stream of women in political parties, unions and federations; and the stream of women of the 'popular'[2] classes who, in their roles as mothers, are gaining their citizenship and becoming aware of their gender subordination. Hence the movement does not reflect a homogeneous process but rather a plurality of processes that demonstrate the diverse and contradictory realities in which women find themselves and which generate different subject-positions that cannot simply be reduced to those of gender[3] (Mouffe, 1990). Within each stream, gender relations survive in their own particular ways.

These streams generate multiple spaces, more symbolic than geographical. They are cultural constructions, points of reference (Melucci, 1989) that express the distinctive ways in which women are articulating their different life experiences. The social, cultural, ethnic and geographic plurality of the greater women's movement structures the political and intellectual developments of Latin American feminism (Vargas, 1991). From the beginning, this heterogeneity served as a basis for recognizing diverse identities and multiple senses of collective action. Nevertheless, this plurality often presents difficulties. The feminist movement has generated practices that are as authoritarian as those it challenged.

The Origins of the Movement

The origins of the feminist movement in Latin America reflect the characteristics of a large sector of the female middle class, rebellious and doubtful of the traditional patterns that mark the destinies of women in our societies. They are mostly intellectual women who have had significant political experience throughout the 1970s, mainly in groups among the 'new left'. This large female sector, inspired by modernism, demanded universal equality as the basis for women's full citizenship. Taking up this demand, feminists took the first big step towards neutralizing the differences between the sexes. Their goal of full citizenship for all was effectively a demand for total equality in societies where an incomplete modernization had marginalized entire sectors of the population.

Paradoxically, feminists' demands for universal equality and citizenship made women themselves invisible. It became clear that the feminist proposal must acknowledge this differentiation and distance itself from the paradigm of a unique subject that represented the universal interest and demanded emancipation in the name of all the oppressed. Thus, the feminist movement developed along a dual course: on the one hand, it attempted to overcome sexual differences through the recognition of universality, while on the other hand, it acknowledged the importance of difference and the urgency of specifying universality. This tension between the universality of the modernist project — necessary but nonetheless partial — and the necessity of recognizing difference and securing distinct and defined spaces, led to great difficulties within the feminist movement.

Because of the great weight carried by universality and a political culture that denied difference, the movement began to express differences more in relation to external parties and states than among women themselves (Barret, 1990: 312). At times, this unintentionally bestowed privileges on certain women and deprived other women of power. In many cases, differences were translated into the presumption of a feminine essence that united all women regardless of race, class or status. We were different from men; our sensibility and subjectivity united us in our personal and political lives. From this perspective, women who did not give priority to the question of gender, who accommodated themselves to the masculine world, who were basically family oriented, were seen to be participating in a form of false consciousness and in need of consciousness raising. A new 'vanguard' was in place.

However, even if the feminist movement took on a new approach and refused to accept those positions which considered women's problems to be secondary, we did not entirely relinquish the fascination of finding global explanations to the subordination of women. There was a strong temptation to search for universal answers: first patriarchy and then gender[4] were offered as the sole explanation for women's subordination. Perhaps this was inevitable in an early stage characterized by a momentary 'fission' of the social dynamics

(Gramsci); it permitted a period of intense theoretical discussion and autonomous militancy. The focus on patriarchy put the question of the subordination of women on the agenda all over the continent. But the focus on women's subordination alone overlooked other social disabilities that women suffered. This brought the movement dangerously close to the reductionism feminists had so highly criticized.

It is in the relationship of the feminist movement with other women's sectors and with other currents of the broader social movements that the influence of populism on one hand, and the 'vanguardist' vision of the left on the other, can be most clearly seen. This emphasis on an equality that did not take account of social differences among women led to an assumption that the processes of change should be more or less homogeneous for all women. The problem of difference was thus temporarily solved through a process which established the pre-eminence of gender. The remaining task was to concentrate on the practices that explicitly touched upon the question of gender in order to advance the development of a new identity among women.

Thus, despite the break with ruling political parties and despite feminists' criticism of the totalizing and vanguardist visions of the political parties, the same logic persisted in feminist assessments of women's reality. Somehow an idea kept floating around, an idea that implied that:

> . . . a fair social order would be one imposed by the oppressed majorities led by [enlightened] vanguards that, by their actions, would not only be remedying ancient inequalities and iniquities but also, by this same action, would cause truth to triumph. (Piscitelli, 1988: 75)

In Latin America and the Caribbean, as Feijóo first pointed out, feminism 'sensed, with difficulty and great exertion, that the only way for feminists to get out of the intellectual ghetto was to incorporate the consideration of the problem of the region's most vulnerable women into the project of feminism' (Feijóo, 1990). Yet ghosts of the past remained. Overtures towards women from the popular classes were based more on the memories of earlier practices — which concluded that only the popular classes held the real possibility of change — a sense of guilt among many feminists for belonging to the middle class, and the need to prove that we were not merely influenced by foreign feminism. We were eager to demonstrate our sensitivity to the reality of poverty and inequality in our own countries. This came out of our previous party experiences and as a result of our life experiences.

At the same time, this caused the development of two polarized visions. The first idealized women's social practices, especially those of the popular women; we quickly discovered the similarities between our own personal processes and those of the 'others': 'curiously, feminism fell again and again into a ciphered lecture whose key lay in the idea of resistance. Thus, small actions . . . became indications of ways in which women resisted oppression, practices which were simultaneously feminine and classist' (Feijóo, 1990). The second expressed scepticism about subordination and resistance, which were seen as two opposite conditions that were mutually exclusive, with no middle ground, no ambiguities and no mutual influence.

For a long time, these restrictive visions of gender made us concentrate on one type of woman more than on another. By emphasizing the experiences of housewives in lower-class households, popular education became a panacea for changing consciousness. The feminist programme tended to confuse this emphasis on daily life and on alternative values with sanctifying their micro-experiences, and immediate feminine perceptions with strategies for change.

THE FEMINIST ENCOUNTERS

These visions have been nurtured and expressed in a cumulative sense in the different Feminist Encounters which took place between 1981 and 1990 in Latin America. Only when the movement expanded and assimilated more women of different ethnic backgrounds and classes did we recognize how limited diversity within the movement had been.

In analysing the quantity and quality of the participants in the different Encounters, we can find the best examples of this growing complexity. In every case the number of participants has been astounding and the cause of disorganization due to the lack of foresight. In Colombia, 150 women were expected and nearly 230 arrived. In Lima 350 were expected and 650 arrived. In Brazil 700 were expected and nearly 1,000 arrived; in Mexico there were 1,500 participants, while in Argentina 3,000 women from different classes, ethnic groups and sexual preferences arrived.

The Feminist Encounters have become a barometer for measuring the evolution of the movement; they demonstrate its strength and limitations. I shall look at the significance of each Encounter in terms of theoretical advances and the subjective climate of feminist opinion, but I shall concentrate on the last two encounters since I believe that, after ten years of existence, those two condense some of the initial tendencies and display some of the knots – past and present – that still impede the movement.

The idea of holding encounters developed at the beginning of the feminist movement. Groups in different countries recognized the need for more direct interchange. Living in similar realities, we had similar reactions to the conditions we shared and we wanted to hold periodic reunions. Until then, we had always met abroad,[5] in places that were friendly enough but still not entirely ours. We wanted to have our own space for this interchange. At that time the experience we had was limited and quite primitive; apart from Brazil, Mexico and, to a lesser extent, Venezuela, the feminist groups in the region had developed a certain permanence only one or two years before. They had very little clarity about the construction of a regional movement; they were still highly influenced by left-wing parties, although the need for autonomy was becoming clear. That is why, at that stage, definitions such as socialist, popular, revolutionary feminist, etc. were the labels we gave ourselves to make our feminist definition more palatable to us. Yet we were all seeking other answers and in some way breaking through the old political paradigms.

In 1981 the First Encounter of Feminists of Latin America and the Caribbean was held in Bogotá; it was undoubtedly a landmark, offering:

> . . . the possibility of a first time, a first opening of Latin American feminism towards the world . . . . It wielded the magic of inception and in this sense it was also unique, unrepeatable . . . . Bogotá marked the era of the recuperation of spaces for women, of a very special space . . . . It marked the moment of an unorganized assault on order; the era when work became song and celebration, when reason was de-sacramentalized and put in its place; it showed itself to be impoverished and it was enriched . . . . Bogotá was the first vivid experiment in this enormous sense of women being together. It was the first time in which all expectations were shattered. (Kirkwood, 1986: 214)

In the midst of this feeling of discovery and expectation, Bogotá had at least two characteristic features: on the one hand, we experienced the wide and generous recognition of 'sisterhood', the explosion of affection and the self-affirmation of knowledge and of a space for women; on the other hand, in relation to this newly discovered sisterhood, we developed a collective sense of Good and Evil, an idea of a *complete and immediate* revolution (Kirkwood, 1986: 215). We developed an impatience to mark our space, to protect ourselves from the powers outside that were an obstacle to our own development, our own proposals and our own truth. The need to deny differences and to mark out territory took the form, perhaps rightly at that initial moment, of a confrontation between feminists and women from political parties in defence of the newly asserted autonomy of the feminist movement. This autonomy, which constituted an affirmation that was vital to the development of the movement, still contained, however, defensive and exclusive elements which were difficult to resolve at this first stage. Autonomy was perceived as an end in itself:

> In our past practice we were accustomed to putting our feminist identity in front of any debate – label first – as if with this we could cut off any influence from outside. And in this struggle, many times we forgot to seek consensus, to find women from inside the parties who did not define themselves as feminists although they accepted that feminism was a political movement that questioned power relations, oppression and exploitation, the domination of some people over others and one human over another. (Villanueva, 1990)

The argument between feminists and women politicians revolved around the question of 'double militancy'.[6] Many party members chose to stay outside this recently discovered sisterhood, but many others, defending 'double militancy', stayed in the movement.

The Second Feminist Encounter in Lima in 1983, marked the moment for restructuring questions and answers and thus for disentangling the knots: 'In Lima, the demand for answers and for the formulation of new, complex questions engendered new feminist political strategies. We suffered exasperation to know it all, to solve even the questions that cannot be answered. Headache' (Kirkwood, 1986: 215). This was the Encounter at which it seemed absolutely necessary to demonstrate – through the presence and persistence of patriarchy – feminism's capacity to provide analyses of women and of society, to contribute to the theoretical status of the movement. Twenty simultaneous workshops that had been set up previously and run by Latin American and Caribbean feminists analysed patriarchy. A rich discussion emerged and revealed the global concept of that period: the segmentation of women's reality into specific themes which only made sense in the light of patriarchal categories.

The confrontation between party women and feminists took place at the end of the Encounter during the last plenary meeting. The fundamental knot was the question whether class or gender was the ultimate cause of the subordination of women. The meeting was a difficult and unpleasant experience, demonstrating widespread intolerance.[7]

The Third Feminist Encounter was held in Bertioga, Brazil, in 1985.[8] It was there that some women resisted the structured forms of organization, the perception that women's subjectivity was a fundamental element in their lives, and recognized the necessity of stimulating the equal participation of all women, thus generating a space and a climate to ensure that 'each woman would participate equally, for herself, without hierarchies of any kind. No woman was accorded a greater or lesser status because of her feminist militancy or political party experience or because she was an eminent specialist' (document from the Third Encounter, 1985).

In these three Encounters some of the issues that colour the movement to this day appeared. Each Encounter complemented the deficiency of the former, not always aiming for continuity but recognizing the distance we had come and presenting itself as an alternative. Face-to-face affection, affirmation of collectivity and sisterhood as expressed in Bogotá all underlay the search in Lima for a theoretical axis that would explain the reality of women. The quest continued in Bertioga with the rejection of structured and individualized forms, the affirmation of equality among women and a certain discomfort with difference. Independently of the advances which permitted each Encounter to take place, and which allowed the feminist movement throughout the continent to consolidate itself, establishing networks, promoting initiatives and developing new proposals, the three Encounters also brought new arguments and theories for interpreting the world and the movement.

This theoretical aspect undoubtedly gave a consistent ideological base to the feminist movement in its first stages of development; perhaps this was necessary in order to face the loss of social legitimacy that being a feminist at that time implied, to deal with the insecurity produced by expressing ourselves in ways so far unknown for us. But this ideological consistency began to carry 'the seal of the absolute', of not seeing others, of feeling that to open up to an understanding of a plural and complex growth was to lose our basis, our sisterhood, our own alternative. Therefore, if it is true that part of the movement and part of each one of us instinctively wanted to walk the path of diversity and to question the absolute, another part of the movement and of each of us wanted to renounce differences and find universal truths.

This is why we arrived at the Fourth Feminist Encounter – in Taxco, Mexico in 1987 – with an almost intuitive determination to distance ourselves from past practices. It was here that Latin American feminists confronted a dark and defensive imaginary politics which many felt was keeping us from advancing to more democratic processes. Mexico was also the scene of the first confrontation, both jolting and enriching, with diversity.

Obviously, with 1,500 women attending the Encounter, the kind of participants was diverse. Besides the autonomous feminists, there were many women from political parties, women from squatter settlements, labourers, women from non-governmental organizations, women with government positions, women immersed in wartime situations (Central America), women from countries with socialist governments (Cuba and Nicaragua), each of them bringing in a whole range of experiences, new ideas, new doubts, and few answers. The lesbians had held their own Encounter previous to this meeting (the First Lesbian Encounter of Latin America and the Caribbean), making the themes and visions more complex. The Encounter in Argentina, with nearly 3,000 women,[9] consolidated the tendency towards pluralism that had arisen in Mexico in 1987.

The tension between homogeneity and diversity appeared not so much in the issues presented, all of which converged, as in the strategies that each group pursued. Thus, a fundamental feature of the Encounter in Mexico was pluralism in the widest sense of the word. It seemed as if all the cultural, political, social and economic characteristics of the continent sought expression in the feminist space. Some wanted to preserve a delineated feminist space while others wanted to create alliances among women from different classes and ethnic groups within Latin America.

MYTHS OF THE FEMINIST MOVEMENT

In the climate of the Fourth Encounter, participants reflected on the 'myths' which crystallized the tension between the political ideals and the social practices of the feminist movement. It became clear that the feminist utopia was in crisis. 'Today we are witnessing a blockade of different perspectives. It is difficult to find another epoch when the sense of development or, if you wish, the "faustian" sense of our history seemed so diminished. Today we live with the feeling of having lost the future' (Weffort, 1990: 36). This may be why we experienced a growing difficulty in thinking about the impossible: our visions of the future seemed dim and contradictory. Visions of utopia, if not completely absent, seemed opaque (Lechner, 1986).

In the face of this, the feminist movement generated its own mechanisms of compensation. A utopia emerged, not based on alternative rationalities but on the mystification of modernist rationality. It began to be defined more in terms of what was *not* wanted than in terms of what was truly desirable. How could we imagine a different world when our reality was full of fears and defences? With two interrelated approaches, the movement drew close to a threatening reality, trying to hide our fear by appealing to compensatory and impoverished interpretations of this movement. Day by day and country by country, we sought guides for our social practices and yet distanced ourselves from the true contents of the societies from which we came.

Instead of recognizing the contradictions that we were living, we constructed myths[10] about what we were as a movement. These myths – and many still exist – did not constitute a utopia but rather a new vanguardism that excluded difference. The myths carried within them a counter proposal to patriarchal power that claimed a feminine capacity that could not be overtaken by contradictions, an essentialism that some authors have called 'womanism' (Lamas, 1990). These myths included a vision of the future in which homogeneity, and not difference, would ensure equality and power. They led us to claim that:

> Feminists are not interested in power.
> Feminists do politics in a different way.
> All feminists are equal.
> There is a natural unity in just being women.
> Any small group is representative of the movement.
> Women's spaces in themselves guarantee positive processes.
> Because I as a woman feel something, it's valid.
> The personal is automatically political.
> Consensus is democracy.

None of these statements is true: we have innate contradictions; we adopt traditional patterns of behaviour when we get involved in politics; not all women are equal, although this affirmation might provoke authoritarian replies that deny our differences. A consensus may hide a profoundly authoritarian practice when it serves to silence differences. Unity among women is not a given but rather something to be constructed on the basis of our differences. Feminism is not a question of building a politics *of* women *for* women, but should be something that men can also embrace. Our personal sentiments, our subjectivity, can also become arbitrary when considered only in their individual dimensions. The personal has the potential to become the political only when it combines itself with both conscience and action. The 'myths' document had a great impact on the movement: it became a 'tool of interior advance of the movement: it broke the barriers of romanticism and candy-coating' (Tornaría, 1991: 3).

FROM MYTHS TO THREATENING DIVERSITIES

In 1990 we arrived in San Bernardo, Argentina, to celebrate the Fifth Feminist Encounter. In the three years since the gathering in Taxco, the political climate in Latin America had come to value democracy much more than before; the crisis of the authoritarian governments contributed to this, as did the processes of democratic transition, the fall of Eastern European regimes, and the crisis of the left all over the continent. The general disenchantment – influenced by the deepening economic crisis and by the loss of legitimacy of the political institutions – reinforced our dissatisfaction with analyses based exclusively on class struggle and confrontation, and gave prominence to more democratic and pluralistic conceptions.

In this climate, the feminist movement was able to spread and to contribute to the changes. It could extend itself into new spaces and reach new women who brought different life experiences, different subjectivities and different realities to feminist debates. This meant that some myths were revised, reformulated, confronted, although it was not possible to overcome a utopian vision based solely on a universal femininism.

In Argentina the process of disenchantment and evasion expressed a tension which was already present within the movement but now welled up much more strongly than before – the problem of respect for diversity. The expansion of the feminist movement in Latin America in this period consolidated and generalized the process we had begun in Mexico: those present at the Fifth Encounter were not only feminists from autonomous groups and full-time feminist centres with an explicit militancy centred around the problem of gender. Now the composition was different. Besides Christians, ecologists, pacifists, researchers, lesbians, heterosexuals, Central Americans, women from the Southern and the Andean regions, mostly from an urban and middle-class culture, there were now black and indigenous women from Brazil, Honduras, Mexico, Peru, Bolivia, Argentina. Women came from settlements in Guatemala, Mexico, Brazil, and from unions in Argentina, Uruguay and Peru. Old and new themes were discussed, compared and co-ordinated. For the first time, feminist academics held their own workshops. Militants from political parties gathered to design feminist strategies in their own parties. Indigenous women brought up the themes of racism, ethnicity and culture. Parliamentarians and autonomous feminists who had participated in designing their governments' policies towards women became interested in analysing their experiences. Lesbians held a workshop on lesbophobia within the feminist movement. The 'esoterics' or spiritual feminists organized beautiful candlelight ceremonies on the beach at night.

It was also a less ideological Encounter, one without great overarching theories, one interested in responding to and defining specific strategies to confront concrete and fixed problems. We established new dates for demonstrations throughout Latin America: there was a specific day dedicated to the Latin American struggle for abortion rights, and another to analysing and denouncing the image of women as presented in the media. New networks were constructed which embraced the diversity of those who attended the conference – networks for feminist historians of Latin America and the Caribbean; for feminists in political parties; for the defence of the environment; for academic researchers. The fact was that all the women, in their enormous diversity, were interested in being there, in taking part, in being recognized within the movement. All of them were seeking – far more explicitly than ever before – new strategies to interact with women from different cultures, so that they could be valid representatives to society as a whole.

At the same time, many demanded, as their right, a space within the feminist movement. They criticized the old leadership and their organization, they expressed resentment at the money which the original feminist groups had and they did not. All of them, or almost all, considered themselves feminists in their own way, wearing their differences and their individuality on their sleeves. This explosion of plurality in action underwrote the search for answers at this Encounter, but the conditions under which the gathering was held contributed more to fragmentation than to the recognition of plurality.[11] The subjective urgencies of some confronted the subjective urgencies of others. It was as if, symbolically, everyone was fearful that her own purity would be contaminated by someone else's (Lechner, 1989).

The Fifth Encounter ran the risk of being a 'dis-encounter'. The difference already apparent in Mexico between those who wished to determine the feminist field and ensure a clear-cut commitment free of compromises with the feminist project, and those who – surprised and uncomfortable as they were with the expansion of plurality – still supported it, manifested itself here with increased strength and tension.

The workshop document, *Feminism in the 90s: Challenges and Proposals*, tried to respond to fears that gender might be lost in demands for attention to race, ethnicity and class. The tension seemed 'to be working itself into the movement's wounds' (Tornaría, 1991: 3). Yet, in spite of the difficulties, we knew that our inability to accept differences within the movement reduced our possibility of conceiving a future where reciprocal recognition and plurality were fundamental elements.

The challenge remains to be met at the next Feminist Encounter in Central America. The rules of the game are no longer defined by the original group that organized the early Encounters. The movement will have to take its direction from those who form it now. There is no longer room for a small group to take charge: we are confronted with a social dynamic in which all the women who feel themselves part of the movement are beginning to enter a dialogue on equal terms.

BY WAY OF CONCLUSION

> The force of democracy is, for the countries of Latin America, the force of hope. (Weffort, 1990)

This complex process of the development of social movements in Latin America is now at the crossroads of two historical stages: that of incomplete modernism and a new one, yet to be defined, whose beginnings seem to express themselves in postmodernism. We are seeing the end of the transition to an incomplete modernity which leaves us fundamental tasks to complete at the same time that it leaves us with the limitations to its rationality. This modernity, in its truncated development, has retained all the pre-modern, patriarchal, anti-democratic elements of restricted interests, of traditional society, of the state and the collective mentality mired in the past. We are also witnessing the rise of postmodern disenchantment, with problems, horizons and characteristics still waiting to be defined in Latin America.

The debate on diversity within the feminist movement is marked by the ambivalence of this transition from one stage to another. Because of this, respect for diversity has become the crux of the process by which we must complete unfinished tasks and formulate proposals for future forms of organization that will include different kinds of women. This will not be easy but on our success rests the democratic egalitarian society which we need to construct all over Latin America.

The dilemma is not a simple one. To accept pluralism without a collective order and without orientation towards action could condemn us to fragmentation. And it may mean succumbing to another grave temptation: that of total relativism, of giving up the possibility of constructing a movement. Because it is not a question of abandoning the ethical-political project of emancipation, it is not merely a question of constructing a movement sustained by more pluralistic visions, but also of facing differences rooted in the ancient inequalities within our continent, which modernization did not address and which affect women in a deep and particular manner. It is, thus, a question of 'a new way of thinking about the political universalism of the enlightenment, about the ideas of individual and collective self-determination, about reason and about history' (Wellmer, 1988: 136).

How can we find a new way of imagining Latin America? How can we recover the vision of a viable and democratic future when the economic, social and political conditions of the continent seem to militate against it?

> Those who accept that the consolidation of democracy is not here yet must also admit the fragility of the democratic conquests realized up to now and, thus, of the possibility that there shall be crises and eventually reverses. Finally . . . democracy was never conceived here as the only road towards the construction of societies and states . . . the democratic struggles of the last decades, no matter how fundamental, have not managed to exorcise all our old authoritarian demons. (Weffort, 1990: 36)

How can we clear a way at this historical crossroad? The feminist movement must know how to navigate between hope and disenchantment. The feminist movement in Latin America is based on a plurality that needs to be expanded in all its dimensions. This is more feasible if it abandons the romantic and essentialist myths about women's condition and rejects the ghost of old paradigms. It is essential to recognize at this stage of feminism that the movement cannot be based only on a single dynamic or on an exclusive, privileged axis, but must be grounded in the articulation of differences, of the multiple and diverse rationalities already present within it.

The coexistence with other social movements offers an enormous wealth because it reveals that we are living in a period where a plurality of rationalities is being developed in the political field, rejecting the notion of a single political logic (Lechner, 1988). There will be many more women all over the continent expressing multicultural perceptions and revealing a variety of complex differences. New participants will demand their own space. We must work out new ways of meeting, of keeping that plurality from washing us away, of creating institutions that can combine pluralism with individual choice and initiative.

Between now and the next Feminist Encounter, we have time to produce a collective democratic order within the movement; one that is not defined on the basis of a single identity, be it normative or mythical, but on the basis of multiple identities and ways of achieving our emancipation.

NOTES

1. Populism adopted 'distributionism' as its economic policy and substituted imports for production as the model for development, accepting the state as the final arbiter of all decision-making.

2. Here used in the sense of 'underprivileged'. In Latin America, the 'stream of popular women' (*vertiente de mujeres populares*) refers not only to their large numbers within the population but also to their economic deprivations.

3. Perhaps one could talk about various women's social movements, but that would mean placing each of the currents in parallel and exclusive dynamics. On the contrary, the currents intersect one another; they permanently speak to and contradict one another. This is why I prefer to talk about one women's social movement.

4. Obviously, I am not unaware of the importance of the category of gender within feminist theory. My reservations, like those of many other feminists, are about considering gender to be the ultimate and fundamental factor in explaining women's lives.

5. It was no coincidence that the proposal of Venezuelan feminists to organize the Latin American Feminist Encounters was put forward by the Latin American

feminists in Copenhagen in 1980, during the meeting of the Alternative Forum at the midway point of the International Women's Decade. There, for the first time, we discovered ourselves as a Latin American group: Peruvian, Chilean, Colombian, Dominican, Puerto Rican, Mexican, Brazilian, Venezuelan, exiled Latin and Chicano women. In 1981 the Colombian women met the challenge and organized the First Encounter of Feminists from Latin America and the Caribbean.

6. 'Double militancy' is a tension specific to Latin American countries where the level of politicization of the society is quite high. Basically, it refers to the simultaneous and militant participation in different groups such as political parties and the autonomous women's movements.

7. Profound intolerance, since many militant party members left no space for reconciliation. We did not feel at the time that this boded well for a constructive plurality but rather that it was paralysing, that it wanted to destroy what we were struggling so hard to construct. There was also intolerance on the part of some of the feminists, not only in confronting the party women but also in challenging the Encounter itself for being too theoretical, too structured, too rigid, too different from Bogotá. As a member of the organizing committee of the Second Encounter, my personal dismay was so grave that I could only reconcile myself to the richness of the Encounter two months later, when Julieta Kirkwood offered me her extraordinary article 'The Knots of Feminist Wisdom' ('Los nudos de la sabiduría feminista').

8. Julieta Kirkwood died a short time before the Encounter in Brazil. Her analysis of the knots in the movement as displayed at the Encounters only reached the one held in Lima.

9. The presence of so many women is even more significant since the majority of them pay their own travel cost. The cost of registration and of room and board are quite low because the seat always looks for some kind of financial help. Even so, each Encounter generally represents a significant expense for each participant. A chartered trip is organized in each country well in advance so as to save money, seeking the cheapest ways to travel, promoting festivals or other activities to raise funds, etc.

10. These myths were expressed in the document 'From Love to Need' ('Del amor a la necesidad'), a collective work prepared by eleven women during the Feminist Encounter in Taxco in 1987.

11. The 3,000 women were spread out over more than twenty small hotels, the luckiest being housed within twenty city blocks, the less lucky in a neighbouring town. Space could not be found for some workshops; others brought women together not necessarily out of interest but out of convenience, because they were close at hand and avoided long walks and vain searches. It was certainly not the best location for encouraging respect for diversity.

REFERENCES

Barret, M. (1990) 'El concepto de la diferencia', *Revista Debate Feminista* 1(2).

Calderón, F. (1988) 'América Latina, identidad y tiempos mixtos, o cómo pensar la modernidad sin dejar de ser boliviano', in *Imágenes desconocidas: la modernidad en la encrucijada postmoderna*, pp. 225–9. Buenos Aires: Ediciones CLACSO.

Feijóo, M. (1990) 'La identidad popular en América Latina', Lima (mimeo).

Guzmán, V. (1990) 'Paradigmas del conocimiento e investigación de género', internal document. Lima: Flora Tristán.

Harding, S. (1990) 'Feminism, Science and the Anti-enlightenment Critiques', in L. Nicholson (ed.) *Feminism and Post-modernism*. London: Routledge.
Kirkwood, J. (1986) *Ser política en Chile.* Santiago de Chile: Ediciones FLACSO.
Lamas, M. (1990) 'Editorial Comment', *Revista Debate Feminista* 1(2).
Lechner, N. (1986) *La conflictiva y nunca acabada construcción del orden democrático*, Centro de Investigaciones CISE. Spain: Ed. Siglo XXI.
Lechner, N. (1988) 'El desencanto post-moderno', in *Imágenes desconocidas: la modernidad en la encrucijada post-moderna*, pp. 126–37. Buenos Aires: Ediciones CLACSO.
Lechner, N. (1989) *Los patios interiores de la democracia.* Santiago de Chile: Ediciones FLACSO.
López, S. (1990) 'El Perú de los 80: sociedad y estado en el fin de una época', in *Estado y sociedad: relaciones peligrosas.* Lima: DESCO.
Melucci, A. (1989) *Nomads of the Present*. London: Radios.
Mouffe, C. (1990) 'La radicalización de la democracia', *Revista Leviatán* 41(II): 85–98.
Piscitelli, A. (1988) 'Sur, post-modernidad y después', in *Imágenes desconocidas: la modernidad en la encrucijada post-moderna*. Buenos Aires: Ediciones CLACSO.
Quijano, A. (1988) 'Modernidad, identidad y utopía en América Latina', in *Imágenes desconocidas: la modernidad en la encrucijada post-moderna*, pp. 17–24. Buenos Aires: Ediciones CLACSO.
Tornaría, C. (1991) 'Los gozos y las sombras de un encuentro fraterno', *Mujer/FEMPRESS* 11.
Vargas, V. (1991) 'The Women's Movement in Peru: Streams, Spaces and Knots', *European Review of Latin American and Caribbean Studies* 50: 7–50.
Vega, J. E. (1988) *Signos y designios en la sociedad latino-americana.*
Villanueva, V. (1990) 'Autonomía feminista y partidos políticos', Lima.
Weffort, F. (1970) 'El populismo en la política brasileña', in *Brazil hoy*, pp. 54–84. Mexico City: Ed. Siglo XXI.
Weffort, F. (1990) 'La América equivocada', in *Estrategias para el desarrollo de la democracia: en Perú y América Latina*. Lima: Instituto de Estudios Peruanos/Fundación Friedrich Naumann.
Wellmer, A. (1988) 'La dialéctica de modernidad y post-modernidad', in José Pico (ed.) *Modernidad y post-modernidad*. Madrid: Alianza Editorial.
Yeatman, A. (1990) 'A Feminist Theory of Social Differentiation', in *Feminism/Postmodernism*. New York and London: Routledge.

Virginia Vargas is a founder of the Flora Tristan Feminist Centre and of the Peruvian feminist movement. She has published several books in Spanish, including *El aporte de la Rebeldia de las Mujeres* and *Como Cambiar el Mundo sin Perdernos* (1989 and 1992), as well as numerous articles in English. Address: Centro Feminista Flora Tristan, Parque Hernan Velarde 42, Lima 1, Peru.

Development and Women's Emancipation: Is There a Connection?

Valentine M. Moghadam

INTRODUCTION

In recent years the concept of development – and before that, modernization – has encountered serious criticism (Apter, 1987; Marglin and Marglin, 1990). It has been pointed out, quite correctly, that within national societies, development has all too often been an élite affair, out of touch with the needs and aspirations of the poor and working classes, arrogant and heavy handed. The terms 'development' and 'modernization' obscure the relations of exploitation, unequal distribution of wealth and other disparities (not to mention environmental degradation) that ensue. And what is there to say after decades of development, when Third World societies are mired in and forced to accept the policing role of the World Bank and IMF in order to get their balance of payments in order? Finally, there is a strand of feminist thinking which argues that development has historically brought about the domination and domestication of women (Mies, 1986; Shiva, 1988). It is argued that the private/public split, whereby the latter became the domain of men while women were relegated to the former – although men were in control – came with modernity and development, as did the nature/culture dichotomy. Within the field of women-in-development, some have argued that economic development has everywhere resulted in marginalization of women from production (Boserup, 1970; Leacock, 1975) or their exploitation as cheap labour (Fernández-Kelly, 1983; Fuentes and Ehrenreich, 1983). This is a rather dire assessment of development and its consequences.

In terms of research, development studies has of late been beset by theoretical problems. Where do we go after the end of the great

Development and Change (SAGE, London, Newbury Park and New Delhi), Vol. 23 (1992) No. 3, 215–255.

'metanarratives' – or competing paradigms – of modernization theory and dependency theory, neither of which was able to fully account for industrialization in South-East Asia or continued underdevelopment elsewhere? In modernization theory explanations too often seemed 'actorless'; urbanization, bureaucratization and the other components of modernization appeared driven by inexorable impersonal forces rather than by the interests and actions of states, classes and other social actors. The possibility that twentieth-century patterns of development might take forms that were distinctly different from earlier patterns was neglected as were questions of the impact of position in the international system on development possibilities (Evans and Stephens, 1987). Dependency theory and world-system theory were improvements, but the premise that external factors determine the dynamics of domestic development eventually proved unsatisfactory. More recently, it has been suggested that developmental paths should be seen as historically contingent (Booth, 1985; Mouzelis, 1988; Evans and Stephens, 1987).

On the other hand, Marx's description of how competition led to the concentration and centralization of capital often seems to have an automaticity which negates the possibility of diverse, historically contingent developmental outcomes. Consider the following passage from *The Communist Manifesto*, 1848:

> The bourgeoisie, by the rapid improvement of all instruments of production by the immensely facilitated means of communication, draws all, even the most barbarian, nations into civilization. The cheap prices of its commodities are the heavy artillery with which it batters down all Chinese walls. . . . It compels all nations, on pain of extinction, to adopt the bourgeois mode of production. (Marx and Engels, 1969: 112)

Given what has happened to Eastern Europe and the Soviet Union, the above proposition is actually quite reasonable. In the Marxist paradigm, history is seen as the growth of human productive power; forms of society rise and fall according to their ability to promote, or prevent and discourage, that growth (Cohen, 1978). It is, of course, supremely ironic that the concept of the fettering of the forces of production and their replacement by new relations of production capable of unfettering the subsequent development of the forces of production, would be applied to a so-called socialist context. But it does suggest the continuing relevance of Marxism's attention to both capitalism on a world scale and socio-economic contradictions in a national context.

Indeed, the Marxist paradigm is quite useful to development studies, as it offers a rigorous theoretical framework (including a dialectical method) that is suitable for social science research, for politics, and, I shall argue, for policy formulation. In terms of its analytic powers, the Marxist approach combines agency and institutional constraint (the structure/action dialectic), as well as historical evolution. It requires social actors with conflicting interests. It assumes that there is an international political economy which has little respect for national borders and which must be understood as a whole. It also seriously considers historical factors: historical evolution, or the trajectory of a society, is analysed in a way that would reveal the central structural determinants of that evolution. And while Marxism does not allow for indeterminacy and contingency, it is not incompatible with the idea of unintended consequences of actions or policies. It remains a powerful explanatory framework.

But there is something else that is compelling in the Marxist framework, and that is its emancipatory content. This it shares with feminism. Both are emancipatory theoretical traditions. Both identify specific forms of oppression in the existing world – the oppression of women in the case of feminism; class oppression, particularly of workers, in the case of Marxism.[1] Both theoretical traditions believe that the forms of oppression on which they focus should and can be eliminated. As Erik Olin Wright (1990) has recently put it, both feminism and Marxism see the active struggle of the oppressed groups at the core of their theory as an essential part of the process through which such oppression is transformed. And intellectuals working within both traditions believe that the central reason for bothering to do social theory is to contribute to the realization of their respective emancipatory projects.

This article examines the emancipatory content of development from a Marxist-feminist perspective, and focuses on its implications for women. My argument is a two-fold one which correlates women's status to form and stage of development: (1) the process of development has contributed to the dissolution of classic patriarchy in most parts of the world; (2) further socio-economic development, including paid employment for women, contributes to gender equity and emancipation of women. The first part of the hypothesis can be fairly easily substantiated by the historical record. The second part is admittedly tentative and will require more time to observe and assess the impact on gender inequality of the development process.

Nevertheless, I advance the proposition on the basis of recent studies from various parts of the world on trends in gender relations and the status of women, and in order to draw attention to positive (if unintended) features and effects of development.[2] The relation between development and women's emancipation is neither direct, automatic nor unilinear. Intervening factors such as economic crisis, cultural revivalism and political instability could worsen women's status. But I will argue that development erodes classic patriarchy, even though new forms of gender inequality emerge and class differences are intensified, and I propose that the long-term trend is towards less rather than more gender inequality, because development provides women with education, paid employment and a wider range of life-options.

Before proceeding, it is necessary to define development. My definition of development is a broad process of economic and social change, usually promoted by technological advancement but crucially affected by changes in social structure, property rights and social relations and cultural understandings. In addition to capital and class, states and revolutions play a role in development and change. This is a sociological approach to development, which differs from the typical development economics approach. Today many development economists focus on GNP, sectoral growth rates and a balanced budget as indicators of development. But the sociological definition of development is broader and our approach more comprehensive, for we are interested in 'society' as well as 'economy'.[3] Whether of a capitalist or socialist type, development is constituted by industrialization, urbanization and proletarianization, resulting in mass education and mass employment. This was the process that unfolded in the countries of what used to be called the First World and the Second World. A similar process has been taking shape in the so-called Third World, although under different historical conditions and within the confines of a world system in which they are disadvantaged.[4]

As part of my definition of development, I also wish to distinguish genuine development from distorted development, from what Samir Amin calls 'maldevelopment', and from reversals to development such as have occurred during the 'lost development decade' of the 1980s due to debt servicing and structural adjustment. Although both socialist and capitalist development have entailed industrialization and 'modernization' of agriculture, capitalist development has rather uniquely deployed an array of strategies of surplus extraction and labour control, including the utilization of family labour, the creation of vast informal sectors and chronic unemployment. This is not what I mean by genuine development. Under these sorts of accumulation regimes, any positive consequences for women are unintended and limited. Development must be seen first and foremost as human development: the satisfaction of basic needs, attention to quality of life, putting people first, creating the possibility for autonomy and action. The question that has preoccupied many students of development since the Second World War is not simply the abstract one of whether 'actually existing development' is good or bad (for it has been both), but how to support the liberation of people from hunger, poverty, illiteracy and disease – and what the responsibilities and roles are of states, élites and international organizations. In this connection, an analysis of structures, functions and relations of exploitation, such as provided for by a Marxian development approach, need not refrain from offering policy recommendations towards the betterment of groups of people.[5]

The status of women has been tied to and shaped by forms of production and property relations. Changes in production and distribution, including macro-level changes in demography, technology and the economy, and changes in consciousness and political forces have also affected the sexual division of labour, gender systems and the status of women. Historically, the transition from simple hunting and gathering communities to agrarian technology entailed a major shift in gender relations, what Engels (1975) called 'the world-historical defeat of the female sex' and what Gerda Lerner (1986) has called 'the creation of patriarchy'. With the rise of capitalism, patriarchy in Western Europe declined and was replaced by systems of gender inequality. Subsequently, gender relations and the position of women have been affected by urbanization, industrialization, the expansion of wage labour, warfare and political conflict. Notions of female equality and autonomy – the essence of feminism – and of course the women's movement, evolved with modernity and development (Chafetz and Dworkin, 1986). A similar, though not identical, trajectory may be observed in parts of the Third World. Indeed, in the Middle East, the erosion of classic patriarchy through the process of socio-economic development may be one cause of the rise of reactive Islamist movements (Mernissi, 1987; Moghadam, 1991a). This has also been suggested for South Asia (Chhachhi, 1991; Vaid and Sangari, 1991). Elsewhere in the Third World, such as in Latin America, development processes and women's participation in paid employment in the formal sector seem to have positive effects on family relations and the sexual division of labour within the household (Finlay, 1989; Safa, 1992).

PATRIARCHY

My definition of patriarchy is also a specific one, with a precise historical and anthropological meaning, influenced by the writings of Mann (1986), Lerner (1986), Caldwell (1982), Giele (1977) and Kandiyoti (1988).[6] Mann's elaboration of the trajectory of patriarchy historically and cross-culturally provides a particularly useful framework for exploring the relationship between development and the status of women. Mann has identified and traced the interrelations of five principal stratification nuclei – five collective actors that have impacted on gender/stratification relations over recent history. They are: the atomized 'person' (more pertinent to liberal, Western society); the connected networks of household/family/lineage; genders (the male and female sexes given social power significance); social classes; and nations and nation-states (Mann, 1986). In the patriarchal society power is held by male heads of households, and there is clear separation between the 'public' and the 'private' spheres of life. In the private sphere of the household, the patriarch enjoys arbitrary power over all junior males, all females and all children. In the public sphere, power is shared between male patriarchs according to whatever other principles of stratification operate. No female holds any formal public position of economic, ideological, military or political power. Indeed, females are not allowed into this public realm of power. (It goes without saying that men have the monopoly on the means of violence.) Whereas many, perhaps most, men expect to be patriarchs at some point in their life cycles, no women hold formal power. Within the household they may influence their male patriarch informally, but this is their only access to power. Contained within patriarchy are two fundamental nuclei of stratification: the household/family/lineage and the dominance of the male gender (Mann, 1986).

Social stratification was thus two-dimensional. One dimension comprised the two nuclei of household/family/lineage and the dominance of the male gender. The second dimension comprised whatever combination of 'public' stratification nuclei (classes, military élites, etc.) existed in a particular society. The latter dimension was connected to the former in that public power-groupings were predominantly aggregates of household/family/lineage heads. But apart from this, the two dimensions were segregated from each other.

Mann notes that this is an ideal-type. But it has not been so far from historical reality, from the first written records emerging from Mesopotamia around 2500 BC, to Western Europe up to the eighteenth century AD. His study is also consistent with Gerda Lerner's (1986) treatise on the creation of patriarchy. Ellen Meiksins Wood (1988) has also argued that there is a disposition to male dominance inherent in the relation between the pre-capitalist peasant household and the world of landlords and the state. The organization of society in general, and specifically the nature of the ruling class, places a special premium on male domination. Patriarchal societies sharply distinguished the public from the private; in the public sphere power relations have been overwhelmingly between male household-heads (patriarchs); and the private sphere has usually been ruled formally by a patriarch. In this context, there is no basis for collective action by women. If women sought to influence public power, they had to go through patriarchs (Lerner, 1986). Gender, though fundamental to stratification, was asymmetric: men could act, women could not.

Historically, property rights in land and livestock were often accompanied by property rights in labour – including property rights in women and children (Sacks, 1982). With the rise of patriarchy, women and children were assimilated in the concept of property. Engels's famous argument about the 'world-historical defeat of the female sex' with the rise of private property included the explanation that the sexual double standard was a device to ensure legitimacy of inheritance in the male line. The preoccupation with virginity, the honour–shame complex in the regions along the Mediterranean, practices such as cliterodictomy, foot binding and purdah, and other forms of control of women are among the aspects of patriarchy.[7]

In modern times, as the particularism of agrarian societies gave way before the universal and diffused stratification of modern society, stratification became gendered internally. This occurred with the entry of women in the public sphere. Mann notes that in Western Europe, from about the sixteenth to the eighteenth centuries, the stratification system changed under the pressure of emerging capitalism, first in agriculture and then in industry, as more of economic life became part of the public realm. The particularistic distinction between the public and the private was eroded, first by employment trends and the emergence of more universal classes, secondly by universal citizenship by all persons in the nation and thirdly by the nation-state's welfare interventions in the 'private household/family'. Mann's model thus posits a trajectory from patriarchy to neo-patriarchy to a stratification system based on gendered classes, 'personhood' and the nation. In as much as his model underscores the central structural determinants of the trajectory, it is parallel to the Marxian historical-structural approach.

In his studies of fertility patterns, the demographer John Caldwell (1982: 158, 162) refers to a patriarchal belt covering North Africa and South-West and South Asia. The anthropologist Jack Goody (1990), while dissenting from some aspects of Claude Lévi-Strauss's theory of the exchange of women and the incest taboo, also utilizes the term 'patriarchal' (again, in its strict sense) in a descriptive manner as part of his explanation linking systems of marriage and the family in pre-industrial Europe as well as in Asia and Africa to systems of production. Patriarchal families engage in transactions such as dowry, brideprice or bridewealth, or other kinds of prestations (Goody, 1990: 13–16). A relevant discussion of contemporary patriarchy is also provided by Kandiyoti (1988), who refers to 'a belt of classic patriarchy' which stretches from northern Africa across the Middle East to the northern plains of the Indian subcontinent and parts of (rural) China. 'Classic patriarchy' is reproduced through the operations of the patrilocally extended household, and is tied to the reproduction of the peasantry in agrarian societies. The patriarchal extended family gives the senior man authority over everyone else, including younger men, and entails forms of control and subordination of women which cut across cultural and religious boundaries. The social structures in this belt are characterized by their institutionalization of extremely restrictive codes of behaviour for women. It should be noted that both Muslim and non-Muslim societies are encompassed in this belt. What the societies have in common is the practice of rigid gender segregation, specific forms of family and kinship and a powerful ideology linking family honour to female virtue. Men are entrusted with safeguarding family honour through their control over female members; they are backed by complex social arrangements which ensure the protection – and dependence – of women (Kabeer, 1988; Mandelbaum, 1988). In contemporary Muslim patriarchal societies, such control over women is considered necessary in part because women are regarded as the potential source of *fitna*, that is, moral disorder or anarchy (Sabbah, 1984; Ghoussoub, 1987; Mernissi, 1987).

As Stacey (1983) found for China, patriarchy originates in a family and social system in which male power over women and children derives from the social role of fatherhood, and is supported by a political economy in which the family unit retains a significant productive role. Young brides marry into large families, gain respect mainly via their sons and late in life acquire power as mothers-in-law. In patriarchal settings, women's life-chances are restricted. One typically finds an adverse sex ratio, low female literacy and educational attainment, high fertility rates, high maternal mortality rates and low female labour force participation in the formal sector. Demographic facts about societies such as Afghanistan, Pakistan, Bangladesh and north India suggest 'a culture against women', in which women are socialized to sacrifice their health, survival chances and life-options (Papanek, 1989). The systematic food deprivation of women *vis-à-vis* men in many societies (particularly that of girls *vis-à-vis* boys in South Asia, West Asia, North Africa and rural China) is discussed in Miller (1981), Harris (1986) and Drèze and Sen (1989). These are areas where 'classic patriarchy' is strongest. Blau and Ferber (1992) cite a recent study of 144 countries confirming earlier research that showed a positive relation between women's labour force participation and the ratio of women to men in the population. The paper points out that women, when they are in the main 'only' wives and mothers, and not seen as economically active, are so short-changed in the allocation of resources that their chances for survival are reduced. Drèze and Sen (1989: 58) point out that 'there is considerable evidence that greater involvement with outside work and paid employment does tend to go with less anti-female bias in intra-family distribution'. They present a table which compares the ratios of economic activity rates (roughly pertaining to outside work, including paid employment) of women *vis-à-vis* men, and the ratios of female life expectancy to male life expectancy. The ranking of the different regions in terms of life expectancy ratios is almost the same as that in terms of activity rate ratios (Drèze and Sen, 1989: 59). In a recent paper on women and work in India and Bangladesh, Chen (1991) quotes Miller (1981: 117) that where female labour force participation (FLP) is high 'there will always be high preservation of female life, but where FLP is low, female children may or may not be preserved'.

Functionalist explanations for patriarchal forms of household organization and gender inequality stress their 'efficiency', 'complementarity' or time-honoured character. Asymmetries in legal rules and asset allocations tend to be downplayed if not denied in such explanations. In describing customs among the Durrani Pushtuns of north-central Afghanistan, anthropologist Nancy Tapper writes: 'The members of the community discuss control of all resources – especially labor, land, and women – in terms of honour' (Tapper, 1984: 299). In the context of a discussion of the contested custom of brideprice, she states that women are given for brideprice or in compensation for blood, and that this 'maintains a status hierarchy' among the households. Interethnic hostility is also described in functionalist terms. In Afghanistan, ethnic identity consists of claims to religiously privileged descent and superiority to all other ethnic groups. This extends to the absolute prohibition on the marriage of Durrani women to men who are of a 'lower' ethnic status. Following from this functionalist reasoning, the attempted abolition of brideprice and other reforms pertaining to marriage by Afghan revolutionaries in 1978 is criticized for its impact on ethnic relations. Tapper writes that 'any substantial alteration in the meaning of marriage within these groups (perhaps by the implementation of marriage reforms) could lead to a complete restructuring of ethnic relations' (Tapper, 1984: 304). Indeed.

Functionalist anthropology notwithstanding, Afghanistan presents an extreme case of contemporary 'classic patriarchy'; it is also one of the poorest and least developed countries in the world. Afghan patriarchy is tied to the prevalence of forms of subsistence such as nomadic pastoralism, herding and farming and settled agriculture, which are organized along patrilineal lines. Historically, Afghan gender roles and women's status have been tied to property relations. Property includes livestock, land and houses or tents. Women and children tend to be assimilated into the concept of property and to belong to a male (Anwar, 1988; Griffiths, 1981; Male, 1982; Nyrop and Seekins, 1986; Tapper, 1984). Gender segregation, veiling and female seclusion exist, though they vary by ethnic group, region, mode of subsistence, social class and family. Among Ghilzai, women are veiled or are secluded from men to whom they could be married. Men also avoid women who stand in the relationship of potential mate to them (Nyrop and Seekins, 1986: 127). Among the Pushtuns studied by one anthropologist, a bride who does not exhibit signs of virginity on the wedding night may be murdered by her father and/or brothers. This is not the case, however, within the Paghmanis and Absarinas, smaller ethnic groups studied by the same anthropologist (Nyrop and Seekins, 1986: 127).

The control of women in Muslim societies is commonly but erroneously attributed to Islam. It is best understood in terms of socio-economic structure and stage of development. The French ethnologist Germaine Tillion (1983) has pointed out that Meditteranean peoples (including Muslims) favour endogamy, and endogamy increases the tendency to control women in tightly interrelated lineages. Nikki Keddie (1990) writes that nomadic tribal groups have special reasons to want to control women and to favour cousin marriage. Pastoral nomadic tribes, the most common type in the Middle East, trade animal products for agricultural and urban ones. The cohesion of tribes and subtribes is necessary to their economy, which requires frequent group decision about migration. To make decisions amicably groups closely tied by kin are desirable. The practical benefits of close kinship, Keddie argues, are surely one reason cousin marriage has long been preferred among Middle Eastern people: it encourages family integration and co-operation. Keddie feels that controls on women are connected to the pervasiveness of tribal structures in the Middle East, and notes that even though most nomadic women are not veiled and secluded, they are controlled (Keddie, 1990).

Kandiyoti's research comparing the status of Turkish women in nomadic tribes, peasant villages, rural towns and cities reveals that the influence of the patrilineal extended household is pervasive in all sectors, but is less so in the towns and cities because of neo-local residence and the diminished importance of elders. It is true that compared to peasant and nomadic women, urban women play a sharply reduced role in the productive process, even though they are more likely to head their own households. But peasant and nomadic women do not receive recognition for their own labour, not even for their offspring, as these belong to the patrilineal extended family. Berik (1985) informs us that in many parts of rural Turkey, women have been traditionally called the 'enemy of the spoon' referring to the fact that they will share the food on the table without contributing economically to the household. Berik's study of carpet weavers in rural central Anatolia reveals that the labour power of the female weavers, and the wages that accrue to them, are controlled by male kin (Berik, 1985, 1987). This pattern has also been found for Iran (Afshar, 1985b) and Afghanistan (Moghadam, 1989). This results from the collusion of the partial penetration of capital with existing patriarchal ideology and family control of women. Patriarchy crumbles under the weight of urbanization, industrialization and proletarianization.[8]

REVOLUTIONS AND MODERNIZING STATES

Concepts of women's emancipation and the decline of patriarchy have come about through gradual development processes and through conscious action, whether by states or by popular movements. In this section I consider the contribution to the emancipation of women of nationalist movements, revolutions and of developmentalist regimes.

In a recent paper, Erik Olin Wright has argued that feminism and the elimination of 'gender oppression' is more viable than Marxism and the elimination of class oppression. One reason why this is so, he argues, is that the prospects for women's liberation 'depend crucially on consciousness raising and emancipatory struggles' (Wright, 1990: 19). His paper is concerned with the prospects of feminism and Marxism in contemporary advanced industrialized societies, and presumes a certain level of socio-economic development. I agree that gender equality is more viable than, say, workers' control, because class oppression and not gender oppression is central to the capitalist system of economic organization. I will return to this presently. But what I want to emphasize here is that the prospects for women's emancipation are very much tied to macro-level change processes such as industrialization, urbanization, revolution, modernizing regimes and welfarist states. In some of the advanced industrialized countries, notably Scandinavia, welfare states have played an important role in relieving women of some of the responsibilities for childcare and other forms of care-giving. In the former German Democratic Republic, as Einhorn (1989) explains, a policy of combating sex discrimination, indeed of positive discrimination towards women, had been in place since 1949.[9]

Elsewhere, and particularly in patriarchal contexts, nationalist movements and developmentalist states – both socialist and non-socialist – have been crucial agents of the advancement of women through the encouragement of education and employment. In many Third World countries, including Middle Eastern societies, feminism and nationalism were linked (Jayawardena, 1986). Concepts of the emancipation of women came about in the context of nationalism and anti-colonialism, state-building and self-conscious attempts towards modernity in the early part of the century; male feminists were especially instrumental in problematizing the Woman Question. Revolutionaries or nationalists who equated national progress with the advancement of women included the Bolsheviks in Russia, Kemalists in Turkey, Maoists in China, Tunisia under Bourguiba and South Yemen under the Marxists. Turkey and Tunisia replaced the Islamic personal status laws (based on *Sharia*, Islamic canon law derived from the Koran) with a civil code of law regulating personal and family relations and equalizing the duties and responsibilities of the sexes. In Turkey this was accomplished with the republican reforms and development of a militant secularism after 1926; in post-independence Tunisia, polygamy and unilateral divorce were abolished and the state assumed a stance strongly in favour of women's emancipation.

In Iran in the 1930s, the first Pahlavi monarch, a somewhat poor imitation of Ataturk, forcibly removed the veil from women in public.[10] The second Pahlavi state granted women the right to vote in 1962 and in 1967 introduced the Family Protection Act which limited polygamy, allowed women to initiate divorce and increased their child custody rights after divorce or widowhood. However, the Shah himself was opposed to 'women's lib' and frequently derided the demands of Western feminists. Moreover, his reforms were in place for only ten years and did not have widespread impact. When the Khomeinists assumed power in 1979, one of their first steps was to abrogate the Family Protection Act. It should be noted, though, that the very first act of opposition to the Islamists – and this at the height of the new regime's popularity and support – came from educated middle-class women, in early March 1979. These were the women who had been the principal beneficiaries of several decades of modernization. Development – however limited and skewed in its Iranian variant – combined with state reforms had allowed a segment of the female population upward social mobility through education and employment, and created a stratum and generation of women who opposed veiling and rejected Islamist exhortations that working women in the civil service return to the joys of domesticity and raise committed Muslims. These women were subsequently silenced – or imprisoned, killed or exiled. But in an interesting twist (and a further illustration of the interplay of structure, consciousness and agency), it is educated and employed Islamist women in Iran – university professors, members of parliament, the widow of a former prime minister – who are now demanding a modification of the rigid gender rules which were implemented in the early 1980s (Tohidi, 1990; Gerami, 1990; Moghadam, 1988, 1991b).

In many Muslim societies, the active role of the state in national development has meant that for many women it is no longer a male guardian – father or husband – who is the provider, but the state. As Fatima Mernissi remarks:

> The North African woman of today usually dreams of having a steady, wage-paying job with social security and health and retirement benefits, at a State institution; these women don't look to a man any longer for their survival, but to the State. While perhaps not ideal, this is nevertheless a breakthrough, an erosion of tradition. It also partly explains the Moroccan women's active participation in the urbanization process: they are leaving rural areas in numbers equaling men's migration, for a 'better life' in the cities – and in European cities, as well. (Mernissi, 1984: 449)

The most striking changes in the status of women have come about in the context of developmentalist socialist revolutions and regimes. In China the unfolding of large-scale historical processes – such as the breakdown of the Chinese imperial state, the beginning of industrialization, the rebuilding of the nation-state, Western cultural imperialism, urbanization, the dissemination of women's education and the crisis of the élite family – had weakened traditional constraints on female behaviour and helped women of various classes step across the boundary between the domestic and the public domains (Gilmartin, 1989). But the Communist Party of China accelerated the process first within its own ranks, and then, after assuming state power, throughout the country. The target was the feudalistic patriarchal household, especially in the countryside (Croll, 1984). Collectivization, wages for women and ideological campaigns were essential elements of this concerted effort to attack patriarchy and raise the status of women.[11]

Russia is the other well-known example of concerted efforts on the part of a developmentalist socialist state to emancipate women. Goldman (1989) has described the bold and audacious reforms in the family and in land ownership. The Bolsheviks were motivated by both an ideological commitment to egalitarianism and a practical need to expand the base of their support and enlarge the labour force. In the case of both China and Russia, principle and pragmatism combined to improve the status of women vastly. I do not think that anyone would seriously argue that the position of women in Russia and China was better before the Communists came to power.

Maxine Molyneux (1986) has argued that revolutionary governments tend to see the importance of reforming the position of women in the first period of social and economic transformation in terms of helping to accomplish at least three goals: to extend the base of the government's political support; to increase the size or quality of the active labour force; and to help harness the family more securely to the process of social reproduction. The case of South Yemen is instructive. In November 1967 the National Liberation Front (NLF) came to power after five years of guerrilla fighting and terminated 128 years of British colonial rule in South Yemen. The People's Democratic Republic of Yemen (PDRY) was born. In June 1969 the revolutionary government took a more radical turn, which aimed at 'the destruction of the old state apparatus', the creation of a unified, state-administered legal system and rapid social structural transformation. The pre-revolutionary social order was seen as an obstacle to economic development and social reform, which required the active participation of women. Kin control over women and the practice of seclusion had consequently to be transformed. In this context the Constitution of 1970 outlined the government's policies towards women, and a new Family Law was promulgated.

In the constitution women were referred to in terms of two main roles envisaged for them by the revolutionary government – as 'mothers' and as 'producers'. Article 7, which described the political basis of the revolution as 'an alliance between the working class, the peasants, intelligentsia and petty-bourgeoisie', went on to add that 'soldiers, women, and students are regarded as part of this alliance by virtue of their membership in the productive forces of the people' (Molyneux, 1985: 159). Women were thus recognized as forming part of the 'working people'; the constitution, in giving all citizens the right to work and in regarding work as 'an obligation in the case of all able-bodied citizens', called upon women not yet involved in 'productive work' to become so.

According to the preamble of the Family Law, the 'traditional' or 'feudal' family is 'incompatible with the principles and programme of the National Democratic Revolution . . . because its old relationships prevent it from playing a positive role in the building up of society'. The law began by denouncing 'the vicious state of affairs which prevails in the family', and proclaims that 'marriage is a contract between a man and a woman who are equal in rights and duties, and is based on mutual understanding and respect'. It established the principle of free-choice marriage; raised the minimum legal age of marriage to sixteen for girls and eighteen for boys; abolished polygamy except in exceptional circumstances such as barrenness or incurable disease; reduced the dower; stipulated that both spouses must bear the cost of supporting the family's economy; ended unilateral divorce; increased divorced women's rights to custody of their children (Molyneux, 1985: 155–6).

As in Soviet Russia and China, family reform was seen simultaneously as a precondition for mobilizing women into economic and political activity and as an indispensible adjunct of both economic change and social stability. The introduction of the new Family Law in the PDRY involved challenging both the power of the Muslim clergy and orthodox interpretations of Islam. After 1969 the government sought to curb the institutional and economic base of the traditional clergy and transferred its responsibilities to agencies of the state. Religious education in schools was made the responsibility of lay teachers. Kin, class and tribal control over women were outlawed and to some degree delegitimized. Women were classified in new ways – as workers, national subjects, political subjects – in order to help construct the new order. Most revolutions and many nationalist movements have combined a developmentalist orientation and concepts of women's rights. This has frequently unshackled women from patriarchal binds.

DEVELOPMENT, EMPLOYMENT AND WOMEN'S EMANCIPATION

A major conundrum in the field of women-in-development remains whether economic development helps or harms the lot of women in developing countries. The goal of 'integrating women in development' has come under attack by some feminist researchers of Latin America, Asia and Africa.[12] One group argues that women have indeed been integrated into development – much to their disadvantage, as they have become the latest group of exploited workers, a source of cheap and expendable labour (Elson and Pearson, 1981; Fuentes and Ehrenreich, 1983; Nash and Fernández-Kelly, 1983; Jain, 1990). Another group argues that development, especially modernization of a capitalist kind, has everywhere reduced the economic status of women, resulting in marginalization and impoverishment (Ward, 1984; Sen and Grown, 1987). A further indictment of integration into development and into the world system is that recession and the debt crisis during the 1980s have placed disproportionate burdens on women, especially poor women but including working women. Similarly, there has been disagreement regarding female proletarianization and the effects of employment. On one side there is the premise that 'the female labour force participation rate as the measure of women's economic status is . . . arguably the key one of the various indicators of the quality of life for women' (Joekes, 1987: 21). On the other side is the assertion that 'waged employment rarely represents a liberation for Third World women' (Mitter, 1986: 63).

It is interesting to note that some of the most vocal critics of female industrial employment have been socialist feminists. In this regard they diverge from Marx's view of the capitalist mode of production as an historical advance over feudal bondage (notwithstanding his trenchant critique in *Capital*). They also diverge from Engels's view that women's participation in factory wage labour emancipates them from domestic slavery and patriarchal arrangements (see Lim, 1990). Apart from this view of historical evolution, what is especially useful in the Marxist paradigm are the concepts of the dialectic and contradictions – as opposed to various binarisms and dichotomies – which both predict and explain the simultaneous existence of positive and negative, exploitative and liberating features and consequences of capitalist development.[13]

It may be useful to examine the women-in-development debate further. Writing for INSTRAW, a UN agency dealing with women, Joekes (1987) proposes that women's social and economic positions are improved most directly by their involvement in paid work. Here Joekes explores the impact of export trade, international finance and technology upon women's paid employment in agriculture, industry and services in Asia, Africa and South America. The study found a strong association between the growth of manufactured exports and the growth of female industrial employment where wages are higher than in agriculture or services. It argues that women's improving economic position is directly related to international factors, including investment by transnational corporations. The study concludes with recommendations for policies to protect gains and improve women's conditions. Lim (1990) points out that the lower wages women receive in export industries than in manufacturing as a whole does not mean that these women workers are poorly paid relative to all others in the economy. She points out that in Mexico, women working in the *maquiladoras* along the US border typically earn at least the legal minimum wage. 'In a country where unemployment runs as high as 40% and barely half of those who have jobs earn the minimum wage, this puts them in the top quartile of the national income distribution. The same is true in Bangkok or Manila' (Lim, 1990: 109). According to one UN study, 'Prima facie, one gets the impression that women employed by TNCs are better off than those employed by local enterprises, the level of their wages being higher than those of their counterparts employed by domestic firms. However, the average wages for women in TNCs are far less than those of male workers, ranging from 50% to 75% of male wages in comparable occupations' (*The CTC Reporter*, No. 26, 1988: 33).[14]

The advantages to women of paid work are borne out by a recent sociological study of women, work and family in rural areas of the Dominican Republic. Finlay (1989) set out to understand the traditional division of labour and decision-making within rural Dominican households, and to see the changes that occur when women move from traditional roles into the market economy as wage earners. To that end, she conducted a survey of two groups of women in Azua: 'community women' and women employees of the export-processing agri-businesses. Her interest was in the effects of this type of wage work on the traditional division of labour, on family structure, and on the attitudes, standard of living and aspirations of the women themselves. The results are intriguing. In the author's own words: 'the division of labour within the home seems to have undergone important changes within workers' families. The workers themselves were less likely to assume full responsibility for all domestic work than were the community sample women' (Finlay, 1989: 139). Significantly, the workers also had more power and control over resources within the family, with the effect that children and the family in general were better off – a conclusion also reached in a series of studies edited by Bruce and Dwyer (1988). And because workers were more likely to limit their fertility, the infant mortality rate was lower as a result. The workers in Finlay's study also had higher aspirations for their children, in terms of both occupational and educational hopes.

Other studies support this trend. Safa (1992) reports that women factory workers in export manufacturing in the Caribbean use their earnings and the family's increased dependence on them to bargain for increased authority and sharing of responsibility within the household. This is in part linked to the failure of men to fulfil their role as economic providers, and the high rates of unemployment in the region. She further argues that women's increased ability to contribute to family income may challenge traditional patriarchal authority and lead to more egalitarian family structures. A study of Turkish women factory workers showed that 'married women factory workers in Bursa have gained a considerable degree of power over decision-making in their families as a result of their employment. Over half the married women who were interviewed reported that they and their husbands took decisions together and often consulted each other' (Ecevit, 1991: 77).

A recent quantitative study of labour supply in rural Tanzania demonstrates the constraints on the supply of female labour resulting from marriage arrangements whereby men who own land acquire control over the labour of their wives and subsequently their children (Smith and Sender, 1990: 1337). The authors explain that women who enter wage work are typically not married, or divorced, or deserted, or widows whose deceased husbands did not leave them (or, more precisely, their sons) adequate resources, or do not undertake unpaid work for men. The authors criticize the notion that 'resistance to proletarianization' enables peasant households to enjoy a superior quality of life, for this implies that women enjoy a superior quality of life as a result of restrictions which confine their labour to household production. They conclude that: 'It is arguable that the reverse is more likely' (Smith and Sender, 1990: 1340).

It should be noted that the process of female proletarianization differs from male proletarianization. Unlike men, female proletarians do not undergo a process of separation or dispossession from the means of production, as they typically do not hold possession or control of it as pre-capitalist peasant producers. A proletarianized woman can sell her labour power to any capitalist whereas a female peasant producer labours under a particular configuration of male power relationships within the family (Bryceson, 1985). While the proletarianization of women entails labour control (as it does for men), wage work also provides prospects for women's autonomy – a factor that does not obtain for men.

A growing number of studies confirm that women do well when given opportunities to be independent and to earn income, and that they are generally better off in paid employment than in unpaid family labour, informal sector type activities, outwork or 'micro-enterprises' (small-scale income-generating activities favoured by certain aid agencies). The extent to which paid work enhances women's social power depends very much on whether it provides for women the experience of being active agents in a public process. A recent study of household decision-making regarding the factory employment of young female members suggests that seeking factory employment is not necessarily done in tandem with parental visions of a daughter's role or a family economic plan (Wolf, 1990). In her comparative study of Java and Taiwan, Wolf found young women who disobeyed and rebelled against parental control; she also found, mainly in Java, that most young women were motivated to seek factory employment for individual social and economic reasons, not for the betterment of the family economy. In Taiwan, however, she found that the patrilineal and patrilocal kinship system socializes daughters to be filial and to pay back what their parents incurred in bringing them up; this is what largely motivated female factory employment there (Wolf, 1990: 54).

Development, including technological change, is a contradictory process which both displaces *and* provides additional employment for women. Weil (1992) reports that in Sub-Saharan Africa, women have been displaced as imported lager beer has replaced the traditional beer brewed by women, and in West Africa, cheaper imported soap has taken over markets serviced by women who have long made soap from palm oil and wood ash. On the other hand, while still relatively rare in Africa, the export-processing zone in Mauritius has provided additional employment for over 22,000 workers, some 80 per cent of whom have been women.

While one would not want to romanticize factory work – there is certainly much that can be done to improve conditions – there is growing evidence from around the world that employed women, including working-class women with factory jobs, value their work for the economic independence and family support it provides, and for the opportunity to delay marriage and child-bearing. In many countries, young women in particular are able to escape restrictive family circumstances and to enjoy 'horizon-broadening' experiences and the companionship of other women (Joekes and Moayedi, 1987). Paid employment also provides opportunities for women's self-organization as women workers. Mitter quotes the young woman vice-president of the Bangladesh Garment Workers Federation, referring to the expansion of export-oriented garment production in Bangladesh: 'These jobs have been catalysts for a bigger struggle for women's independence' (Mitter, 1986: 75). Paid employment also has socially useful consequences: there are strong linkages between female education and employment on the one hand, and lower fertility and infant mortality rates (not to mention maternal mortality) on the other.[15]

It is of course understood that the structure of opportunities in the formal sector is limited by gender bias and occupational sex-typing (which is the cause of the earnings gap). Further determinants of women's access to employment and economic resources are the macro-economic environment (which shapes the employment structure), the state and legal system (which could act as facilitator or impediment), the class context (work for middle-class women is as a rule better than work for proletarian women) and the specific form of paid work (e.g. factory work is very different from outwork). It should also be stressed that the transnational firm does not guarantee stable, long-term employment (for men or for women). Thus the work in a transnational or world-market factory is often highly stressful and without benefits or advancement, or even assurance of a future (ILO/UNCTC, 1988). The expansion of female employment in the formal sector is also constrained by what Afshar has called 'a coincidence of interests between capital and male policy-makers' (Afshar, 1985a: ix) which has resulted in the creation of a female domain in subsistence agriculture responsible for reproducing and nurturing a large reserve army of cheap labour.

One may therefore propose that in the short term, the relationship between development and women's status is an empirical question which seems to depend on a number of factors. First, there is the class factor. Middle-class women generally benefit more from development than do proletarian and peasant women, whether in terms of income, status, working conditions or quality of life. In many developing countries, middle-class women work in the public sector, such as in government agencies, where conditions are better and jobs more secure than they are for proletarian women in the private sector. Second, the type of development strategy is key. Oil-centred industrialization, as has proceeded in most of the Middle East, has tended to marginalize women, and import-substitution industrialization through capital-intensive technologies has favoured male labour over female labour. In many Middle Eastern countries, women's share of the measured labour force is considerably below the Third World average, and women's participation in industrial production is insignificant (see Moghadam, 1992b). Studies indicate that export-oriented industrialization is more conducive to increased female employment (Joekes and Moayedi, 1987). Third, the structure of pre-industrial relations, and women's pre-existing positions in their communities, provide important clues as to the impact of development on women's status. The mobility and autonomy women enjoyed in the Andes, south India or in parts of Sub-Saharan Africa prior to colonialism and modernization stand in contrast to the situation of women in the belt of 'classic patriarchy'. Women in the Andes (Bourque and Warren, 1981) or in the Pacific (Gailey, 1987) lost status with colonialism and development, but in the Middle East, most of South Asia, Central Asia and East Asia, where the control of women was strongest, development would be more likely to improve their situation by disrupting patriarchal controls.

With regard to wage employment and women's status in Turkey, Abadan-Unat (1981: 127) refers to the existence of 'archaic and patriarchal family structures' as obstacles to the transformation of women's status. Kandiyoti has argued that we cannot speak of a simple decline in women's status with the transition to an urban wage labour economy because capital penetration introduces considerable heterogeneity into the gender division of labour. This is illustrated in her empirical study of Turkish women in shanty-towns, lower middle-class and traditional middle-class women, and educated middle- and upper-class women (Kandiyoti, 1977, 1980) and her discussion of village patriarchy (Kandiyoti, 1984). The contradictory and class-specific consequences of development and women's employment have also been described by Papanek (1985). She notes that in many developing countries, such as the West Asian and South Asian countries she has looked at, educated women from the middle class have been entering modern-sector employment in increasing numbers. Many of these women come from families where paid jobs for women were unacceptable in earlier generations.

> Their entry into the paid labour force has occurred in response to two factors. First, demand for educated female labour has increased as a result of the expansion of the modern sector [and the state]. Second . . . aspirations have risen and now increasingly require cash incomes beyond those earned by adult male family members. . . . On the other hand, uneducated women – mostly poor – have lost their traditional earning opportunities, partly as a result of accelerated technological innovations and other changes brought about by development.

> Poor, uneducated women obviously do not compete for the same jobs that have become available for educated middle-class females. Much of the work poor women have depended on in the past is now being done by men or machines. (Papanek, 1985: 134)

Although women's status is changing and variable in the Middle East, North Africa, West Asia and South Asia, patriarchal structures persist with implications for female educational attainment, employment and fertility. Many demographic studies of developing countries, including summaries and reports of the World Fertility Survey of 1977–82, have found that fertility and non-agricultural labour force participation are negatively related (Anker et al., 1982; Anker, 1985; Bodrova and Anker, 1985; McDonald, 1985; Sathar et al., 1988). Middle Eastern countries have lower non-agricultural female labour force participation and higher fertility rates than do other areas. In this case causality must be sought in the type of development strategy pursued (oil-centred and limited industrialization), which has had limited success in eroding patriarchal kinship arrangements and Islamic family law. Development, broadly defined, and its concomitant, female employment, would alter such a situation in women's favour. Further industrialization in West and South Asia would integrate more women into paid employment in the formal/modern sector of the economy, which would in turn have other socially positive effects (including lower fertility). The emancipatory effects for women are self-evident. When paid work provides the only means for open female participation and interaction in a cultural milieu otherwise characterized by rigid sex roles and gender constructs, then in countries such as Iran, Afghanistan, Pakistan, Saudi Arabia, Jordan and Algeria, where women constitute less than 10 per cent of the measured labour force, 'integrating women in development' is fairly revolutionary in its implications.

'FLEXIBILITY', ORGANIZED LABOUR AND WOMEN WORKERS

Where subcontracting is favoured by multinationals and domestic firms, this has dubious implications for women's employment and emancipation, and adverse implications for the position of labour as a whole. One consequence of the increasing incorporation of women into the labour force under conditions of 'flexibility' is to weaken the power of organized labour. Standing (1989) has argued that what he calls global feminization through flexible labour results from structural adjustment policies and the need to cut labour costs in order to meet increasing international competition from developing as well as advanced industrial societies. Standing cites a number of factors such as the growth of export processing, labour market deregulation through subcontracting and the informal sector, and cuts in government expenditure that contribute to the rising participation rates of women and the falling participation rates of men. If, as Standing suggests, women are being substituted for men in various occupational categories, then this may be a reflection of and contributing factor to the erosion of trade union strength in those regions.

It is true that in many places women constitute a cheap labour reserve which is difficult to organize, since many work in the informal economy or in areas like seasonal agriculture or export processing where labour unions are prohibited or politically controlled.[16] It is no doubt also true that low-wage female employment is a management strategy against male 'labour aristocracies'. Historically, capital has maintained what Marx called the reserve army of labour and what Standing (1987) defines as vulnerable groups in urban labour processes. This has served to divide the working class, keep wages down and increase profits. The growth of informalization of work, and the deployment of female labour in this process, is by no means a desideratum from a Marxist-feminist perspective. Low-wage, part-time or informal sector work is not incompatible with patriarchal arrangements and is not conducive to the goals of equity and empowerment of women. The latter is accomplished in part through stable and properly remunerated employment.

If 'cheap female labour' is displacing organized male labour, the onus should be on the trade unions to take women workers more seriously and indeed to organize them. Safa (1992) argues that at present women workers in many areas have no adequate vehicles through which to express their grievances or to transform their sense of exploitation (which is very real) into greater class solidarity. She concludes: 'Until the claims of women workers are given the same legitimacy as those of men, and not regarded as supplementary or subsidiary, women will continue to be treated primarily as a source of cheap labour.' Similarly, Rohini asserts that:

> Unless women organise and press the trade-union movement to oppose the gender division of labour in all its aspects, it is likely that not only women workers but all workers will continue to suffer the consequences, and the possibilities inherent in the entry of women into the labour force of manufacturing industry will not be fully realised. (Rohini, 1991: 285)

In conclusion, development entails integration, marginalization, *and* exploitation – for male and female producers and workers. But the specificity of women's oppression is that (unlike male labour) their subjugation is rooted not in capitalism, which it long predates, but in patriarchy; not in the wage relations between capitalist and worker, to which gender is not central, but in the domestic relations between men and women; not in the workplace, where sexism is but one of the many forms of division and discrimination, but in the patriarchal household (Kusterer, 1990). If kinship systems operate so as to construct women as a subordinate gender (Whitehead, 1984: 189), then capitalism constructs the working class as the subordinate class. Gender is not central to capitalism as class is, but gender bias is clearly present in all cases. It is present in policies that *exclude* women from economic participation, and in management strategies that *include* women as cheap ('flexible') labour and a divisive element. Capitalism of course exploits labour – that of men and of women – but it is essentially indifferent to the labour it exploits. It utilizes differences within the working classes – differences based on race, ethnicity, gender, skill – but gender is not central to the wage relationship as is class. Capitalism exploits labour and is uninterested in the welfare of people. But it also provides the conditions for the eventual demise of patriarchy, and for the betterment of women *as women*. As development increases, and as women are drawn in greater numbers into paid employment and public life, their subjugation *as women* is undermined and gender roles and constructs change. This is why, to return to Wright's discussion of the viability of the feminist project, gender inequality, versus the Marxist project, the abolition of class exploitation, the former is indeed more viable in a capitalist context.

An empirical indicator of this trend towards less rather than more gender inequality is that since the 1960s literacy and education among women worldwide has increased, even though male–female ratios in attainment remain very unequal in the Third World. The female share of the labour force has also increased everywhere, even though women tend to be clustered in 'feminine' white-collar occupations and low-wage service jobs (ILO/INSTRAW, 1985).

Evidence is accumulating to suggest a trend whereby countries with higher levels of economic development, industrialization and urbanization are more likely to increase gender equality (Kim, 1990). If the long-term trend in development is to enhance the status of women, in the short-term setbacks and failures are inevitable, and call for the attention of concerned and committed researchers and practitioners.

STRUCTURAL ADJUSTMENT, PRIVATIZATION AND DEVELOPMENT PROSPECTS

In the 1980s, most developing countries experienced rising indebtedness and suffered substantial setbacks in growth and development. In some cases economic contraction and declines in living standards have reached astounding proportions. The response of the World Bank and IMF was to provide for both short-term relief and long-term restructuring of developing country economies through stabilization and adjustment lending policies. Structural adjustment lending was defined as 'non-project lending to support programs of policy and institutional change necessary to modify the structure of an economy so that it can maintain both its growth rate and the viability of its balance of payment in the long term' (Joekes, 1989: 12), and has come in the form of structural adjustment loans (SALs) or sectoral adjustment loans (SELs). Although these adjustment loans have different maturities, come from different sources and are used in different ways, they all have policy conditions attached to them which have had direct impact on women's lives – on their workloads and on their incomes. The main thrust of the IMF stabilization programmes has been to cut back on expenditure, through controls on credit creation and public expenditure levels, reduction in subsidies, especially food subsidies, and cuts in real wages and public sector employment. In addition, the programmes include measures to encourage resource reallocation to more productive uses and the internationally traded sector, through devaluation, price decontrol and wage restraints. Longer-term measures include financial reforms. Clearly, these programmes would have implications for women as producers, consumers, household managers, mothers and care-givers.

The emphasis away from project investments in favour of increased efficiency in public expenditure has on the whole increased inequality and poverty and adversely affected women's economic status. Indebtedness and the concomitant structural adjustment policies have resulted in greatly reduced allocation of resources to social reproduction. In Jamaica, a decline in the ratio of health personnel to population has made it almost impossible for women to have access to important health services. A now classic study by UNICEF (1987) argues that adjustment policies in most cases have aggravated the situation of the poor, and that reductions in spending on social programmes have had a particularly detrimental effect on children. Real wages have dropped, access to health and to education has been reduced for the poor and the middle class, and in various countries the decline in infant mortality has slowed down or has stopped entirely. This has been the case where there have not been poverty-targeted measures to alleviate the impact of structural adjustment. (Zimbabwe provides an encouraging exception: see UNDP, 1990: 35.) In a country with extreme inequality of income, the situation has been exacerbated by the dynamics of adjustment programmes, to the point where the society is truly fractured into two: the well-to-do middle and upper middle classes who have maintained in many cases and even improved their incomes in US dollar terms, and the rest of the population who have borne the brunt of the devaluations and the reduction of public expenditure on health and education (Levitt, 1990: 1593). One effect of the economic crisis has been to curtail opportunities in paid employment and to open up more self-employment activities. But the array of informal sector activities – street vending, petty commodity production, personal services and small-scale transportation – is notoriously precarious. Returns are often minimal, people are overworked and there is no security (Safa, 1982; Sethuraman, 1981; Portes, 1983). Weil (1992) argues that the primary effect of adjustment programmes, through the contractionary aspects of stabilization, has been to reduce the amount of credit available. Without special attention, women tend to be crowded out of formal credit markets. This is a vivid illustration of how free market policies are not only biased in general, but biased against women.

The declines in per capita income so closely associated with the debt crisis, particularly in Latin America and Africa, have disrupted virtually all aspects of women's lives, forcing them to shoulder extra burdens to keep families afloat. Women have to work much longer hours in and outside the home and often suffer physically and emotionally as a result. This drain on women's time, resources and energy also inhibits their ability to participate in political life and hence to have an influence in changing the policies which affect them so adversely. The crisis has diminished educational and economic opportunities for young women, thus affecting their future ability to contribute to society on an equal basis with men. Reductions in public expenditure adjustment have more often than not included cuts in food subsidies, and devaluation leads to increases in all imported goods, including food. Certain groups of women, particularly women in poor urban households and female heads of households, are especially adversely affected by increases in the price of food. So are women with special nutritional needs, i.e. pregnant and nursing women. This could and should be offset by food programmes for this group of women in the midst of austerity.

The resulting undercapitalization of women's production, transformation and marketing activities constrains national growth potentials. Structural adjustment further exacerbates this bias by overlooking, if not denying, women's access to and consumption of the type of productive resources and services such as extension, credit and input subsidies that are targeted to export production. In so far as this limits women's productivity, adjustment policies are sabotaging their very goals of stable long-term growth (Joekes, 1989; Commonwealth Secretariat, 1989: 4). Strategic policy intervention is thus required to prevent or at least reduce the adverse effects of adjustment on women and on national development.

Some of these strategic interventions have been suggested by the UNICEF (1987) report. They include more expansionary macroeconomic policies aimed at sustaining levels of output, investment and human need satisfaction over the adjustment period; the use of 'mezo' policies to determine the impact of policies towards taxation, government expenditure, foreign exchange and credit (among others) on the distribution of income and resources; sectoral policies focusing on small farmers and informal sector producers in industry and services; improving the equity and efficiency of social sector spending; compensatory programmes to protect basic health and nutrition of those with low incomes; monitoring of the human situation. A WIDER project based on the adjustment experience of eighteen countries concluded that a 'socially necessary growth rate' of 5.5 per cent in GDP terms is needed to provide basic needs, reduce unemployment, and improve income distribution – but this requires a massive annual transfer of capital from the North (Taylor, 1990).

Debt and austerity have undone a great deal of the advance in human development attained in previous decades. The 1980s have been called the Lost Development Decade, and even the World Bank has noted that poverty has increased dramatically (World Bank, 1990). In this context gains in women's status – such as increased employment in the public sector and the formal private sector, access to state-funded education and health – have been lost in many countries. A similar pattern of development reversals and adverse social consequences may be observed in the former socialist countries now undergoing privatization and the transition to a market economy. Especially where 'shock therapy' has been applied, notably Poland, the results have been widespread unemployment, the rise of poverty and homelessness and a denial to women of the social benefits they enjoyed in the previous systems (Moghadam, 1992a). Neither structural adjustment in developing countries nor the privatization crusade in the former socialist countries is consistent with the definition and goals of development presented in this article.

Austerity and structural adjustment have placed enormous pressures on Third World women, forcing them to devise all manner of survival strategies. But these measures have also sparked public protests, initiated by women and by men. Bread riots and austerity protests, also known as 'IMF riots', have occurred in numerous countries (Walton and Ragin, 1990). Women have been present in all forms of collective protest and resistance, from the establishment of communal kitchens in Lima, Santiago and other Latin American cities to participation in organized movements and in street demonstrations (Eckstein, 1989; Safa, 1992). Indeed, Eckstein reports that in Mexico City, women in the city's largest shanty town have protected their community against land developers attempting to evict families. In Brazil, women's community organizations have engaged in political campaigns to improve standards of living. In Asia, too, women have been involved in collective action in response to austerity and policies of stabilization and adjustment. Thus, while structural adjustment has victimized women (and men, and children), it has also emboldened them to take action and to act politically (Daines and Seddon, 1991).

FEMINIST STRATEGIES FOR DEVELOPMENT

Genuine human development encompasses more than GNP growth, more than income and wealth and more than producing commodities, accumulating capital and balancing budgets. Development is about people and societies, about quality of life and the enlargement of human capabilities and people's choices. The authors of the *Human Development Report* (UNDP, 1990) argue that to live a long and healthy life, to be educated and to have access to resources needed for a decent standard of living are the most critical of human capabilities and choices. Additional choices include political freedom, guaranteed human rights and personal self-respect. Development enables people to have these choices, by creating a conducive environment for people, individually and collectively, to develop their full potential and to have a reasonable chance of leading productive and creative lives in accordance with their needs and interests. 'Development is ultimately . . . [a matter] of the capacity of a society to tap the root of popular creativity, to free up and empower people' (Levitt, 1990: 1594). Proposing an improvement in the status and lives of the poor and working classes has often been viewed as a threat by those people who have more status, wealth or power. But development *has* come about, and it has done so as a result of collective action, or through responsible state systems and popular participation. An external environment that is at least not hostile is also a prerequisite.

Since the political and social status of women is secondary to that of men in most societies, proposing an improvement in their status could similarly be viewed as a threat to the status quo. But women – as women and as workers – have demonstrated a capacity for collective action through their participation in movements and organizations for change. Women are not only victims of bad policies, but actors in their own right and agents of social change.[17] Moreover, as a result of women's movements and of the efforts of various UN agencies, élites are beginning to recognize the practical benefits of gender awareness and of increased attention to women's work and women's lives. They are more cognizant that women tend to spend a high proportion of earnings to improve family well-being, and that development programmes or changes in laws, regulations and customs to build women's economic productivity and improve their earning capacity will have direct benefits for families as well (Blumberg, 1989). Both the imperatives of distributive justice and concerns about societal development call for women's access to productive resources (employment, training, credit, land, extension services, legal reform), access to basic goods and services (household needs, education, health) and external resource flows (such as debt reduction). In turn, these contribute to the long-term goals of gender equity and the empowerment of women.

'Integrating women into development' thus remains not only a valid goal but a radical one, as it challenges social and political structures, the distribution of wealth, and cultural mores (Charlton, 1984). An effective strategy must integrate economic, political, legal and cultural aspects at the domestic, regional and international levels. Interventionist policies are needed to make more progress towards gender equity and the emancipation of women. The long-term goal of social equity and full participation of women in decision-making processes requires a number of concrete measures in the immediate and medium term which are especially crucial in developing countries:

- The protection of women's existing sources of livelihood.
- The elimination of discriminatory legislation in the ownership and control of productive assets.
- Agricultural incentives.
- Investment in rural infrastructure and services.
- Land reform.
- Improving employment opportunities and work conditions of women in the formal sector.
- The support of extra-household forms of organization of women's labour and assisting with self-employment.
- Public works programmes.
- Ensuring access to health and education services.
- Training women teachers who will serve as role models.
- General education on 'women's issues'.
- Shifting resources into primary health programmes.
- Action against the degradation of women through sex-related tourism and prostitution.
- The encouragement of an increased capacity for political empowerment and organization.

The concept of development that emerges from this endeavour is emancipatory; it advances a notion of development and change that is liberating, and a strategy that places people's basic needs and human development first rather than last. A Marxist-feminist perspective recognizes the international and national relations of exploitation and structural constraints but seeks to alter the rules of the game and assist in the process of transformation through strategies and policies to improve the quality of people's lives. A Marxist-feminist development strategy seeks to end the chronic unemployment and underemployment of people, to valorize the work that women perform and to make more equitable the sexual and social divisions of labour; and it seeks a redistribution of wealth and income at the global and societal levels. A Marxist-feminist policy perspective would identify gender-biased projects, seek to strengthen women's positions in the labour market and at the workplace, and suggest ways to redirect government expenditure to support working women.

CONCLUSION

In this article I have asked whether there is a relationship between development and women's emancipation. I have tried to show that, historically, the process of development has entailed both emancipation and exploitation, liberation and oppression, and I have argued this within a Marxist-feminist framework. The negative entailments are well known: the exploitation of the producing classes and the degradation of the environment. In capitalist development especially, the constant search for cheap labour, the manipulation of reserve armies of labour and the persistence of poverty (even in many advanced industrialized countries) have been an integral part of the process. But development – whether capitalist or socialist – has also increased life expectancy, decreased infant and maternal mortality, and enlarged people's choices. This has been especially significant for women, who historically have been the most disadvantaged social group, with a limited range of life-options, and an inability to act autonomously under long-standing patriarchal arrangements. The erosion of classic patriarchy, and women's access to paid employment are critical stages in the movement towards the emancipation of women. Development has differentiated women, but it has also provided them with a wider range of choices and activities. Except in cases of revolutionary outcomes and actions by developmentalist states, these consequences for women have been largely unintended. The point is to recognize in theory the contradictory process of socio-economic development, and to ensure through policy and politics that the positive aspects of the development process continue.

NOTES

1. As is well known, Marxist-inspired development theory (e.g. dependency theory and world-system theory) also examined oppression at the international level, arguing that colonialism and imperialism were responsible for Third World underdevelopment. Some theorists also used the term 'oppressed nations', now out of currency.

2. This article is concerned exclusively with exploring the relation between socioeconomic development and prospects for women's emancipation. I cannot address the many other interesting and related theoretical issues in development studies, such as the relation between development and inequality, multinational investment and national well-being, development and the working class.

3. Among the more sociological of the development economists are Albert Hirschman and Dudley Seers. Alexander Gerschonkron included an historical-comparative sociological approach in his seminal work on late development. Other development economists whose approach is compatible with that taken here are Amiya Bagchi, Ajit Singh and Amartya Sen.

4. Another approach to development has been called 'the new comparative historical political economy' (NCHPE). Evans and Stephens (1987), two of its theorists, identify four areas as research priorities: (1) the role of the state in the process of development; (2) accumulation and distribution, or how the fruits of development should be distributed; (3) the consequences of economic change for political regimes, or the relation between industrialization and political democracy; and (4) the relation between national development and the world political economy. While NCHPE draws heavily on the critiques of modernization theory and as such is inspired by Marxist and dependency points of view, it does not ground itself systematically in familiar Marxian categories. It is unfortunate that in their lengthy literature review, Evans and Stephens completely bypass the WID scholarship and do not take up the gender dimension of economic development and political change. For an elaboration on this, see Moghadam (1990).

5. In an interesting article, Booth argues that the limited utility of Marxism for development sociology lies in its structural-functionalism: its 'metatheoretical commitment to demonstrating the "necessity" of economic and social patterns, as distinct from explaining them and exploring how they may be changed' (Booth, 1985: 761). Booth neglects Marxist theory's concepts of dialectics and contradictions, which provide for a theory of social change (see, for example, Smelser, 1973), unlike standard structural-functionalism in sociology. Furthermore, Booth somewhat surprisingly ignores the political and purposive dimension of Marxism: 'the point is to change things'.

6. My use of the concept of patriarchy differs from that of Sylvia Walby (1990). While sympathetic to her attempt to theorize patriarchy and rescue it from misuse, I am not convinced by her distinction between private patriarchy (with its household mode of production, where women are barred from the public sphere and controlled in a fairly direct way by individual patriarchs) and public patriarchy (in which women

have access to both spheres but are subordinated collectively in the public one). The salience of class and of class differences among women and between women and men in 'public patriarchy' are not accounted for in her schema.

7. On the honour–shame complex in the Mediterranean, see Pitt-Rivers (1977) and Tillion (1983); on purdah see Mandelbaum (1988); on marriage, virginity, bride-price and so on, see Goody (1990); on women and property see essays in Hirschon (1984); on marriage customs in patriarchal Afghanistan, see Kamali (1985).

8. Of course I do not mean uncontrolled urban growth with inadequate services for residents and huge informal sectors, such as we may find in many Third World cities. Nor do I mean by proletarianization, immiseration. Rather, I mean wage employment in the formal sector under proper working conditions.

9. An interesting example of unintended (positive) consequences of policy for women is the case of educational reform in post-war Poland, discussed by Bialecki and Heyns (1991). They discovered that, while the intent had been to provide increased access to higher education to the working class, 'the major egalitarian trend that appears to be a consequence of socialist education is diminished gender inequality. The expansion of vocationally oriented educational programs at both the secondary and post-secondary level was intended to provide a new Communist man with technical skills for productive labour; their major effect seems to have been the displacement of men by women in the conventional academic tracks' (Bialecki and Heyns, 1991: 15).

10. While the Khomeinists would vehemently deny any similarities with the Pahlavis, their *compulsory veiling* of women in the early 1980s was the mirror image of the *compulsory unveiling* by Reza Shah.

11. In more recent years, Chinese modernization, especially the shift from collective farming to family farms, has had negative consequences for women's emancipation, inasmuch as the peasant household is a patriarchal institution headed by a man. I am grateful to Ajit Singh for drawing my attention to this example of retrogression. For an elaboration of the Chinese case, see Davin (1991).

12. See Tiano (1987) for a thorough review of the debates and literature.

13. It may be necessary to point out that my approach to the contradictory process and effects of development differs from that of the late Bill Warren (1980). I am uncomfortable with his generalizations and categorical statements and agree with Booth (1985) that Warren's method of argument takes us from the indiscriminate pessimism of the dependency view of the world to a barely less misleading generalized optimism. Furthermore, I am dismayed by Warren's preoccupation with *capitalist* development, as if non-capitalist development were not possible or desirable.

The framework presented here is also radically different from the old modernization view, which posited an automatic, unilinear progress effected by foreign investment (including the assumption that all women would benefit from the market economy), and was oblivious to relations of exploitation.

14. These observations and arguments obviously contradict the main propositions of dependency thought, which tended to regard foreign investment as leading to underdevelopment rather than development. The positive consequences for women are of course wholly unintended by investors and policy-makers, but can be explained theoretically in terms of the contradictory effects of capitalist development and its tendency to break down patriarchal controls through the proletarianization of women.

15. Joan Robinson's famous quip is apposite here: under capitalism, the next worst

thing to being exploited is not being exploited, i.e. being unemployed.

16. This is not true in India, where the famous Self-Employed Women's Association (SEWA), based in Ahmedabad, has had success in organizing women in the informal sector and supporting co-operatives. But see Westwood (1991) for a discussion of the contradictions of supporting home-based work for women.

17. India provides an interesting case study not only of the contradictory and differential effects of development on women's economic status, social positions and life-options, but also of the emergence of a dynamic women's movement and of activist development researchers promoting women-centred development policies. See, for example, Mehendale (1991), Everett and Savara (1991), Rohini (1991) and Westwood (1991).

REFERENCES

Abadan-Unat, N. (ed.) (1981) *Women in Turkish Society*. Leiden: Brill.

Afshar, H. (1985a) 'Introduction', in H. Afshar (ed.) *Women, Work and Ideology in the Third World*, pp. ix–xvii. London: Tavistock.

Afshar, H. (1985b) 'The Position of Women in an Iranian Village', in H. Afshar (ed.) *Women, Work and Ideology in the Third World*. London: Tavistock.

Anker, R. (1985) 'Comparative Survey', in V. Bodrova and R. Anker (eds) *Working Women in Socialist Countries: The Fertility Connection*, pp. 1–21. Geneva: ILO.

Anker, R., Buvinic, M. and Youssef, N. (1982) *Women's Roles and Population Trends in the Third World*. Geneva: ILO.

Anwar, R. (1988) *The Tragedy of Afghanistan*. London: Verso.

Apter, D. (1987) *Rethinking Development: Modernization, Dependency, and Postmodern Politics*. Newbury Park, CA: Sage.

Berik, G. (1985) 'From "Enemy of the Spoon" to "Factory": Women's Labor in the Carpet Weaving Industry in Rural Turkey', paper presented at the Annual Meetings of the Middle East Studies Association of North America, New Orleans 22–6 November.

Berik, G. (1987) *Women Carpet Weavers in Rural Turkey: Patterns of Employment, Earnings and Status*. Geneva: ILO.

Bialecki, I. and Heyns, B. (1991) 'Educational Attainment, the Status of Women, and the Private School Movement in Poland', paper prepared for the Conference on Gender and Restructuring: Perestroika, the 1989 Revolutions and Women. UNU/WIDER, Helsinki (2–3 September).

Blau, F.D. and Ferber, M.A. (1992) 'Women's Work, Women's Lives: A Comparative Perspective', in H. Kahne and J. Giele (eds) *Women's Lives, Women's Work: Parallels and Contrasts in Modernizing and Industrial Countries*. Boulder, CO: Westview Press.

Blumberg, R.L. (1989) *Making the Case for the Gender Variable*. Washington, DC: Office of Women in Development, Agency for International Development.

Bodrova, V. and Anker, R. (eds) (1985) *Working Women in Socialist Countries: The Fertility Connection*. Geneva: ILO.

Booth, D. (1985) 'Marxism and Development Sociology: Interpreting the Impasse', *World Development* 13(7): 761–87.

Boserup, E. (1970) *Women's Role in Economic Development*. New York: St Martin's Press.

Bourque, S. and Warren, K. (1981) *Women of the Andes*. Ann Arbor, MI: University of Michigan Press.

Bruce, J. and Dwyer, D. (eds) (1988) *A Home Divided: Women and Income in the Third World*. Stanford, CA: Stanford University Press.

Bryceson, D.F. (1985) 'Women's Proletarianisation and the Family Wage in Tanzania', in H. Afshar (ed.) *Women, Work and Ideology in the Third World*, pp. 128–52. London: Tavistock.

Caldwell, J. (1982) *Theory of Fertility Decline*. New York: Academic Press.

Chafetz, J. Saltzman and Dworkin, A.G. (1986) *Female Revolt: Women's Movements in World and Historical Development*. Totawa, NJ: Rowman and Allenheld.

Charlton, S.E. (1984) *Women in Third World Development*. Boulder, CO: Westview Press.

Chen, M.A. (1991) 'A Matter of Survival: Women's Right to Work in India and Bangladesh', paper prepared for the Conference on Human Capabilities: Women, Men and Equality, UNU/WIDER, Helsinki (August).

Chhachhi, A. (1991) 'Forced Identities; the State, Communalism, Fundamentalism and Women in India', in D. Kandiyoti (ed.) *Women, Islam and the State*, pp. 144–75. London: Macmillan.

Cohen, G.A. (1978) *Karl Marx's Theory of History. A Defense*. Oxford: Oxford University Press.

Commonwealth Secretariat (1989) *Engendering Adjustment for the 1990s*. London: Commonwealth Secretariat.

Croll, E. (1984) 'The Exchange of Women and Property: Marriage in Post-Revolutionary China', in Renée Hirschon (ed.) *Women and Property — Women as Property*, pp. 44–61. London: Croom Helm.

Daines, V. and Seddon, D. (1991) 'Survival Strategies, Protest and Resistance: Women's Responses to Austerity and Structural Adjustment', Gender Analysis in Development, sub-series 4. Norwich: University of East Anglia, School of Development Studies.

Davin, D. (1991) 'Chinese Models of Development and their Implications for Women', in H. Afshar (ed.) *Women, Development and Survival in the Third World*, pp. 30–52. London and New York: Longman.

Drèze, J. and Sen, A. (1989) *Hunger and Public Action*. Oxford: Clarendon.

Ecevit, Y. (1991) 'The Ideological Construction of Turkish Women Factory Workers', in N. Redcliff and M.T. Sinclair (eds) *Working Women: International Perspectives on Labour and Gender Ideology*, pp. 56–78. London and New York: Routledge.

Eckstein, S. (1989) 'Power and Popular Protest', in S. Eckstein (ed.) *Power and Popular Protest: Latin America Social Movements*, pp. 1–60. Berkeley, CA: University of California Press.

Einhorn, B. (1989) 'Socialist Emancipation: The Women's Movement in the German Democratic Republic', in S. Kruks et al. (eds) *Promissory Notes*, pp. 282–305. New York: Monthly Review Press.

Elson, D. and Pearson, R. (1981) 'The Subordination of Women and the Internationalisation of Factory Production', in Kate Young et al. (eds) *Of Marriage and the Market: Women's Subordination in International Perspective*, pp. 144–66. London: CSE Books.

Engels, F. (1975) *The Origin of the Family, Private Property and the State*. New York: International Publishers (originally published 1884).

Evans, P. and Stephens, J. (1987) 'Development and the World Economy', Working Paper No. 8/9. Providence, RI: Brown University, Center for Comparative Development Studies.

Everett, J. and Savara, M. (1991) 'Institutional Credit as a Strategy Towards Self-Reliance for Petty-Commodity Producers in India: A Critical Evaluation', in H. Afshar (ed.) *Women, Development and Survival in the Third World*, pp. 239–59. London and New York: Longman.

Fernández-Kelly, P. (1983) *For We Are Sold, I and My People: Women and Industry in Mexico's Frontier*. Albany, NY: SUNY Press.

Finlay, B. (1989) *The Women of Azua: Work and Family in the Rural Dominican Republic*. New York: Westport; London: Praeger.

Fuentes, A. and Ehrenreich, B. (1983) *Women in the Global Factory*. Boston, MA: South End Press.

Gailey, C. Ward (1987) *Kinship to Kingship*. Austin, TX: University of Texas Press.

Gerami, S. (1990) 'The Role, Place and Power of Middle Class Women in Iran', paper prepared for the Conference on Identity Politics and Women, UNU/WIDER, Helsinki (10–12 October).

Ghoussoub, M. (1987) 'Feminism – Or the Eternal Masculine – in the Arab World', *New Left Review* 161 (Jan./Feb.): 3–13.

Giele, J.Z. (1977) 'Introduction: Comparative Perspectives on Women', in J.Z. Giele and A.C. Smock (eds) *Women: Roles and Status in Eight Countries*, pp. 1–32. New York: Wiley.

Gilmartin, C. (1989) 'Gender, Politics, and Patriarchy in China: The Experiences of Early Women Communists, 1920–27', in S. Kruks et al. (eds) *Promissory Notes*, pp. 82–105. New York: Monthly Review Press.

Goldman, W.Z. (1989) 'Women, the Family, and the New Revolutionary Order in the Soviet Union', in S. Kruks et al. (eds) *Promissory Notes*, pp. 59–81. New York: Monthly Review Press.

Goody, J. (1990) *The Oriental, the Ancient and the Primitive: Systems of Marriage and the Family in the Pre-Industrial Societies of Eurasia*. Cambridge: Cambridge University Press.

Griffiths, J.C. (1981) *Afghanistan*. Boulder, CO: Westview Press.

Harris, N. (1986) *The End of the Third World: Newly-Industrializing Countries and the Decline of an Ideology*. Harmondsworth: Penguin.

Hirschon, R. (ed.) (1984) *Women and Property – Women as Property*. London: Croom Helm.

ILO/INSTRAW (1985) *Women in Economic Activity: A Global Statistical Survey (1950–2000)*. Geneva: ILO; Santo Domingo: INSTRAW.

ILO/UNCTC (1988) *Economic and Social Effects of Multinational Enterprises in Export Processing Zones*. Geneva: ILO/UNCTC.

Jain, D. (1990) 'Development Theory and Practice: Insights Emerging from Women's Experience', *Economic and Political Weekly* 7 July: 1454–5.

Jayawardena, K. (1986) *Feminism and Nationalism in the Third World*. London: Zed Books.

Joekes, S. (1987) *Women in the World Economy: An INSTRAW Study*. New York: Oxford University Press.

Joekes, S. (1989) 'Gender and Macro-Economic Policy'. Occasional Paper No. 4. Washington, DC: Association for Women and Development.

Joekes, S. and Moayedi R. (1987) *Women and Export Manufacturing: A Review of the Issues and AID Policy*. Washington, DC: ICRW.

Kabeer, N. (1988) 'Subordination and Struggle: Women in Bangladesh', *New Left Review* 168 (March/April): 95–121.

Kamali, M.H. (1985) *Law in Afghanistan: A Study of the Constitutions, Matrimonial Law and the Judiciary*. Leiden: E.J. Brill.

Kandiyoti D. (1977) 'Sex Roles and Social Change: A Comparative Appraisal of Turkey's Women', *Signs* 3(1): 57–73.

Kandiyoti D. (1980) 'Urban Change and Women's Roles: An Overview and Evaluation', in H.A. Rivlin and K. Helmer (eds) *The Changing Middle Eastern City*, pp. 121–37. Binghamton, NY: SUNY, Center for Social Analysis, Program in Southwest Asian and North African Studies.

Kandiyoti D. (1984) 'Rural Transformation in Turkey and its Implications for Women's Status', in UNESCO *Women on the Move*. Paris: UNESCO.

Kandiyoti D. (1988) 'Bargaining With Patriarchy', *Gender & Society* 2(3): 274–90.

Keddie, N.R. (1990) 'The Past and Present of Women in the Muslim World', *Journal of World History* 1(1): 77–108.

Kim, H.K. (1990) 'The Changing Status of Women: A Cross-National Analysis', paper presented at the annual meetings of the American Sociological Association, Washington, DC 11–15 August.

Kusterer, K. (1990) 'The Imminent Demise of Patriarchy', in Irene Tinker (ed.) *Persistent Inequalities: Women and World Development*, pp. 239–55. New York: Oxford University Press.

Leacock, E. (1975) 'Introduction', in F. Engels *The Origin of the Family, Private Property and the State*, pp. 7–67. New York: International Publishers.

Lerner, G. (1986) *The Creation of Patriarchy*. New York: Oxford University Press.

Levitt, K. (1990) 'Debt, Adjustment and Development: Looking to the 1990s', *Economic and Political Weekly* 25(29): 1585–94.

Lim, L. (1990) 'Women's Work in Export Factories: The Politics of a Cause', in I. Tinker (ed.) *Persistent Inequalities: Women and World Development*, pp. 101–19. New York: Oxford University Press.

McDonald, P. (1985) 'Social Organization and Nuptuality in Developing Societies', in J. Cleland and J. Hobcraft (eds) *Reproductive Change in Developing Countries: Insights from the World Fertility Survey*, pp. 87–114. Oxford: Oxford University Press.

Male, B. (1982) *Revolutionary Afghanistan*. New York: St Martins Press.

Mandelbaum, D. (1988) *Women's Seclusion and Men's Honor*. Tucson, AZ: University of Arizona Press.

Mann, M. (1986) 'A Crisis in Stratification Theory? Persons/Households/Families/Lineages, Gender, Classes and Nations', in R. Crompton and M. Mann (eds) *Gender and Stratification*, pp. 40–56. Cambridge Polity Press.

Marglin, F.A. and Marglin, S.A. (eds) (1990) *Dominating Knowledge*. Oxford: Clarendon Press.

Marx, K. and Engels, F. (1969) 'The Communist Manifesto' (originally published

1848), in *Karl Marx and Friedrich Engels, Selected Works Volume One*, pp. 98–137. Moscow: Progress Publishers.

Mehendale, L. (1991) 'The Integrated Rural Development Programme for Women in Developing Countries: What More Can Be Done? A Case Study from India', in H. Afshar (ed.) *Women, Development and Survival in the Third World*, pp. 223–38. London and New York: Longman.

Mernissi, F. (1984) 'Morocco', in R. Morgan (ed.) *Sisterhood is Global*, pp. 444–53. New York: Anchor Books.

Mernissi, F. (1987) *Beyond the Veil: Male–Female Dynamics in a Muslim Society*, 2nd edn. Bloomington, IN: University of Indiana Press.

Mies, M. (1986) *Patriarchy and Accumulation on a World Scale*. London: Zed Books.

Miller, B. (1981) *The Endangered Sex*. Ithaca, NY: Cornell University Press.

Mitter, S. (1986) *Common Fate, Common Bond: Women in the Global Economy*. London: Pluto.

Moghadam, V. (1988) 'Women, Work and Ideology in the Islamic Republic', *International Journal of Middle East Studies* 20(2): 221–43.

Moghadam, V. (1989) 'Patriarchy, the State, and Women in Afghanistan: Problems and Prospects', submitted to UNICEF/UNIFEM Workshop on Planning and Afghan Women, New York (August).

Moghadam, V. (1990) 'Gender, Development and Policy: Toward Equity and Empowerment', WIDER Research for Action Monograph Series (November).

Moghadam, V. (1991a) 'Islamist Movements and Women's Responses', *Gender & History* 3(3): 268–86.

Moghadam, V. (1991b) 'The Reproduction of Gender Inequality in Muslim Societies: A Case Study of Iran in the 1980s', *World Development* 19(10): 1335–50.

Moghadam, V. (ed.) (1992a) *Privatization and Democratization in Eastern Europe and the Soviet Union: The Gender Dimension*. Helsinki: UNU/WIDER Research for Monograph Series.

Moghadam, V. (1992b) 'Women, Employment and Social Change in the Middle East and North Africa', in H. Kahne and J. Giele (eds) *Women's Work, Women's Lives: Parallels and Contrasts in Modernizing and Industrial Countries*. Boulder, CO: Westview Press.

Molyneux, M. (1985) 'Legal Reform and Socialist Revolution in Democratic Yemen: Women and the Family', *International Journal of Sociology of Law* 13: 147–72.

Molyneux, M. (1986) 'Mobilization Without Emancipation? Women's Interests, State, and Revolution', in R. Fagen, C.D. Deere and J.L. Corragio (eds) *Transition and Development: Problems of Third World Socialism*, pp. 280–302. New York: Monthly Review Press.

Mouzelis, N. (1988) 'Sociology of Development: Reflections on the Present Crisis', *British Journal of Sociology* 35(1): 23–44.

Nash, J. and Fernández-Kelly M.P. (eds) (1983) *Women, Men and the International Division of Labor*. Albany, NY: SUNY Press.

Nyrop, R. and Seekins, D. (eds) (1986) *Afghanistan: A Country Study*. Washington, DC: The American University, Foreign Area Studies.

Papanek, H. (1985) 'Class and Gender in Education-Employment Linkages', *Comparative Education Review* 29(3): 317–46.

Papanek, H. (1989) 'Socialization for Inequality: Entitlements, the Value of Women, and Domestic Hierarchies'. Boston, MA: Center for Asian Development Studies, Boston University.

Pitt-Rivers, J. (1977) *The Fate of Shechem or The Politics of Sex: Essays in the Anthropology of the Mediterranean*. Cambridge: Cambridge University Press.

Portes, A. (1983) 'The Informal Sector: Definition, Controversy, and Relation to National Development', *Review* 7(1): 151–74.

Rohini, P.H. (1991) 'Women Workers in Manufacturing Industry in India: Problems and Possibilities', in H. Afshar (ed.) *Women, Development and Survival in the Third World*, pp. 260–87. London and New York: Longman.

Sabbah, F. (1984) *Woman in the Muslim Unconscious*. New York: Pergamon Press.

Sacks, K. (1982) *Sisters and Wives*. Urbana, IL: University of Illinois Press.

Safa, H. (ed.) (1982) *Toward A Political Economy of Urbanization in the Third World*. Delhi: Oxford University Press.

Safa, H. (1992) 'Changing Gender Roles in Latin America and the Caribbean', in H. Kahne and J. Giele (eds) *Women Lives and Women's Work: Parallels and Contrasts in Modernizing and Industrial Countries*. Boulder, CO: Westview Press.

Sathar, Z., Crook, N., Callum, C. and Kazi, S. (1988) 'Women's Status and Fertility Change in Pakistan', *Population and Development Review* 14(3): 415–32.

Sen, G. and Grown, C. (1987) *Development, Crisis, and Alternative Visions: Third World Women's Perspectives*. New York: Monthly Review Press.

Sethuraman, S.V. (ed.) (1981) *The Urban Informal Sector in Developing Countries: Employment, Poverty and Environment*. Geneva: ILO.

Shiva, V. (1988) *Staying Alive: Women, Ecology and Survival*. New Delhi: Kali for Women.

Smelser, N. (1973) 'Introduction', in N. Smelser (ed.) *Karl Marx: On Society and Social Change*, pp. vii–xli. Chicago, IL: University of Chicago Press.

Smith, S. and Sender, J.B. (1990) 'Poverty, Gender and Wage Labour in Rural Tanzania', *Economic and Political Weekly* 16–23 June: 1334–42.

Stacey, J. (1983) *Patriarchy and Socialist Revolution in China*. Berkeley, CA: University of California Press.

Standing, G. (1987) 'Vulnerable Groups in Urban Labour Processes', WEP Labour Market Analysis Working Paper No. 13. Geneva: ILO.

Standing, G. (1989) 'Global Feminization through Flexible Labor', WEP Labour Market Analysis Working Paper No. 31. Geneva: ILO. (Shorter version in *World Development* 17(7): 1077–96.)

Tapper, N. (1984) 'Causes and Consequences of the Abolition of Brideprice in Afghanistan', in N. Shahrani and R. Canfield (eds) *Rebellions and Revolutions in Afghanistan*, pp. 291–305. Berkeley, CA: University of California International Studies Institute.

Taylor, L. (1990) *Foreign Resource Flows and Developing Country Growth*. Helsinki: UNU/WIDER.

Tiano, S. (1987) 'Gender, Work, and World Capitalism: Third World Women's Role in Development', in B. Hess and M. Marx Feree (eds) *Analyzing Gender*, pp. 216–43. Newbury Park, CA: Sage.

Tillion, G. (1983) *The Republic of Cousins* (trans. Q. Hoare). London: al-Saqi.

Tohidi, N. (1990) 'Identity Politics and the Woman Question in Iran: Retrospect and Prospects', paper prepared for the Conference on Identity Politics and Women, UNU/WIDER, Helsinki (10–12 October).

UNDP (1990) *Human Development Report 1990*. New York: Oxford University Press.

UNICEF (1987) G. Cornia, R. Jolly and F. Stewart (eds) *Adjustment with a Human Face*. Oxford and New York: Clarendon Press.
Vaid, S. and Sangari, K. (1991) 'Institutions, Beliefs, Ideologies: Widow Immolation in Contemporary Rajasthan', *Economic and Political Weekly* (27 April): WS-2–18.
Walby, S. (1990) 'From Private to Public Patriarchy: The Periodisation of British History', *Women's Studies International Forum* 13(1/2): 91–104.
Walton, J. and Ragin, C. (1990) 'Bread Riots, Banks and the Debt Dilemma', *PEWS News* (Winter): 3-6.
Ward, K. (1984) *Women in the World-System: Its Impact on Status and Fertility*. New York: Praeger.
Warren, B. (1980) *Imperialism: Pioneer of Capitalism*. London: New Left Books.
Weil, G. (1992) 'Women in the Economies of Sub-Saharan Africa', in H. Kahne and J. Giele (eds) *Women's Lives, Women's Work: Parallels and Contrasts in Modernizing and Industrial Countries*. Boulder, CO: Westview Press.
Westwood, S. (1991) 'Gender and the Politics of Production in India', in H. Afshar (ed.) *Women, Development and Survival in the Third World*, pp. 288–308. London and New York: Longman.
Whitehead, A. (1984) 'Women and Men: Kinship and Property: Some General Issues', in R. Hirschon (ed.) *Women and Property – Women as Property*, pp. 176-92. London: Croom Helm.
Wolf, D.L. (1990) 'Daughters, Decisions and Domination: An Empirical and Conceptual Critique of Household Strategies', *Development and Change* 21(1): 43–74.
Wood, E. Meiksins (1988) 'Capitalism and Human Emancipation', *New Left Review* 167 (Jan./Feb.): 3-20.
World Bank (1990) *World Development Report 1990: Poverty*. New York: Oxford University Press.
Wright, E.O. (1990) 'Explanation and Emancipation in Marxism and Feminism'. Madison, WI: Department of Sociology, University of Wisconsin (mimeo).

Valentine M. Moghadam is Senior Research Fellow and Coordinator of the Research Programme on Women in Development, United Nations University. She has been at the World Institute for Development Economics Research (UNU/WIDER), Annankatu 42C, 00100 Helsinki 10, Finland, since 1990. Born in Iran, she is the author of many articles on the Iranian revolution, women, and the labour movement in the Iranian context. Her book, *Women and Social Change in the Middle East*, will be published by Lynne Rienner.

The State and the Dialectics of Emancipation

Wim F. Wertheim

There is in Asia less mental resistance to State intervention than in the West, for Asia has a long history of effective and helpful State action.
(Maurice Zinkin in *Asia and the West*, 1953: 214)

INTRODUCTION

Today there is a tendency, not only in Western public opinion, but also among some scholars, to view the state as a negative factor, particularly in relation to economic development. We are confronted with a trend towards neo-liberalism not very different from the mood prevalent during the greater part of the nineteenth century, when the free functioning of market forces was expected to promote real economic development and the role of the state was viewed as marginal at best. The question needs to be asked, however, whether the state cannot, and in the past did not, frequently function as a significant factor in promoting economic development, and sometimes even as an ally of emancipatory forces; and if so, under what conditions this has been the case.

In addressing this question, I use the term 'emancipation' for *any* form of collective struggle of groups that feel themselves to be treated as 'underdogs', fighting against the privileges of the 'upperdogs'. In this sense, emancipation includes a whole range of social groups struggling for recognition as being *at least* equal with those who thus far exercised political, economic or social power over them. One may think of emancipation of labourers, peasants, coloured nations, racial or other ethnic minorities, women, youth and many other categories.

The original meaning of 'emancipation', in early Roman society, was a decision of a master to free a slave belonging to his

Development and Change (SAGE, London, Newbury Park and New Delhi), Vol. 23 (1992) No. 3, 257–281.

patrimonium or *mancipium*, or of a father to grant manumission (full authority over his possessions) to a son who had reached the age of maturity. In nineteenth-century American history, emancipation was still used in the sense of freedom *granted* to slaves through an act of benevolence on the part of those in power, such as President Lincoln's Emancipation Proclamation of 1863. My concept of emancipation does not refer to a liberation of individuals distinguishing themselves from their former peers; nor does it refer to freedom granted from above to a group or category without a struggle for recognition of its right to equality. As a sociological concept, emancipation refers to a collective struggle on the part of a thus far underprivileged group or category.

There is a tendency to restrict the concept of emancipation to the struggle waged by one specific group. In the Netherlands, for example, it is common for the term 'emancipation' to refer in particular to women's liberation. Terms such as the 'Emancipation Council', the 'Under-secretary for Emancipation Affairs', the first and second 'Emancipation Wave' all refer exclusively to the issue of equality for women, although in the nineteenth-century Netherlands emancipation was still used for issues such as the advancement of labourers, Roman Catholics or Jews. More important, from a theoretical point of view, is another restriction, frequently applied by Marxists, who connect emancipation to class struggle. Thus, the revolutions at the end of the eighteenth century are viewed as class struggles between a rising bourgeoisie and a ruling aristocracy. After the bourgeoisie became dominant, it is the proletarian class that is deemed to be struggling for victory. This restriction of the concept of emancipation to class struggle, with the proletarian class as the dynamic force, is much too narrow an interpretation of emancipation as an historical and sociological phenomenon.

Max Weber warned against reification of social institutions, which he called *Kollektivgebilde* (Weber, 1922: 444–6). For example, a bank, a school, a church or a state cannot be viewed as an objective reality within social life. They only represent a certain social reality as long as their existence as such is acknowledged by a broad category of people. Weber advocated that historical institutions be freed from this kind of 'magic spell'; he was aware that *Kollektivgebilde*, with the illusion of imperishability, could easily fade away once people withdrew their support from the dominant power structure.[1] Similarly, the concept of 'class' should not be viewed as an objective reality, with an existence of its own independent from the consciousness of the people involved. This is particularly relevant to the Marxist concept of a class-in-itself, which is supposed to exist independently of any recognition and awareness on the part of its members. This is a fiction – in Weber's terminology a 'magic spell' – the expression of an expectation that in the future the members will become aware of their common interests and thus be transformed into a 'class-for-itself'.

This concept, with its stress upon a demonstrable class consciousness among its members, may be viewed as referring to an objective social reality. Recognizing this does not imply, however, that the Marxist interpretation which looks to a proletarian class as the main agency for revolution and emancipation, can be accepted as valid and satisfactory in the present world situation. In most Third World countries, for example, an industrial proletariat is discernible only in an embryonic state. All the same, even in Mao's China there was an expectancy that 'workers, peasants and soldiers' would lead the society towards its optimum state. Although the Chinese Revolution of 1945–49 was mainly an agrarian revolution, reaching the big towns only in the final phase, Marxist and even Maoist theory claim that the workers' class was the real vanguard of the revolution. In fact it was not the urban workers who ruled the country, but the Communist Party led predominantly by intellectuals – just as in the Soviet Union. Hence the ultimate estrangement between the state and the people.

My interpretation of emancipation does not need a proletariat as a harbinger of paradise. Emancipation is not an ideology, still less a class ideology, but a highly important, maybe even basic, historical and sociological phenomenon; it is in the first place action based and always occurs in terms of a struggle. Emancipation starts from that which people themselves are yearning and struggling for – whatever they view as liberation. The real motive power is of a predominantly mental nature, not the prevalence of a certain material 'mode of production'. Its main roots are in the realm of norms and values. In an earlier study (Wertheim, 1983; see also Worsley, 1984) I distinguished several phases in a number of historical emancipation movements, which can be characterized as follows: (1) fighting for equality; (2) fighting for self-assertion; (3) fighting for a new society, based on solidarity among different groups of former underdogs. Only in the third phase could one speak, to an extent, of a struggle by a class-for-itself, but not necessarily with an industrial proletariat as a vanguard.

Emancipation should be viewed as a fundamental phenomenon in the history of humankind. I do not pretend that it is a consistent and irreversible trend in human history. Emancipation does not aspire at some sort of final apogee, but remains open ended. It will always be a dialectical process, with ups and downs. It is precisely emancipation *struggle*, erupting time and again, which evokes strong counterforces that should be recognized as significant historical phenomena. Nederveen Pieterse (1989/1990) rightly opposes 'empire' to 'emancipation' and 'power' to 'liberation'.[2] Only by developing an insight into this interplay and mutual struggle between two trends, both conceived as key elements in total social evolution, can we arrive at an understanding of the dynamic of social evolution, both on a micro- and a macro-level. The 'teeming millions' of Asia, Africa, South and Central America still stand for 'most of the world' in dire need of emancipation. The original Marxist interpretation of emancipation was above all concerned with the fate of an industrial proletariat suffering from capitalist exploitation. At present, those who 'have nothing to lose but their chains' are not the Western industrial workers enjoying a good deal of social protection, but the innumerable have-nots among the peasantry and the urban subproletariat of the Third World.

The first part of this article sketches the role of the state in economic transformation as an historical phenomenon. I do not pretend to develop a new interpretation of economic history; but only an historical-sociological analysis, starting from the concept of emancipation as defined above, can shed proper light on past and recent processes, including the dramatic changes in the role of the state in some parts of the world over the past few years. Depending upon the historical context, 'the state' may appear in a great variety of forms. The national state was a relatively late phenomenon in world history; even today there are many multinational states, both in and outside Europe. In this article, the term 'state' is generally used in opposition to private market forces, without referring to a specific branch of the state structure.[3]

EARLY MERCANTILISM

The current tendency to view private enterprise as the decisive factor which has propelled Western societies towards economic growth and industrial development, and to discount the role of the state as one of minor significance, is a hangover from the nineteenth century. The one-sided attribution of economic growth to an independent bourgeoisie was not only dominant among defenders of capitalism in that period, but also determined the thinking of Marx and his followers. Nederveen Pieterse (1989/1990) has demonstrated that an exaggeration of the role of the bourgeoisie has equally led to a monocausal conception of the rise of imperialism in the Western world; a thorough reappraisal of the role of the state in Western economic development is long overdue.

Eighteenth-century British state policies included a set of economic practices, supported by its naval power, which have since been labelled 'mercantilist'. In the seventeenth century, India had a distinct lead over Britain in the textile manufacturing industry: 'besides supplying the needs of the local aristocracy and merchants', Indian manufacturers were able to 'meet the demands of traders coming from Europe and other parts of Asia' (Mukherjee, 1958: 195). In the course of the eighteenth century, when the manufacture of textiles began to develop in England, it needed government support to be able to withstand the competition from India. Imports were severely restricted and even the wearing of wrought silk and printed and dyed calicoes from India, Persia and China was eventually prohibited by law (Mukherjee, 1958: 307).[4] A curious element of this policy was that British manufacturers claimed protection against their own compatriots – the British merchants in the service of the East India Company, who had become the main exporters of Indian silks and calicoes into England.

In 1776, Adam Smith's *The Wealth of Nations* was published. His plea for free trade was apparently a sign of a new awareness that British national economic interests no longer needed state protection since Britain was already on the way to becoming the 'workshop of the world' (Smith, 1976). Smith set the tone for a widespread belief that economic affairs should be the exclusive business of private entrepreneurs – an important factor in the decline of mercantilism. This view, which Breman (1990) has called 'the myth of non-intervention', even induced Max Weber to assume that the growth of industry had been entirely the work of capitalist entrepreneurs, led in their endeavour by the 'Protestant Ethic'. In this context, he misread the economic successes of the Dutch during the seventeenth century, the Dutch 'Golden Age'. He attributed the rapid rise of Dutch economic power largely to the Protestant Ethic, although he saw its force as somewhat impaired by the ascent to power of the patrician regents, whom he calls a 'class of rentiers' (Weber, 1956: 43).[5]

Albert Hyma (1942) discusses several instances of state intervention on behalf of Dutch trade, such as the stimulation of the import of large amounts of raw materials and assistance provided to the export of manufactured goods.[6] The officials who played such an active part in the economic growth of the young Republic were vigorous and efficient administrators, wealthy merchants actively interested in trade — and the same 'regents' whom Weber had dismissed as rentiers. Most of them did not belong to the pious Calvinists whom Weber regarded as the initiators of Dutch economic growth; among the leading regents of Amsterdam, for example, the moderates and those sympathizing with the liberal Arminian trends formed the majority.[7]

By the time Britain had become the 'workshop of the world' and had fallen under the influence of the liberalist Manchester School, advocating complete abstinence of the state in economic affairs, the role attributed to government was that of 'nightwatchman'. In the course of the nineteenth century, however, other Western nations developed strategies to counteract British hegemony. In *Das nationale System der politischen Ökonomie* (1841), Friedrich List propagated economic nationalism as a defence against British free trade, recommending neo-mercantilist strategies such as protective tariffs, in order to develop a national industry in Germany (see List, 1920).[8] By the turn of the century the world constellation had changed radically. Until about 1850, England had been the only real industrial power in the world, but in the course of the second half of the century other countries such as Germany, France and the United States, not prepared to become a kind of economic semicolony of the British empire, had all started to stimulate national industrial development through strong government support. In addition to imposing tariffs on industrial products from England, this support also consisted of credit facilities from state banks, and other protective measures.

In the nineteenth century, Japan was the last country in which the industrialization of a large agrarian society was achieved on the basis of a capitalist economy. There, too, the Emperor's authority was invoked to first build a powerful state structure, in order to obstruct the mass influx of cheap industrial products from the West, and to support infant national industries by other means. From the turn of the century onwards there are no further examples of states of substantial size and with a numerous rural population, that managed to escape from a general condition of underdevelopment along the capitalist path.

By exporting cheap home manufactures on a massive scale, the British had succeeded in practically crippling the Indian textile industry. Karl Marx wrote in 1853: 'English interference having placed the spinner in Lancashire and the weaver in Bengal, or sweeping away both Hindu spinner and weaver, dissolved these small semi-barbarian, semi-civilized communities, by blowing up their economical basis' (Marx and Engels, n.d.: 36). Here we find the tragic result of the 'dialectics of world history': the country which had been the main producer and exporter of manufactured textiles a few centuries earlier, had become perhaps the main victim first of British mercantilism and then of British free trade. Preventing the industrial development of colonies became a general pattern; in the Netherlands policies towards the Netherlands Indies were basically no different. The usual colonial pattern consisted of carrying off cheap raw materials from a country where labour was abundant and inexpensive, transforming them in one's own country into industrial products and selling the finished products on a massive scale in captive colonial markets. From the point of view of profit-making this was far more attractive than promoting industrial development in the colonial country – or the semi-colonial one that was nominally independent – especially if overseas transport in both directions could be effectuated by the industrial country's own shipping companies.

In China, the British, through the Opium Wars (which perhaps should more correctly be called 'textile wars'), had succeeded in acquiring *de facto* power in the main Chinese ports, which meant that import taxes upon British industrial products would not exceed 5 per cent. In Japan, however, the attempts of the British and Americans to stifle Japanese efforts to build a competitive industry failed.

THE STATE AS A MOTOR OF EMANCIPATION

Gerschenkron (1962) highlighted the phenomenon that the more backward a country's economy, the more probable it is that industrialization may start with a jump, a sudden spurt, with a high rate of growth in industrial production. He stated that in such rapid development the role of the state increases relative to the initial backwardness. He failed to mention, however, that the enhanced role of the state in this situation was not simply a function of the internal condition of backwardness: state intervention was a necessity on account of external factors such as heavy competition from transnational enterprises, which impaired industrial development both in colonial and semi-colonial countries such as China or the countries of South America.

It was this *economic necessity* to provide protection to the newly developing industries that led to ever increasing state intervention. Given the growing power of transnational capital, the rate of state assistance depended on the historical period in which indigenous industrial development began.[9] Around the turn of the century a point was reached where an industrial sector growing from within no longer possessed sufficient possibilities for independent development. Adverse wind calls for added push, which could only be furnished by increasing governmental protection. The strength of transnational capital had become so overwhelming that in the absence of state support, the emergence of new competing industrial nations could be prevented. Kula (1960) has shown how Poland had more than once been on the verge of entering the company of industrial nations; but each time the effort came to nought, largely due to deadly competition from Western big business.

A crucial case was Czarist Russia. In the 1890s there were certainly politicians, Count Witte among them, who contributed to an early development of Russian industry. But the Russian empire remained a huge, predominantly agrarian society, which twice suffered defeat in war — from Japan and, in the First World War, from Germany. According to Walt Rostow's (1960) theory of the process of economic growth via a 'take-off' period of relatively short duration (two or three decades) Russia had completed its 'take-off' before the Revolution. The message was clear: Russian industry would in any case have entered a phase of 'self-sustained growth', with or without a communist revolution.

Of the four nations which Rostow expected to 'close the technological gap on the West' (Rostow, 1959: 413), only two have succeeded to any substantial extent, and these two giants, Russia and China, both needed radical revolutions. The other countries, India and Brazil, are still suffering from serious underdevelopment and from neo-colonial exploitation. In terms of the magnitude of the task of industrialization, today's four new industrial countries,

(NICs), among them the city-states of Hong Kong and Singapore, can in no way be compared to the large agrarian countries which Rostow saw as candidates for early industrial development (Nolan, 1990: 45ff). A 'take-off' does not occur automatically. As Gerschenkron pointed out, the state had to play an ever increasing role in pushing a largely agrarian society on the road towards industrial development. A radical revolution was needed to create a state strong enough to withstand foreign economic competition, military intervention and subversion, while building a national economy.

Here we have arrived at a basic point in our argument. The two great revolutions of this century – the Russian Revolution of 1917 and the Chinese Revolution of 1945–49 – can, I believe, be viewed as emancipatory movements. During the 1920s advances were achieved in various sectors of the Soviet Union which would have been unimaginable under Czarist rule, such as industrial development, electrification and agricultural mechanization, in addition to an impressive extension of education. But these newly acquired rights had to be protected by a state strong enough to withstand foreign influences from the capitalist world.[10] It is a paradox of history that the foundations for a new state had been laid by Lenin who, in his *State and Revolution* written in 1917, had upheld the Marxist view that a socialist revolution would involve, in the rather near future, the 'withering away' of the state (Lenin, 1932: 16–20).

During Mao Zedong's time as leader of the Communist Party the People's Republic of China was also striving for economic progress and again a powerful government apparatus was needed. In contrast to the Soviet strategy, the Chinese leadership whose victory was, to a great extent, due to the support of the peasantry, adopted policies aimed at satisfying the needs of the rural people, who formed 80 per cent of China's total population. In addition to laying the basis for industrial development, the Chinese leadership promoted modernization of the traditional agricultural implements, realizing that a rapid mechanization of agriculture would result in serious unemployment. However, the People's Republic of China has never known a degree of centralization of government comparable to that of the Soviet Union. The People's Communes enjoyed a certain amount of autonomy: the 'mass line' (from the masses to the masses) meant that people were granted a voice in local affairs.

In the first decade after the Communists came to power, China achieved some notable successes. Despite a setback in the late 1950s, largely caused by the failure of the rash Great Leap Forward of 1958, successful agricultural policies had been fully restored by 1965 (Wertheim, 1965; Dumont, 1965: 216–17). Through improved irrigation and electrification, China achieved self-sufficiency in grain production during the 1960s for a population increasing by some 2 per cent per year. Thus in the twentieth century, in a country inhabited by one-fifth of the total world population, a true process of economic development, concomitant with a strong emancipation upsurge, had been initiated. It went hand in hand with forms of emancipation in a number of fields, and was realized without foreign assistance. In as far as there was repression during that period, it was much less pronounced than during Stalin's reign in the Soviet Union, and it was directed not against the peasantry, but mostly against intellectuals.

In order to appreciate the significance of China's achievements, one only needs to compare its level of development in agriculture and industry with those in India, Bangladesh, Pakistan or Indonesia — countries whose economic level before the Second World War was similar to that of China (Dumont, 1965: 260ff). Although important initiatives were repeatedly undertaken in these countries to promote economic development, an essential element was lacking: no real efforts were made to promote the emancipation of the impoverished rural masses. In India there were serious attempts during the 1950s to foster rapid industrialization, such as the second Five Years' Plan of 1956. But the prevalent social stratification affording privileges to the propertied classes and land-owning castes thwarted any attempts at a radical emancipation of the rural have-nots (Breman, 1985). Political freedom, in the shape of a parliamentary system, did not reach broad sections of the rural and urban masses.

In Indonesia during the 1950s, under President Sukarno's populist regime,[11] there were also moves towards policies aimed at emancipation for the rural population. But since General Suharto became Indonesia's 'strongman' in 1965/66, any chance for the rural masses to pursue collective emancipation from dire poverty and to organize themselves freely, has been effectively thwarted by the 'New Order' regime. Similarly in Pakistan and Bangladesh, where supreme power was for the most part in the hands of military dictators, the 'Green Revolution' initiated around 1970 was pursued in a way that most benefited the land-owning class. All these countries remained subject to economic pressure from the capitalist powers, with the result that their governments were unable to achieve accelerated and sustainable levels of growth.

THE STATE AS A BRAKE UPON EMANCIPATION

The strong state power built in Russia and China in order to protect the revolutionary reforms against enemies from outside, also had the potential to grow into an element *within* the nation, that might become a serious brake upon the emancipation movement which had made the socialist revolution possible. In order to secure their own survival, the Bolsheviks fixed a set of priorities:

> Priority number one was to secure the party's power against internal opposition. This involved the creation of a one-party state, the strengthening of the state bureaucracy in general and of the police apparatus in particular, and the control of the dissemination of information.
>
> Priority number two was to secure the state as such against foreign enemies. This required strengthening the state's military and economic bases. It involved rapid industrialization and its historical concomitant, the expropriation of the peasantry. It also involved the creation of a military machine capable of neutralizing at least enemy military forces. (Wallerstein, 1984: 88)

These priorities were not the only choices available, but they determined the further development of the Russian Revolution. Stalin created an empire that had characteristics reminiscent of the old Czarist regime — the pursuit of centralization, and the powerful influence of the secret police upon the life of individual citizens. The isolation which developed in response to the danger of economic infiltration, and the construction of an economy planned and directed from the centre, contributed to fettering the whole social and political system, causing a rigidity that stifled any possibility of an open cultural atmosphere. In the end, this rigidity assumed such proportions that no room was left for criticism of government policies, or for initiatives from below.

The adoption by this inflexible Soviet society of *perestroika* (reconstruction) as a design for change and *glasnost* (freedom of speech) as a means, has been a surprising development. This cannot be classed an emancipation movement from below: it was a leader from the old establishment who developed these new initiatives. In so doing Gorbachev initially succeeded in acquiring much mass support, but his inability to solve the basic economic problems in the Soviet Union and to handle ethnic conflicts and liberation movements, led to an increasingly chaotic situation and, ultimately, to the dissolution of the Soviet Union as a state. However, it is important to note that in a society such as the Soviet Union, which during the Brezhnev era seemed to be trapped in a hopeless rigidity, a radical urge for renewal could develop, implying many reversals of values and norms. This can be viewed as proof of a vitality and potential for renewal inside a society that originally carried a socialist signature.

Generally speaking, a national state with virtually unlimited power runs the risk of eventual domination by a cumbersome bureaucratic apparatus, particularly when it has been dominated by a single unassailable political party which leaves no scope for criticism from below or from outside. Once industrial development has reached a certain level, the national economic system becomes too complex for centralized management. Is this transformation of the socialist state from motor of revolutionary emancipation to brake upon emancipation an inevitable process? This would support Crane Brinton's thesis that any social revolution must end in a 'Thermidor', a return to 'normalcy' and a kind of 'Restoration' of the pre-revolutionary regime (Brinton, 1965: Ch. 8). No doubt, 'thermidorian' tendencies may be discerned everywhere after a successful socialist revolution. As I have written earlier:

> . . . there were also in China, in the years after the revolution, along with the distinct improvement in material welfare, certain tendencies towards self-contentment, bureaucratic rigidity, a loss of faith in the original revolutionary ideals and an inclination to seek compromises with the realities of life and with the frailties of human nature. (Wertheim, 1974: 333)

In China, however, bureaucratic domination never reached a level comparable to the Soviet Union during the Brezhnev period. From the outset, the Chinese government system has been characterized by a greater degree of popular participation in decision-making than prevailed under Stalin.[12] Yet as early as in the mid-1960s Mao recognized that both the party apparatus and the government bureaucracy ran the risk of an increasing rigidity, and he saw the danger of a new privileged class emerging that could be compared to the 'nomenclatura' which had constituted itself in the Soviet Union as a societal élite. This was the period of serious ideological and political conflicts between the Chinese and the Soviets. Mao severely criticized the tendency among some of his colleagues in the Party leadership, including Liu Shaochi, Chairman of the People's Republic since 1958, and Deng Xiaoping, General-Secretary of the Communist Party, to repress the popular masses (Gray, 1990: 335–6). In Mao's view a new 'bourgeoisie' was developing within the

Party, and in 1966–7 he attempted to reform it from above with the assistance of the Chinese youth who organized themselves as the Red Guards. In some respects Mao's Cultural Revolution could be compared to Gorbachev's *perestroika*. His strategy also included a kind of *glasnost*, in the shape of allowing and advocating the large wall-newspaper's (*dazebao*), which registered complaints about all kinds of abuses. The main difference with Gorbachev is, of course, that whereas the latter aspired at more scope for private initiatives in economic matters, including agriculture, the Cultural Revolution was directed at a strengthening of the socialist element within the Chinese economic system.

The Cultural Revolution ended in an anarchic state of affairs,[13] Mao appearing too old to keep control of further developments. After his death in 1976 Deng Xiaoping, who during the Cultural Revolution had been exposed as a capitalist sympathizer and shorn of his power, soon became the dominant leader of the People's Republic. Around 1980 a true 'thermidorian' reaction won the day; under Deng's influence in the 1980s, the grip of the government on the Chinese economy was appreciably reduced and significant steps were taken towards a more market-oriented economy (Hinton, 1991).

The same tendency was not only advocated by Gorbachev and his supporters in the Soviet Union, but from 1989 onwards, has also been pursued by other countries of Eastern Europe. It is clear that in the past few years particularly in Eastern Europe, emancipatory movements have no longer been directed against Mammon, but rather against Leviathan — the very state which at the inception of the two great revolutions had itself supported powerful emancipatory protest movements.

THE 'SOCIALIST STATE' UNDER ATTACK

Should the popular movements in Eastern Europe which aspire to the elimination of all remnants of communist power, be viewed as emancipation struggles? We must take into account the specific circumstances under which these movements arose and which social groups are most anxious to rid themselves of Leviathan. A final judgement on such issues is hardly feasible so soon after the events; the following observations must remain basically conjectural.

With the exception of the Soviet Union and possibly Yugoslavia, communist rule in Eastern Europe was not the result of a popular revolution, but of the victory of the Soviet Armed Forces at the end of the Second World War. The governments called into being and kept in power by the Soviets were not based on popular consent in the nations which joined the Warsaw Pact. For them, Soviet domination was a kind of foreign rule essentially no different from the German occupation from which they had been liberated. Consequently, Leviathan became the Goliath, the force to be attacked. They had no experience of the other Goliath, Mammon; they had been told that capitalism was wrong, that people suffered from poverty under that system, but official propaganda had lost all credibility.

Now they may gradually realize that delivery to a market economy, to Mammon, involves problems such as mass unemployment, rising prices and withdrawal of subsidies on essential consumer goods, under pressure of the IMF and the World Bank, as well as the privatization of public utilities, which can be seen as: 'nothing more than a cover to grab ever larger sectors of national and global markets: sectors historically deemed inseparable from the national patrimony' (Clairmonte and Cavanagh, 1987: 559). Even Adam Smith believed that the public utility services should remain under the care of the state.

To the question whether the events in Eastern Europe since 1989 might be called a true emancipation movement, the answer is yes, in so far as the movement engendered an urge towards a political democracy. But there are also indications that it is mainly an urban phenomenon, in which the intelligentsia has been most active. In countries where a large percentage of the population still consists of a poor peasantry, as in Bulgaria and Romania, people seem afraid of losing some of the social securities achieved under communism. Poor peasants are less sure that they will benefit from a transition to a market economy, involving cut-throat competition. In most cases, also, the movements do not exceed ethnic boundaries. There is a particularist character to the movements, in which anti-foreign sentiments, or rather antagonism against groups perceived as 'foreign', are playing a prominent role. This tendency had already started in the last years of communist rule, as for example in the anti-Hungarian policies under Ceausescu, or the anti-Turkish policies in Bulgaria. In Yugoslavia there are serious conflicts between the Serbs and other ethnic groups, and in Eastern Germany a general anti-foreign mood is leading to large-scale dismissals and a mass exodus of coloured foreign workers, such as those from Vietnam, Mozambique and Angola.

Religious conflicts, for a long time suppressed under communist regimes, are also coming to the fore, in clashes between Christian and Moslem groups or, as in Yugoslavia, between Roman Catholics and Orthodox Christians. The same pattern of ethnic and religious tensions manifests itself in the former Soviet Union, now that *glasnost* has opened the way to venting real feelings. In the Baltic Republics and in Moldavia, particularist anti-Russian sentiments have developed.

We might therefore count the movements in Eastern Europe among emancipation movements, but within that range they belong to a special category. In 'Emancipation as Motive Power of Human Evolution and Survival' (Wertheim, 1983: 13ff), I divided emancipation movements into three distinct phases, briefly referred to earlier. The characteristics evident in the Eastern European movement are reminiscent of the second emancipation phase, in which group solidarity remains particularistic. In that earlier work I referred to the potential for 'highly aggressive characteristics' within such movements, observing that in cases when it 'may pursue and sometimes achieve a complete physical elimination or expulsion' of a minority, 'the term "emancipation" seems rather a misnomer'. Furthermore:

> Whereas during the first emancipation phase the (integrationist) aims pursued were largely of interest for the well-to-do bourgeoisie, the second phase mostly stresses the interest of a rising petite bourgeoisie. The particularistic approach may benefit these groups, or parts of them, both in the case of withdrawal and in the case of a more aggressive strategy which aimed at a conquest of a measure of political and economic power. But the 'liberation' is mostly not intended for the broad masses of labourers and peasants, nor does it actually benefit them. (Wertheim, 1983: 18)

The term 'rising petite bougeoisie' was used with (poor, agrarian) Third World countries in mind, and is certainly not the most appropriate term in the East European case. But I believe that the characterization of the driving force behind the dismantling of the 'socialist states' in Eastern Europe as a largely urban bourgeois movement can be upheld.

THE STATE AND EMANCIPATION IN THE THIRD WORLD

How far does the East European pattern of rejection of a state power experienced as foreign, as oppressive and inefficient also apply to people of Third World countries? Experience has taught us that for the underdeveloped agrarian countries of the Third World, living under the impact of foreign capitalism in general has highly unfavourable effects. It is not only the rural masses in the densely populated regions of South and South-East Asia that are unable to achieve active, collective emancipation. In the more sparsely populated countries of Africa and South America, too, the dependence upon foreign capital creates a social system marked by gross inequalities, with little scope for emancipation for the rural poor.[14] In the past few decades under this system only two Asian states have achieved the status of NICs: Taiwan and South Korea. The two city-states of Hong Kong and Singapore lack the necessary vast adjoining territories, but even the two remaining 'Little Tigers' are 'not large countries in terms of either population or land area' (Nolan, 1990: 45). There are other relevant factors besides size: 'Location and politics have also been extremely important for the ROK and Taiwan in that, it is argued, their growth was greatly stimulated by inflows of foreign capital related to their strategic position *vis-à-vis* China and North Korea' (Nolan, 1990: 47).

One might compare the effects of this kind of limited external 'patronage' by the United States with the internal situation in an Asian peasant society where only a small number of agriculturists enjoy state patronage. The policies of President Suharto in Java have been characterized as 'cooptation and incorporation of village élites, offering access to credit, subsidies and significant opportunities for accumulation, while at the same time ensuring their dependence on the state' (Pincus, 1990: 24; referring to Hart, 1988: 263, 260). The great majority of small peasants and sharecroppers in Java gain no benefits from this patronage. Similarly, extending aid to agrarian countries such as India or Bangladesh at a rate comparable to what 'the Little Tigers' received would have been impossible even for the United States.

In contrast to the significant amount of support to South Korea and Taiwan, the 'aid' extended to other Third World countries under capitalist conditions has acquired a new dimension in the past two decades with the onset of the debt crisis. Many Third World governments took on sizeable loans in the early 1970s, against low interest rates. When world interest rates soared in the late 1970s, Third World countries which had incurred heavy debts were no longer able to keep up their annual repayments, sometimes not even the interest. Then followed the spiral of new loans, on harsher terms, until the commercial banks pulled out; Third World governments were forced to apply to the IMF and the World Bank for assistance, submitting to onerous conditions such as cutting subsidies for essential consumer goods, making the establishment of sound economic development in these countries impossible (Clairmonte and Cavanagh, 1986; George, 1988).

This may explain why many people in Third World countries – particularly those under a socialist government – with negative experiences of 'market economies' in a more distant past, are less eager to exchange Leviathan for Mammon. In Nicaragua, the Sandinistas, who never aspired at a dictatorial power (Mullenders-Van Lijnden, 1988), lost the national elections in 1990, but retained much support and sympathy among the common people. The main reason for the shift in political allegiance was the hope that this might bring to an end the military attacks of the Contras, and the 'low intensity warfare' waged since the early 1980s by the United States. Mozambique and Angola are now also forced to come to terms with their 'Contras', supported by South Africa, but their concessions are not due to a clear dissatisfaction with socialism among the popular masses.

Maybe in these smaller Third World socialist nations the period of rule has been too short to breed a truly 'thermidorian' or restorative reaction. In any case foreign intervention, either through embargoes (Cuba) or through political and financial support to counterrevolutionary forces (Nicaragua, Angola, Mozambique) seriously impairs the possibility of assessing the extent to which a socialist state *without* interventions might maintain its emancipatory character in the long run. Still less useful as test cases are Asian nations such as North Korea, Vietnam, Cambodia and Laos, where foreign intervention has been rife.

Recent events in China are somewhat ambiguous. There are some striking differences between the developments in China and those in the former Soviet Union: the new political line pursued in China since Mao's death has hardly been characterized by increased openness on behalf of the peasant masses. It is rather the urban élites, including university students and writers, who have gained a certain amount of freedom. Although the so-called 'Wall of Democracy' in

Beijing was soon prohibited, there was a greater openness to cultural and economic influence from Hong Kong and the Western world. However, since the violent clashes of June 1989 even the scant degree of *glasnost* which intellectuals and students possessed, has been on the wane. The dismantling of collective agriculture and the elimination of the people's communes threatens to throw the peasantry back into the 'sack of potatoes' of Marx, as petty landowners with individualistic tendencies, concerned about the material interests of their own small family. Investment in irrigation and in the long-term upkeep of the infrastructure is also being seriously neglected (Hinton, 1991; Petras, 1988).

The Chinese government has been taking some major steps back – particularly since the retreat of Deng Xiaoping from the forefront of Chinese politics – perhaps as the result of its experiences with a market economy in the early 1980s, earlier than the Soviet Union and Eastern Europe. Having granted privileges to the coastal areas at the expense of inland regions during the 1980s, for example, the Chinese are now paying more attention to the inner territories. There even seems to be a tendency to return to some aspects of collective agriculture. A certain revival of veneration of Mao Zedong[15] might also indicate a reverse trend, in contrast to Eastern Europe.

In other parts of the world, the movement to reject socialist states is by no means comparable to the mood in Eastern Europe, reminding us of Maurice Zinkin's assertion that 'there is in Asia less mental resistance to state intervention than in the West, for Asia has a long history of effective and helpful state action' (Zinkin, 1953: 214). Evidence of this includes the huge works of canalization and irrigation constructed in imperial China more than forty centuries ago, during the reign of Emperor Yao, and greatly expanded under subsequent dynasties. What has been disgraced in recent decades is not socialism as an ideology and as a system for balancing the interests of the individual with the interests of a society; it is the *dictatorial* and *intolerant* type of government pretending to dispense supreme wisdom in matters of ideology which has been rejected. This rejection, however, does not basically affect socialism as an emancipatory ideology. It should lead to 'rethinking socialism', as a fundamental aspect of 'rethinking emancipation'.

As Peter Nolan (1990: 60) writes: 'There is nothing intrinsically "socialist" about the state.' Marx and his followers were wrong in stating that the state under capitalism was nothing but a tool in the hands of a dominant bourgeoisie. Emancipation as a social phenomenon is basically a collective effort aiming at thorough control from below of both the state and the market, which by themselves are 'flawed vehicles for achieving social goals' (Nolan, 1990: 60). The dialectics of emancipation imply that under certain circumstances a strong state is required to check market forces standing in the way of emancipation, or to protect the popular masses from catastrophic developments. Among such circumstances would be situations in which the national state has to assume responsibility for taking urgent decisions, such as war and natural disasters. Large sections of the Third World are continuously in this position – at war against nature, against soil erosion, against hunger, disease and urban mass unemployment, and against the neo-colonial forces which dominate the economy. This state of war requires a prompt and efficient style of decision-making and is thus a basic factor in determining the type of government adopted.[16]

It is not the commandeering style of military dictatorship which will be able to resolve the urgent problems confronting their peoples. The authoritarian character of military regimes is their basic weakness. Most of the military 'strongmen' are hard towards the rural and suburban majority; but they tend to be quite soft towards influential elements within their own country and to those outside forces upon which they are dependent. Gunnar Myrdal (1970) has explored the question of the 'soft state' and found it open to exploitation by anyone wielding power, with widespread corruption as a consequence.[17] Joel Migdal (1988) uses examples from different Third World countries to show that social strata such as rich and middle peasants play a critical role even where military rulers attempt to build a 'strong state'.

But both Myrdal and Migdal seem to overlook the most crucial factor responsible for the persistent weakness of most Third World states: their lasting dependence upon foreign capitalist forces. Of the few countries which Migdal considers comparatively strong states, *four* owe that qualification to a socialist revolution – Cuba, China, Vietnam and North Korea (Migdal, 1988: 269). The author does not draw the plausible conclusion that it is not the preceding 'dislocation' which brought about the rise of a 'strong state', but the revolution which brought together emancipatory forces from below. The picture of Third World societies and states as sketched by Myrdal and Migdal may be largely accurate, but without taking account of the importance of the emancipatory perspective in relation to the rural masses of the Third World, the crucial point is lost.

There are further problems for the 'national state' in Third World countries: carrying out legislative measures in a preponderantly agrarian society with a population far removed from central authority is one difficulty. The peasantry is generally only in touch with local or regional officials (Von Benda-Beckmann, 1989), whose interpretation of laws or regulations emanating from the centre may not reflect the original intention. For example, while politicians at the centre may be in favour of legislative measures of an emancipatory nature, authorities on the spot with close ties to the rural élite, may thwart such measures by interpreting the laws in their favour. Attempts to introduce radical land reform legislation are especially vulnerable, as demonstrated by the failure of legislation in favour of tenants in various parts of India during the 1950s, and the silent obstruction of the land reform legislation initiated by Sukarno in Indonesia in the early 1960s, by elements of the regional and local bureaucracy (Baks, 1985; Utrecht, 1969).

Very few states have so far been able to respond adequately to the challenges confronting the Third World. Only a government system responsive to the basic needs of the population may succeed in solving the urgent problems with which the poor nations are beset. The ability to take effective decisions has to be combined with a deep understanding for the existence of independent emancipatory movements, which might originally have been a motive power for the emergence of a socialist revolution. Whenever a state born from such a revolution grows into an independent power susceptible to general stagnation or extreme repression and exploitation, it may itself become an institution against which emancipatory movements are likely to develop.

In view of recent developments, particularly in Europe, one might doubt whether *states* are really the appropriate institutions from which to expect the fulfilment of this difficult role. In the course of history, the state has assumed a variety of shapes, dependent on the extent to which a majority of the people were prepared to acknowledge a political body claiming the authority to govern a certain territory. In several countries of Eastern Europe multinational states are disintegrating under the impact of emancipatory forces of a particularistic, ethnic colouration.

In the Third World, it seems likely that most populations will continue to strive for a total or partial takeover of the present 'weak' states, as their form of emancipatory struggle. A combined action, a kind of 'Rainbow Coalition'[18] might in the future produce a different type of emancipation movement transcending present national borders (Nederveen Pieterse, 1989/1990: 366/67). Similarly, Third World states might combine forces to further their common goals: for example by forming coalitions, as Fidel Castro has suggested, to renounce the burdens imposed upon them by the debt crisis.[19]

In the present world situation, national or plurinational states cannot be dispensed with in the underdeveloped countries: they are needed if only as a check on market forces that are driving society towards environmental disaster through pollution, that promote continued sales of armaments, or that condemn millions of people in Third World countries to lasting poverty and enslavement. The world of today still needs state protection and state activity, but it should be a state which is in turn controlled by strong emancipatory forces and movements from below. Parliamentary democracy of the Western type, implying that following the rules of the parliamentary game is more important than solving urgent problems, is only one of the manifold shapes which these emancipatory forces may assume.

NOTES

1. Also see Wertheim (1974: 89–94), which criticizes the reification of concepts such as 'state' or 'church': 'Reification of social phenomena may serve the interests of those in power; it adds a quality of endurance to the present distribution of positions and roles' (p. 94).

2. The author has rightly criticized my earlier studies on emancipation in so far as my analysis 'stops short of a theory of the state and its relative autonomy in a global context' (Nederveen Pieterse, 1989/90: 83).

3. In my historical survey I have followed Nederveen Pieterse in using the term 'Leviathan', coined by Hobbes (1950) for the state, and the term 'Mammon' for capital, representing market forces.

4. See also Karl Marx in *New York Daily Tribune*, 11 July 1853 (Marx and Engels, n.d.: 46ff). Wallerstein (1980) pays only sporadic attention to the British efforts to stop the import of textiles from India; his attention is mainly concentrated upon the British competition with France and the Dutch Republic.

5. Wallerstein is guilty of the same misconception: see 'The Three Instances of Hegemony in the History of the Capitalist World Economy', in Wallerstein (1984).

6. For a more detailed elaboration of the Dutch case during the seventeenth century, see Wertheim (1964: 147–50).

7. As early as 1909, Weber was criticized by the historian Felix Rachfahl for his deficient treatment of the Dutch case. For Weber, however, this criticism was not a

reason to reconsider his tenets; evidently he was simply irritated by what he felt as an attack upon his authority in scholarly matters (Rachfahl, 1909, 1910; Weber, 1910a, 1910b). Also see Elias (1903: LII, n. 5).

8. Wallerstein (1979: 29) writes: 'Mercantilism now became the major tool of semiperipheral countries to become core countries thus still performing a function analogous to that of mercantilist drives of the late seventeenth and eighteenth centuries in England and France.'

9. Also see Eisenstadt (1966: 46–7). For a fuller discussion of Gerschenkron's and Eisenstadt's theory, see Wertheim (1974: 78–83).

10. See 'Socialist States: Mercantilist Strategies and Revolutionary Objectives' in Wallerstein (1984). In Wallerstein (1979: 31) the author remarks that the Russian 'state managers' made use of 'the classic technique of mercantilist semi-withdrawal from the world economy'.

11. On the concept of populism, and the inclusion of Sukarno among populist leaders, see Worsley (1967: 128–30) and Wertheim (1974: 245–54).

12. Franz Schurmann (1971) quotes from the 'Party Rules' of the Eighth Party Congress (1956). According to him the weight of emphasis is put on the need to strengthen 'democracy': 'The Party must take all efficacious measures to develop internal Party democracy, to encourage the positivism and creativity of all Party members, basic-level Party organizations, and local organizations. . . . Only in this way can the relationships between Party and people be broadened and strengthened . . . and can the Party actively respond to all kinds of concrete conditions and local peculiarities, can Party life become spirited . . . all Party members and all Party organizations must undergo supervision from the top down and from the bottom up.' See also Skocpol (1979: 286–7). During a field trip to China in 1979 on behalf of UNRISD, I got the impression that the 'mass line' was still effective: see Wertheim and Stiefel (1983).

13. An excellent description of the period can be found in Hinton (1983). Fang and Fang (1986) mention a Xinhua News Agency report 'that 34,274 people had been "persecuted to death" – in other words, died unnaturally – during the ten years of the Cultural Revolution. This is possibly a conservative figure.'

14. Frank (1970) defined the impact of foreign capitalism upon the 'periphery' as a 'development of underdevelopment'.

15. 'Portraits and busts of Mao can be found in millions of peasants', herdsmen's and workers' homes and on many a party committee wall' (Hinton, 1991: 163). See also Hager (1989).

16. For a more extensive treatment of this subject of urgency, see Wertheim (1984), an abridged version of which was made a subject for internal debate among experts by UNRISD, Geneva, in *Dialogue about Participation* (1981 No. 1) and in subsequent issues of *Dialogue*.

17. A typical example is Suharto's 'New Order' regime in Indonesia; see Robison (1986).

18. The term 'Rainbow Coalition' has been used in the United States for a movement called into life by Jesse Jackson, as a 'common struggle of all progressive forces, whether they are black or white, male or female, green or red'.

19. As Clairmonte and Cavanagh (1986) wrote: 'Debt repudiation stands out as the only ethically feasible and rational solution for the Third World.'

REFERENCES

Baks, C. (1985) 'An Interpretation of Growing Landlessness among Adivasis of South Gujerat, India', in V. Sutlive et al. (eds) *Modernization and the Emergence of a Landless Peasantry: Essays on the Integration of Peripheries in Socio-Economic Centers*. Williamsbury: College of William and Mary, Dept of Anthropology.

Benda-Beckmann, Von F. (1989) 'Scapegoat and Magic Charm: Law in Development Theory and Practice', *Journal of Legal Pluralism* 28: 129–48.

Breman, J. (1985) *Of Peasants, Migrants and Paupers; Rural Labour Circulation and Capitalist Production in West India*. New Delhi: Oxford University Press.

Breman, J. (1990) 'The Colonial State and the Labour System', paper presented at the Workshop on Capitalist Plantations in Colonial Asia, Amsterdam (September).

Brinton, C. (1965) *The Anatomy of Revolution*. New York: Random House.

Clairmonte, F. and Cavanagh, J. (1986) 'Third World Debt: The Approaching Holocaust', *Economic and Political Weekly* 21(31): 1361–64.

Clairmonte, F. and Cavanagh, J. (1987) 'Global Economic Debacle and Corporate Power', *Economic and Political Weekly* 22(13): 559–63.

Dumont, R. (1965) *La Chine surpeuplée — tiers monde affamé*. Paris: Ed. du Seuil.

Eisenstadt, S.N. (1966) *Modernization: Protest and Change*. Englewood Cliff, NJ: Prentice Hall.

Elias, J. (1903) *De vroedschap van Amsterdam, 1578–1795*, Vol. 1. Haarlem.

Fang, P.J. and Fang, L.G.J. (1986) *Zhou Enlai — A Profile*. Beijing: Foreign Languages Press.

Frank, A.G. (1970) *Latin America: Underdevelopment or Revolution? Essays in the Development of Underdevelopment and the Immediate Enemy*. New York: Monthly Review Press.

George, S. (1988) 'Third World Debt: The Moral and Physical Equivalent of War', *Who Owes Whom?* (Spring): 3–10.

Gerschenkron, A. (1962) *Economic Backwardness in Historical Perspective*. Cambridge, MA: Belknap Press.

Gray, J. (1990) *Rebellions and Revolutions: China from the 1800s to the 1980s*. Oxford: Oxford University Press.

Hager, M.M. (1989) 'Reading the Tea Leaves of Protest', *Monthly Review* 41(4): 24–32.

Hart, G. (1988) 'Agrarian Structure and the State in Java and Bangladesh', *Journal of Asian Studies* 47(2): 249–67.

Hinton, W. (1983) *Shenfan: The Continuing Revolution in a Chinese Village*. New York: Random House.

Hinton, W. (1991) *The Privatization of China: The Great Reversal, 1978–1989*. London: Earthscan.

Hobbes, T. (1950) *Leviathan: Or the Matter, Forme and Power of a Commonwealth, Ecclesiastical and Civil*. Oxford: Clarendon Press (first edn 1651).

Hyma, A. (1942) *The Dutch in the Far East: A History of the Dutch Commercical and Colonial Empire*. Ann Arbor, MI: Wahr.

Kula, W. (1960) 'Les débuts du capitalisme en Pologne dans la perspective de l'histoire comparée', text of lecture read at the Polish Academy in Rome.

Lenin, V.I. (1932) *The State and Revolution*. New York: International Publishers (first edn 1917).

List, F. (1920) *The National System of Political Economy*. London: Longman (first edn 1841).

Marx, K. and Engels, F. (n.d.) *On Colonialism*. Moscow: Foreign Languages Publication House.

Migdal, J.S. (1988) *Strong Societies and Weak States: State–Society Relations and State Capabilities in the Third World*. Princeton, NJ: Princeton University Press.

Mukherjee, R. (1958) *The Rise and Fall of the East India Company: A Sociological Appraisal*. Berlin: Deutscher Verlag der Wissenschaften.

Mullenders-Van Lijnden, L.C.W. (1988) 'Mass Organization and the Revolutionary Transformation Process in Nicaragua', unpublished doctoral dissertation, Leeds University.

Myrdal, G. (1970) *The Challenge of World Poverty: A World Anti-Poverty Program in Outline*. New York: Pantheon Books.

Nederveen Pieterse, J. (1989/90) *Empire and Emancipation: Power and Liberation on a World Scale*. New York: Praeger; London: Pluto Press.

Nolan, P. (1990) 'Assessing Economic Growth in the Asian NIC', *Journal of Contemporary Asia* 20(1): 41–63.

Petras, J. (1988) 'Contradictions of Market Socialism in China, Part I', *Journal of Contemporary Asia* 18(1): 3–23.

Pincus, J. (1990) 'Approaches to the Political Economy of Agrarian Change in Java', *Journal of Contemporary Asia* 20(1): 3–40.

Rachfahl, F. (1909) 'Calvinismus und Kapitalismus', *Internat. Wochenschrift für Wissenschaft, Kunst und Technik* III (39–43).

Rachfahl, F. (1910) 'Nochmals Calvinismus und Kapitalismus', *Internat. Wochenschrift für Wissenschaft, Kunst und Technik* IV (22–25).

Robison, R. (1986) *Indonesia: The Rise of Capital*. Asian Studies Association of Australia.

Rostow, W.W. (1959) 'Rostow on Growth', *The Economist*, 15 and 22 August.

Rostow, W.W. (1960) *The Stages of Economic Growth: A Non-Communist Manifesto*. Cambridge: Cambridge University Press.

Schurmann, F. (1971) *Ideology and Organization in Communist China* 2nd edn. Berkeley, CA: University of California Press.

Skocpol, T. (1979) *States and Social Revolution: A Comparative Analysis of France, Russia and China*. Cambridge: Cambridge University Press.

Smith, A. (1976) *An Inquiry Into the Nature and Causes of the Wealth of Nations*. Chicago, IL: Cannan (first edn 1776).

Utrecht, E. (1969) 'Land Reform in Indonesia', *Bulletin of Indonesian Economic Studies* 5(3): 71–88.

Wallerstein, I. (1979) *The Capitalist World Economy: Essays*. Cambridge: Cambridge University Press.

Wallerstein, I. (1980) *The Modern World System, Vol. 2, Mercantilism and the Consolidation of the European World Economy, 1600–1750*. New York: Academic Press.

Wallerstein, I. (1984) *The Politics of the World Economy*. Cambridge: Cambridge University Press.

Weber, M. (1910a) 'Antikritisches zum Geist des Kapitalismus', *Archiv für Sozialwissenschaft und Sozialpolitik* XXX: 184ff.

Weber, M. (1910b) 'Antikritisches Schlusswort zum Geist des Kapitalismus', *Archiv für Sozialwissenschaft und Sozialpolitik* XXXI: 554ff.

Weber, M. (1922) *Gesammelte Aufsätze zur Wissenschaftslehre*. Tübingen: Mohr.

Weber, M. (1956) *The Protestant Ethic and the Spirit of Capitalism*. London: Allen and Unwin (first edn 1904/5).

Wertheim, W.F. (1964) 'Religion, Bureaucracy and Economic Growth', in W.F. Wertheim (ed.) *East–West Parallels: Sociological Approaches to Modern Asia*, pp. 147–63. The Hague: Van Hoeve.

Wertheim, W.F. (1965) 'La Chine est-elle sous-peuplée? Production agricole et main-d'oeuvre rurale', *Population* 20(3): 477–513.

Wertheim, W.F. (1974) *Evolution and Revolution: The Rising Waves of Emancipation*. Harmondsworth: Penguin.

Wertheim, W.F. (1983) *Emancipation in Asia: Positive and Negative Lessons from China*. Rotterdam: CASP Publications, Erasmus University.

Wertheim, W.F. (1984) 'Tensions between Urgency and Democracy', ZZOA Working Paper No. 45. Amsterdam: University of Amsterdam.

Wertheim, W.F. and Stiefel, M. (1983) *Production, Equality and Participation in Rural China*. London: Zed Press.

Worsley, P. (1967) *The Third World*. London: Weidenfeld and Nicolson.

Worsley, P. (1984) *The Three Worlds: Culture and World Development*. London: Weidenfeld and Nicolson.

Zinkin, M. (1953) *Asia and the West*. London: Chatto and Windus.

Wim F. Wertheim (Gen. Foulkesweg 225, 6703 DJ Wageningen, The Netherlands) was born in 1907; he graduated in law from Leiden University in 1930, served as a member of the judiciary in the Netherlands Indies from 1931 to 1936, and was Professor of Law at Batavia from 1936 to 1942. After the Japanese occupation, he was appointed Professor of Asian Sociology and Modern History, University of Amsterdam (1947–1972). His publications include *Indonesian Society in Transition* (1959), *East–West Parallels* (1964), *Evolution and Revolution* (1974) and *Emancipation in Asia* (1983).

Theories of Development and Politics of the Post-modern — Exploring a Border Zone

David Slater

Across the various arenas of development theory, and in particular with reference to those of a radical, Marxist or neo-Marxist origin, a rather pervasive sense of crisis and in some cases disenchantment continue to characterize present debates. In one current, initiated by Booth (1985), and continued by Vandergeest and Buttel (1988), Sklair (1988) and Corbridge (1990), discussion of a so-called impasse in development sociology, with suggestions for its transcendence, has raised a series of issues concerning the theorization of dependent development, (post)-imperialism, class, power and socialism. In other longer studies similar themes have been firmly placed on the agenda, as the texts of Becker et al. (1987), Hettne (1990), Kay (1989) and Larrain (1989) demonstrate. Interestingly, although there have been some recent hints of possible connections with the poststructuralist and post-modern literatures, in the main these readings of development and its conceptualization have largely remained outside those other analytical domains, or at the least very much on the periphery.

On that other side, the most well-known exponents of post-modern interpretations, as well as their critical discussants, have tended to remain rather silent on Third World development, except for occasional linkages through the works of literary theorists such as Said (1985a) and Spivak (1987). Is there then, in the post-modern genre, a residual universalism or ethnocentrism which has so far remained submerged from the deconstructive view? Furthermore, is there a potential basis, within post-modernism, for a possible reconstruction of critical development theory, so that the apparent 'impasse' can be bypassed or displaced? While the potential encounter between feminism and post-modernism is already being

Development and Change (SAGE, London, Newbury Park and New Delhi), Vol. 23 (1992) No. 3, 283–319.

explored (Fraser and Nicholson, 1989), development theory and the post-modern have, overall, moved along separate tracks.[1]

My purpose here is as follows. I intend to explore what I refer to as three crossings of a border zone. The border zone is constituted by the potential intersections between critical development theory and post-modern perspectives, and in this case the three 'crossings' that I have chosen for analysis are: (1) the troubled conceptualizations of centres and peripheries, including some brief remarks on the global dimension in development debates; (2) questions of agency and power; and (3) meanings of democracy and socialism. Obviously the analytical terrain is extensive, and therefore I limit myself to certain controversial themes, the treatment of which is vital for any reconstruction of critical development theory. In my view this reconstruction or transformation can be most usefully approached within a perspective that is post-Marxist, as I shall attempt to illustrate.

PERIPHERAL MEANINGS AND MEANINGS OF THE PERIPHERY

Cocks, in her book on the 'oppositional imagination', makes the point that 'the political advantage in looking at peripheries and extremities is that power is exposed in what it drives from the center of life to the edges, and in what it incites as its own antitheses' (Cocks, 1989: 4). In an earlier text, the Uruguayan writer Galeano (1983: 184), expressed a similar notion commenting that 'in the outskirts of the world the system reveals its true face'. But can the 'edges', the 'outskirts', have another meaning? In the context of an exchange of letters on South Africa, Laclau (1990: 159) suggests that it is always the 'anomalous' or 'peripheral' case which reveals that which does not appear immediately visible in what seem to be more 'normal' cases. For instance, the struggle against the exclusionary logic of racism in South Africa reveals the hidden forms of the same logic in our societies, while American aggression against the Sandinista regime laid bare the ultimate limit of liberal regimes, as the Spanish Civil War exposed the fragility and ambiguity of Western democratic values in the 1930s. Thus, Madrid, Managua and Soweto are more than 'precise geographical locations in a neutral space, they are the names of political trenches indefinitely expandable to all latitudes; they are, in short, the names of the frontiers through which our own political identities are constituted' (Laclau, 1990: 159–60). To what extent then do post-modern[2] readings take these kinds of frontiers into account, especially when they emerge from within peripheral societies? Or, expressed somewhat differently, given the idea that, as Ross (1989: vii) remarks, 'postmodernist culture' has advertized itself as 'decentered, transnational and pluralistic', to what extent can we therefore conclude that this culture signifies an end to Western ethnocentrism?

In outlining a response to these questions, I want to consider some of the texts of those authors who are most closely associated with the post-modern interruption, namely, Baudrillard, Lyotard and Jameson. This consideration will also be linked to aspects of poststructuralism. The picture drawn will be symptomatic rather than systematic, and in subsequent sections I shall return to these and other related writers.

Although the work of Foucault is more customarily situated in poststructuralist rather than post-modern thought, there are significant imbrications. This is especially the case if one accepts the idea that post-modernism is not simply an exit from modernity, but rather an internal rift or fissure, which if interpreted creatively can stimulate the rethinking of the political. In a text which dates back some two decades, Foucault (1970: xxiv) wrote that, 'in attempting to uncover the deepest strata of Western culture, I am restoring to our silent and apparently immobile soil its rifts, its instability, its flaws; and it is the same ground that is once more stirring under our feet'. But it can be argued that it is in the context of that stated intention of uncovering the deepest strata of Western culture that the contours of a Eurocentric focus can be discerned. For Spivak (1988a: 291), Foucault's project has tended to foreclose a 'reading of the broader narratives of imperialism', and as she expresses it 'to buy a self-contained version of the West is to ignore its production by the imperialist project'. This incisive criticism goes together with an unequivocal recognition of Foucault as a brilliant thinker of 'power-in-spacing'. The problem for Spivak is the need to chart all those diverse expressions of what she refers to as that 'sanctioned ignorance' of the imperialist project.[3]

In contrast to Foucault, Derrida has given more time to investigating the often complex nature of ethnocentrism in the texts of some influential European thinkers. For example, he effectively deconstructs the sentimental ethnocentrism of Lévi-Strauss, noting how the critique of ethnocentrism, a theme so dear to the author of

Tristes Tropiques, 'has most often the sole function of constituting the other as a model of original and natural goodness'. Non-European peoples were to be studied, after Rousseau, as the 'index to a hidden good Nature, as a native soil recovered . . . with reference to which one could outline the structure, the growth, and above all the degradation of our society and our culture' (Derrida, 1976: 114–15). In Lévi-Strauss's own words, 'if the West has produced anthropologists it is because it was so tormented by remorse' (quoted in Derrida, 1976: 337). In this kind of vision, 'non-Western' peoples are essentialized around notions of the nobility and goodness of the primitive; contradiction and difference are erased from their histories.

The critical importance attached by Derrida to these kinds of issues is supported by his stand on apartheid (Derrida, 1985), expressed in an essay on the 'last word in racism', which contrasts markedly with the innovative orientations of much if not all of the recent work of certain key post-modern philosophers.

With Baudrillard, for instance, there are a number of curious ironies. Unlike many other radical European intellectuals of the 1970s, Baudrillard developed a critique of Marxism which emphasized the romanticization of productivity, the inability to conceive of an alternative social and political practice that went beyond the 'mirror of production'. For Baudrillard (1975: 17), Marx had only provided a critical theory of the mode of production, but not of the principle of production – 'revolutionary discourse' was reinforced as a language of productivity. Further, and in relation to the specific theme of this section, Baudrillard confronted not only the universal presumptions of historical materialism but also the ethnocentrism of Western Marxism. Of the former he writes that in Marxism, 'history is transhistoricized: it redoubles on itself and thus is universalized'. This is the case since in historical materialism critical concepts, such as labour power and surplus value, are not seen as explosive and mortal, but are constituted as universal, expressing an 'objective reality'; they thus cease to be analytical, and the 'religion of meaning begins' (Baudrillard, 1975: 47–8). On the issue of ethnocentrism, Baudrillard first interrogates Western culture in general, writing that other cultures were entered into its museum 'as vestiges of its own images . . . it reinterpreted them on its own model, and thus precluded the radical interrogation these "different" cultures implied for it', and 'its reflection on itself leads only to the universalization of its own principles' (Baudrillard, 1975: 88–9). It is then argued that the limits of the materialist interpretation of earlier societies are the same because in the last analysis historical materialism simply 'naturalizes' earlier societies 'under the sign of the mode of production'; these societies and those of the Third World are not comprehended – rather they become that other territory within which the analysis of the economic contradictions of Western societies is projected and implanted.

It is now a somewhat strange irony – and there are others as Gane (1990) shows – that Baudrillard has recently been selected by Spivak (1988b: 18) to serve as an example of the discourse of post-modernism with its 'sanctioned ignorance' of the history of imperialism. Spivak quotes from Baudrillard's 1983 essay on the 'silent majorities', where there is indeed no recognition of the movements of resistance of Third World peoples, and wherein for Baudrillard in general 'the mass is only mass because its social energy has already frozen', and this during the phase of mass media culture, of the 'glaciation of meaning' (Baudrillard, 1983: 26, 35). However, in this same essay, Baudrillard does refer to the way in which colonization 'violently initiated . . . primitive societies into the expansive and centrifugal norm of Western systems' (p. 59). Hence, it can perhaps be better argued that Baudrillard has been aware of the realities of the colonialist and imperialist project, with its conquests and violence, but that in his more recent work he is silent on the reality of resistance and the mobilizations and actions of the subaltern groups of the periphery, a point to which I return in the discussion of agency and subjectivity.[4] Baudrillard's silence on resistance may not be unrelated to his recent and deterministic statement that 'the countries of the Third World will never internalize the values of democracy and technological progress' (Baudrillard, 1989: 78). Again the South becomes the object of a familiar Eurocentric condescension.[5]

In contrast to Baudrillard, in Lyotard's work the Third World is largely present through its absence; it is only in the interstices of the argument that reference to peripheral societies emerges. Apart from a passing reference to some Brazilian work on education and the state (p. 32), Lyotard's (1986) analysis of the post-modern condition, as stated at the outset, deals with the 'most highly developed societies'. However, there are some revealing passages, where, for example, it is suggested that knowledge, 'the principle force of production', is the 'major bottleneck for the developing countries' (Lyotard, 1986: 5), or, in his discussion of science and legislation, the remark that, since the time of Plato, the languages of science and of ethics and politics both stem from the same perspective or 'choice' – 'the choice called the Occident' (p. 8). This comment, coming across as somewhat sardonic in the context of his critique of Habermas, is developed further in a series of contrasts between 'traditional' and 'developed' knowledges. The former are exemplified through extracts from the research of anthropologists on other peoples, and a link is made, for example, between the narrative of the Cashinahua Indians, with their initiation ceremonies, rituals and monotonous chants, and a kind of knowledge which is akin to nursery rhymes (Lyotard, 1986: 20–2). We subsequently discover a fleeting reminder of the cultural imperialism of Western civilization (p. 27), but the tendency to essentialize the 'traditional' and the 'developing', or in another more philosophical book (Lyotard, 1988a: 156), 'savage narratives', sits uneasily with the declared 'war on totality' (Lyotard, 1986: 82).[6]

From a different point of departure, Jameson, as a key figure of the post-modern turn in literary theory, would be difficult to include in the category of Lyotard's (1986: 41) people who have lost the nostalgia for a 'lost narrative'. In a number of articles, he has posited the need for a conception of the 'social totality' (Jameson, 1988: 355), stressed the importance of analysing global capital and class (Jameson, 1986: xiv) and reaffirmed the need for 'systemic transformation', adding too a belief in the future re-emergence of a new 'international proletariat' (Jameson, 1989a: 44). Also, in contrast to Baudrillard and Lyotard, Jameson's interventions rarely marginalize the Third World; in fact he has underlined the crucial interlocking of First and Third World realities, writing that in terms of culture, awareness is central, and 'it would not be bad to generate the awareness that we in the superstate are at all times a presence in third world realities, that our affluence and power are in the process of doing something to them' (Jameson, 1989b: 17).[7] In these interpretative traces there is a clear connection with Deleuze and Guattari's (1984) theoretical contextualization of the Third World, which largely follows Samir Amin's earlier work on accumulation and unequal development, an influence which reoccurs in their more recent text on capitalism and schizophrenia (Deleuze and Guattari, 1988).

From this introductory and necessarily brief commentary on some representations of the post-modern genre, it would appear that for Baudrillard and Lyotard, if not for Jameson, the relationship with the Third World as 'other' is enigmatic and ambiguous and certainly not free from Eurocentric traits. Western ethnocentrism is certainly not explicitly defended, in the style of Rorty (1985: 166), nor reluctantly accepted, as by Lévi Strauss.[8] At least in the earlier Baudrillard as well as in the writings of Jameson, the subordinating nature of the West's encounter with the periphery is dealt with or at least alluded to, in contrast to, for example Berman (1982), whose treatment of modernity is expressive of ethnocentric nostalgia.

Other writers who have been concerned to map the terrain of the post-modern stress the importance of other non-Western cultures, arguing that such cultures 'must be met by means other than conquest or domination' (Huyssen, 1984: 51). Huyssen is here influenced by Ricoeur, who at the beginning of the 1960s announced the demise of the West's 'cultural monopoly', noting that suddenly it becomes possible that there are just *others*, that we ourselves are an 'other' among others; for Ricoeur this was cause for a dispirited sense of loss – 'all meaning and every goal having disappeared, it becomes possible to wander through civilizations as if through vestiges and ruins' (quoted in Owens, 1985: 57–8). This comment leads Owens to suggest a connection with the post-modern condition, whereby Ricouer's idea of loss 'anticipates both the melancholia and the eclecticism that pervade current cultural production' (Owens, 1985: 57–8). What Huyssen and Owens both omit to mention is that the connection between the sense of loss of mastery, of monopoly, of cultural hegemony and a resigned melancholy, is reflective of an ethnocentric imperative.

How then are these newly surfaced scepticisms and spreading interrogations of modernity seen in the periphery? What relevance do post-modern politics have for Third World societies?[9]

Richard (1987/88), writing from Chile, has provided a series of penetrating observations on the ambiguities of post-modernism. She argues that although the post-modern critique of the universalizing project of capitalist modernity has been politically enabling in one sense, on the other hand, there has also been a tendency to dissolve centre–periphery distinctions, whereby the realities of imperialist domination have been reabsorbed and neutralized within an apparently equivalent set of 'other' images and meanings. Post-modernism may well stress specificity, regionalisms, social minorities, the marginal and political projects which are local in scope, but the fact is that 'no sooner are these differences – sexual, political, racial and cultural – posited and valued than they become subsumed into the meta-category of the "undifferentiated", which means that all singularities immediately become indistinguishable and interchangeable in a new sophisticated economy of "sameness"' (Richard, 1987/88: 11). For Richard, post-modernism 'defends itself against the destabilizing threat of the "other" by integrating it back into a framework which absorbs all differences and contradictions . . . the centre through claiming to be in disintegration still operates as a centre, filing away divergences into a system of codes whose meanings, both semantically and territorially, it continues to administer by exclusive right' (Richard, 1987/88: 11).

Despite these criticisms, Richard also sees some positive potential in post-modernism noting that it offers the chance to reconsider all that was unsaid in the project of modernity. Moreover, it is still possible to inject those opaque and resistent areas of post-modernism with the potential for new and 'as yet undiscovered meanings' (Richard 1987/88: 12). Similar echoes of open and innovative critique come from other Latin American intellectuals (Arditi, 1987; Brunner, 1987; Calderón, 1987; Hinkelammert, 1987; Reigadas, 1988), who tend to express a double or ambivalent attitude towards notions of post-modernism.[10]

As Richard indicates, one political element of the post-modern sense, the displacement and undermining of the modern certitudes of universal projects, is emancipatory in relation to the older themes of modernization theory. But, in addition, it is also enabling in its destructuring of Marxist totality. Conversely, when the realities of oppression and subordination, especially, for example, as they are expressed in and through global politics, are occluded or anaesthetized, post-modern politics becomes a barrier to emancipatory modes of thought and practice. Taking the post-modern in its potentially enabling sense, and referring back to critical development theory, there are three points I would like to make.

1. It can be argued that given the pronounced post-modern emphasis on plurality, difference, heterogeneity and the marginal, it might be expected that critical analysis from the South would be read and learnt from. The contribution of Third World intellectuals is not something for an exotic supplement, nor for a sentimental celebration; there is heterogeneity and difference here too. What does need saying is that within the central arena of critical or Marxist development theory cognizance and recognition of those other debates and investigations are frequently absent. One could take many examples,[11] but since I am considering questions of the

'peripheral' and the 'political', I would like to refer to the Peruvian intellectual Mariátegui, whose rethinking of Marxism in the historically concrete conditions of Andean America, gives us several seeds for further reflection in the present and for the future.

Mariátegui, and here there is an interesting parallel with Marx's later writings on Russia,[12] did not intend to parachute the categories of *Capital* into his reading of Peruvian society. Influenced by Gramsci as well as by Sorel, he was also concerned with the questions of political consciousness, culture, nationalism and historical specificity. Mariátegui realized the profound significance of indigenous culture in the political construction of a revolutionary imaginary; moral and cultural leadership required a symbiosis between organic intellectuals and the subaltern groups of Andean Peru. Such an intertwining could project a collective sense of national and popular emancipation. It was his emphasis on concepts of the 'national' and the 'popular' that led the Comintern to denounce him for his 'populism'.[13] In his attention to national sovereignty and the anti-imperialist struggle, Mariátegui viewed politics as an intrinsically creative activity.[14] And, as Aricó (1985: 90) reminds us, in his suggestive article on Marxism in Latin America, it is that singular relation between Marxism and subjectivity that erases from Mariátegui's texts the 'patina of time'.

2. Taking one example of a voice from the periphery has given me my second point, which concerns the power of political forces emerging within the South itself, and in the specific context of anti-imperialism and the struggles for popular self-determination. Given the enunciated interest of the post-modern in the 'marginal' and the 'different', it ought not to be an impossible step to consider the relevance of national-popular resistances. To what extent this might take place will naturally depend on the discourses within which 'post-modern politics' may acquire meaning, since there is no *one* post-modern politics, just as there is no *one* politics of poststructuralism. Equally, of course, national-popular resistances never have a fixed political content since their meaning is always the product of a continuous struggle.

Pitted against such a view one can find, within some streams of development theory, an implacable resistance to any deviation from the centrality of class and of internationalism. For Harris (1986: 202), speaking of the post-war period, the 'cause of socialism became swamped by the politics of nationalism and national liberation'. For others like Becker (1987), populism is an ideological distraction from the necessary pivot of history – class. But if critical development theory is to move on, it can be argued, and I develop these points in more detail below, that a renewed understanding of politics and civil society, freed from the circumscribing influence of class analysis, is crucial for a deeper comprehension of the possible meanings of 'development'.

3. My third point relates to the international or global dimension in radical theorizations of development. Since the withering away of earlier ideas concerning metropolis–satellite relations and the dynamics of 'internal colonialism', analysis of changes in the internationalization of capital, or the 'international division of labour', came on to centre stage, and with such effect that some commentators referred to the 'vortex of globalism'. As has been widely argued, the mainstream of Marxism has been flawed, *inter alia*, by its essentialization of the economic. This particular critique has been predominantly rooted in the general theoretical debates about power, agency, subjectivity and movements, and only rarely has the context been taken from globalist perspectives on capitalist economy.

From Jameson's work, taken as an illustration, we can only find a reinforcement of the emphasis on global capital. He suggests, for instance, that 'for the moment, global capital seems able to follow its own nature and inclinations'; on the same page he argues that 'local struggles and issues are not merely indispensable, they are unavoidable' and 'politics has to operate on the micro- and the macro-levels simultaneously' (Jameson, 1989a: 44). On the global level we have capital that follows its own 'nature and inclinations', abstracted and set above discourse and social subjectivity; but then at the same time politics has to operate simultaneously at the micro- and macro-levels (local and global). At that global level there is an analytical void which is filled by a structure or a system which is named 'capital', and which stands in for politics at the macro-level. When, as mentioned previously, Laclau (1990) refers to, for example, Managua as the name of a frontier through which our own political identities are constructed, he is also hinting at another blank analytical space – that of a critical geopolitics.[15] Managua, or 'The Nicaraguan Revolution', as a political symbol and event, cannot be effectively understood under the rubric of 'global capital', just as the Revolution's destabilization cannot be explained by that capital's presumed inclinations or imperatives. Rather, specific social agents, present both inside and outside particular institutions, and adhering to a discursive strategy of destabilization, were able to deploy that strategy in a series of successful practices. Agents acting in concrete ways with specific effects, rather than the impact of an abstraction, give effective meaning to geopolitics.

These ideas, which are expressive of poststructuralist thought, as well as being linked to the recent project of Laclau and Mouffe (1985) and Laclau (1990) to develop a post-Marxist perspective, can be connected to the conceptual directions of a new literature on international/intertextual relations (Der Derian and Shapiro, 1989). Ashley (1989), in his innovative chapter on 'poststructuralism, man and war', suggests that 'the appropriate "place" of poststructuralism in the study of global politics is neither domestic nor international . . . it is the "non-place" defined in terms of the ever problematical difference between the two' (Ashley, 1989: 285) – the unstable 'border line' between domestic and international politics. For Ashley, the analytical centrality of the state in international relations ought to be displaced, just as the androcentric conceptualization of 'Man' needs to be decentred. Connolly (1989), in his discussion of ideology and difference in global politics, follows many of the ideas developed by Ashley but rightly, in my view, detects a theoretical postponement, wherein the apparent inability to establish secure ontological ground for a theory links with the 'obligation to defer infinitely the construction of general theories of global politics'; and it does so, Connolly adds, 'during a time when the greatest dangers and contingencies in the world are global in character' (Connolly, 1989: 336).

Returning to the domain of development theory, it seems clear that the potential relevance of the new agenda in international relations has not yet been envisaged.[16] Instead, the global remains attached to the economic, so that inspiration tends to be derived, as one example, from authors who develop a distinction between regimes of accumulation and modes of regulation, in an examination of global fordism (Lipietz, 1987). Connolly (1989: 338–9), in his thoughts on the post-modern, contends that in a time of closure and danger, the 'political task' is to 'open up that which is enclosed, to try to think thoughts that stretch and extend the normal patterns of insistence'. In this spirit, I would argue that it is necessary to open up, extend, deconstruct and displace Marxist development theory so that new territory can be explored.[17]

In concluding this section of my discussion, I want to refer to a recent essay on international politics, in which the necessity for a new cognitive mapping of global relations is called for, and in which the place of the periphery, in this case Latin America, is alluded to. Tomassini (1990), in summarizing a 1989 Latin American collection of articles on modernity and post-modernity, calls our attention to the revalorization of democracy, to the dynamics of plurality, to new uncertainties and openness, to the relativization of mechanistic paradigms of the past and to the emergence of new social movements within a rethinking of political culture. These signposts put us on track for my second 'border crossing' which intersects with the first.

POWER, SUBJECTIVITY AND RESISTANCE

Paradoxically, it is in Jameson, one of the most prominent thinkers of the post-modern, that we can find one of the clearest statements of the centrality of class and the mode of production. He states that, 'Marxism as a coherent philosophy (or better still, a "unity of theory and praxis") stands or falls with the matter of social class'; and he further connects this with the contention that, 'the posing of the category of "mode of production" as the *fundamental* one of Marxian social analysis and the endorsement of a "problematic" that asks such systemic questions about contemporary society would seem to remain *essential* for political people who are still committed to radical social change and transformation' (Jameson, 1986: xiv–xv; emphasis added).

Echoes and reassertions of this position reverberate through the extensive literature of development studies, including discussions of social movements. Arrighi et al. (1989), in their book *Antisystemic Movements*, unambiguously set down that 'class struggle is the pivotal process of the capitalist world-economy' (p. 67). Subsequently, they suggest that social movements form through the 'structurally shifting loci of class struggle' (p. 76). Sklair (1988), in his response to Booth's (1985) article on Marxism and development sociology, prioritizes the social relations of production and class struggle. Symptomatically, when ideas from feminist theory are introduced, he posits their compatibility with class analysis, and the examples he gives all relate to the connection between gender and the economy. The theorization of subjectivity, so important in feminist theory, is left out of account.[18] Finally, in two recent texts which deal largely, although not exclusively, with the Latin American case, Kay (1989) and Larrain (1989) underline in different ways the central essence of class for any radical analysis.[19]

As a way of ordering the argument, I want to mention four main problems with the centrality of class analysis.

1. *Class*, as an abstract concept or mental construct, is not capable of social action or agency, just as *gender* does not act, but women and men do. Equally, in contrast with a political party, trade union, state agency or firm, etc., classes as social aggregates do not have any means of taking decisions or acting upon them.

2. It is assumed that classes have 'objective interests', which result from the overall structure of class relations, and which then function, *a priori*, as the necessary basis for the mobilization of actors, divorced from any analysis of the varied constitution of the social subject or the dynamic of collective wills. The failure of classes to become conscious of their 'interests' gives rise to the notion of 'false consciousness'.

3. It is further presupposed that a class in struggle, for instance the proletariat, has a consciousness that emanates from or is centred at the point of production. In this way, a fixed foundation is assigned a pre-given significance in the analysis and interpretation of consciousness.

4. Lastly, the proletariat, or more broadly defined, the working class, has been conceptualized as *the* privileged revolutionary social subject, thus dispensing with the need to explain the processes whereby varying forms of political subjectivity are constituted, and through which the propensity to act collectively may emerge in certain specific circumstances.

In considering the contrast between class and social movement, Laclau (1989: 65–6) asks the question: is it classes or social movements that constitute the fundamental agents of historical change? This question '*presupposes* what is fundamental: the obviousness and transparency of the category "class" '; thus what is required is a realization that the category 'class', 'far from being obvious, is already a synthesis of determinations, a particular response to a more primary question of social agency' (p. 66). Whereas classical Marxism gave an objective meaning to history, which subsequently 'operated as an unquestioned transcendental horizon in the analysis of concrete social processes',[20] Laclau (1990: 161), in his development of a post-Marxist perspective, stresses the radical contingency of that horizon. Thus the historical conditions for the constitution of social agents or subjects must be first analysed.

A crucial theme in all the discussions of class and agency relates to the ways in which 'structure' and 'subject' are conceptualized and theoretically deployed. According to Mouzelis (1988: 122), in his critique of Laclau and Mouffe's (1985) book on hegemony and socialist strategy, Marx's work as a whole provides the 'conceptual means for looking in a theoretically coherent manner at social formations and their overall reproduction/transformation from both an agency and a structural/institutional point of view'. Laclau's (1990) reply to this point is very relevant; he rightly states that Mouzelis does not attempt to give any examples from Marx's work which would show the presence of the 'conceptual means' to establish a logical coherence between the two dimensions of agency and structure. As Laclau (1990: 222) argues, there is a dualism in Marx – a consideration in some texts of the importance of the agent, and in others of the overriding impact of the structure, but there is no theoretical integration of the two. Laclau continues by stressing the fact that their own approach attempted to elaborate a 'unified theoretical framework and language which allow both the agency and the institutions to be conceived within them' (p. 223). Rather than seeing agents and structures as two separate entities, the following points are advanced; that 'there are merely relative *degrees* of institutionalization of the social, which penetrate and define the subjectivity of the agents themselves'; and 'that the institutions do not constitute closed structural frameworks, but loosely integrated complexes requiring the constant intervention of articulatory practices' (Laclau, 1990: 223). It is here too that the meaning of the political becomes crucial.

In classical Marxism, and in much of today's alternative development theory, the political is either a superstructure, or a subordinated sector of the socio-economic, being explained according to the supposedly objective tendencies of the latter. But in the contemporary period, the political is being increasingly seen as a dimension rather than a level. With the multiplication of sites of social struggle, or the growing subversion and dislocation of the social, the political can be inscribed in a broad range of social spheres. Thus, for instance, what is and is not political at any moment changes with the emergence of new questions, posed by new modes of subjectivity, e.g. 'the personal is political'. But also the 'political' does not eliminate the social conditions from which its question was born; gender, sexuality, religious belief, the 'milieu' may become political but they are not only political. This means that the political is not just restricted to the domain of the state, nor is it, as Mouzelis

(1988: 120) would like to sustain, separate from the economy as a 'permanent feature of advanced capitalism'.

In classical Marxism the subject is absorbed by the structure, but conversely this does not have to mean that the subject in capitalist society is free from the effect of the structure; there is always a 'relative structuration' as seen, for example, in the effects of increasing commodification or the bureaucratization of social life. These tendencies can generate the bases for the emergence of antagonisms, but that possible emergence has to be placed in the context of subjectivity – there is no predetermining social logic.

Before dealing with some aspects of subjectivity and change, I would like to take up some of the ideas forwarded by Laclau (1990) in his treatment of aspects of the structure of capitalist society, and in particular the issue of bureaucratization. This will give me a link to some facets of state power, a topic of primary importance for development theory, and a consideration of this modality of power can lead us back to questions of agency and resistance.

The growing bureaucratic unification and control of social relations in contemporary societies does not have to be seen as something which reflects a totalizing trend. As Laclau (1990: 53) suggests, on the one hand, 'administrative standardization in a single power centre is increasingly questioned by the internationalization of political and economic relations', and on the other, 'that bureaucratization produces resistance by those suffering its effects'. As regards the former point, this can be taken to mean that with a process of rapid internationalization, some might say globalization, the 'national framework' has been transformed into 'just one of the forces to be taken into account in the determination of structural change' (Laclau, 1990: 53). Subsequently Laclau (1990: 58–9), using ideas from recent work on 'disorganized capitalism', goes on to list some of the main features of the contemporary period, referring to a series of socio-economic trends such as changes in the international as well as spatial division of labour, the organization of production, occupational structures and so on.[21] With these trends acting as a backdrop to the argument, Laclau goes on to stress the fact that we are faced with a decline, both absolute and relative of the 'decision-making power of the national state as a centre of regulation of economic life' (Laclau, 1990: 58–9). It is not a collapse in which a once absolute power is transferred *in toto* to the multinational corporations, but a decline.

There are two comments I would make concerning the national

state and bureaucracy. First, the juxtaposition of the thesis that there is a growing bureaucratization of social life with the proposition that the decision-making power of the national state, as regards the regulation of economic life, is in decline, raises the issue of the characterization of types of power within the state. For example, there may well be an increase in the power of surveillance over the citizen, but at the same time the nation-state's power over the organization of production, not to mention monetary flows, in an increasingly global economy, can well be seen as in decline. And in peripheral societies this is even more the case. But again it can be argued that this potential differentiation of types of power can be most appropriately understood in the context of discourse and agency.

For example, a grouping of social agents, let us say, within a political party, which shares at a certain moment a common set of beliefs, attitudes, visions concerning a project of intervention, may constitute a regime. In other words, within the arena of the national state this grouping will have the opportunity or the space to deploy a particular political discourse. Such a deployment can be seen as a continuation of previously sedimented meanings, or in other instances there can be an attempt to rearticulate and transform meanings – to develop a hegemonic project which is not restricted to one area of intervention, for example, the economy, but is constructed around a broader conception of political leadership. Within that project, as can be seen in the example of Thatcherism, conceptions of individuality, of bureaucracy, of welfare, of the nation, of the family, of wealth and poverty and so on are deployed within an unstable ensemble of linguistic and extralinguistic practices. The will to deploy discourse is the will to power, but in this case that power will relate to different spheres, to military questions, to issues of controlling the citizen, to reshaping economic policies and to international relations. And between those different spheres there will be dissonances of meaning, conflicts and openings for critique and displacement.

My second point touches on the centre–periphery divide and its relevance for a discussion of the power of the state. In Laclau's comments on the national state and also on bureaucratization, the potential meaning of such a divide is left out of account. In an earlier article (Laclau and Mouffe, 1987), the state is envisaged as being constituted around the principles of division of powers, universal suffrage, multiparty systems, civil rights, etc. The radical democratization of society, which they associate with a variety of autonomous struggles and the increasing capacity of social agents involved in these struggles for self-management, does not have to pass through a 'direct attack upon the State apparatuses but involves the consolidation and democratic reform of the liberal State' (Laclau and Mouffe, 1987: 105). This conceptualization of the 'liberal State' has a blank space, the name of which is institutionalized violence.

Even for the advanced capitalist societies, their notion of the liberal state, within which the factor of coercion and the very real existence of repressive apparatuses are neglected, evokes too consensual an impression.[22] For the societies of the capitalist periphery the above notion of the 'liberal State' is hardly apposite, and would also conflict with their earlier identification of the predominance of 'brutal and centralized forms of domination' in these kinds of societies (Laclau and Mouffe, 1985: 131).

In the above sketch I have looked at a few aspects of a certain kind of power — the power over — but there is also a power to act, to be able to resist, and this leads us to the issue of social movements. First, however, I want to reconnect with the post-modern literature, and ask the question: how do authors such as Baudrillard, Lyotard and Jameson situate the realities of resistance in their work, especially in the context of the periphery?

In contrast to the classical Marxist canon, in which the subject has been absorbed by the structure, in Baudrillard the subject has vanished in an 'ecstasy of communication'. The psychological dimension is no more; public spaces disappear, as the new advertising, with its omnipresent visibility of enterprises, brands and the social virtues of communication, invades everything; sexual obscenity has degenerated from being hot and carnal to 'cold and communicational, contactual and motivational'; finally, the message no longer exists, it is the medium that imposes itself in its pure circulation — potential 'ecstasy' (Baudrillard, 1985). In this essay, Baudrillard presents the reader with a finely tuned dystopia. Elsewhere, on the revealing edges of his disenchanted thought, he avers that while the 'international style is now American', the American model now 'universal', there is no longer any real opposition — 'the combative periphery has now been reabsorbed (China, Cuba, Vietnam)' Baudrillard (1989: 116). Is there perhaps nostalgia for a lost narrative?

In the two works I previously commented on, Lyotard (1986, 1988a) gives little importance to opposition or resistance, but in the

1988 text, conflict, dispute and politics are examined in different ways, without a unilinear structure of presentation. More concretely, in a recent interview, he repeats his view that modern intellectuals were Enlightenment figures, securing their legitimacy in the 'grand metanarrative of emancipation'; there was always a foundational meaning, what Laclau would call an original ground, and this was the 'emancipation of humanity from poverty, ignorance, prejudice and the absence of enjoyment' (Lyotard, 1988b: 302). What is left for Lyotard is the minimum requirement for a 'politics of resistance'. This is defined not only in relation to the defence of elemental liberties, but also as a resistance in and through writing. The real political task today, therefore, is 'to carry forward the resistance that writing offers to established thought, to what has already been done, to what everyone thinks, to what is well-known, to what is widely recognized, to what is "readable", to everything which can change its form and make itself acceptable to opinion in general'. The artist, the writer, do not, for Lyotard, owe this resistance to the community but 'to thought itself' (Lyotard, 1988b: 303), like the figure of Winston in Orwell's *1984*.

I want to make three points here; (1) Lyotard, as opposed to Baudrillard, still believes in the primacy of resistance – there is no 'implosion of the social'; (2) an unhelpful split is registered between community and 'thought in itself' – the two can be creatively interwoven; and (3) there is no reference to the historical or empirical investigation of resistance or to the actual movements, as well as individual intellectuals, who make it happen. This last remark brings us to Jameson.

In an intriguing interview with Stephanson, Jameson (1989b: 16) says that the 'political movement going on today – such as there is – is in places like Nicaragua and South Africa . . . it is not a matter of cheering for third world countries to make their revolutions; it is a dialectical matter of seeing that we here are involved in these areas and are busy trying to put them down, that they are part of our power relations'.[23] Jameson continues by suggesting that there is a third possibility beyond the 'old bourgeois ego and the schizophrenic subject of our organization society today' (a reference to Deleuze and Guattari): 'a *collective subject* decentered but not schizophrenic'. This subject, according to Jameson, emerges in 'certain forms of storytelling that can be found in Third World literature, in testimonial literature, in gossip and rumours, and in things of this kind' (Jameson, 1989b: 21). This romanticization of the Third World other stems partly from a lofty sense of cultural supremacy, but also perhaps from what Said (1985b: 149) has forthrightly referred to as a 'cloistral seclusion from the inhospitable world of real politics'. Not only do the subaltern speak, they can also analyse, reflect and move.

If it is the case that these three authors of the post-modern, despite the significant differences amongst them, do not give us many clues for a consideration of the importance of resistance, perhaps we should broaden the question and ask: is it possible to acquire a general sense of how the political meanings of the post-modern might aid us in thinking about subjectivity?

Subjectivity, seen as a process, can be interpreted in terms of the individual's conscious and unconscious thoughts and emotions, within which ideas of identity and of ways of understanding and expressing the sense of relation to the social 'outside' are particularly significant. From the post-modern reading, as well as from the closely connected currents of poststructuralist thought, there is no longer any essentiality of subjectivity or a central privileged core which radiates meaning to the outer spheres of the individual's consciousness. A riddle of post-modern politics can be expressed through the question: 'what do a trade union member, an unemployed worker, a Tory, a racist, a Christian, a wife-beater, and a consumer all have in common?' The answer is, of course, that they can all be the same person, or expressed more precisely, they can be variously defined from 'one discursive moment to the next' (Ross, 1986: 99).

Thus it can be argued that in each individual there exist multiple subject positions corresponding both to the different social relations in which the individual is inserted (for instance, in terms of gender, race, production, nationality, regionality and so on) and to the discourses that constitute these relations. All these relations are the site of subject positions and every social agent is therefore the bearer of many subject positions rather than one. Moreover, each subject position is itself the point of various possible discursive constructions; thus the subjectivity of a given social agent can never be finally fixed. The idea of differential positionalities located within the space of the social subject connects with the notion of the 'de-centering of the social subject'.

This approach to the construction of identities is also very relevant for the understanding of new social movements and the rethinking of democracy. For example, subjects constructed on the basis of certain rights can experience a situation in which those rights and identities are threatened or undermined by the spread and incursion of other social forces, institutions or practices. This negation can form the basis for the emergence of an antagonism; for example, the cases of the development of human rights movements, of squatter movements and the ecological movement can be seen in this context. On the other hand, there can be a situation wherein subjects who have been constructed in subordination by one set of discourses are, at the same time, interpellated as equal by other discourses. This for Mouffe (1988) is evidence of a 'contradictory interpellation', since although like the first form a particular subject position is being negated, in this instance it is the 'subjectivity-in-subordination' that is negated, providing the possibility for its deconstruction and challenging. This second form of antagonism can be exemplified in relation to the women's movement, anti-racism and ethnic minority movements, and earlier national liberation movements of the Third World. Always, of course, there will be a complex relation between the basis for the antagonism and its discursive representation, since nothing is predetermined. For example, the curtailment of basic civil rights can be given a legitimated meaning by being articulated within an authoritarian discourse of political order and national security; here the act of curtailment is presented as a necessity in the struggle against a constructed 'national enemy'.

These elements of an approach to subjectivity contrast markedly with the customary perspective to be found in radical development theory. Here, the subject is prevailingly a class subject, essentialized and centred. One of the fascinating stories of the class analysis of Third World societies has revolved around notions of marginalization. To what extent was it possible and desirable to apply the concepts of an industrial reserve army and relative surplus population to societies that had not undergone a thoroughgoing process of capitalist transformation? Was it possible to talk of a marginal mass or a marginal pole of the economy? How were these other people who did not easily fall into the customary categories of traditional Marxian class analysis to be explained? Traditionally, the 'informal' and the 'marginal' have been concepts used to supplement the central categories of class, but the presupposed supplementary, extrinsic character of these groups has always had a subversive effect on the explanatory effectiveness of class analysis. In addition, the potential subversiveness of the 'marginal', as social subject, has, at least in the past, been more of a concern for the liberal scholar and politician, while in Marxist work the focus of attention has been much more towards the problems of economic classification.[24] Ironically, it is in today's neo-liberal discourse that the marginal and the informal are romanticized in both an 'economic' and a 'political' sense; namely, as bearers of productive initiative outside the regulatory and restrictive attention of the state, and as the new expression of individualism, creativity and personal advancement in a hostile world – De Soto's (1989) by now renowned if not luminous 'other path'.

Intriguingly, in post-modern accounts, the 'marginal' is very much 'in'. To be on the margins is to be in a position which opens up greater possibilities of insight and critique; as Yúdice (1989: 216) nicely puts it, in a certain way the post-modernist has taken the old negative myths of marginality and turned them on their heads,endowing them with a subversive and positive sense. Sometimes, however, this can divert analytical attention away from the different contexts in which subaltern groups are forced to survive, to become, for instance, 'squatter-wise', in conditions of increasing social polarization, political instability and material deprivation. Moreover, 'bucking the system' has a plurality of meanings, from, for example, the use of inside information to make a million in the stock market, to the moonlighting activities of low-income immigrant workers.

In the development literature there is an emerging sense that concepts such as 'class', 'masses' and 'marginality', are no longer fully sufficient for the analysis of change. Gradually interest in social movements is growing. I would argue that to a considerable extent this interest is combined with the rise of democracy as a parallel theme of enquiry. Aronowitz (1989: 61) underscores the importance of such an imbrication, and goes on to add that the 'new social movements speak in postmodern voices; they enter the national and international political arena speaking a language of localism and regionalism'. The potential interconnections among (new) social movements, democracy and post-modern politics signal the need to move on to the third and last border crossing.

DEMOCRACY AND SOCIALISM – FOR A MERGING OF HORIZONS

For the persevering Marxist, socialism can still be the ultimate, fixing horizon. For a post-modernist like Baudrillard, socialism can be the eclipsed dream of a faded past. For today's advocate of neoliberalism, socialism is the *gulag* and democracy lives as an emaciated formality.

For Laclau (1990: 82), the state of social struggles in the contemporary world at least 'create the preconditions for a radicalization of democracy'. The multiplication of sites of political struggle and the construction and articulation of new identities open up the possibility for a more emancipatory vision of democracy. Mouffe (1989: 44), in her attempt to trace out some of the implications of post-modern philosophy for radical democracy, advances a similar argument noting that a strategy for a politics of radical democracy would need to 'abandon the abstract universalism of the Enlightenment, the essentialist conception of a social totality, and the myth of a unitary subject'. Where would this leave the idea of socialism? Does it have a future in the radical democratic imaginary? And in peripheral societies does the struggle for socialism always have to terminate in the fortress state?

In the radical literature on Third World development there has always been a strong tendency to defend the achievements of post-revolutionary societies. If, for example, one surveys the Marxist and related literature on Cuba, the heralding of the social and economic improvements of over three decades of revolution overshadows any critical consideration of the absence of plurality, difference and discursive openness. Conversely, in the mainstream literature of development studies, the emphasis on the authoritarian nature of the one-party state is not infrequently used to blot out any of the relevance of the welfare achievements of the Cuban Revolution, as well as the impact of over thirty years of United States hostility.

The presence of a totalizing imperative in socialist thought has a long history. In the Cuban case it was concisely expressed by Fidel Castro, in his speech to the 1975 Congress of the PCC, when he declared that the Party was the 'synthesis of everything', embodying the 'Soul of the Revolution' (Castro, 1976: 231–2). But, in the Cuban case, the attempt to encompass the whole is not only found in the speeches of the maximum leader of an institutionalized revolution but also in the writings of its foremost guerrilla leader. Che Guevara, in his celebrated essay on man and socialism in Cuba, where he stressed the importance of moral incentives, also wrote that 'we are looking for something new that will permit a complete identification between the government and the community in its entirety' (Guevara, 1988: 7). This notion of a complete identification does away with the need to maintain a distinction between civil society and the state, and further still the force of the mechanism of identification implies that nothing will escape state power; as Guevara put it: 'society as a whole must be converted into a gigantic school'. It is then within the realm of this discourse that the prosecution of economic and social development comes to be equated with socialism.

As has been argued over a long period of time, liberalism produced the myth of a society that was organized and developed as a result of free competition between independent owners and in which the state limited itself to ensuring that the rules of the game were respected, and to protecting persons and property. Socialist thought demonstrated that the crises of the capitalist system were not accidental but structural, and that there was a radical opposition of interest between those who possessed the means of production and those who did not. However, this kind of argument in no way abandoned the idea that reality was to be revealed at the level of the economy. Correspondingly, as Lefort (1986: 276–7) convincingly argues, since the centre of the theoretical and political universe remained the economy, it became much more likely that when a situation arose in which private property was abolished and in which class antagonisms could no longer be deciphered in the known context of capitalism, critical thought would be disarmed. Moreover, this meant that the emergence of new relations of exploitation and oppression in the post-revolutionary society remained opaque because the primary sphere of reality had already been cordoned off by the limits of the economy.

Examining the role of the Party in the post-revolutionary period, it can be suggested, following Lefort's general thesis, that its initial success as a political force can be associated with the following three features: (1) its capacity to identify with the revolution, so it is envisaged as a power able to effect both a radical break with the past and a radical founding of a new world; (2) its ability to fuse together the demand for social transformation with the claim to have a superior knowledge of history and society; and (3) its capacity to conceive of itself and to make manifest its claim to be the depository of socialist legitimacy and truth (Lefort, 1986: 283). These features are particularly apposite in the Cuban case, and in the way that revolution was institutionalized, as in other cases too, it is possible to identify three tendencies.

First, there is a trend towards the continual displacement and then transcendence of the divisions between the state and civil society, political and administrative power, and the state bureaucracy and the party (Polan, 1984). As an eventual condensation, power comes to be materialized in one organ (or in extreme cases in one individual) that has the supposed capacity of concentrating and representing in itself all the forces of society ('the Party is the synthesis of everything').

Secondly, the principle of antagonisms internal to society is denied. There are no longer any contradictions within the organization of production or the general structure of society. We have arrived at a classless society. This was also, of course, seen as an inevitable result of revolutionary change; Mao, for example, wrote in 1938 'once man has eliminated capitalism, he will attain the era of perpetual peace' (quoted in Alker et al., 1989: 152).

Finally, the notion of social heterogeneity, as far as it radically contradicts the image of a society in harmony with itself, is rejected. The negation of heterogeneity, and of difference, the imperative of societal harmony and the fortification of a Marxist-Leninist conformity foreclose the development of political culture, of alternative socialist as well as democratic thought. When the paralysis of official doctrine is publicly recognized, and when the need for structural reform is accepted, the radical sources of alternative thought and vision have already been terminally crippled if not erased. The political landscape is so riven by the official contours of 'scientific socialism' that a move to its perceived opposite, capitalism, is starkly reinforced.

Turning briefly to democracy, it has been argued, since Poulantzas, that the struggle to combine a transformed representative democracy with direct democracy could provide a more liberating goal than the orthodox socialist vision. In many traditional Marxist accounts there has been an inclination to establish a fixed frontier between the institutions and norms of bourgeois democracy on the one side and the principles of socialist organization on the other. However, the development and significance of the institutions of representative democracy can be closely connected with the struggles and impact of popular movements, and interpreted as an arena within which attempts to articulate socialist and democratic ideas are both possible and desirable. Nevertheless, it would of course be shortsighted to believe that majority influence or control, won by left-wing forces acting within these institutions, could of itself provide a sufficiently stable and secure basis for a successful project of radical societal transformation. History already has enough examples of such a dream being transformed into the nightmare of state terror.

From one useful point of view, the principles of democracy as a system are succinctly discussed by Bobbio (1989). In his text on dictatorship and democracy, he delineates the latter in terms of the combination of procedures required for arriving at collective decisions in a way which secures the fullest possible participation of interested parties. At a minimum, democratic procedures include equal and universal suffrage, majority rule and guarantees of minority rights, which ensure that collective decisions are approved by a substantial number of those expected to make them, the rule of law, and the constitutional guarantees of freedom of assembly and expression. Specifically on direct democracy, Bobbio is of the view that rather than seeing this form as a substitution for representative democracy, it reflects a trend towards the transfer of democracy from the political sphere to the social sphere where the individual is regarded as multifaceted. Consequently, 'current forms of democratic development . . . should be understood as the occupation of new spaces' (Bobbio, 1989: 156).

How is it possible to make a link between these general indications on democracy and political change at the periphery? In the above commentary on revolution and socialism, I made a few remarks on the Cuban experience; in relation to democracy, the Nicaraguan experiment contains a number of illustrative pointers.

For the 1979–89 period, a number of writers have employed the concept of popular hegemony to attempt to characterize key aspects of the Sandinista project. The hegemonic aspect of the project concerned the construction of a new subjectivity relating to: (1) the articulation, consolidation and institutional embodiment of collective forms of problem identification, discussion and decision-making; and (2) the constant maintenance of an anti-imperialist position with regard to defence of the national territory, the redirection of social and economic development and the preservation of a revolutionary and democratic state. As an objective the political construction of new social identities traversed both the popular organizations operating in an emerging civil society and the organs of the post-revolutionary state. Such a phenomenon developed from a situation where an original popular-democratic insurgency had led to the seizure of state power; but that capture, in contrast to the Cuban case, did not usher in a period of political closure. In fact, the coexistence of both representative and direct forms of democracy provided a key facet of the originality of the Sandinista project. However, geopolitical circumscription, with the continuing disruption of war and socio-economic destabilization, coupled with a growing dislocation between the party in power and the grassroots organizations (exacerbated by a show of overconfidence by some leaders of the government) brought to a halt this innovative experiment in post-revolutionary democracy.

In general, it can be argued that in the important sphere of the organization of the economy the deployment of neo-liberal discourse constitutes a barrier to the extension and deepening of democracy (Cunningham, 1987). However, as I have argued above, this ought not to be taken to mean that socialism must be automatically democratic. The socialist organization of production can certainly coexist with the lack of democracy in many other spheres of social life, as can be illustrated from the Cuban case. In this context, therefore, we can suggest, with Laclau and Mouffe (1987: 104), that, 'the compatibility of socialism and democracy, far from being an axiom, is the . . . result of a hegemonic struggle for the articulation of both'.

In bringing this brief consideration of democracy and socialism to a close, it is worthwhile referring to three dimensions of change in the critical discussion of socialism and emancipation (Laclau, 1990: 225–6).

1. In contrast to previous times, it is now more relevant to talk of 'emancipations' rather than 'emancipation'. In place of the fundamentalist perspective which has always prioritized the supposed centrality and universality of one kind of struggle (the class struggle), today any struggle is by definition partial; it can never hope to absorb the meaning of all struggles; the agents of struggles are neither transcendental nor omnipotent.

2. Although struggles are partial they are nevertheless tending to be extended to more and more subject positions, with the implication that the articulation of these positions is becoming more complex and more open. Again this does not imply any necessarily progressive imprint since the very openness goes together with a

variety of positions and horizons, some of which are far from being emancipatory.

3. Finally, in Laclau's phrase, it is now possible to talk of the 'deuniversalization' of the socialist project. 'If socialism is part of what we have called the "democratic revolution", socialist demands can only be articulated to other democratic demands of the masses, and these will vary from one country to another' (Laclau, 1990: 225) – for instance, demands in a country subject to colonialism or racist subordination will not be the same as in a West European-style liberal democracy.

On the one hand, these ideas imply and carry with them a crisis in the political representation of the future – they announce the end of one transcendental horizon – but on the other, they point to the possibility of a more genuinely emancipatory future, freed from the predetermined fixity of the political. Equally, however, they raise the question of the possible modalities and content of 'democracy' itself, including the notion of a 'radical democracy'. Future political horizons also need to be thought of in relation to the ethics of change and the complexities of political cultures.

TRAVELS ON THE BORDER – THE NEED FOR DIALOGUE

Chambers (1990), in his journey across the landscape of post-modern culture, writes: 'to break with a unilateral sense of history means to abandon a metaphysical purpose mirrored in the passage of time . . . it means to renounce a knowledge that already knows its scope and to respond to the importance of those uncertain, decentered and ambiguous margins and borders that exist at the edges of time, obscured by the unswerving light of "progress" ' (Chambers, 1990: 109). The 'post-modern' escapes unequivocal definition. It has, as Hebdige (1988: 181–2) writes, a proliferation of meaning, or what Hassan (1985: 121) called a certain semantic instability, foreclosing the possibility of any lasting consensus of meaning. For Hebdige, and I think this is important, the degree of semantic overload and complexity surrounding the term 'post-modernism' signals the emergence of a site of dispute and contention which is regarded by a significant number of people as important enough to be worth struggling and arguing over. In the direction of what I would call a constructive, enabling approach to the term 'post-modern', I would like to argue as follows.

It seems to me that a rethinking of the political in critical development theory is quite crucial. This does not mean that all one has to do is state a political position, as if this was somehow a substitute for theory, as is sometimes implied. Rather, the excavation of hidden meanings, the analysis of organizing concepts of the economic, the consideration of the prioritization of themes for research, a focusing on the imagery of transformation, will all reveal a significant adherence to the metanarrative of classical Marxism. Ironically perhaps, for parts of the world where political meaning has been and remains so rich in diversity and wider relevance, radical theorizations have so often tended to be couched in the predictable language of class and capital. The unpredictable potency of human agency has so often been anaesthetized and absorbed into the narrative of capital accumulation and class struggle.

Other writers, starting out from a different point of departure, have attempted to identify some of the shortcomings of radical dependency perspectives, while at the same time suggesting a way of interpreting the 'post-modern condition' in the Third World. Apter (1987: 20), in his book on rethinking development, defines violence, which can be seen as 'one expression of the negative side of development', as a 'postmodern' condition. Violence, for Apter, is a diagnostic phenomenon, which he sees in relation to marginalization, terror and protest. It would be misleading to equate violence with the term 'post-modern', not only because of the variety of meanings this term has, as I have demonstrated in this article, but also because the dark side of modernity has also been violent, dissolving the grounds for Apter's distinction. Moreover, it is worthwhile remembering that the literature on modernization theory carried with it a stunning idealization of the already modernized society, especially the United States, and a characteristic silence concerning the violence used by First World societies in the diffusion of their 'modernizing' mission. The deployment of terror has not been historically restricted to the actions of individuals, militant groups and military dictatorships; it has been one of the emblems of the imperial state.

It is also important to guard against the idea that there is a First World–Third World schism between 'paradox' in one and 'fortress' in the other (Pêcheux, 1983); that in the Third World people know how to resist and to fight, whereas in the First, movements have acquired a greater degree of reflexive maturity and complex interweaving that leads to all kinds of paradoxes. The complexities of social movements on the periphery (Arditi, 1987; González, 1987; Jelin, 1990; Vargas, 1991; Viola, 1988) cannot be forced into the limiting terms of terror, violent protest and armed rebellion. The struggles for democratic transformation take many forms, connecting *inter alia* with ecological, women's, urban, ethno-regionalist and human rights issues.

Having travelled through parts of the border zone between Marxist development studies and post-modern politics, some might want to erect a fixed frontier to defend the fortress of historical materialism. But the walls of that fortress are already crumbling. On the other side, some post-modernists might argue that the fortress was built to defend the dream of a revolutionary apocalypse, and its walls have already long gone. It does not have to be this way. A post-modern politics, as I have tried to show, can also be enabling in the sense of an emphasis on iconoclastic questioning rather than predetermination, on openness rather than pre-empting closure, on plurality rather than essentialism. Also, in the turn to a subversive questioning, there is a potentiality, and it is only a potentiality since some post-modern writing is androcentric as well as ethnocentric, to undermine the universalist projections of the white Western male heterosexual. One key element of any discussion of emancipations in the plural must surely include a radical deconstruction of these kinds of projections, made as they are in the heartlands of Western academia.

But I would also argue that a post-Marxist perspective, within which there is a displacement and reproblematization of the Marxist tradition, can be highly relevant at this juncture. The rejection of Marxism *in toto* serves only to maintain the myth of its coherence and unity. The post-Marxist does not dogmatically affirm the unity and coherence of Marxism, but specifies its plurality. As Laclau (1989: 77) puts it, 'to set the historical limits of marxism is to reestablish a living dialogue with that tradition, to endow it with a certain contemporaneity against the timelessness that its orthodox defenders attribute to it'. Post-Marxism is not ex-Marxism. Concepts of 'hegemony', of 'historical bloc', of 'collective wills', of 'organic crisis'; analyses of political culture as in Gramsci or Mariátegui; Luxemburg on centralization and decentralization; Marx on the Russian commune and so on, all retain their relevance. Interpretative amnesia is a recipe for dogma and a gateway to the historical impoverishment of a rich political tradition. However, it is also here that an enabling post-modern reflection can continually help us to rethink any post-Marxist perspective. That sense of continuous subversion and analytical interrogation is crucial in helping us to avoid the formation of new fixities and normalizing protocols of interpretation.

Finally, there is this. Post-Marxists, post-modernists and development theorists too, ironically, can learn from the periphery. As Gadamer (1979: 272) once wrote, in a much broader context, 'to acquire a horizon means that one learns to look beyond what is close at hand – not in order to look away from it, but to see it better within a larger whole and in truer proportion'.

NOTES

1. One of the exceptions to this can be found in some of the more recent work of Apter (1987), which I shall briefly refer to later on in the paper. Nederveen Pieterse (1989/90: 51) comments that in the debate between modernism and post-modernism Third World issues are 'literally absent from the discussion . . . it is an all-Western debate, an Occidental quiz, with Western answers to Western questions'. To this one should add that much critical or Marxist development theory proceeds as if the above debate was not relevant to its concerns.

2. I prefer to retain the hyphen in the post-modern, in the way that Jencks (1989) puts it, i.e. by stressing the double coding or double meaning, whereby post-modernism entails both the continuation of modernism as well as its transcendence; it seems to me that there is also here a link with the way Laclau and Mouffe (1985) use the term post-Marxist to denote both a continuation of some elements of Marxism together with its transcendence or displacement.

3. This does not mean of course that the concepts developed by Foucault are only relevant in a Western context, but that the critical investigation of discourses of sexuality, of confinement, of truth, of caring, did not connect with the critique of Eurocentric discourses of colonialism and imperialism. Interestingly, in Foucault's preface to Deleuze and Guattari's (1984: xi) *Anti-Oedipus* it is commented, and this was written at the end of the 1960s, that 'at the gates of our world, there was Vietnam, of course, and the first major blow to the powers that be'. But here, inside our walls, perhaps it could be argued that Vietnam was not at the gates of 'our world' but very much inside it as the peripheral recalcitrant other of resistance.

4. It might be added here that Spivak (1988a) also tends not to deal in any detail with the realities of resistance in Third World societies, and even feels obliged to ask the question 'can the subaltern speak?' The impact of contemporary social movements, from ecological through urban and ethno-regionalist to gender issues, is largely left out of account, helping to evoke an unreal sense of quiescence.

5. In a parallel fashion, some of Baudrillard's recent views on feminism have expressed a certain patriarchal persuasion – see the interview entitled 'Politics of Seduction' in *Marxism Today* (January 1989: 54).

6. In a useful examination of Lyotard's 'postmodern condition', Connor (1989:

32) observes that while both science and Cashinahua narrative say 'We do what we do, because that's the way we do it . . . the difference between them is that, where the Cashinahua's modes of communication and exchange form a comfortingly self-identical whole, such that their collective lives are dominated by one language game, postmodern society encompasses a multitude of different, incompatible language-games, each with its own untransferable principles of self-legitimation. . . . We have seen, therefore, a shift from the muffled majesty of grand narratives to the splintering autonomy of micronarratives.' In parentheses Connor adds that for Lyotard the Cashinahua stand for a 'magical equivalent of the unspoilt linguistic innocence of all primitive peoples'; the phrase 'linguistic innocence' connects with Derrida's previously noted criticisms of Lévi-Strauss/Rousseau on the 'innocent primitive'.

7. Whether or not one agrees with Jameson's portrayal of Third World realities would take us into a longer discussion, and I shall be returning to aspects of his argument later; in passing it can be noted that in his foreword to Lyotard's 'postmodern condition' he writes of the global expansion of capitalism 'which now specifically penetrates the hitherto pre-capitalist enclaves of Third World agriculture' (Jameson 1986: xiv) – he leans here on Mandel's (1975) *Late Capitalism*.

8. This is a reference to Lévi-Strauss's attempt to differentiate racial prejudice from ethnocentrism, wherein he states that the latter can be seen in terms of 'common inclinations and attitudes which would be illusory to imagine that some day humanity could or would wish to overcome' (quoted in Policar, 1990: 100).

9. In their introduction to the theory and politics of post-modernism, Boyne and Rattansi (1990: 34–6) allude to the connectivities between the critique of Western imperialism and discussions of the 'other'. However, not only do they minimize the contribution of Western intellectuals in the critique of colonialism and imperialism, but also, and perhaps more symptomatically, they say nothing about the contribution of Third World intellectuals to this critique, except for those who are actually resident in the First World such as Said and Spivak. Further, they do not seem to be aware of the ethnocentric traits of post-modern writing, as opposed to the more overt Eurocentrism of the defenders of Western modernity and projects of radical Enlightenment.

10. In a rather resigned vein, Brunner (1987: 39) notes, for example, that in Latin America, 'we are condemned to live in a world where all images of modernity and modernism come to us from outside, and become obsolete before we can materialize them; we find ourselves trapped in a world where every symbol evaporates into air – *América Latina*: a project of echoes and fragments, of utopias and pasts, whose present we may only perceive as a continual crisis'. A more hopeful less lugubrious sentiment is found in Arditi (1987).

11. In the widely disseminated debates on underdevelopment and *dependencia*, starting in the late 1960s, the First World discussion evolved around the ideas of a limited number of authors whose work had been published in English. The original richness and complexity of the Latin American tradition was largely bypassed as caricature was added to simplification, acquiring terminal crystallization in the work of Warren (1980) and Booth (1985). Fortunately, in Chilcote (1984) and especially Kay (1989) the reader is provided with a long-overdue rectification, which gives back to this literature its historical dignity.

12. For example, in his 1881 letter to Vera Zasulich, Marx wrote that 'the commune is the fulcrum for social regeneration in Russia' – see Shanin (1983: 124). His close analysis of the then 'peripheral' case of Russia helped Marx to modify his earlier more

universalist views. Again there is a link with Laclau's idea of the frontier effect of the peripheral case.

13. In a rather bizarre continuation, some of today's development theorists, who aspire to the Marxist label, dismiss the *dependentistas* for being 'populists' who want 'absolute sovereignty', which the reader is informed 'simply cannot be had'. Apparently, Cardoso, with his historical-structural method, departs from rigorous class analysis, and falls for national-populist inspiration. These and other strictures are to be found in Becker's (1987: 203–25) article on post-imperialism — I shall take up the theme of class analysis further on.

14. In an editorial written in 1928, Mariátegui (1987: 249) stated that what he referred to as Indo-American socialism had to be created through giving life to their own reality in their own language.

15. This 'space' is already the subject of new theorizations which have appeared in the last few years; for a beginning, using ideas from Foucault and Derrida, see, for example, Ashley (1987), as well as the interesting articles of Dalby — for example, Dalby (1988).

16. For an indication of the new agenda the reader might consult, among others, George (1989), Rosenau (1990) and Walker (1989).

17. Continuing his comments on the need for openness, Connolly advances a few critical remarks on 'the modernist', which *mutatis mutandis*, can be appropriate for those traditional carriers of Marxism; he writes that 'the modernist . . . often worries that if a transcendental standard cannot be proven (or at least proven to be "presupposed"), then all hell will break loose'; he goes on: 'the political danger resides not in the closure of identity and difference but in the hell of an infinite openness' (Connolly, 1989).

18. One ought not to assume that this does not happen when the writer is a woman; Eckstein (1989), for instance, in her introduction to a study of social movements in Latin America adds gender to class analysis as a supplement — the problematic is not displaced and the rich insights on power and identity, coming out of women's studies, find no space in Eckstein's text.

19. Elsewhere, I have provided a critical review of these two interesting contributions — see Slater (1990).

20. Such a position can be found expressed in the work of Harris (1986) and Warren (1980).

21. These trends are dealt with by Lash and Urry (1987), as well as by Offe (1985).

22. In one of Gramsci's passages on the nature of the state, he uses the by now well-known phrase, 'hegemony protected by the armour of coercion'; he goes on to note that 'it is possible to imagine the coercive element of the State withering away by degrees, as ever-more conspicuous elements of a regulated society . . . make their appearance' (Gramsci, 1971: 263). So far, there are few examples of such a development.

23. Jameson fudges his position on this somewhat by adding that the United States has become the 'biggest third world country, because of unemployment, nonproduction, the flight of factories, and so on' (Jameson, 1989b: 17). The alterity of the Third World is de-differentiated in a way that is reminiscent of Deleuze and Guattari (1988: 468–9) who suggested that there are many internal Third Worlds within the centre.

24. For an interesting critique of this kind of approach, see Camacho's (1990) recent article, which looks at 'political informality', social movements and violence; the context is largely a Colombian one.

REFERENCES

Alker, H.R., Jr, Biersteker, T.J. and Inoguchi, T. (1989) 'From Imperial Power Balancing to People's War: Searching for Order in the Twentieth Century', in J. Der Derian and M.J. Shapiro (eds) *International/Intertextual Relations – Postmodern Readings of World Politics*, pp. 135–62. Lexington, MA: Lexington Books.

Apter, D.E. (1987) *Rethinking Development – Modernization, Dependency and Postmodern Politics*. Newbury Park, CA: Sage.

Arditi, B. (1987) 'Una gramática postmoderna para pensar lo social', in N. Lechner (ed.) *Cultura política y democratización*, pp. 169–88. Buenos Aires: CLACSO.

Aricó, J. (1985) 'El Marxismo en América Latina', *Opciones* 7: 72–91.

Aronowitz, S. (1989) 'Postmodernism and Politics', in A. Ross (ed.) *Universal Abandon? – The Politics of Postmodernism*, pp. 46–62. Edinburgh: Edinburgh University Press.

Arrighi, G., Hopkins, T.K. and Wallerstein, I. (1989) *Antisystemic Movements*. London: Verso.

Ashley, R.K. (1987) 'The Geopolitics of Geopolitical Space: Toward a Critical Social Theory of International Politics', *Alternatives* XII: 403–34.

Ashley, R.K. (1989) 'Living on Border Lines: Man, Poststructuralism and War', in J. Der Derian and M.J. Shapiro (eds) *International/Intertextual Relations – Postmodern Readings of World Politics*, pp. 259–321. Lexington, MA: Lexington Books.

Baudrillard, J. (1975) *The Mirror of Production*. St Louis, MO: Telos Press.

Baudrillard, J. (1983) *In the Shadow of the Silent Majorities*. New York: Semiotext(e).

Baudrillard, J. (1985) 'The Ecstasy of Communication', in H. Foster (ed.) *Postmodern Culture*, pp. 126–34. London: Pluto Press.

Baudrillard, J. (1989) *America*. London: Verso.

Becker, D. (1987) 'Postimperialism: A First Quarterly Report', in D. Becker et al. (eds) *Postimperialism*, pp. 203–25. Boulder, CO: Lynne Rienner.

Becker, D., Frieden, J., Schatz, S.P. and Sklar, R.L. (eds) (1987) *Postimperialism – International Capitalism and Development in the Late Twentieth Century*. Boulder, CO: Lynne Rienner.

Berman, M. (1982) *All that is Solid Melts into Air – The Experience of Modernity*. London: Verso.

Bobbio, N. (1989) *Democracy and Dictatorship*. Cambridge: Polity Press.

Booth, D. (1985) 'Marxism and Development Sociology: Interpreting the Impasse', *World Development* 13(7): 761–87.

Boyne, R. and Rattansi, A. (1990) 'The Theory and Politics of Postmodernism: By Way of an Introduction', in R. Boyne and A. Rattansi (eds) *Postmodernism and Society*, pp. 1–45. London: Macmillan.

Brunner, J.J. (1987) 'Notas sobre la modernidad y lo postmoderno en la cultura latínoamericana', *David y Goliath – Revista de CLACSO* 52: 30–9.

Calderón, F. (1987) 'América Latina: identidad y tiempos mixtos o cómo tratar de pensar la modernidad sin dejar de ser Indios', *David y Goliath – Revista de CLACSO* 52: 4–9.

Camacho, A. (1990) 'Informalidad política – movimientos sociales y violencia', *Nueva Sociedad* 106: 36–49.

Castro, F. (1976) 'Report of the Central Committee of the Communist Party of Cuba to the First Congress', First Congress of the Communist Party of Cuba, Havana (December). Moscow: Progress Publishers.

Chambers, I. (1990) *Border Dialogues – Journeys in Postmodernity*. London: Routledge.

Chilcote, R. (1984) *Theories of Development and Underdevelopment*. Boulder, CO: Westview Press.

Cocks, J. (1989) *The Oppositional Imagination – Feminism, Critique and Political Theory*. London: Routledge.

Connolly, W. (1989) 'Identity and Difference in Global Politics', in J. Der Derian and M.J. Shapiro (eds) *International/Intertextual Relations – Postmodern Readings of World Politics*, pp. 323–42. Lexington, MA: Lexington Books.

Connor, S. (1989) *Postmodernist Culture – An Introduction to Theories of the Contemporary*. Oxford: Blackwell.

Corbridge, S. (1990) 'Post-Marxism and Development Studies: Beyond the Impasse', *World Development* 18(5): 623–39.

Cunningham, F. (1987) *Democratic Theory and Socialism*. Cambridge: Cambridge University Press.

Dalby, S. (1988) 'Geopolitical Discourse: The Soviet Union as Other', *Alternatives* XIII: 415–42.

Deleuze, G. and Guattari, F. (1984) *Anti-Oedipus – Capitalism and Schizophrenia*, with a preface by Michel Foucault. London: Athlone Press.

Deleuze, G. and Guattari, F. (1988) *A Thousand Plateaus – Capitalism and Schizophrenia*. London: Athlone Press.

Der Derian, J. and Shapiro, M.J. (eds) (1989) *International/Intertextual Relations – Postmodern Readings of World Politics*. Lexington, MA: Lexington Books.

Derrida, J. (1976) *Of Grammatology*. Baltimore, MD: Johns Hopkins University Press.

Derrida, J. (1985) 'Racism's Last Word', in H.L. Gates, Jr (ed.) *'Race', Writing, and Difference*, pp. 329–38. Chicago, IL: University of Chicago Press.

De Soto, H. (1989) *The Other Path – The Invisible Revolution in the Third World*. New York: Harper and Row.

Eckstein, S. (1989) 'Power and Popular Protest in Latin America', in S. Eckstein (ed.) *Power and Popular Protest – Latin American Social Movements*, pp. 1–68. Berkeley, CA: University of California Press.

Foucault, M. (1970) *The Order of Things – The Archaeology of the Human Sciences*. New York: Random House.

Fraser, N. and Nicholson, L. (1989) 'Social Criticism without Philosophy: An Encounter between Feminism and Postmodernism', in A. Ross (ed.) *Universal Abandon? – The Politics of Postmodernism*, pp. 83–104. Edinburgh: Edinburgh University Press.

Gadamer, H.-G. (1979) *Truth and Method*. London: Sheed and Ward.

Galeano, E. (1983) *Days and Nights of Love and War*. London: Pluto Press.

Gane, M. (1990) 'Ironies of Postmodernism: Fate of Baudrillard's Fatalism', *Economy and Society* 19(3): 314–33.

George J. (1989) 'International Relations and the Search for Thinking Space: Another View of the Third Debate', *International Studies Quarterly* 33(3): 269–79.

González, L. (1987) 'Por un feminismo afrolatinoamericano', *ISIS International* IX: 133–41.

Gramsci, A. (1971) *Selections from the Prison Notebooks*. London: Lawrence and Wishart.

Guevara, E. (1988) *Socialism and Man in Cuba*. Sydney: Pathfinder (first edn, 1965).

Hassan, I. (1985) 'The Culture of Postmodernism', *Theory, Culture and Society* 2(3): 119–31.

Harris, N. (1986) *The End of the Third World – Newly Industrializing Countries and the Decline of Ideology*. London: Tauris.

Hebdige, D. (1988) *Hiding in the Light – On Images and Things*. London: Routledge.

Hettne, B. (1990) *Development Theory and the Three Worlds*. Harlow: Longman.

Hinkelammert, F.J. (1987) 'Utopia y proyecto político – la cultura de la postmodernidad', *Nueva Sociedad* 91: 114–40.

Huyssen, A. (1984) 'Mapping the Postmodern', *New German Critique* 33: 5–52.

Jameson, F. (1986) 'Foreword', in J.-F. Lyotard (ed.) *Postmodern Condition*, pp. vii–xxi. Manchester: Manchester University Press.

Jameson, F. (1988) 'Cognitive Mapping', in C. Nelson and L. Grossberg (eds) *Marxism and the Interpretation of Culture*, pp. 347–57. Urbana, IL: University of Illinois Press.

Jameson, F. (1989a) 'Marxism and Postmodernism', *New Left Review* 176: 31–45.

Jameson, F. (1989b) 'Regarding Postmodernism – A Conversation with A. Stephanson', in A. Ross (ed.) *Universal Abandon? The Politics of Postmodernism*, pp. 3–30. Edinburgh: Edinburgh University Press.

Jelin, E. (ed.) (1990) *Women and Social Change in Latin America*. London: Zed Press.

Jencks, C. (1989) *What is Post-Modernism*? London: Academy Editions.

Kay, C. (1989) *Latin American Theories of Development and Underdevelopment*. London: Routledge.

Laclau, E. (1989) 'Politics and the Limits of Modernity', in A. Ross (ed.) *Universal Abandon? The Politics of Postmodernism*, pp. 63–82. Edinburgh: Edinburgh University Press.

Laclau, E. (1990) *New Reflections on the Revolution of Our Time*. London: Verso.

Laclau, E. and Mouffe, C (1985) *Hegemony and Socialist Strategy*. London: Verso.

Laclau, E. and Mouffe, C. (1987) 'Post-Marxism without Apologies', *New Left Review* 166: 79–106.

Larrain, J. (1989) *Theories of Development*. Cambridge: Polity Press.

Lash, S. and Urry, J. (1987) *The End of Organized Capitalism*. Cambridge: Polity Press.

Lefort, C. (1986) *The Political Forms of Modern Society – Bureaucracy, Democracy, Totalitarianism*. Cambridge: Polity Press.

Lipietz, A. (1987) *Mirages and Miracles – The Crises of Global Fordism*. London: Verso.

Lyotard, J.-F. (1986) *The Postmodern Condition – A Report on Knowledge*. Manchester: Manchester University Press.

Lyotard, J.-F. (1988a) *The Differend – Phrases in Dispute*. Manchester: Manchester University Press.

Lyotard, J.-F. (1988b) 'Interview', *Theory, Culture and Society* 5(2–3): 277–309.

Mandel, E. (1975) *Late Capitalism*. London: New Left Books.

Mariátegui, J.-C. (1987) *Ideología y política, colección obras completas*, Vol. 13. Lima: Amauta (first edn 1969).

Mouffe, C. (1988) 'Hegemony and New Political Subjects: Toward a New Concept of Democracy', in C. Nelson and L. Grossberg (eds) *Marxism and the Interpretation of Culture*, pp. 89–101. Urbana, IL: University of Illinois Press.

Mouffe, C. (1989) 'Radical Democracy: Modern or Postmodern?', in A. Ross (ed.) *Universal Abandon? The Politics of Postmodernism*, pp. 31–45. Edinburgh: Edinburgh University Press.

Mouzelis, N. (1988) 'Marxism or Post-Marxism?', *New Left Review* 167: 107–23.

Nederveen Pieterse, J. (1989/90) *Empire and Emancipation: Power and Liberation on a World Scale*. New York: Praeger; London: Pluto Press.

Offe, C. (1985) *Disorganized Capitalism*. Cambridge: Polity Press.

Owens, C. (1985) 'The Discourse of Others: Feminists and Postmodernism', in H. Foster (ed.) *Postmodern Culture*, pp. 57–82. London: Pluto Press.

Pêcheux, M. (1983) 'Ideology: Fortress or Paradoxical Space', in S. Hänninen and L. Paldán (eds) *Rethinking Ideology: A Marxist Debate*, pp. 31–5. New York: International General.

Polan, A.J. (1984) *Lenin and the End of Politics*. London: Methuen.

Policar, A. (1990) 'Racism and its Mirror Image', *Telos* 83: 99–108.

Reigadas, M.C. (1988) 'Neomodernidad y postmodernidad: preguntado desde América Latina', in E. Mari (ed.)? *Postmodernidad*, pp. 113–45. Buenos Aires: Editorial Biblos.

Richard, N. (1987/88) 'Postmodernism and Periphery', *Third Text* 2: 5–12.

Rorty, R. (1985) 'Habermas and Lyotard on Postmodernity', in R.J. Bernstein (ed.) *Habermas and Modernity*, pp. 161–75. Cambridge: Polity Press.

Rosenau, P. (1990) 'Once Again into the Fray: International Relations Confronts the Humanities', *Millenium: Journal of International Studies* 19(1): 83–110.

Ross, A. (1986) 'Discussion of Hegemony and Socialist Strategy', *M/F – A Feminist Journal* 11/12: 99–106.

Ross, A. (1989) 'Introduction', in A. Ross (ed.) *Universal Abandon? The Politics of Postmodernism*, pp. vii–xviii. Edinburgh: Edinburgh University Press.

Said, E. (1985a) *Orientalism*. London: Penguin Books.

Said, E. (1985b) 'Opponents, Audiences, Constituencies and Community', in H. Foster (ed.) *Postmodern Culture*, pp. 135–59. London: Pluto Press.

Shanin, T. (ed.) (1983) *Late Marx and the Russian Road – Marx and the 'Peripheries of Capitalism'*. London: Routledge and Kegan Paul.

Sklair, L. (1988) 'Transcending the Impasse: Metatheory, Theory and Empirical Research in the Sociology of Development and Underdevelopment', *World Development* 16(6): 697–709.

Slater, D. (1990) 'Development Theory at the Crossroads', *European Review of Latin American and Caribbean Studies* 48: 116–26.

Spivak, G. (1987) *In Other Worlds – Essays in Cultural Politics*. London: Methuen.

Spivak, G. (1988a) 'Can the Subaltern Speak?', in C. Nelson and L. Grossberg (eds)

Marxism and the Interpretation of Culture, pp. 271–313. Urbana, IL: University of Illinois Press.
Spivak, G. (1988b) 'Subaltern Studies: Deconstructing Historiography', in R. Guha and G. Spivak (eds) *Selected Subaltern Studies*, pp. 3–32. Oxford: Oxford University Press.
Tomassini, L. (1990) 'La política internacional después del muro', *Estudios Internacionales* XXIII(91): 281–338.
Vandergeest, P. and Buttel, F.H. (1988) 'Marx, Weber, and Development Sociology: Beyond the Impasse', *World Development* 16(6): 683–95.
Vargas, V. (1991) 'The Women's Movement in Peru: Streams, Spaces and Knots', *European Review of Latin American and Caribbean Studies* 50: 7–50.
Viola, E. (1988) 'The Ecologist Movement in Brazil (1974–1986): From Environmentalism to Eco-politics', *International Journal of Urban and Regional Research* 12(2): 211–18.
Walker, R.B.J. (1989) 'History and Structure in the Theory of International Relations', *Millenium – Journal of International Studies* 18(2): 163–83.
Warren, B. (1980) *Imperialism – The Pioneer of Capitalism*. London: Verso.
Yúdice, G. (1989) 'Marginality and the Ethics of Survival', in A. Ross (ed.) *Universal Abandon? The Politics of Postmodernism*, pp. 214–36. Edinburgh: Edinburgh University Press.

David Slater is Associate Professor of Social Geography at the Interuniversity Centre for Latin American Research and Documentation (CEDLA), Keizersgracht 395–397, 1016 EK Amsterdam. He is the author of *Territory and State Power in Latin America – The Peruvian Case* (Macmillan/St Martins Press, 1989) and editor of *New Social Movements and the State in Latin America* (Foris/CEDLA, 1985).

Abstracts

Jan Nederveen Pieterse. Emancipations, Modern and Postmodern

This is a reflection on contemporary reorientations in emancipatory thought and on the concept of emancipation, as a vantage point from which to review changing critical practice and theory. Emancipation as a concept is juxtaposed to liberation, participation, empowerment, resistance. It is situated historically by reviewing several episodes of emancipation: the extension of political and social rights to the bourgeoisie, workers, women, slaves, Jews and Catholics in the wake of the American and French Revolutions, class struggles, national movements, and in recent times, new social movements. Leading theories have been liberal equal rights theories, Marxism, nationalism (anticolonial movements included) and, in recent times, poststructuralism, post-Marxism and social movement theory. Is it possible to differentiate between modern and postmodern emancipations? There may be a pattern in that the former tend to view power as a promise, adopt a single paradigm of emancipation and a totalizing project, while the latter tend to pose power as a problem, and are self-reflexive, and self limiting in their aspirations.

Alberto Melucci. Liberation or Meaning? Social Movements, Culture and Democracy

This article shows how the teleological idea of liberation as a final stage of history, a main legacy of modern thought, has been challenged by contemporary social movements. Recent forms of collective action, by their very existence, offer to the rest of society new meanings that reverse those imposed by a power increasingly based on the manipulation of cultural codes. In a global world the field of social conflicts is a cultural arena in which social actors are engaged in struggles for the construction of meaning. The notion of democracy has then to be redefined: when power is concerned with the control of cultural codes, the main role of social movements is that of making power visible and of opening up civil society as the public space for societal debates.

Sudipta Kaviraj. Marxism and the Darkness of History

Marxism should be seen as a discourse, that is, as containing diverse possible ways of articulating its major ideas. Traditionally, Marxist historical thinking has been seen as an inheritor of the enlightenment tradition of historical optimism. There is, however, a second, self-critical and self-doubting tradition of rationality, and

Development and Change (SAGE, London, Newbury Park and New Delhi), Vol. 23 (1992) No. 3, 321–324.

Marxism should be read through this second strand. If so read, it would abjure its common stance of cognitive and moral immodesty, and recognize that one cannot be right about history at one go, but work through recursive corrections of earlier beliefs. Recursivity is built into historical rationality. The history of communism is then seen through this view. Finally, it suggests that basic reworking is required in several major areas of Marxist historical thinking.

Bhikhu Parekh. Marxism and the Problem of Violence

The collapse of communism in the Soviet Union and Eastern Europe raises important questions about the validity of the central doctrines of the Marxist tradition. Part of the reason for this collapse had to do with the pervasive terrorism of the communist states. By and large communists took an historicist, utilitarian and positivist view of violence, and the roots of such an ill-considered and incoherent theory lie in Marx's own thought. Marx's excessive preoccupation with the 'next stage' of history and his failure to provide regulative moral principles paved the way for the utilitarianism of the left and historical consequentialism. As a result, he provided no theoretical and institutional safeguards against the misuse of violence. His followers remained trapped within historical utilitarianism and were unable to mount a systematic critique of state terrorism.

Ernesto Laclau. Beyond Emancipation

This article tries to probe the internal inconsistencies of the category 'emancipation' and to develop, out of the latter, the alternative strategic moves which become possible for a radical democratic politics. It starts by enumerating six distinctive features of the concept of emancipation and shows how they are organized around two of these: the dimension of *ground* and the *dichotomic* dimension. They are strictly incompatible with each other, because the radical character of the act of emancipation requires that the latter takes place at the level of the ground of the social, while the concept of ground excludes the notion of a radical chasm. From this point on, the article shows how these two dimensions subvert and at the same time require each other. This double movement deconstructs the notion of 'emancipation' but at the same time makes possible, precisely as the result of these deconstructive operations, the elaboration of new forms of struggle, based in a plurality of partial emancipations and no longer in the ideal of 'Emancipation' (with a capital E).

David E. Apter. Democracy and Emancipatory Movements: Notes for a Theory of Inversionary Discourse

This article examines relationships between emancipatory movements and democracy in terms of two models; institutional democratic and inversionary discourse, the one based on equilibrium principles and the other disjunctive. Both models are provided with a 'pedigree' which suggests how they evolved analytically. Each is first considered as a self-contained system and then both are discussed in terms of their dynamic interaction. The analysis is designed to suggest how institutional democracies respond systematically to emancipatory movements, and how the latter contribute to and enlarge the scope and practice of democracy itself.

Sandra Harding. Subjectivity, Experience and Knowledge: An Epistemology from/ for Rainbow Coalition Politics

Feminist researchers, theorists and activists in the dominant social groups have increasingly come to an understanding that if there is no universal or even typical 'man' and his unified and uniquely legitimate reason, then neither can feminists assume that the subject of feminist projects of knowledge-seeking and social transformation is universal or typical 'woman' and her unified and uniquely legitimate reason. The logic of feminist criticisms of androcentric humanism returns to challenge the remnants of humanism within feminist analyses. This article explores how one leading feminist theory of knowledge – feminist standpoint epistemology – can be developed away from its humanist origins and towards notions of knowers, the known and processes of gaining knowledge that are more compatible with the kinds of coalition politics emerging among the new social movements.

Virginia Vargas. The Feminist Movement in Latin America: Between Hope and Disenchantment

This article analyses the development of the feminist movement in Latin America over the last decade. It does this by examining the discussions and documents of the five Latin American feminist assemblies held in Colombia, Peru, Brazil, Mexico and Argentina, since 1981. It is stated that the feminist movement in the continent has taken shape in a situation of incomplete modernization, that it has contributed to the destruction of the old paradigms and certainties, and that it has allowed for the plurality and diversity of social life. But it is argued, at the same time, that the movement has maintained certain reductionist practices; and that these obstruct the recognition of diversity and plurality within it. The Latin American feminist movement thus finds itself presently at an historical crossroads. Its further development cannot be based on a single dynamic, nor found on one privileged and exclusive axis. Its growth depends, rather, on the articulation of the differences – of the multiple and diverse discourses – that can already be found within the movement.

Valentine M. Moghadam. Development and Women's Emancipation: Is There a Connection?

This article addresses a major conundrum in the women-in-development literature: the question of the relationship between socio-economic development and women's status and well-being. At a macrosociological level of analysis, the trend has been to emancipate women from patriarchal constraints, to improve their life-chances and to provide them with a wider range of choices and life-options. At an empirical level, the effects of development are variable by class, with some groups of women benefiting more than others. The article also discusses the effects of development on women's status in terms of unintended consequences and purposive action. The benefits accrued to women in the course of socio-economic development (industrialization, urbanization, proletarianization) are largely unintended, whereas in cases such as revolutions or legal reform, the explicit intent is to achieve women's liberation, gender equality, or the full participation of women in national development. Finally, the article criticizes the 'maldevelopments' of the 1980s as setbacks both to national development and to women's emancipation, and proposes steps to undo the damage.

Wim F. Wertheim. The State and the Dialectics of Emancipation

This article first attempts to elucidate the concept of emancipation as a sociological phenomenon, analysing it as a universal human urge for liberation, as distinct from the Marxian concept of class struggle. The main question posed by the article is whether the state is to be viewed as an ally of social emancipation or as an adversary. In spite of a widespread opinion to the contrary, the author argues that in Western history, industrial development was due only in part to private entrepreneurship, and that government support was in fact an indispensable precondition. During the twentieth century, the state could be seen functioning as an ally of, and motor for, social emancipation; it was gradually transformed, however, into a brake upon emancipation. Finally, the author argues that in the Second and Third Worlds, the state still has important stimulating and protective functions to perform.

David Slater. Theories of Development and Politics of the Post-modern – Exploring a Border Zone

This article explores three crossings of a border zone: this zone is constituted by the potential intersections between critical development theory and the post-modern interruption. The three 'crossings' analysed are: the troubled conceptualizations of centres and peripheries, including a brief consideration of the global dimension of development debates; questions of agency, power and resistance, including some comments on class and marginality as relevant in peripheral societies; and differential meanings of democracy and socialism. The illustrations used in the analysis largely come from Latin America, and the perspective adopted can be represented in terms of one possible interpretation of post-Marxism.